TREASURER'S AND CONTROLLER'S DESK BOOK

Daniel L. Gotthilf

Prentice-Hall, Inc.   Englewood Cliffs, N.J.

Prentice-Hall International, Inc., *London*
Prentice-Hall of Australia, Pty. Ltd., *Sydney*
Prentice-Hall of Canada, Ltd., *Toronto*
Prentice-Hall of India Private Ltd., *New Delhi*
Prentice-Hall of Japan, Inc., *Tokyo*
Prentice-Hall of Southeast Asia Pte. Ltd., *Singapore*
Whitehall Books, Ltd., *Wellington, New Zealand*

© 1977 *by*
Prentice-Hall, Inc.
Englewood Cliffs, N.J.

Fourth Printing . . . . . September, 1979

Library of Congress Cataloging in Publication Data

Gotthilf, Daniel L
    Treasurer's and controller's desk book.

    Includes index.
    1. Finance--Handbooks, manuals, etc. 2. Business
enterprises--Finance--Handbooks, manuals, etc.
3. Controllership--Handbooks, manuals, etc. I. Title.
HF5550.G68   658.1'5   76-45327
ISBN 0-13-930727-3

Printed in the United States of America

About the Author

Daniel L. Gotthilf, CPA, is Vice President, Treasurer, and Director of Savin Business Machines Corporation. Mr. Gotthilf's areas of responsibilities with Savin, for the past ten years, have ranged from accounting services, data processing, personnel, budgeting and forecasting,to systems and procedures.

His early business years were spent in public accounting practice and as an internal operational auditor. Prior to joining Savin he served as Controller for Universal Laboratories and as Treasurer and Controller for Technical Tape Corporation.

Mr. Gotthilf was an honor graduate of the University of Michigan School of Business in 1948 and subsequently obtained a Certificate in Programming and Data Processing Analysis from New York University. The author is a frequent lecturer before the American Management Association on a wide range of financial subjects and has written numerous articles for business and financial journals.

FOREWORD

As I read the manuscript of Dan Gotthilf's *Treasurer's and Controller's Desk Book,* I became more and more impressed with the title of his book. Whether you are a Treasurer or a Controller, or you're on your way to becoming one or the other, this is the book you should have on your desk.

Here is a book that is not intended to be read at one sitting. It is based, to a large extent, on the author's own business experiences, and trying to read it straight through would be like trying to live your lifetime in one day.

This book is a practical, how-to-do-it working tool, full of procedural guidelines, helpful hints and warnings of pitfalls to avoid. It devotes a chapter to each major responsibility of the Treasurer or Controller, each supported by numerous forms and workpapers in a most comprehensive Index of Working Aids showing just how to get each job done.

Mr. Gotthilf has covered critical functions—providing an encyclopedic volume answering key questions that a Treasurer or Controller might be called upon to meet in his day-to-day challenges. It is an excellent guide to the performance of a financial executive's everyday duties, and I recommend that this book be kept right at the reader's findertips. It belongs in every financial library.

Ted Reynolds

Treasurer
Hazeltine Corporation

What This Book Will Do For You

The responsibilities of the Treasurer and Controller have been defined by the Financial Executives Institute (FEI). These duties encompass the management and direction of the enterprise, and they are, in effect, the province of any over-all business owner, manager, generalist, financial executive or entrepreneur.

This book was written to provide the practical methods, procedures and systems for the acceptance and successful performance of all financial responsibilities—to present them in one place, in one handy desk book. The desk book is an "idea bank" of fingertip answers to everyday firing line challenges. The narrative is followed by an Index of Working Aids, a unit of well over 100 exhibits and instant retrieval informational schedules to illustrate the key points, in chapter sequence. This permits successful researching of problems in seconds. You will want to keep this desk book close at hand—for instant reference as well as re-acquaintance with an ever-widening scope of responsibilities.

In one illustrated source book, you now have set forth all the many and varied facets of the treasury and controllership functions—for example, in chapter order, the key subjects are:

Banking and short-term borrowing arrangements

Long-term borrowing

Credit and collection

Insurance coverage

Cash forecasting

Formulating the operating plan

Controlling operations

Reporting the result of operations

Tax policies

Operational audits

Special areas of responsibility

Mergers and acquisitions

Records retention and filing

Data processing control

Stock option planning.

This book gives you practical, no-nonsense approaches to handling the pertinent responsibility. The book is conveniently indexed and cross-referenced to enable you to look up any subject matter and find the right chapter and page number. The page then refers you to the Index of Working Aids for the precise schedule, exhibit or graph that you need.

Problems are a part of management. Solving them quickly is a part of good management. The *Treasurer's and Controller's Desk Book* is the manager's everyday tool to achieve this.

Here are some examples of what you will find:

How to set up most of your bank accounts to avoid the need for reconciliations monthly, through *Color Coding and Imprest Accounts*. How to apply for and get bank loans by supplying the right information, in advance. You'll also find a simple, accurate and proven Accounts Payable "jacket". Control System—a supervisor to insure prompt payment to your vendors. (See Chapter 1)

A critique of the various borrowing devices is examined, and methods are presented to compare the alternatives of borrowing short-term or *Long-Term Borrowing*, through mortgages, sale and lease backs, straight debt, debt with "kickers" or equity. A Term Sheet on a typical long-term loan is presented. All the alternatives are presented here in one section for simple comparison. (See Chapter 2)

Four unique methods of *Credit Granting* to customers, to enable you to broaden your sales base with very little risk or cost. (See Chapter 3)

Four types of Catastrophe Insurance are reviewed with a view to a 25% premium savings. A typical schedule of *All Required Insurance Coverage* to completely protect the enterprise is submitted. You may not be adequately covered now, or you may be over-insured. The exhibited insurance schedule is a checklist to be used to compare your present coverage. (See Chapter 4)

A working illustration on *Projecting Cash Requirements*, focusing on the details of accounts-receivable collections. Longer-term cash requirements are related to the Operating Plan, with illustrations of the technique used, showing the Statement of Source and Utilization of Funds. Techniques to meet unexpected cash shortages are outlined, and practical tips are presented to insure that your cash forecasts are accurate. (See Chapter 5)

Step-by-step detail and building blocks for constructing the Operating Plan. You will find here all the basic rules to construct the budget and profit plan and to tie it in to the Operating Plan. The detailed *Working Tools of the Budget* are presented together with the ways to make them work. These ways include lines of authority and proper division of responsibilities. A successful Operating Plan depends on these. If you employ these techniques, you can build a solid framework for the entire corporate structure. (See Chapter 6)

The veritable framework of the Company . . . the trucks to carry the mail. These consist of the definitions, uses and examples of the *Policy Manual, Procedures Manual, Organizational Charts, and Position Descriptions*. No organization can operate efficiently, some cannot operate at all, without them. They delineate the place and responsibilities of the individual within the corporate structure. (See Chapter 7)

Twenty-five *Reports and Graphs* for getting the story of the results of operations across to top management. Each report speeds up the transmission of clearer, more concise information to the user, allowing for corrective action based on realistic data. Reports are designed to present information by exception, rather than masses of detail. (See Chapter 8)

The financial and tax accounting aspects of five major *Tax Shelter Areas* are discussed as they relate to most businesses—the WHTC, DISC, Capital Gains versus Sales, not "effectively connected" and the Captive Finance Subsidiary. One or more may give you a real tax-saving payoff of significant proportions. (See Chapter 9)

How to identify those headquarters departments requiring audit. An actual *Field Operational Audit Procedure* and a reporting system are illustrated. These procedures prevent fraud and insure that your Operating Plan is not subject to mechanical failure. (See Chapter 10)

How to monitor loans to employees. A system is presented for Product Pricing Control with illustrated forms and a detailed procedure. A *Philosophy of Management* is described, to set the tone for the company. Checklists are given for control of external audits, inventories, and for cost reduction programs. (See Chapter 11)

How to make tax-free *Mergers and Acquisitions.* This presents a mathematical evaluation formula for judging the feasibility of such acquisitions. Once having decided to acquire, you have a checklist to help you evaluate the operations and finances of the acquiree. A proven motivational device is presented to encourage the acquired owner, and an actual letter memorandum of acquisition agreement is illustrated. (See Chapter 12)

Records that you must retain, and for how long. This explains how to establish a good current filing system and explores a microfilm retrieval system which is inexpensively implemented. (See Chapter 13)

The entire *Data Processing* function, in both the large and small business, is explored. An organizational chart of the typical department is exhibited as well as status reports to control the flow of work coming out of the data processing department. Whether to automate or not is defined. Security safeguards against theft and fire are explained. (See Chapter 14)

Three innovative *Non-Qualified Stock Option Plans* are reviewed in the light of tax and stock market dictates. These will motivate and induce managers to remain with the Company. Both the financial and tax aspects of each plan are examined. A stock purchase plan for all employees is examined. It gives everyone a real stake in the operation and makes the lowest level employee profit conscious. (See Chapter 15)

All chapters are amply supported with references to Procedures, Forms, Exhibits and carefully delineated instructions, which are arranged for easy reference in an Index of Working Aids at the rear of the book. These tools will save countless hours of procedural flow-charting and forms design. The Index of Working Aids brings all Forms and Exhibits together in one place, sub-divided by Chapter, making a fast and easy reference tool.

Daniel L. Gotthilf

To my wife Dottie,
for her unflagging support
during the many hours devoted to writing this book,
and for the index

CONTENTS

Implementing and Administering Tax Policies and Procedures *(cont.)*

10. Organizing the Operational Audit **143**

11. Supervising Special Administrative Areas of Responsibility **153**

CHAPTER 1

Maintaining and Administering

Banking and Financial Arrangements

THIS typical treasury function involves specifying which banks and financial institutions to use, maintaining relations with them, handling and controlling the actual flow of cash through the company involving accounts payable, payrolls, petty cash, interest and dividends. This responsibility encompasses the concepts of budgeting and cash planning, the control over collections, and provision for the prevention of fraud involving cash. The Controller usually develops the budget and is responsible for operational disbursements involving payrolls and trade accounts payable. The Treasurer retains banking liaison and overall control of company funds. They must work in close collaboration to insure that all the responsibilities are being acquitted as called for in the company Position Descriptions, with nothing falling through the cracks due to undesignated tasks. This is a chapter on the source and control of "money," the life plasma of any business organization.

BANKING AND INSTITUTIONAL RELATIONS

The financial relationship is concerned with the company's banks, investment bankers, and institutional lenders such as insurance companies.

The financial officer of the company must develop a relationship of informality, trust, knowledge and confidence with the suppliers of his funds. All of the following should be used to achieve this relationship:

1. Once-a-month business meetings, sometimes at the company, sometimes at the bank.

2. Semi-annual meetings involving all major financial lenders, both long- and short-term.

3. Special group meetings, as required, to present new programs.

4. Luncheon meetings for discussion of one or two brief subjects, monthly or as the need arises.

5. Social meetings, evenings, with wives included, usually at dinner or some sporting event, for brief discussions on one or two business topics.

A warm and friendly business relationship, and no more can be developed using these approaches. I would not suggest any further fraternity, such as invitations to cocktail parties, or week-end home visits, unless they are sought out by the lender. Even in such cases, they should best be kept to an occasional meeting. This type of additional intimacy can place an unnecessary strain on the relationship which could have the opposite effect one is seeking. The association is better built on a social engagement.

Your lender should never be made to feel that you are seeking him out, currying his favor or using any other blandishments to gain your own ends. On the contrary, your frequent meetings and lunches, and occasional social evenings, always involving a business discussion, will impress him with your devotion to your company and attention to the responsibilities of your job. To what end? Why all this? If handled right, you will accomplish a great deal:

1. Your banker, through these frequent meetings, will practically become another member of your management team, at no cost to the company. You are effectively expanding the depth of your management.

2. The time to explain your program is considerably shortened, since your man already has a detailed, intimate knowledge of your company. Your own time, therefore, may be utilized more efficiently.

3. The lender, due to the frequency of these meetings and the sometime social aspect of them, has an opportunity to assess your own competence and intelligence, and your ability to react to varied situations. This, in turn, will permit him to rely on that competence and intelligence in making his commitments to your company.

4. At monthly and group meetings, your bankers will meet your entire management team. These meetings will have been structured to allow all sections of management to participate. The banker will appreciate the involvement of total management in the financial affairs of the company.

5. The company's bankers, through their frequent and total involvement in company affairs, will be of great assistance in long-range planning, acquisitions, and alternative marketing strategies and can better recommend their total banking services, which are considerable, to a company which they understand well.

6. Your banker, in essence, will become expert in your business or industry, because of your assistance. His own career path will be eased, and you will have an invaluable financial colleague who can help ease your way, within your own company or another with which you may become associated in the future.

The cultivation of this association should be an on-going thing, whether or not the firm is currently borrowing or anticipating raising additional equity. There may be no need for banking services today, but there surely will be in the future. The banking relationship may be almost impossible to establish on short notice when it is needed. It must already be in place.

Bankers develop confidence in a company when detailed financial information is presented to them on a continuing basis. This provides support for loans they have made or will make, keeps them continually informed, permits them to monitor progress, and gives them confidence in the integrity of the company. Bank credit agreements frequently call for quarterly internal financial statements and year-end certified audit reports. Monthly statements are better, however, to accomplish the above ends, and they should be offered to banks even though they are not specified in any agreements. As a minimum, the following financial data should be submitted:

1. Monthly Operating Statement (P&L), compared to budget.

2. Monthly Balance Sheet.

3. Monthly narrative report consisting of a brief, few lines explanation for any significant changes in key balance sheet items or in variation from budgeted operations.

4. Monthly Statement of Changes in Financial Position, or some other acceptable variant on the statement of source and application of funds.

5. Schedule of Bank Credit Agreement Limitations (see Exhibit 1-a) showing restrictions and limitations set by the bank and the company's performance vis a vis them.

Most companies prepare most of this data monthly, as a matter of routine, so that no extra effort need be expended to supply it to the banks. The availability of it will satisfy the most stringent requirements. Additional schedules may be made available on request, to suit the type of loan being made. These could include inventory schedules, 90-day cash forecasts, 12-month cash requirements projections, and 12-month operating statement projections.

SUMMARIZING AND SCHEDULING CREDIT AND LOAN ARRANGEMENTS

Bank agreements, credit and security agreements, and debt arrangements are generally lengthy documents, replete with representations, warranties, and restrictive covenants. The agreement, itself, is not a working document and needs to be reduced to a manageable form, so that that those workers involved in administering the agreement may find their way through it. Usually, a 100-page document can be outlined and summarized in five or six pages. Article and Section numbers of the agreement can be referenced to page numbers and a brief summary given of pertinent paragraphs. A Credit and Security Agreement Summary is illustrated at Exhibit I-b. Its use will save hours in searching out those clauses which are needed for ready reference.

Similarly, the schedule of limitations or restrictions under the agreement,

Exhibit I-a, should be circulated to all executives and decision makers, to be used as a gentle reminder of prior commitments when negotiating new contracts and commitments. The treasurer will monitor this schedule monthly and will alert other officers of approaching limits.

An overview should also be taken of cash in major bank accounts and of current short-term borrowings from banks under the terms of existing bank agreements. These schedules are maintained on a daily basis and present a running history of bank balances and daily borrowings. They are illustrated in Exhibits 1-c and 1-d. The treasurer utilizes them in maintaining balances requirements, transferring funds between banks, and limiting borrowings to obtain maximum utilization of the float. Each column on the Bank Borrowings schedule is supported with a detailed page showing all deposits and disbursements into that bank, summarized on a daily basis, which enables a better estimate of outstanding checks which affect the float. The supporting page is shown at Exhibit 1-e. Note that the total ties in to the appropriate column of 1-c. Additional supporting schedules can be prepared to supplement I-e, showing areas of the country to which checks have been mailed—an indicator of how quickly they will be returned through the Federal Reserve system.

These summary schedules should be posted with all bank reconciliation adjustments and agreed to financial statement balances for cash and bank debt at month end. When this is done, they serve as a valuable audit trail at fiscal year end and are useful in composing the footnote to financial statements relating to bank balances and/or bank debt.

INCREASING CASH FLOW THROUGH BANKING ARRANGEMENTS

Having established the basic bank borrowing agreements and the summary schedules to monitor cash and bank debt, you may now devote your attention to maximizing cash utilization. The schedules in Exhibits 1-c and 1-d are merely starting points. There are at least five additional methods of increasing cash flow through unique banking arrangements:

1. *Lock Box Banking*—Companies with customers outside their immediate metropolitan area should explore the flow of customers' checks from the mailing point through the Federal Reserve Banking System. Most banks perform lock box services or will refer you to a bank which does. Setting up a lock box usually involves giving the bank an entire month's receipts, either checks or data processing runs, showing amounts and dates received by territory. If your system does not provide for territory coding, envelopes may be saved for an entire month, date stamped with receipt and check amount. The bank will process these through their lock box computer program and will output a report showing the optimum locations for lock box accounts. This report allows for mailing time and the lag in clearance through the Federal Reserve System. Such a report is reproduced at Exhibit 1-f, evidencing in the case of the company exhibited, that San Francisco, Chicago, and New York provide fastest

clearance of funds. Customers are then instructed, at the time they are invoiced for merchandise, to remit to a special lock box account number at a particular post office address. The bank is authorized to pick up checks at the lock box post office and deposit them in a special box bank account. Funds are then cleared from this special lock box bank account in the company's regular general account on a routine basis. A complete set of lock box instructions is delineated at Exhibit 1-g. These instructions not only provide the mechanics of the operation but also the internal accounts receivable control which is needed.

Lock Box Banking, in addition to clearing funds more quickly, offers the following advantages:

a. Checks are picked up at the post office on Saturdays, which companies do not normally do.

b. The possibility of employee fraud is eliminated. Only bank employees handle checks and the bank is responsible for defalcations. The company can save the cost of employee dishonesty bonds or similar insurance.

c. The company saves the cost of establishing internal control procedures between accounts receivable and accounting departments since there is no actual handling of cash or checks.

d. Checks are deposited on a timely basis. The company is not concerned with key employee illness or other factors which could delay timely deposits.

Lock Box Banking advantages may usually be obtained without cost to the company. The cost of the bank's services will usually be met by the balances in the lock box account. This enables the company to still obtain greater balances utilization, on an overall basis, plus the above advantages.

2. *Zero Balance Accounts*—These are usually ancillary accounts, in addition to the company's principal or general account, used for petty cash, freight payments on a weekly basis, travel expense accounts, municipal tax payments, payrolls and other frequently used special accounts. They are, therefore, working bank accounts which are not used to carry balances but are kept at zero. A letter of instructions is given to the bank, authorizing them to make transfers before the close of banking business, each day, in an amount sufficient to cover the checks returned for payment to the zero balance account. A limit is usually placed on the amount which may be transferred, say $5000, and any larger transfers must be approved by a signatory. Transfers are made from the general account, where balances are normally maintained, and advice of such transfer is forwarded to the treasurer's department on a daily basis. Thus, maximum utilization of cash is the result, as small balances need not be carried in these operating accounts in anticipation of checks being returned.

3. *Imprest and Color-coded Accounts*—Imprest accounts are similar to zero balance accounts in that the amount of the deposit exactly equals the checks written. The difference however, is that imprest account deposits are made at the time checks are written, or a few days after, when they are expected to be returned for payments. They do not provide quite as much cash utilization as zero balance bank accounts, but

in those cases where the bank is not equipped or prepared to make pre-authorized zero balance transfers, the imprest method gives the nearest result.

Imprest bank accounts may frequently be used with color-coded checks. Bank reconciliations are completely unnecessary with imprest or zero balance accounts, since the daily deposit exactly equals the daily disbursements. When used in conjunction with color-coded checks, the amount outstanding from any given month may be easily calculated. Normally, six different color codes will suffice for an account without too much activity, changing color each month. A large national payroll account, serving many branch office locations, could use nine colors to allow for lost checks and late stragglers beyond the six-month period. Each month, the canceled checks are totaled by color and subtracted from the total of checks originally written. The difference is the amount outstanding to be carried forward to next month. Color-coded checks may then be arranged in numerical order and filed. After two months of no activity in a particular color, the outstanding checks may be canceled, stop payments issued, and the bank balance adjusted. The individual outstanding check should then be investigated to determine why it hasn't been returned. In the case of payroll checks, this may indicate some flaw in the system for handling checks sent to terminated employees at remote offices. The color-coded check, therefore, serves to eliminate the traditional bank reconciliation, substituting instead adding machine tapes, and also as an internal control system review.

4. *Petty Cash Accounts*—These accounts are best handled on an imprest or zero balance basis. Maximum cash utilization is obtained by well documented procedures on when to use petty cash or to pay through the company's general account. When petty cash is used as a checking account, rather than as a true cash box, bills tend to be paid more promptly than they would through the general account. In the case of a company with a great many field offices and remote locations, there can be hundreds of petty cash checking accounts, all paying vendors bills more quickly than necessary. Here are a few simple rules for controlling petty cash payments, which may be adapted to suit any particular company:

a. Invoices in amounts over $50 may not be paid through petty cash fund checks (to avoid too prompt payment of larger invoices).

b. Invoices in amounts under $50 *must* be paid through petty cash fund checks (to avoid the unnecessary expense of purchase requisitions, purchase orders, receiving reports and vouching for payment).

c. Collect freight bills may not be paid through petty cash funds. Vendor shipments should be made freight prepaid and billed back on vendor invoice. Inter-branch shipments should be freight prepaid by the shipping branch. All this avoids duplicate freight payments and the need for checking every freight bill to determine whether it is a proper charge or whether it has been paid by another branch or the headquarters office.

d. Expense reports which require higher approvals (above that of the office administering the petty cash fund) may not be paid through petty cash. This keeps proper controls on excess Travel & Entertainment expense spending.

e. A petty cash voucher must be made out for each disbursement, and this must be supported by a vendor's receipt. Hence, two documents are needed, one from the approver and one from the vendor.

f. Petty cash reconcilations must be submitted with each reimbursement request, and these should be home office audited to verify conformity to procedures.

g. Petty cash reimbursements must be made at least once a month (to avoid a requirement to establish a larger fund than necessary. Like inventory, a faster turnover requires less investment).

5. *Accounts Payable Imprest Accounts*—The company's principal account for bill payments is the Accounts Payable bank account. The volume and activity is such that it may not be operated as a zero balance account. However, operating it on an imprest basis, making daily deposits in the same amount as daily disbursements, will provide maximum cash flow. This can be further increased by using the schedules of Bank Borrowings in Exhibit 1-c and the detailed support in Exhibit 1-e. Deposits into the imprest account can be written and timed, based on the section of the country to which the disbursement was sent.

FINANCIAL ARRANGEMENTS WITH VENDORS AND PAYMENTS CONTROLS

Payments to vendors are most frequently made in accordance with the terms on the vendor's invoice—in short, to accommodate the vendor. This is not the best way. Vendors' terms are myriad. This means an assortment of data processing runs and different check writing dates during any month. Instead, the company as the buyer can generally set its own terms of payment to suit its own data processing or accounts payable system. If the method of payment is consistent, the vendor will usually accept it. If not, the Purchasing Department can usually educate the vendor to acquiesce and, on occasion, may find it necessary to replace the vendor.

A good company method is one which provides for two general payment periods per month. Bills for net payment (no discount) are paid on the 25th of the month following receipt in the accounts payable department. Bills with discounts are paid on the 10th of the month following receipt. Note that the controlling date is not the date of the vendor's invoice but, rather, the date received in the accounts payable department for processing. This schedule can be varied somewhat in the vendor's favor by using a 5th-of-the-month cut-off date—invoices received in accounts payble by the 5th of the month are considered as received in the prior month. This type of variation, though, is not at all necessary to gain vendor acceptance, unless the company deals with many vendors who traditionally complete heavy shipments during the last few days of each month, thereby throwing their billings in to the first of the following month.

The results of such a payment system are to translate 30-day terms from the vendor into payments of 25 to 55 days, and 10-day discount terms into 10-to 40-day discount terms, plus the added savings of only two processings per month. There are also considerable time savings in tracing unpaid invoices through the system using a two-payment system.

An adjunct to a two-payment system usually would provide for a payments run every Friday. This would handle freight bills which carry an ICC payment requirement of seven days, and expense reimbursements to employees which need prompt payment. Certain classes of trade accounts payable may also be coded to fit into the Friday payment runs. These might be utility bills or personnel recruitment agency bills which usually require more immediate payment.

At any rate, it is obvious that with a firmly established payment schedule, suited to the company's own data processing or accounts payable system, significant extra cash utilization may be obtained. This will, of course, require the support of the Purchasing Department in establishing these terms with vendors. But even where they have not been pre-established, vendors will rarely complain if the method is consistently followed.

The Purchasing Department can contribute even more to additional and repetitive cash savings by specifying discount terms with all new vendors and insisting on them in renegotiating contracts with old vendors. Once the discount terms are negotiated, the vendor may very well consider that he has given the customer a price discount, but he tends to forget about it on subsequent reorders or on new jobs. The effect is the same as if the company had received a permanent price reduction. Purchasing may take a firm stance in this regard, even refusing to do business with those vendors who do not allow such cash discounts.

The vendor's arguments against allowing discount terms can be easily overcome by the Purchasing Manager. This will require his education by the Controller on the advantages to the seller of allowing such discounts. Breathes there a financial officer who has never agonized over whether or not to allow such discounts to the company's own customers. Here are some of the arguments in favor of allowing discount terms of say, 2/10/eom:

1. Customers who can afford to pay sooner do not, unless discount terms are made available to them.

2. Customers who cannot afford to pay sooner will do so, diverting funds from other vendors not offering discounts.

3. A 2% discount for payment within 10 days gives the vendor the use of 98% of the money for an extra 20 days.

4. While this has a cost of 37% per annum ($2 for 20 days = $36 for a 360-day year, or 37% on $98), the company probably earns close to this on its invested capital.

5. A faster turnover on trade accounts receivable gives the balance sheet a better look and is the mark of a well managed company. Banks and investors have more confidence.

6. Less credit need be used to carry receivables, allowing the company to borrow for more important needs, such as capital expenditures or research and development.

7. Vendor's sales are probably increased when discounts are allowed, as customers tend to purchase in larger amounts to achieve greater savings. This, at least, is valid in the first fiscal period in which the discount is initiated.

8. In the case of customers who are able to take discounts but do not, there is no certainty that payment will be made on the net due date, 30 days after shipment. There is no incentive to make payment on the net due date, and no penalty for failure to do so, Consequently, if a more attractive alternative appears, funds may be diverted.

9. On an after tax basis, the 2% discount is really a 1% discount for most companies, assuming a 50% tax rate, and the 37% effective rate is really half that.

Compromises will occasionally have to be made in the two-payment system described above, probably with a few key vendors. In these cases, the responsibility for such special payment terms is a treasury function. When payment methods are varied, an attempt should be made to fit the new method in to the existing accounts payable system. For example, if a key vendor will not permit payments on the 25th of the month following, but offers instead that shipments of the preceding month be paid twice during the following month, a good compromise would be to pay on the 10th and 25th of the following month, as these are regular data processing run dates. Shipments from the 1st to the 15th could be paid on the 10th of the following month (a 25- to 40-day payment span), and shipments from the 16th to the 31st could be paid on the 25th of the month following (again a 25- to 40-day span).

Improper planning or unforeseen circumstances will sometimes dictate a change in some key vendor payment terms. When this happens, the vendor should be contacted personally by the treasurer and advised, with complete candor, as to the reason for the delay, how long it will last, whether it will recur next month. Advance notice to the vendor is a courtesy to permit proper cash planning on his part.

With banking and other borrowing relationships established to provide for the ebb and flow of funds required to operate your company, an accounts payable system must be defined to provide for payments to vendors on a prompt and accurate basis. Any accounts payable system, whether manual or automated, will provide for the following controls:

1. Date-in stamp the receipt of the vendor's invoice.

2. Require a receiving report for all invoices except repetitive utilities or services.

3. Agree bills of ladings, packing slips, and receiving reports as to quantities and whether freight is prepaid or collect to each other and to purchase orders.

4. Agree vendor's invoice to purchase order as to quantity, price, freight and terms of payment, extensions.

5. Indicate initialed approval of the above audits through an approval stamp.

6. Provide for a schedule of payments within the defined payment system, say on the 10th and 25th of the month following.

7. Provide for two-signature check signing control, at specified dollar levels.

8. Reconcile key vendor statements monthly to avoid unrecorded liabilities.

9. Research unmatched receiving reports monthly to avoid unrecorded liabilities.

10. Research unmatched invoices monthly to insure vendor payment in accord with terms.

11. Provide for routine duplicate invoice payment checks, using a computer edit and/or a manual check-off list showing that the invoice has not been previously paid. The check-off list would include:
    a. Petty cash vouchers.
    b. Paid bill file.
    c. Unmatched invoice file.
    d. Invoices in process of payment.
    e. Purchase order files—completed and open.
    f. Original approver—does he recall invoice?
    g. Receiving report records.

12. Maintain a payment history file for key vendors, to include all non-receiving report repetitive utility and services vendors.

13. Provide a chart of accounts code for all accounts payable vouchers to allow easy manipulation of data.

Computer-oriented systems maintain payment history files easily, on tape or disk. The problem is more complex in a manual system. Some sort of record control is necessary to verify that payment has been made for the variety of repetitive services that are intangible in nature—rent, financing payments, utilities, repairs, medical services, personnel recruitment agencies and a host of others. The problem can be extremely severe in the case of an installment obligation, say 60 payments of $100 each, monthly. An example of this type of payment could be rent for premises, a premises cleaning and maintenance service, or an installment loan to finance a delivery truck. The company may have a coupon book to use for each monthly payment; the landlord may bill monthly for rent and so, too, may the cleaning service. Even with such billing by the vendor, there is usually no receiving report for such services rendered, no purchase requisition or purchase order, no inventory control and, generally, no positive way to determine that a duplicate payment is not being made, or that one of the repetitive payments has not been missed. A good manual historical record is an accounts payable "jacket," simply a manila folder in which each payment is recorded and which accompanies the check to the check signer as proof that proper payment is being made. A jacket page is shwon at Exhibit 1-h. The elements and advantages of the jacket system are:

1. A brief, one-paragraph description heads up the jacket page, explaining the service being rendered, showing the requirements for monthly payments and bearing the original approver's signature. The criteria as to whether or not to use a jacket are: a) the services are repetitive, even if not in the same dollar amount; b) the services are intangible, hence no product has been delivered and no receiving document will be prepared; c) an invoice may not be rendered by the vendor (even if it is, and criteria a and b are met, the jacket system is to be utilized).

2. If there is a predetermined contract amount, a declining balance column is used

to show the remaining contract amount and to insure that payments beyond the final one are not made.

3. Payment information is shown each month—month being paid, date paid, check number, amount, remarks. Payments are serially numbered.

4. Supporting documentation, such as a contract copy or original Purchase Order copy, is stapled on the left-hand side of the jacket.

5. The jacket is forwarded, monthly, with the check request, as authority for payment of a service without an invoice and/or a receiving report.

6. Jackets are scheduled for payment on the first of each month. A master listing of all jackets is maintained. Jackets pulled for monthly payment are compared to the monthly listing to ascertain that none are missed.

These elements will be included in any automated system, as well, in the form of computer edits and maintenance of a history file that may be recalled on request.

CONTROL PROCEDURE FOR THE FINANCIAL ASPECTS OF CONTRACTS

All contracts will have financial aspects which affect the responsibility of the Treasurer or Controller. Some contracts are directly financial in nature and will not directly concern other departments—insurance policies, bank credit agreements, leases for premises. Other contracts are working tools for other departments, such as a manufacturing contract, but will be used by financial officers to establish terms of payment, or to audit costs.

Proper contract administration will therefore require the following steps:

1. The originals of contracts should be retained in permanent files by the Chief Executive Officer, usually the President of the company. Copies should be retained by the general or in-house counsel and the Chief Financial Officer, with other copies being distributed to concerned parties, including the Treasurer and Controller.

2. These copies should be maintained in working files, in alphabetical order, by the Treasurer or Controller.

3. Working summaries (see Exhibit 1-b) should be prepared for operating personnel.

4. Pertinent dates, including renewal or termination dates, should be "tickled" for proper review.

5. Completed contract copies should be removed from the open files and refiled in an alphabetical Closed Contracts file, kept as a permanent record.

6. Corporate policy should be written specifying which corporate officers may sign contracts. This should be published in the Policy Manual (Chapter 7).

7. Contracts should be reviewed for payment requirements and a determination made whether to include in the accounts payable "jacket" system.

Contracts which are similar in nature, numerous, and special purpose, should be separately filed and administered. This would include insurance policies (see Chapter 4) and landlord/tenant leases for premises.

If the company maintains a great many premises locations, leases may be filed separately by the real estate administrator, or by the accounts payable supervisor, since monthly payments are the responsibility of that department under the jacket method of payment. The Controller, however, should maintain a checklist in processing each lease, to include the following:

1. Insurance coverage is provided in accord with the terms of each lease, both as to property damage and liability. This usually requires that a copy of the lease be sent to the insurance department or the company's insurance broker.

2. Dates for termination of lease, or exercise of renewal options, are "tickled". Termination dates should be tickled 120 days prior to the end, to allow time to search for new premises, if necessary.

3. An Accounts Payable "jacket" is established to provide for repetitive monthly rental payments, with a copy of the lease filed in the jacket. It is best to pay the initial rent from the date of signing to the end of the calendar month, say from March 18th to the 31st, thereafter paying on the 1st of each month on a calendar basis.

4. The lease is recorded on a special Leased Premises summary sheet, showing all pertinent information such as location, square footage, cost per foot, monthly rent, landlord's name, lease period, and any renewal options. This is seen at Exhibit 1-i. It is a convenient summary to use for a great many locations and is also useful in calculating the company's amounts payable under lease obligations (long-term indebtedness) for the Annual Report and 10K, annually for the next two years and thereafter through five years.

INVESTING SHORT-TERM FUNDS

Proper cash management will occasionally produce excess cash. This may arise due to the timing of long-term debt offerings or equity issues, or simply because of the cyclical nature of the business. Excess short-term funds may be invested in a variety of ways to produce income or reduce costs for the company:

1. Short-term bank debt may be temporarily reduced to save on interest costs.

2. Heavier purchases of inventories may be made if there is an expectation of inventory cost increases. This should be examined in the light of the cost of carrying additional inventories. These excess inventories should be planned to liquidate themselves in 90 days.

3. Marketable securities may be purchased, consonant with the degree of risk you are prepared to assume. This may include tax-free municipal bonds and other Moody's-rated industrial bonds. Commercial Paper is also issued by rated businesses at somewhat higher rates of return, with little risk.

4. Short-term interest-bearing Certificates of Deposit are available from banks for 30-, 60- and 90-day periods.

5. If the company purchases from overseas markets, excess dollars may be used to purchase currency in forward markets, at today's prices, thereby hedging against currency fluctuations.

6. Link-financing transactions may be negotiated with other companies. You establish an interest-bearing Certificate of Deposit with a bank specified by the other company. The bank makes prime rate loans to the other company, using your deposit in times of tight money conditions. You receive points or a fee from the other company which, combined with your interest on the CD, gives you a higher rate of return than you could normally obtain. When negotiated with a customer, the device cements a selling relationship. When done with a vendor, it assures a supply of the merchandise you buy and provides additional surety of the receipt of your points or fee through your right to offset against payments due to the vendor.

7. Excess bank balances may be carried with your working banks, at no interest income to you, to compensate them for those times when you may have to operate with less than the required balances.

8. The company may purchase its own securities and resell them at a later date, subject to meeting SEC requirements. The shares may also be issued to employees under incentive or stock option programs. Such a purchase reduces the number of outstanding shares and thus increases earnings per share.

OTHER SHORT-TERM BORROWING TECHNIQUES

In addition to usual bank financing and the maximum utilization of cash within the company, there are a number of other techniques that may be explored to raise short-run monies. When used in this context, short-run is intended to mean for periods of one year or less. Some of the methods below may also be translated into long-term arrangements with proper contract provisions:

1. *Equipment Lease Financing*—may be done with a variety of equipment leasors, to finance furniture and fixtures, materials handling and manufacturing equipment, with monthly payments from 1 to 5 years. Financing rates are quoted as "add-on" rates and range from 6% to 10% add-on, which translates to almost double that for simple interest. The yield to the lessor is highest on a shorter-term lease. The obligation is not reflected on the balance sheet and may usually be in addition to existing bank credit lines. More is discussed in the chapter on Long-Term Borrowings.

2. *Commercial Financing*—may usually be done for periods of at least one year, and thereafter may be terminated with little notice. This involves borrowing on trade accounts receivable, usually 80% advances on those receivables which are not more than 90 days past due, at a cost which is 150%-200% of bank prime interest rates. Such a rate can work out to 1% on net sales. Added features of financing can be revolving inventory loans to provide greater borrowing capability.

3. *Factoring*—is a variant on commercial financing, with the major difference being that the receivables are actually sold to the factor, collected by the factor, and

rates are somewhat lower than charged by commercial finance companies. Since the receivables are sold with recourse, factoring works best when the receivables are of high quality.

4. *Commercial Paper*—may be issued by the company to obtain funds to supplement bank borrowings. This is generally confined to companies in the $100 million sales level, issuing paper in the aggregate of $10 million in lots of $100,000. The paper may be issued for any number of convenient months and the rates paid depend on the credit of the issuer and the length of time for which issued, but the rates are traditionally in the area of prime.

5. *Letters of Credit*—are guarantees of payment by a bank on submission of proof of shipment or other performance. They avoid the necessity of the company paying cash in advance of shipment and tying up funds that could be used to better advantage in the business. Banks charge a fee and a rate for bankers' acceptances arising after shipment which, in combination, is always approximately the same as prime.

6. *Link Financing*—as described above, may be used on the other end of the transaction, to borrow money based on the credit of a customer or supplier. The cost is always in excess of prime, due to the points or fee paid to the supplier of the Certificate of Deposit.

7. *Inventory Reductions*—may be planned for limited periods of time to free funds for short periods of time. A comparison must be made of the risk associated with short inventories and the cost of other short-term fund raising alternatives.

8. *Bank Balances*—may be worked down, provided that banks understand that the shortfall will be made up with excess balances being carried at a later date.

9. *Treasury Stock*—previously acquired, may be resold, subject to SEC regulations, or issued under incentive or stock option programs.

There are other short-run management expedients which may be employed to increase cash availability. These involve the proper deployment of the resources of the company in any given department. Accounts receivable turnover may be increased by mounting a special-effort collection campaign with past due customers owing in excess of specific amounts. A national service department may embark on an overtime program to repair and make salable the company's product, thereby increasing inventory turnover and freeing up cash. The customer service department may "blitz" the issuance of credit memos to customers for returned merchandise and billing adjustments, thereby making it easier for the collection people to enforce prompt payments of trade accounts receivables. Proper cash flow, in other words, is directly affected by the total management approach which is concerned with all facets of the operation of the company.

PRACTICAL POINTERS

Banking and financial arrangements are concerned not only with establishing credit lines and relations with bankers but with methods to obtain maximum utilization of cash through the use of special bank accounts and vendor payment systems. The company's cash is affected by its contractual relationships which are administered by the Treasurer and Controller. Short-term borrowings are often necessary to augment normal bank credit lines and, occasionally, temporary imbalances create extra funds which need to be employed effectively. A solid measure of the level of performance of the Treasurer and Controller is the efficacy with which these functions are handled.

CHAPTER 2

Long-Term Borrowing Techniques

THE Treasurer's primary function, the first one listed in the FEI's definition, is the Provision of Capital . . . . to establish and execute programs for the provision of the capital required by the business, including negotiating the procurement of capital and maintaining the required financial arrangements. The need for capital may be considered to be short-term or long-term, some organizations even classifying a medium-term need. Short-term capital requirements, those needed to supply the company for the coming year, were discussed in Chapter 1. Anything longer than one year, we shall consider as a long-term need. The medium-term need may be defined as one to three years, usually by stable companies that utilize long-range planning techniques of five years or longer. Some of the short-term devices discussed in the first chapter, such as equipment lease financing and the use of commercial paper, are often continuing and revolving in nature and so may be considered to be long-term. This chapter will discuss the various capital alternatives, their advantages and disadvantages, their cost, accounting considerations, and how to choose the best alternative.

Types of long-term borrowing include the following:

1. Equity.
2. Bank debt.
3. Straight debt.
4. Debt with equity.
5. Installment loans and leases.
6. Acquisitions.

EQUITY

Equity tops the list. You may not ordinarily think of it as long-term debt, but it really is the ultimate and longest-term debt, and usually the lowest cost. Unlike other debt, shareholders do not acquire the right to the repayment of a fixed amount of principal and interest but, rather, the shareholder has the right to share in the company's fortunes, whatever they may be. If the company is successful, his share in that success will be much greater than the lender's fixed interest. If the company fails and is liquidated, he will suffer a much worse fate since he stands behind, or junior to the lender's principal and interest before the shareholder can be paid whatever remains of the company's assets, if anything.

Stream of Earnings Approach

The cost of equity, when viewed from a cash flow standpoint, is the least expensive cost of any capital available. This cost includes the underwriting spread, legal, accounting, and printing costs, as well as the cost of future cash dividends. In a growth company, or one which stresses the price of its publicly traded shares, dividends may never be paid and equity is veritably the cheapest capital, its issuance costs being minimal.

Conceptually, however, all of the earnings belong to the shareholders, and the cost of equity is equal to the minimum rate of return that the company must earn on the equity funds to avoid any fall in the market price of the company's stock. Expressed as a formula, the cost of equity capital is

$$\frac{Ea}{P}$$

in which Ea is expected earnings per share and P is current stock price. This concept is acceptable when you view the value of any share to its owner as a claim on a stream of company earnings, rather than a claim upon cash flows from the company in the form of dividends. Using the claim on earnings concept, let us compute the cost of raising capital in an example:

> A company decides to raise $1 million of new equity at a time when its stock is selling for $12 per share, it has 1 million shares issued and outstanding, and it earns after taxes $1 per share (its price/earnings ratio is therefore 12). The new shares will probably have to sell at a more attractive price than the current $12, say $10 and, so, 100,000 new shares must be issued to raise the required $1 million.
>
> There will now be 1,100,000 shares outstanding, and if earnings remain the same at $1 million, the earnings per share will fall from $1 to $0.91 ($1,000,000 ÷ 1,100,000), and the price of the stock will fall from $12 to $10.92 (12 x $.91). The cost of this equity may then be said to be 8.3% ($0.91 ÷ $10.92) (using the formula Ea/P).

In the calculation above, note that we have used the old reported earnings of $1 million, but our formula calls for Ea or anticipated earnings. One must assume that the company has no need to raise $1 million of additional equity unless it has a productive use for that capital, one which will produce additional earnings for the company. The effect on earnings per share of these new earnings will offset the fall in earnings per share that results from selling the additional shares. If the earnings on the new capital are high enough, they will fully offset the effects of the dilution caused by selling the new stock, and shareholder wealth will be unaffected. Therefore, Ea, or expected earnings, may be assumed to be those earnings which will cause zero dilution in the price of the shares held by existing stockholders. Using this assumption, the cost of equity may then be determined to be:

> Earnings per share continue at $1 or $1,100,000, the price of the stock remains at 12 times earnings or $12, and the cost of this equity may then be said to be the same 8.3% as before ($1 ÷ $12). Obviously, the price per share has increased in proportion to the earnings per share and the cost of equity remains constant. The cost of this capital would rise only in the event that earnings continued at $1 million and an earnings per share of $0.909 would result ($1,000,000 ÷ 1,100,000). The capital cost would then be 9.1%, assuming a stock price of $10 per share, based on the current market price at which the new shares were sold.

The price/earnings ratio, expected, then is the determinant of the cost of capital, based on the expected stream of earnings. Examining this further, you may determine this to be the least costly alternative, depending on that p/e ratio, especially when related to the cost of other debt. If long-term institutional debt is available at 7%, this would be preferred to an 8.3% cost of equity. On the other hand, if the p/e ratio were 20, the cost of equity would be 5% ($1 per share ÷ $20 per share), and this would appear to be the most desirable alternative.

Cash Flow from Dividends Approach

Another approach, as inferred above, for dividend paying companies, or those which are expected to pay dividends, is to cost the equity based upon the cash flows expected from dividends, using the formula:

$$V = \frac{Do}{k\text{-}g}$$

in which

V is the present value of the stock
Do is the current annual dividend
k is the investor's required rate of return
g is the rate of earnings growth, which is less than k, say 6%.

Then, in the example above,

Ea/P equals 8.3%. Assuming a dividend of 10¢ per quarter were paid,

$$k = \frac{Do}{V} + g = \frac{.40}{12} + 6\% = 3.3\% + 6\% = 9.3\%$$

Either approach to the cost of equity may be used, depending on whether or not dividends are expected.

Cost of Retained Earnings

A sub-set of equity is retained earnings, after tax profits which have been plowed back into the company, rather than distributed to shareholders through cash dividends. The cost of these funds is the same as externally raised equity, except that earnings paid out in dividends are subject to double taxation. The company pays a tax on the pre-dividend income, and the individual pays a tax on the dividend. Retained earnings, however, avoid this double tax. Thus, the cost of retained earnings (which may be considered to be internal equity compared to raising external equity) is the cost of raising external equity times the reciprocal of the average tax rate of the company's stockholders. For example, if the cost of raising equity were 8.3% as in previous examples, and average shareholders were in a 30% tax bracket, then the cost of retained earnings is:

$$8.3\% \times (1.0 - .30) = 8.3\% \times .70 = 5.8\%$$

This method may not be used for single proprietorships, partnerships, nor corporations that elect to be taxed as partnerships, as they are not subject to the double tax.

BANK DEBT

Demand loans, short-term bank borrowings, are the most common form of bank debt. Banks generally initiate their borrowing relationships with short-term debt. As confidence is built, banks will participate in longer-term relationships, usually two- or three-year revolving credits. By revolving credit, I mean those loans which have a debt ceiling in dollars, funds being lent on a formula, say total dollar value of receivables and inventory. The loan fluctuates, up or down, based on the formula and subject to the lending limit, and the overall agreement may run for a year, or two, or three. It is a term loan, by any definition, despite the revolving nature of the collateral, since the company's borrowings will tend to remain the same from year to year. At any rate, given constant collateral conditions, the loan will remain approximately the same, being reduced only by profits which are turned back into the operations.

Even short-term bank debt may be considered long-term under certain conditions. Demand notes may not be called and 30- or 60-day notes are continually revolved. If the loan is outstanding more than a year or is contemplated to be, then it is term in nature. Many banks lend short-term for 11 months, with a requirement that the loan be paid off for 30 days and then renewed. The payoff may be from corporate working capital or another bank. Cash may be generated internally, using inventory and accounts payable methods described in Chapter 1, in anticipation of the payoff. Or, a line of credit may be established, but not used, with another bank or two, being used for the paydown. In this event, the short-term debt is extended beyond a year, almost indefinitely, and the loan may be characterized as long-term for all practical purposes. Your accountants will, of course, continue to classify it as short-term.

Short-term debt of this nature is usually available only when a good credit rating is presented. The debt carries a favorable interest rate and may not be secured. The revolving credit, on the other hand, is secured, and contrary to most long-term debt, carries a higher rate than short-term borrowings. The revolving credit also is subject to specific operating constraints, which may be onerous to the management but which, generally, bankers will consider to be prudent restrictions necessary to protect their secured interest. These include requriements to maintain net worth and working capital at pre-determined levels, debt to equity limitations, and limits on capital spending. An example of these constraints is shown in the Schedule of Limitations Under Bank Agreement at Exhibit 1-a. The cost of this type of long-term bank debt is simply the interest rate, expressed as the formula:

$$k = I/P$$

where k is the rate of return; I is the annual interest cost, and P is the total value of the debt—in short, the simple interest rate. This cost, and this formula, may be considered to be valid where the company maintains a stable amount of debt; as one bank loan is paid off it is replaced with another. If the debt is one-time, that is not replaced, its true cost is not the simple interest rate but such cost must consider the expected outflows and the discount rate which makes these outflows just equal to the net proceeds obtained from the lending source. In short, the outstanding loan balances must be discounted to a present value basis.

From an accounting standpoint, revolving loans may usually be treated as long-term liabilities if they have a maturity of more than one year and the borrower has the right and a clear intention to renew or revolve the loan.

STRAIGHT DEBT

Straight debt refers to long-term borrowing in the form of bonds, notes, or debentures, without options, warrants, stock or other equity features attached to it. Straight debt is available from private individuals, funds, institutions, or insurance companies. It may be new debt or a refunding of an older bond issue.

Features

The bond is, in essence, an interest-bearing IOU. The IOU contains stipulations as to the principal sum to be repaid, dates of repayment, specific claims or liens against assets, and protective covenants. The protective covenants are a normal feature since the bond is a long-term investment with risk presumed to increase as the time-span of the investment increases. Typical covenants are:

1. Duties of the trustee.

2. Limitations on further borrowing.

3. Minimum financial ratios.

4. Limitations on cash dividends.

5. Sinking fund requirements.

6. Callable features.

7. Public registration.

A Term Sheet containing typical restrictive covenants is illustrated at Exhibit 2-a. This exhibits the terms, conditions and covenants for convertible senior subordinated notes. While there are additional features which relate to their convertibility, straight debt carries the same type of covenants.

The above general terms are characteristic of all long-term debt. There are, though, distinct features to various types of bonds, as discussed below:

1. *Mortgage Bonds*—give the lender a specified claim against stipulated real assets of the borrowing corporation, presumably reducing the risk to the lender. Such bonds may be open-end (more bonds of the same priority may be issued against the specified assets), or closed-end. Open-ended bonds imply that the borrower was in a strong borrowing position at the time of original issuance. When closed-end bonds are issued, if the corporation needs to raise additional long-term debt, it must issue bonds against different assets or must subordinate them to the original issue. If the borrower was in a weak borrowing position, such bonds may contain an "after-acquired property clause," meaning the lenders receive a claim against the specified assets in existence when the loan was made and all other assets of the specified type acquired at a later date as long as the bond issue is outstanding.

2. *Collateral Trust Bonds*—are similar to mortgage bonds in that they give the lender a claim against specified assets. The difference is that collateral trust bonds secure financial assets, stock and bonds, whereas mortgage bonds secure physical plant and equipment.

3. *Equipment Trust Certificates*—are like mortgage bonds in that they give the lender a claim against equipment, such as rolling stock (used mostly by the railroads). The main difference is that title to the equipment belongs to the lender, rather than the corporation, until the debt is finally paid off. To this extent, they may be considered to be lease financing. This variant on mortgage bonds arose as corporations found a need to raise new funds to finance the purchase of new equipment without having the property come under the after-acquired clause described above.

4. *Debentures*—are unsecured bonds that carry no claim against any specific assets. The lender may look only to the earning power of the corporation for repayment. Such bonds are usually issued by firms with strong earnings and low risk ratings. They also usually carry more restrictive covenants than mortgage bonds, though not always, due to the strong bargaining positions of the issuers.

5. *Subordinated Debentures*—are also unsecured and carry only a secondary claim against the corporation's earnings or its assets in liquidation. Such bonds carry an increased risk to the lender and, hence, usually give him a greater rate of return.

The corporation views these as near equity, ranking ahead of preferred and common stock, but behind all other secured and unsecured debt. These are usually issued when existing bond indenture agreements prohibit the issuance of additional debt having an equal claim against the corporation's earnings and assets. Several stages of subordination may be used, resulting in layers of subordinated debt with titles like "second subordinated debentures" and "third subordinated debentures." Successive subordination usually results in higher interest rates. Rates are often reduced on subordinated debentures by combining them with a convertible feature.

6. *Income Bonds*—are debt security wherein the interest payment depends on earnings. There is no legal obligation for interest payments unless earnings are adequate enough to permit such payments. These bonds are appropriate for companies with large fixed-capital investments and large fluctuations in earnings, or for emerging companies with the expectation of low earnings in the early years. Railroads, hotels and motels have used Income Bonds for these reasons. The interest on such bonds, like the dividend on preferred stocks, may be cumulative or noncumulative. Because of the added flexibility such bonds give to the corporation, they usually carry a higher interest rate than all other bonds. Many corporations have used Income Bonds to retire preferred stocks, since the interest paid on the bond is tax deductible but the preferred dividend is not.

The Cost of Debt

This is not simply the interest rate paid for funds, nor even the after-tax rate, but rather is based on the expected costs, or outflows and the discount rate that makes these outflows exactly equal to the net proceeds of the loan. This is a discounted cash flow concept and may be expressed by:

$$P_o = \frac{C1}{(1+k)^1} + \frac{C2}{(1+k)^2} + \ldots + \frac{Cn}{(1+k)^n}$$

where:

    P_o = net proceeds in year o
    $C1$ = total cost in year 1 and so on
    k = the discount rate; the pretax cost of the debt funds

For example:

assume a $1 million bond issue, for 20 years, with a sinking fund of $50,000 per year, a 7% interest rate, and an annual cost of mailing, administering and handling the bonds of $30,000 (total cost of the bonds is $70,000 interest + $30,000 handling, or $100,000), then

the cost of the bonds will be the discount rate, k, determined from the above equation, or:

$$\$1,000,000 = \frac{\$100,000}{(1+k)^1} + \frac{\$100,000}{(1+k)^2} + \ldots + \frac{\$100,000}{(1+k)^{20}}$$

which is 7.5%.

This type of discounted cash flow calculation is readily available from many time-sharing computer services at a small monthly cost of as low as $80. Such calculations are also available on electronic calculators, hand models, like the Hewlet-Packard HP 80 selling at about $400. The calculation can be done in minutes with these aids.

On the other hand, if it is assumed that the company has perpetual debt, or revolves its debt by paying off one issue and replacing it with another, or does not use sinking funds, or pays off a final balloon amount with another issue's proceeds, then the cost of debt is simply the interest rate using the formula $k = I/P$ as set out on page 36, which is a pre-tax expression. This may be translated to an after-tax amount by:

a. for large firms in a 48% bracket = $k \times (1 - 0.48)$

b. for firms earning under $25,000 = $k \times (1 - 0.26)$

The above rates assume bonds sold at par. If they are sold at a premium or discount, then P, the total value of the debt must be adjusted by the average of the bond's current sale price and its maturity value, and I, the annual interest cost must be adjusted by adding or subtracting the effect of the difference between the proceeds of the debt and the amount of principal that will eventually have to be refunded.

DEBT WITH EQUITY

Subordinated Debentures, as described previously, are near equity in that they rank just ahead of preferred and common stock, but behind all other debt as to a claim on the corporation's earnings or assets in liquidation. Income Bonds, too, are close to preferred stock in nature, but neither Income Bonds nor Subordinated Debentures create or eventually result in the lender having equity in the corporation. There are types of debt that do give this result.

1. *Convertible Bonds*—are the debt equivalent of preferred stock, differing from preferred in that before conversion they have the characteristics of debt. The conversion feature sets out circumstances when, at the option of the holder, the bonds may be converted into common shares. Convertibility is expressed as a price (say $20 a share, meaning a $1000 bond may be converted into 50 shares), or as a ratio (say 50 common shares per $1000 of face value of the bond issue). The conversion price may vary over the life of the security, specifying a higher conversion price or a declining conversion ratio, reflecting the expectation of a higher common stock price over the years as corporate earnings increase. The value of a convertible bond may be based only on its interest rate and the current rates of interest in the capital market, this value giving the bond's value on a yield basis. This value usually provides a downside floor on the value of the bond. It also has an alternative value based on its conversion price, say convertible into 50 shares with a market value of $15 equals $750. The two values are not the same and the bond will tend to sell for close to the higher of the two. If the bond sells on a conversion basis and the price of the common stock falls, the bond price will fall, too, but not below its yield basis. In the absence of a call provision, the bond probably will not be converted as its value will rise whenever the

common stock rises. Thus, the lender enjoys all the capital appreciation on the common, without converting and without even losing the convertible's limited downside risk. In this case, the bondholder would convert only if the dividend yield on the common were to be greater than the interest yield on the bond—an unlikely circumstance. When the company calls the bond for conversion, the holder's decision is based on the comparison of the current call price and the market value of the stock, plus taxes and transaction costs. The corporation will consider the use of convertible bonds when:

a. Increased debt is desirable but difficult or expensive. It may be difficult due to existing indenture restrictions in previous bond issues or simply because interest rates are too high. The equity feature and the possibility of capital appreciation because of the convertibility make a lower interest rate possible.

b. The corporation desires to sell common stock but the price of the common is too low or market conditions do not permit the sale of straight equity. The company is willing to pay the interest cost on the bond, temporarily, as it believes all the bonds will eventually be converted into common. The use of a call feature may force such conversion. The effective cost of this type of equity is reduced, prior to conversion, as the interest paid is tax deductible.

The conversion price must be set carefully if the company desires to attain its objectives of converting its bonds into common stock at the appropriate time. This requires a sensitivity to the technical aspects of the bonds as well as the capital and money markets which is usually best fulfilled by a competent investment banker. A miscalculation will mean:

a. If the conversion price is too high, the conversion value of the bond may never reach its call price and the issue will be uncallable. The company is then saddled with continuing debt.

b. If the conversion price is set too low, the corporation will not achieve its objective of selling its common stock significantly above the current depressed market price. The cost of this type of equity may be too high.

2. *Debt with Warrants or Options*—is a bond issue with an option to buy common stock in the corporation at a stated price. The bond may be any of several types, and the warrant may be for a fixed period of time, or indefinite. They may also be at a single stated price or varying on an increasing scale, based on the expectation of the company for higher prices. They usually are exercisable at 10% to 25% above the present market value price of the stock. The warrants may be detachable from the bond and, therefore, separately tradable, or may be permanently attached and not separable from the bond. This should not be confused with a convertible security which gives the right to change or exchange the bond for stock under certain conditions. The warrant, on the other hand, gives a right to buy, not exchange.

Debt with warrants offers certain advantages:

a. The investor has greater flexibility than with convertibles as the warrants may sometimes be detached and traded separately.

b. The exercise of the warrant produces additional cash for the company; the conversion of convertible debt does not.

As with conversion, exercise of the warrants presupposes a rise in the stock price above the warrant price.

c. The use of warrants may permit a company to issue bonds when it would not otherwise be considered strong enough to do so.

d. The use of warrants may offset the higher rate the corporation might have to pay without the warrants in view of a weak financial position.

Debt with warrants, however, has the following disadvantages:

a. Stock price may have a ceiling while there are outstanding warrants. As the stock price tends to rise above the warrant price, warrant holders will exercise. The resultant exercise dilutes total holdings and tends to depress the price of the stock. Hence, a market value of the stock tends to be established at a level slightly above the exercise price, not higher, until all the warrants are exercised.

b. It is more costly to issue new stock while there are outstanding warrants since the market price of the stock is depressed due to the warrants.

Accounting for Convertible Debt and Debt with Stock Purchase Warrants

Accounting Principles Board (APB) Opinion No. 14 sets forth the accounting principles and rules for dealing with convertible debt and warrants.

No portion of the proceeds from the issuance of convertible debt securities should be accounted for as attributable to the conversion feature. This is a different position from that originally taken under paragraphs 8 and 9 of Opinion No. 10, since suspended, which advocated that the conversion feature be given accounting recognition. Since Opinion 10, experience has indicated that the debt and conversion option are inseparable and so Opinion 14 and its new requirements better reflect both the theoretical situation and the practical considerations. Expressed simply, this means that since there is no discount set up on the issuance of the convertible, there is no loss in profits in later years through amortization of this discount as a charge to earnings.

The Board also reaffirmed in this opinion its previous position regarding debt issued with detachable stock purchase warrants. The proceeds should be allocated to the debt *and* to the warrants based on their respective values at the time of issuance or shortly thereafter. The value attributable to the warrants is to be accounted for as paid-in-capital, with the resulting discount, or reduced premium, treated as debt discount. Once again, any debt discount must be amortized as a charge against future earnings and will serve to reduce earnings per share.

However, when warrants are not detachable from the debt, and the debt security must be surrendered in order to exercise the warrant, the two securities are taken together and are the equivalent of convertible debt—hence there is no attribution to the warrant. If there is a choice and market conditions and interest rates permit it, the warrants should be attachable to avoid a future reduction in earnings per share due to amortization of debt discount.

It is not always possible to clearly identify every type of debt security, as to its broad classification. There are many types of debt with varying conversion features, stock purchase warrants, or a combination of such features. In such case, proper accounting dictates looking to the substance of the transaction. For example, if convertible debt is issued at a substantial premium, there is a strong presumption that such premium represents paid-in-capital and that a portion of the proceeds should be accounted for as being attributable to the conversion feature.

INSTALLMENT LOANS AND LEASES

Installment loans are those obligations payable over a period of years, usually one to five, on a periodic basis, usually monthly or quarterly. While such loans may require payments during the current twelve-month period, they are included in the discussion in this chapter on long-term borrowings, since the major part of such loans is given long-term classification on the balance sheet.

As used in this context, installment loans would include Equipment Trust Certificates (discussed on page 37) and Equipment Lease Financing (see page 29), and any other type of capital equipment purchasing which would include a payment schedule with installments.

The most common type of installment financing is equipment leasing. It offers these decided advantages:

1. Leasing is available to companies of any size, and particularly to smaller companies that are not large enough to do bond issues and to newer companies that have not established a track record which would enable them to sell bonds.

2. The lease liability need not necessarily be shown on the balance sheet. When it is not, the corporation's debt capacity is increased. Present accounting principles require that the lease be capitalized if it is, in fact, an installment purchase. Leases, however, are so varied in their terms, nature and purchase options that they can readily be constructed so as to preclude capitalization and balance sheet presentation.

3. Lease payments are fully tax deductible. If the lease period is shorter than the useful life of the equipment, this will supply greater tax deductions than would depreciation if the asset were purchased outright with proceeds from a bond issue.

4. 100% financing of the equipment, usually with little or no down payment, is available on terms tailored to the user.

5. Most loan indenture agreements and restrictive covenants do not prohibit debt created through leasing, or if they do, a ceiling is set to permit significant amounts of such leasing.

6. Debt financing through the use of leasing does not contain restrictive covenants. There are no limitations on debt to equity, working capital, or dividends.

7. There is no tax problem at audit time over lease payment deductions, as there well might be over useful life and the amount of depreciation claimed.

8. The lease may be structured to provide higher book income in the early years than under outright ownership. The early years' rental payments are generally less than the combined interest expense and depreciation under ownership.

9. State and city franchise and income taxes may be reduced as the property factor, one of three, is reduced.

There may be some disadvantages to leasing, including:

1. Residual rights to the property may be lost at the end of the lease period. In a pure lease, the lessee may have renewal rights or the right to purchase, but these rights require the payment of additional sums.

2. Rentals under the lease may exceed comparable debt service. The lessor probably had to borrow the financed amount and tacked on a profit, structuring his required lease payments to meet this total. If the corporation borrowed its own funds for the purchase, it could avoid the profit factor.

3. There is a loss of operating flexibility and less protection against obsolescence. If a new and better piece of equipment were to become available, it might not be possible to sell or exchange the old equipment. This can be avoided if the lessor will allow a trade-up to newer equipment and will execute a new lease.

4. The lease payment is based on a fixed interest rate. If the cost of money declines, and with it interest rates, the lessee continues to pay the same amount. If, on the other hand, the asset had been purchased outright and financed, the debt could probably be refinanced at a lower rate in a declining money market.

5. There may be a loss of tax benefits which would accrue due to using accelerated depreciation and high interest deductions on the debt in the early years. This would produce a short-term cash advantage if the equipment were bought instead of leased.

Leverage Leasing

The Leverage Lease is a major new financial vehicle for companies involved in making significant capital investments. Such leases are those in which the funds for the purchase of the leased property are provided in part by one or more third parties (loan participants) in addition to the financing institution (the owner or equity participant). Under these leases, a major portion of the lease payments may be typically assigned to these third parties as repayment of their investment, together with interest thereon. If the lessee defaults, the loan participants generally have no right of recover against the owner participant. The loan participant must look only to the lessee and his first lien on the property. The owner participant's return on its investment usually includes some portion of the lease payments, in addition to the income tax benefits during the lease period, as well as proceeds from the sale or re-lease of the property during or at the end of the lease period. The income tax benefits, obviously, are the investment tax credit, depreciation using fast methods, and the related high cash flow in the early years.

Structuring a leveraged lease is a complicated process, requiring thorough familiarity with legal, tax, and accounting details. Because of these complexities, firms have come into being which specialize in structuring this type of lease. The leveraged lease offers a good return to the investor through the utilization of tax benefits, and a lower than normal cost to the lessee. Accounting for leverage leases follows the general rules for lease accounting, discussed below.

Accounting for Leases

Accounting Principals Board Opinion No. 5, Reporting of Leases in Financial Statements of Lessee and subsequent APB Opinion No. 31, Disclosure of Lease Commitments by Lessees, sets forth the accounting rules for treatment of leases in the balance sheets of the lessees, and other statements.

Effectively, these require complete disclosure of lease commitments which are non-capitalized, to enable users of the statements to assess "the present and prospective effect of those commitments upon the financial position, results of operations, and changes in financial position of lessees." Total rental expense affecting operations for the period reported on must be stated; minimum rental commitments under all noncancellable leases should be disclosed for each of the succeeding five fiscal years, each of the next three five-year periods, and the remainder as a single amount. Disclosure must also be made as to renewal or purchase option terms, related guarantees, restrictions on dividends or other debt, and other pertinent information necessary to evaluate the effect of lease commitments upon the financial position. The Board has also recommended the disclosure of the present value of the commitments to assist in evaluating the credit capacity of the lessee and for comparing the lessee's financial position with that of similar entities who use other means of financing to obtain the use of property.

The SEC, moreover, in accounting series releases has set forth a requirement for complete disclosure on the part of public companies, in both Annual Reports and the Form 10-K.

Most public accounting firms recommend the capitalization of leases which are, in actuality, installment purchases of property. Consequently, whether or not the lease is capitalized, present accounting principles and SEC rules require a complete disclosure of the commitments. Since the terms and conditions of every lease may vary, the substance of each transaction must be analyzed to determine whether capitalization is appropriate. The Financial Accounting Standards Board (FASB) is considering the subject of capitalization of leases, and current accounting pronouncements should be reviewed at the time of presentation of financial statements to ascertain that conformity to current accounting rules exists.

Along these same lines, the accounting profession, through the AICPA, is giving current consideration to the presentation of renewable short-term debt on the balance sheet. Conventional thinking indicates that revolving loans and installment purchases may receive long-term debt presentation, below the line, if it is due more than one year from the end of the fiscal year, the lender is financially able to renew the obligation, and the borrower intends to so renew. Accounting pronouncements in this area, too, should be reviewed closely at statement time to enable the company to avail itself of the most favorable presentation in keeping with proper accounting principles.

Sale and Lease Back

A form of leasing is the sale and lease back and, in nature, it is similar to the Mortgage Bond or the Equipment Trust Certificates described previously. It is, however, often accomplished quickly, with little cost, and without any elaborate bond indenture.

Owned property, like land, buildings or equipment, may be sold to an independent finance company at a high percentage of its appraised value, say 80% (subject to negotiation and often contingent on the credit of the owner), and the resultant cash received may be more than original cost if the property has appreciated in value, either as a result of inflation or economic utility. The property may then be leased back, usually for terms of three to eight years.

This is an excellent device to use in inflationary times. The property will usually have appreciated far over its cost, providing windfall cash on the sale. If the property has a long future life or is not expected to be replaced, then the debt incurred on the sale may be paid over future years of the lease with inflated dollars.

Such leases are as varied as the parties desire to have them. Factors receiving particular attention in negotiation are the term of the lease, the rate, and the residual value or renewal option at the end. The rate will be determined by the utilization either party may have of the investment tax credit and depreciation. Sale and lease backs may be structured as leveraged leases and, on occasion, may even be structured as straight debt.

When structured as straight debt, a tax-oriented partnership is usually found to purchase the equipment. The equipment is sold for 8% to 10% cash, the balance due on two notes. One of the notes is amortizing, the other is a non-recourse balloon note. The amount of the monthly rental is set at a level exactly sufficient to pay for the interest and amortization on both notes. At the end of the lease back period, usually five years on this type of program, the balloon note is canceled, and since it is non-recourse, the equipment reverts to the company. The company may account for this as a straight long-term loan, at an interest rate substantially below bank prime, not even accounting for the sale and lease back for financial accounting purposes. For tax purposes, the company will pay a capital gain on the sale and will lose the depreciation advantages of owning its equipment. It may also have an investment tax credit and depreciation recapture. These tax disadvantages will be offset by the higher monthly rental which is a tax deductible charge. The entire transaction can be structured with no unfavorable tax aspects.

The lenders, on the other hand, receive the full tax benefits and cash flow advantages of the tax-sheltered partnership, including depreciation, investment tax credit, and other benefits depending on the structure of the transaction.

The Captive Finance Subsidiary

Companies that manufacture equipment which qualifies for investment tax credits may find it advisable to establish a wholly-owned finance subsidiary. The parent will sell the equipment to the sub., taking full accounting sale treatment. The finance sub. will then lease the equipment to the ultimate user, with these advantages:

1. The finance subsidiary can support a debt to equity ratio greater than the parent's.
    a. Finance subs. do no report traditional balance sheets showing current assets and liabilities. Instead, all assets and liabilities are lumped in a group, without the current classification.
    b. Banks and institutions will traditionally lend at least 2 to 1 on debt to equity, since the subs. assets are always accounts receivable (leases receivable) and are usually secured by the equipment underlying the lease.

2. The customer receives terms of payment in accordance with the lease, from one to five years. This is a great marketing device which the parent would not ordinarily supply.

3. The finance subsidiary usually has an independent name, which facilitates its collection activities against slow-paying lessees.

4. The parent treats the sale to the sub. as a sale, taking in to income the full profit on the sale. This usually requires that the parent's salesman has negotiated a full-pay-out lease with a third-party customer, using the subsidiary's lease document.

5. The finance subsidiary need not be consolidated with the parent, avoiding the necessity of picking up the long-term lease receivable and the short-term bank borrowings used to finance such receivables. If consolidated, this would kill the parent's current ratio and hurt its own credit capability. The authority for non-consolidation is found in Accounting Research Bulletin (ARB) No. 51, which exempts finance companies and insurance companies from the normal consolidation rules.

6. The finance subsidiary may utilize finance lease accounting, for financial accounting purposes, which would permit it to reflect higher earnings in the early years.
    a. Sum-of-the-digits accounting methods are proper, to match income in the early years to the higher debt balances.
    b. The sub. may reflect acquisition costs of new leases by front-loading income with a portion of the unearned interest income.

7. The finance subsidiary may utilize operating lease accounting for tax purposes, reflecting less income and taxes in the early years. It may also reflect income on a cash basis, eliminating unpaid lease receivables (past-dues) from its determination of income.

8. The subsidiary may file a consolidated tax return with its parent, despite not consolidating for financial accounting purposes. This will permit the consolidated group to use the tax losses of the subsidiary which usually result in the early

years, and the investment tax credit may be utilized, it otherwise being lost to the parent. This is a tremendous benefit.

The captive finance subsidiary, then, if properly structured, offers immediate cash flow, tax advantages, and permanent investment tax credit benefits, while providing long-term financing to the company's customers. The use of a subsidiary permits the company to obtain bank financing and long-term institutional money more readily than through the parent. A word of caution, however: such a subsidiary is "capital intensive" requiring increasing amounts of borrowings each year to continue to finance the installment sales to the parent's customers. This requires a constant and inexorable fund-raising effort on the part of the subsidiary, year in and year out. This is difficult to accomplish in tight money times and requires careful long-range planning to provide advance funds to weather the tight money times. A way out of this eventuality is participation on a 50-50 partnership basis with an independent finance company, preferably a public company, which is in the business of raising funds in the public markets on a continuing basis. In any event, the wholly-owned finance subsidiary could be set up for as short a period as three or four years to obtain the significant advantages offered, and then discontinued, if tight money markets persist.

The American Management Association offers several excellent seminars on leasing and the benefits of establishing a captive finance subsidiary. Since it is so highly specialized a field, the responsibility for the project should be placed in the hands of the Treasurer or Controller who should personally supervise the project and be prepared to devote most of his time to establishing the project, to include:

1. Formation of the corporation and qualification in required states

2. Design of the lease, guarantees, and other legal documents

3. Establishing the format for tax and financial accounting

4. Creating the marketing plan and promotional literature

5. Setting appropriate and competitive rates

6. Structuring the debt and equity aspects

7. Preparing short-and long-term operating and cash projections

8. Establishing the short- and long-term lending relationships

ACQUISITIONS

Acquisitions are usually thought of as being made to increase earnings, to diversify products, to vertically integrate, to acquire assets, and sometimes, even for the sake of creating excitement in a company's stock. Rarely are they considered as an alternative to the issuance of long-term debt, but this effect often results and, indeed, is often sought by the purchaser. Long-term debt may be acquired through acquisitions if:

1. The acquired company is in the business of obtaining long-term debt on a continuing basis. Examples are a fixed asset company—say steel or rail, which makes major investments in fixed assets through such borrowings, or a finance company which is capital intensive and constantly raising funds to operate. The acquirer may use these relationships to obtain direct debt or debt funnelled through the subsidiary.

2. The acquired company may manufacture a product which is marketed or used in manufacturing by the parent. If such a product has been long-term financed by the subsidiary, the parent has, in effect, obtained long-term financing for its product, due to the intercompany eliminations in consolidation.

3. The parent, by issuing stock at the cost of equity previously described in the Equity section, has obtained all of the assets and liabilities, including the long-term liabilities of the acquired company.

Acquisitions may be treated as Purchases or Poolings of Interest, for accounting purposes, in accord with APB Opinion No. 16. In a pooling, an acquiring company takes the assets of a merged company onto its own books at their original cost. This has sometimes allowed a company to issue stock at a worth much more than the original cost of the acquired assets and then to sell the assets at present value and take the difference as a profit. It has also been possible to include the profit of an acquired company in an annual report, even though the pooling occured at the end of the fiscal year reported on. Opinion No. 16 requires that either the pooling or purchase method be used, not a combination; pooling may be used only if companies combine through an exchange of common stock, subject to certain restrictions. All other business combinations must be accounted for as purchases. In purchase accounting, any difference between the price paid and the value of tangible and identifiable intangible assets acquired, as goodwill, must be systematically written off against future earnings for a period not to exceed 40 years. Moreover, under Opinion No. 16, it is not possible to include the profits of an acquired company in net income reported to stockholders if the pooling took place after the end of the year reported on.

INTEGRATION OF LONG-TERM BORROWINGS
INTO THE LONG-RANGE CASH FORECAST

Forecasting cash requirements is discussed in Chapter 5. One of the considerations used in preparing the long-range forecast is a determination of the long-term debt required to support the company's operating programs over the period of years studied. That chapter discusses long-range planning techniques which translate themselves into financial statements, including statements of operations, balance sheet, and statement of changes in financial position. These statements give the absolute amount of cash required. The Treasurer must determine the mix between short and long-term debt and the different types of each.

With the financially strong company, the choices are varied and the Treasurer's decision is based on a mix which results in the lowest borrowing cost over the period, or if not the lowest cost, a mix which will assure a reasonably low cost and provide open avenues for future financing. For example, some short-term debt, at higher than long-term rates, may be desirable to protect short-term bank commitments which may be required to meet contingent cash shortages.

For the company which is not the highest credit rated, the choice is not so much a choice as it is a dictum of market conditions. The weaker company may not be strong enough to negotiate institutional debt over an eight- to ten-year period; stock market conditions may be wrong for an equity offering, and the clear choice would then be a convertible debenture. Or, under these same conditions, the company may be too small to negotiate a convertible or debt with warrants. In this case, revolving bank debt would be the appropriate answer. A revolver could be augmented with leasing to acquire new equipment, or a sale and lease back, and some of the continuing or revolving devices described in Chapter 1—commercial financing, factoring, inventory reductions, and accounts receivable reductions. The point is, despite market fluctuations, a thorough understanding of the avenues for creation of debt will provide the path to successful, low-cost financing for the enterprise.

CHAPTER 3

The Direction of Credit Granting

and Accounts Receivable Collection

THE FEI Treasurership functions listing in the "Treasurer's and Controller's Functions Defined by the Financial Executive Institute" describes the Credit and Collections function as "to direct the granting of credit and the collection of accounts due the company, including the supervision of required special arrangements for financing sales, such as time payment and leasing plans." Closely juxtaposed to this function is that of applying accounts receivable collections to the accounts, creating the aged trial balance of accounts receivables and associated accounts receivables reports. The latter function, relating to receivables application and related reports, is the responsibility of the Controller, as part of the Protection of Assets and Reporting and Interpreting function. The Position Description of the Treasurer, addended to the above, includes this function of credit and collection (the seventh major duty listed), and the Controller's Position Description, likewise, includes the responsibilities for protecting assets and reporting results.

This chapter will examine these functions, with emphasis on:

1. Credit granting procedures.

2. Collection procedures.

3. Special arrangements for credit.

4. Internal control (fraud and asset protection).

5. Essential Reports to Monitor Performance.

1. CREDIT GRANTING PROCEDURES

Any good credit-granting system is inextricably combined with a good order-writing discipline. The order, after all, contains the key elements which will, later, be necessary to insure collection, as well as the key information needed to analyze the order to determine whether credit may even be granted. Such a system also provides for automatic approvals or rejections, based on standard criteria. This makes it possible for line employees to pass most of the orders, without review by a manager.

A procedure applicable to retail (ultimate consumers) accounts and to dealers (distributors) is shown at Exhibit 3-a. This contains the following features:

1. The order must be in writing, legible, legally signed, with an accurate address, and must have a purchase order number in certain cases (large companies and institutions).

2. A letterhead order blank from customer is required, and for new accounts, our company's own order form must be signed. This assures that our special terms and conditions are agreed to.

3. Special order forms supplied by us may be needed for special products to obtain conformity to their unique features.

4. Some orders require telephone confirmation. These are usually large dollar orders. The confirmation nails down the order, makes certain there are no salesman's misrepresentations and that the customer clearly understands his obligations.

Try This Helpful Hint: The confirmation call is ostensibly made under the guise of asking to obtain marketing information—why this particular machine was bought; did it replace another; what application will it be used for; are you satisfied with its potentials?—then a segue into the details of the confirmation.

A Confirmation Call procedure and checklist is shown at Exhibit 3-b.

Key Point: The Confirmation Phone Call checklist can serve as a valuable collection tool in the event of future misunderstandings or disputes. You have the date, person spoken to, and a record of the points you have confirmed to the buyer.

5. Customer's purchase order number is important, is again stressed as it was in 1. above.

6. Merchandise returns result in credits and must be handled promptly to keep the customer's account clean and to avoid unnecessary collection action.

7. Returns which are accepted result in credits, and this is akin to signing a check in favor of the customer. Therefore, such returns require special authorization procedures.

8. Freight policy and FOB points control the passing of title—an important point in any collection action. Proper billing of freight and conformity to company policy are important sources of revenues.

9. Even exchanges are inevitable in any company which vends a product which is not immediately consumed. Even exchanges require tight control to prevent the shipment of unbilled merchandise. The danger, of course, is that a replacement shipment may be made at no charge, without the defective product ever being returned. This is best controlled by requiring that all even exchanges be both billed and credited. As a matter of convenience, even exchanges can be allowed, without billing, but with adequate documentation, for limited amounts, say up to $500. For higher-priced items, every shipment should be invoiced. When the

authorized defective product is returned, a credit may then be issued. A separate procedure should be published to set forth the governing rules.

10. Companies selling products nationally are subject to a multitude of diverse and sometimes confusing state tax laws. Laxity in obtaining sales or use-tax exemption certificates can cost the company dearly, years later, when the state performs a tax audit. In some states, labor services are taxable, in others, not. In some, the value of traded-in equipment is a deduction from sales, in others, not. Specific instructions must be issued to those responsible in each state, and conformity to the instructions must be periodically monitored. Obtaining the proper exemption certificates must be an on-going program to avoid losses through future state tax audits.

11. Orders from ultimate users are shipped if credit is approved after referring to a current statement of account. If the account has no past record, credit is not checked, in this example, for amounts up to $150. This avoids the expense of checking credit on a vast number of small orders. The risk of loss is spread among many small accounts.

Orders are carefully checked by a bank and two trade references.

Note This Important Point: Good trade references cannot overcome a bad bank reference. A good bank reference is normally enough to blunt trade references which are not the best. A good bank reference cannot offset bad trades.

Helpful Hint: The trade references should not be a utility or his landlord. He must pay these on time every month. Good references are his printer, stationer, major supplier.

Avoid This Pitfall: Be selective and careful about accounts in business less than a year. (50% fail within the first year). Moreover, an account in business exactly one year is to be evaluated differently from an account one to five-years old.

12. Contracts which renew automatically, from year to year, may require special procedures. For example, if your product is one which requires periodic service or maintenance, do you want to hold up such maintenance if the customer is delinquent on his supply account payments? Perhaps the customer forgot that his contract renewed automatically and he was questioning your invoice.

Watch Out For This: You may turn a customer over to a collection agency because of non-payment. But if you have a service contract which automatically renews at the end of a year, he will receive a billing for the renewal which will age as current in your trial balance. Be sure to stop automatic renewal billings on collection accounts.

13. Large accounts require special attention and should be handled by exception.

14. Special types of customers present special problems in various industries. Any special terms must be handled by exception.

Avoid This Pitfall: Do not permit *anyone* to set special terms or change standard terms. If you do, you will find every salesman or division selling on a different basis with no uniformity. This may lead to anti-trust violations, with special customers receiving preferred treatment. It may also lead to a slow-down in receivables turnover without your knowledge of the reason for it.

15. Large customers or distributors (not ultimate users) require special attention and separate credit procedures. These are set forth.

Helpful Hint: Credit Limits for dealers, over a specified amount, and any increases thereon, should be approved by the Treasurer. This will avoid a concentration of too much credit in one account, will backstop a line credit manager's decision, and, mostly, will avoid unexpected large bad debt losses.

16. Collection Procedures are discussed in the section below.

2. COLLECTION PROCEDURES

We have observed that any good credit granting system is combined with a good order-writing discipline. Equally important, it must be combined with a good collection system. The account receivable function consists of getting the order, credit-approving it for shipment, and then collecting it.

IT'S NOT A SALE UNTIL IT'S COLLECTED! Accordingly, the Order Writing and Credit Procedures described in Exhibit 3-a include a collection procedure in pages 8 and 9 of the procedure.

Page 8 relates to a "field" procedure for collections. In the procedure illustrated, all collections are handled centrally, at the headquarters (home office) location. But headquarters personnel must have the cooperation and aid of field personnel. Hence:

Field people receive aged trial balances and issue credits necessary to keep accounts receivable clean. Commissions are charged back to salesmen after 90 days delinquency, so they are involved to rectify the situation. Collection, thus, becomes a company-wide function, involving sales as well as administrative personnel.

Case in Point: One company's top marketing management decided that salesmen would not be involved in collection activities, that the salesman's job was to sell and not take time away from selling effort to see that customers paid for previous sales. As a result, commissions were not charged back for uncollected accounts. Within 90 days, there was a sharp increase in past due receivables which seriously affected the company's cash position. The President made an immediate decision to revert to the previous system. Within 30 days, receivables and cash position had improved. The key to the improvement was involvement of salesmen in collections through the possibility of commission charge backs.

Field collection procedures must be an integral part of a central collection effort. That central effort may be through division headquarters or at the corporate home office, but it is centralized. As a matter of simple internal control, the office that creates the sale should not be responsible for collecting for the sale or even for issuance of credits related to that sale (as a matter of convenience, the field may have limited authority to issue credits up to specific amounts, but never to negate the sale). This construction is not opposed to the responsibility accounting concept that those responsible for the profits in any profit center should control all activities of that profit center. Responsibility accounting is rife with examples of divided responsibility to achieve better internal control and corporate goals. For example, headquarters may control all cash and make all disbursements to achieve greater liquidity; payrolls may be accomplished centrally because of central computer capability; capital expenditures are a corporate decision-making responsibility in almost every company. So too, the sale is maintained inviolate by divorcing the collection function from the selling function.

A centralized Collection Procedure is at Exhibit 3-c. The key elements of this procedure are listed below, numbers conforming to those in the procedure:

1. Statements of account are prepared twice a month, timely. You can't collect without fast, accurate information.

2. Dunning is computer automated. The first 75 days of dunning is on a form-letter basis.

3. The system provides for special terms, these varying by type of company or industry.

4. Legal collection action is a possibility which is pointed out to the customer after 60-days delinquency. This period may vary with each company, but the important point is to adhere to a fast policy.

   Do Not Permit Accounts To Be Months Old Without Legal Action

   If your collection activity is slipshod, your accounts will work you to the end. You will, effectively, be financing them.

5. Delinquencies are not always a simple past due matter. Sometimes the company is at fault and all sources must be researched to resolve any problems for which we are responsible. This requires field support.

6. The field office is alerted to the possibility of legal action. This means a salesman's commission charge back and a possible lost account.

7. At this time, telephone contact is made with the delinquent customer, commissions are charged back, and third party collection action is commenced. The account is now considered "doubtful."

8. The field is involved in special problems as a result of the dunning procedure.

9. A dun master list is used to control all accounts who are now doubtful.

10. Field offices receive copies of the dun master list.

11. The field may cross-reference the dun master list to the detailed statement of account.

12. The entire cycle consumes about 120 days. Disputes are jointly resolved by a high marketing manager and the Credit Manager.

13. In some geographical areas, regional credit offices are established. This allows for closer contact with our field office and the customer. These area offices report to the Home Office Credit Manager, in keeping with the divided responsibility concept.

3. SPECIAL ARRANGEMENTS FOR CREDIT

Any credit granting procedure should possess the attribute of flexibility. There are always special types of accounts, special terms, special problems. Page 9 of Exhibit 3-a, Order Acceptance Procedures, provides for this, in that larger orders receive special attention in paragraph 4. Similarly, paragraph 5 provides for exception control over special terms. Special arrangements for credit may be categorized below:

a. Dealer or Exception Accounts—being those in a special category or above a specified credit limit. These are handled by exception. It is necessary to review every order against the credit limit and to know the status of the open account aging, instantly. Normally, computer processing does not permit this instant capability, due to the processing time and delaying editing routines. Moreover, most computer routines monitor and update billings, rather than open orders which may be in process. If your computer system does not possess instant review capability (usually only with on-line CRT systems), here is a simple manual control monitoring system:

1. Process all orders and payments through a Special Accounts desk, where they are initialed before being passed on to normal order processing and cash application desks.

2. Special Accounts (SA) desk receives a bi-weekly or semi-monthly aged trial balance. Thus, if any checks or orders in 1 above by-pass SA, they will appear on the next trial balance within 2 weeks.

3. SA desk pencil-posts each check and order to the aged trial balance (these are larger accounts and there is usually only 1 check a month and one or two orders) and visually sights the adjusted balance, giving effect to unposted checks and unshipped orders. A credit decision may now be made.

4. On receipt of the bi-weekly aging, SA desk examines pencil notations on the old aging and carries forward any notations that have not yet been billed or posted.

5. Orders in excess of established credit limit are referred to the Credit Manager for review and, if more than a temporary increase in credit limit, to the Treasurer for formal increase in the credit line.

Helpful Hint: Larger credit limits may be set, and increased sales obtained from special accounts, if these credit devices are considered:

• Financing statement filings (UCC-1's) covering liens on inventory and accounts receivables, and Security Agreements, to define conditions of default.

• Personal Guarantees

• Subordination agreements covering officer or stockholder loans

• Signed statements of personal net worth (fraudulent statements may permit criminal actions, if desired)

- Cross-corporate guarantees for parents of subsidiaries or corporations with interlocking directorates
- Securities may be held in escrow with blank signed stock powers, to cover his corporation's stock or his personally owned securities.
- Second mortgages on property may be obtained. While these will not normally be foreclosed, in a bankruptcy you will be paid out of any remaining value in the property, instead of standing unsecured.
- Notes receivable to cover long past due items. This insures automatic monthly payment without chasing the account. It also prevents claims against defective merchandise if collection ensues.
- Conditional Sale instruments to keep title from passing until paid. Product may, thus, be repossessed, limiting your loss.

b. Leasing—as described in Chapter 2, page 42, is a corporate borrowing technique. The corporation may use it, equally as well, as a marketing or credit granting device, with the same advantages accruing to the lessee. Independent leasing companies will carry the customer for periods ranging from 12 to 60 months, usually on full pay-out leases, for almost any kind of machinery, equipment or product which is not immediately consumed. Your salesman makes a normal sale, also obtains the customer's signiture on the lease, and these advantages result:

1. You invoice the leasing company and take full accounting treatment for a sale.
2. The customer receives terms on payment, up to 60 months.
3. The cost of carrying the account over the extended time period is borne by the customer. This cost is expressed as an add-on interest rate. As a rule-of-thumb, simple interest rates are slightly less than double the add-on rate. For example, 6% add-on is less than 12% simple yield. Leasing yields, for full pay-out leases, generally run from 12% to 18% for 60-month leases. Shorter-term leases carry higher yields, as much as 30%, to cover the cost of processing the lease for a short period.
4. The monthly customer's payment is expressed as a specific dollar amount of rental. The customer does not usually consider the interest rate, only the dollar rental amount.
5. There may be a residual value or purchase option, say 10%, at the end of the lease. The customer would have to pay this 10% to take title. This residual value can belong to the corporation, rather than the leasing company, resulting in a hidden profit at the end of the lease. The amount of the residual depends on market conditions and the utility of the equipment, as well as its useful life.
6. The customer is not required to put up front money to purchase this asset. This makes for an easier sale.
7. The corporation can often receive a broker's commission from the leasing company for carrying its lease forms, again resulting in additional hidden profit for the company.
8. The leasing company is independent of the corporation, which makes collection easier. The company cannot also take the same tough posture in collection which the independent finance company takes.

9. Not all of your customers will request that the leasing company pass through the investment tax credit. Where this is not passed through, the leasing company obtains a tax benefit. You can negotiate a rebate on this—again more hidden profits.

10. The leasing company, being in the finance business, is better able to weather tight money times and may be able to "commit" itself to keeping a supply of leasing money available for your customers. Thus, if you were funding your own time-financing program, money availability might dry up more quickly than under a leasing company commitment.

Beware This Pitfall: Many states charge a use tax on the amount of monthly rentals, rather than a one-shot tax on the sale price of the equipment. Be sure you do not invoice and collect the sales tax from the leasing company in such states. Bill your equipment without such tax. The lessor will collect the use tax from the lessee and remit it to the taxing authority. Any national lessor can supply a list of the required states.

c. Revolving Inventory Plans—are a form of floor-planning devices used to aid your customer, usually a dealer or distributor, in carrying your inventory. These plans may be administered through an independent leasing company, a captive finance subsidiary (as described in Chapter 2 page 46), or directly by the company. The features of such a plan are:

1. Customer is permitted to pay over a period of months, usually 12 to 36 months.

2. Customer signs and a financing statement is filed (UCC-1) to protect the company's title to the equipment.

3. Rates paid by customer are based on add-on rates and yields for the period financed.

4. A lease or conditional sale document is signed by customer, further protecting your title.

5. Payments are made monthly, until the equipment is sold. At the time of sale, the lease may be paid off and discontinued (non-revolving plan), or a new piece of equipment may be shipped to distributor, serial numbers substituted on the old lease, and monthly payments continued (revolving plan).

6. If dealer sells the equipment under a lease to a consumer, he merely sends in the lease and receives a check for the difference between his cost of the equipment and the price for which he sold it under the lease.

7. The customer should be audited two to three times per year to ascertain the location of equipment. It should be in inventory. If not, the dealer is given 10 days to pay for it. Repeated infraction of inventory sales without payment should result in dropping him from the program.

8. These are full pay-out purchases by your dealer, not subject to the return of equipment. Accordingly, dealer is responsible for all local sales and use taxes, insurance, and the condition of the equipment.

Avoid This Pitfall: These are full pay-out leases and the dealer should really capitalize these leases and treat them as balance sheet assets and liabilities. In most cases, however, dealers use these as off-balance sheet items. They do not appear. In analyzing a dealer's credit, remember to check on his floor-planning commitments. His liabilities may be drastically understated.

d. Recourse and Buy-Back Commitments—cover the gamut of selling and credit granting plans where the customer, again usually the dealer or distributor, has the right, or a limited right, to put back merchandise to you, the seller. These plans may include:

1. Agency sales—to an individual who acts as your agent in reselling your product. These may not be accounted for as sales until sold to the ultimate consumer.

2. Consignment sales—almost exactly the same as agency sales. These usually carry a memorandum invoice and are not booked as a sale until the consignee reports monthly that they have been sold.

3. Buy-back commitments—cover sales wherein the buyer is given an unadulterated right of return if a third-party sale does not result. Jewelry and seasonal products are usually sold this way to department stores. Variants on this device may prove useful sales tools and may permit accounting treatment as a sale, provided a satisfactory estimate of returns can be made, and a reserve established against such returns.

   In one variation, the amount of the buy-back commitment is drastically reduced after day one, and remains the same for six months. It then reduces, straight-line to zero, over months seven through eighteen. This permits the company to take 1/3 (6/18) sale and income treatment immediately, the balance over the last 12 months, under the most conservative treatment. Given a proper experience factor, the entire amount may be booked subject to a suitable reserve being established for returns. This type of variation on the buy-back commitment is shown at Exhibit 3-d. Note that further protection is provided for the company in that equipment must be return on a first-in, first-out basis.

   The AICPA is currently studying Recognition of Revenue Where Right of Return Exists. Existing or contemplated credit or marketing programs, embodying these features, should be considered as temporary pending the release of official AICPA pronouncement is this area.

   The buy-back commitment has these advantages:
   a. It is easier to convince the dealer to buy the product.
   b. The dealer can obtain bank financing more readily, as he substitutes your buy-back commitment for his credit.
   c. As a practical matter, if monitored properly, very few items are returned.
   d. The cost to the dealer of this plan is based on low bank rates, rather than the higher leasing company rates found in other time-payment plans.

4. Recourse—is a device the company may use with leasing companies or financing institutions to encourage them to extend credit to the company's customers, usually dealers.

   If the dealer does not pay, the company is on recourse and must pay. The lender, thus, has the protection of both you and your customer. As with buy-back commitments, such transactions may not be booked as sales unless a reserve is established against potential returns. Experience may indicate that bad debts and returns under recourse arrangements are no worse than under normal sales without recourse. In this case, a full sale results with a usual small charge to the bad debt provision and increase in the allowance for doubtful accounts.

e. The Captive Finance Subsidiary—has been discussed in Chapter 2, page 46, as a borrowing technique, and should be reviewed in the context of a credit granting device. Credit is, after all, totally dependent on the company's ability to borrow.

The captive finance sub. serves the same purpose as the independent leasing company described in the leasing section on page 56, above, with all the advantages set forth on page 46. However, with regard to the comparison between an independent leasing company and a sub., the captive can offer these decided advantages:

1. The company is responsible for its own financial destiny and has the responsibility to supply its own funds to support a time-financing lease program. It is not subject to the outside pressures occasioned by an independent leasing company which may be unsuccessful in obtaining funds or may have other priority commitments.

2. The sub. can obtain better leverage on its debt to equity borrowing formula than the parent. This should result in a lower cost of money and either lower rates for the customer, or more profit for the sub.

3. The captive may utilize operating lease accounting for tax purposes, availing itself of depreciation benefits, and it may report on a cash basis for tax purposes, obtaining cash flow benefits. These benefits accrue to the parent in a consolidated tax return, rather than to the independent leasing company.

4. The captive will use finance lease accounting for financial statement purposes, creating faster income in the earlier years, and producing more income for the parent who is reporting on an equity basis for the income of the sub.

5. The captive obtains the use of the Investment Tax Credit on purchases from the parent, albeit at the parent cost, not selling price. The ITC is lost on the sale to an independent lessor, unless a separate rebate is negotiated. Even then, the rebate becomes taxable, whereas the ITC is an "after-tax" item, a direct reduction in taxes. You would have to negotiate twice the benefit, assuming a 50% tax rate, to obtain the same benefit as the ITC.

f. Special Terms of Sale—may be granted to customer at no real cost to the company. These may sometimes be dressed as attractive marketing programs, giving the salesman an opportunity to ease the customer into the sale. For example, a company which customarily sells on net 30-day terms may offer:

1. 1/3 cash down, 1/3-30 days, 1/3-60 days, or

2. 1/2 cash down, 1/2-60 days, or

3. 1/2 cash down, 1/4-30 days, 1/4-60 days.

In the first two cases, you will average 30 days, in the third case, slightly better. The customer may very well view these as an improvement over net 30-day terms and certainly ought to have the option, at no cost to the company.

Be Careful of This: If you customarily report agings on a 30-day basis, these accounts will flip over into past due columns, subject to routine dunning. There is nothing which aggravates a customer more than being dunned when he isn't past due. Special activity codes are required to permit proper computer or manual aging for such terms. For example, if your system is a manual one, you could provide for the letter A to be posted to the customer's statement, signifying 60-day terms. When aging, any invoice marked A would be aged by a date plus 30.

Similarly, you may want to offer a discount for payment within 10 days (see page 24 for a discussion of the cost and disadvantages of cash discounts). Or you may have two different discount programs, say 2%-10 days and 1%-20 days. Further, your discount may apply only to certain products, not your entire line, and, in fact, your usual terms of sale may vary from product to product or line to line. All of these situations dictate the establishment of a special activity code, thereby flagging the special terms, and allowing the computer or manual system the opportunity to properly monitor the taking of improper discounts or any special aging requirements.

4. INTERNAL CONTROL (FRAUD AND ASSET PROTECTION)

The essence of internal control in an accounts receivable operation is found in the following areas:

a. Order Entry—A separate order department records the receipt of a properly-credit-approved order. A fraudulent receivable (as might be used in a lapping fraud) cannot be created without a properly approved order.

b. Billing—A separate department (separate from credit or collection), it may be part of order entry, records the invoice. Each shipment must be assigned a sequential number by shipping personnel. This number becomes the Bill of Lading number as well as the invoice number. Each number must be accounted for monthly. Unaccounted-for numbers are carried forward as outstanding to next month.

The combination of order entry and sequential billing control avoids fraud by:

1. Insuring that every shipment is billed. No product goes out the back door without being billed.

2. Avoiding the setting up of a fraudulent receivable. Strangely enough, some companies can be invoiced, and they will pay those invoices. Checks can be received, pocketed and later cashed, and then the fraudulent invoice can be credited out.

c. Credit Adjustment Control—The function of issuing credit to customers, should be kept separate from the accounts receivable function. It may be part of the billing department, but is entirely separate from the credit, collection, or cash application operations. Standards for the issuance of credits should be established to include:

1. Authorized higher approvals for allowances.

2. Authenticated, sequentially controlled receiving reports to support merchandise returns, these being issued only by receiving departments in warehouse locations.

3. Limited write-off authority, say up to $25, may be given to the collection department, as an exception to the above rules. This will allow for minor,

on-the-spot adjustments. It will create customer good will and provide for faster collection of receivables do to minor disputes and problems.

These standards assure that billed items will be collected and will not be credited illegally. The system can only be broken through collusion on the part of two or more persons and two or more departments.

d. Application of Cash Receipts—The function of applying cash as a reduction to the customer's account receivable is a function normally handled within the accounting section. If handled as a part of the Credit and Collection department, there must be a division of responsibility from the collection section. A basic cash application procedure is set forth at Exhibit 3-e, the numbers below conforming to those in the procedure:

1. The mail room merely slits envelopes, not removing checks or contents. This is done to avoid unauthorized handling of checks and to avoid separation of checks from remittance advices.

2. In this procedure, with cash being applied in a separate accounts receivable department, the checks are initially taped in the accounting department to gain control of them.

3. Checks are then photocopied in the cash application section of the accounts receivable section. This is done to enable the actual checks to be deposited and postings to be made from the copies.

4. Checks are now machine endorsed and meter counted to tie in to the number of check copies made, the number of checks taped by the accounting department, and the number on the meter. This assures that no checks are lost. Checks are hand delivered for deposit back to the accounting department, which deposits the checks before the close of bank on the same day.

5. Cash is now posted from check copies.

6. Special cash application procedures are delineated in this section, with particular attention being paid to on-account or unapplied cash, in a-c. Special transaction codes are used in d for analysis work (such as, is discount taken, is it paid in full, which product line is paid?). Sections e and f assure that all payments will be identified promptly. Section g provides for on-the-spot minor adjustments for allowances, and section h provides for approvals for allowances of greater amounts. All totals are carefully controlled in i through m to tie-in the amount of the checks and the adjustment to the accounts receivable records. A careful, daily filing system is established in n, for the purpose of rechecking on errors. Retention of these records can be established in accord with each company's need, but two years is the normal retention period. Most collection actions have been completed or are well on the way by the end of two years.

Avoid the Following Pitfall: Files of check copies and remittance advices are very voluminous and must be filed carefully, with plenty of room for retrieval and expansion. Avoid unauthorized entry into this file. If you don't, you'll attempt retrieval at a critical time and won't be able to locate the needed check copy. These files may be maintained in the cash application section, rather than the main file department.

Try This Helpful Procedure: Support the write-off of allowances in g, and larger adjustments in h, with rigid rules as to whether items should be written-off, credited, or charged to the allowance for doubtful accounts. Minor allowances do not usually provide for reductions in gross product-line sales. Consequently, analyses of net sales can be fuzzed up by such allowances. Moreover, a separate procedure is needed to prevent the issuance of credits covering accounts in "doubtful," as these do not appear as bad-debt write-offs to support IRS deductions for bad debts. The following Write-Off and Credit Memo Policy could be adopted:

a. Write-offs up to $25 may be authorized by cash application personnel, without other approvals, as a charge to Sales Returns and Allowances.

b. Write-offs from $25 to $300 will require the approval of the Assistant Manager of the department (either Credit & Collection or Accounting, depending on where the basic responsibility lies). Such write-offs will require separate product-line analysis by dollars and units, through credit memo issuance.

c. Write-offs of $300 and up need the appropriate department head's approval, and credit memos must be issued.

d. Write-offs of accounts in "doubtful" (that is, having been placed for collection with legal or third party collection agencies) may not be handled through the issuance of a credit memo. These will be journal-entried as a charge to the allowance for doubtful accounts.

e. Annual write-offs of doubtful accounts should be made, as in d. above, based on a review of collection activity. Such write-offs, if still alive as to collection, may be transferred to a suspense ledger where they may be controlled for continued collection, though completely written-off. This annual write-off will support, and should be compared to, the aggregate annual provision for bad debts taken for tax purposes.

5. ESSENTIAL REPORTS TO MONITOR PERFORMANCE

The Treasurer's performance is measured by his success in collecting receivables—hence, turnover of receivables to sales and bad debt write-offs. The Controller requires reports on total receivables to verify asset balances, and he reports operating results pertaining to amounts of receivables, collections, credits, past due accounts, and bad debt reserves. Essential reports prepared by the Controller, for his own use, and that of the Treasurer and the Credit and Collection Manager are:

a. Aged Trial Balance (Exhibit 3-f)—used by Collection personnel as a collection aid, by Credit personnel to approve credits on reorders, by Accounting personnel to prove out totals of sales, cash, and receivables and to estimate appropriate provisions for bad debts.

b. Aged Trial Balance Summary (Exhibit 3-g)—used by the Treasurer and Credit and Collection Manager to monitor changes in the trends of past due receivables.

These columns are easily adapted to graphs to present a visual picture of the trend lines. The detailed report in Exhibit 3-f is summarized and posted to this report, monthly, to present a continuing progress report on the changing ages of receivables.

c. Sales to Cash Analysis (Exhibit 3-h)—used by the Treasurer and Collection Manager as a summary report to show overall collections related to overall sales. This report is for a company with a normal 60 day collection period. Columns 2 and 3 show monthly sales and cash collections, respectively. Column 4 represents three months of sales, including the current month. Thus, the figure of $11,749 in col. 4, line 21, is the sum of column 2, lines 19, 20, and 21, this being Sept., Oct., and Nov. sales totals. Column 5 represents three months of cash collections, lagged sixty days. Thus, the figure of $12,093 in column 5, line 20, is the sum of column 3, lines 20, 21, and 22, this being Oct., Nov., and Dec. collections.

In this report, the assumption is made that sales, say in Aug., Sept., and Oct., totaling $11,554 (col. 4, line 20), resulted in collections in Oct., Nov., and Dec. (a 60-day lag) of $12,093 (col. 5, line 20). The difference between these sales and lagged collections is an average in collections of $539 (col. 6, line 20), and a cumulative *monthly* cash average collected of $675 (col. 7, line 20). Note that the cumulative figures in column 7 are divided by three to obtain a monthly figures. Thus, $539 ÷ 3 = $180, which, added to the previous cumulative total of $495, equals $675.

An average in 3 month collections indicates that the 60-day turnover is being bettered. Further, at a glance, column 7 indicates whether we are collecting more than we are selling, an indication that our past due collection efforts are bearing fruition.

Try This Helpful Report: It's a one-liner which permits you to monitor performance at a glance, without getting lost in the welter of a mass of figures.

d. Percentage of 61 Plus Days Old to Total A/R (Exhibit 3-i)—used by the Treasurer and Collection Manager to follow the trend in various agings. This exhibit shows the 61 plus days old accounts. This means 61 days past the due date or 91 days from date of invoice (assuming net 30-day terms). This same graph may be used to plot 91 plus days past due, and 121 plus past dues. The numbers are obtained from the appropriate column of the Aged Trial Balance Summary (Exhibit 3-g). High points on the graph may be marked to explain the effects of economic conditions, changes to more liberal credit terms, a systems failure, or ineffectual performance. Low points may indicate more rigid credit terms, introduction of discount terms, effective performance, an improvement in economic conditions, or a change to an improved system.

e. Percentage of 61 Plus Days Old Collected (Exhibit 3-j)—used as with the previous exhibit to spot the trends in collections related to accounts which are 61 days past due. Numbers are obtained from a Cash Receipts report (not illustrated here) showing the aging of cash collections, that is, relating the cash to the age of the invoice to which it applies.

If a computer run is not available to provide this report, it may be obtained using the following calculation and simply refering to the Aged Trial Balance Summary (Exhibit 3-g): Last month's 31 Plus past due column becomes this month's maximum 61 Plus past due amount, if nothing were collected. Compare this result to the actual amount of the 61 Plus past due shown in the summary, and the difference is added or subtracted to last month's 30 Plus column to obtain the total amount of 61 Plus past dues which were collected.

f. Monthly Analysis of Doubtfuls (Exhibit 3-k)—used by the Treasurer and Collection Manager to monitor the status of doubtful accounts (those in the process of third-party collection action)—amounts collected, percent collected, amount of new doubtfuls, amounts written off to the Bad Debt reserve.

g. Doubtful vs. Bad Debt Reserve (Exhibit 3-l)—used by the Controller and Treasurer to constantly review and test the amount of the reserve (allowance for bad debts) against the total of receivables which may ultimately be charged to that reserve.

Avoid This Pitfall: The company's independent accountants may require an addition to the reserve to cover non-doubtful accounts, on the expectation, based on experience, that some of these accounts will become doubtful. The monthly bad debt provision should provide for this, if necessary.

h. Schedule of Bad Debt Reserve—Annual (Exhibit 3-m)—used as an adjunct to the previous exhibit, showing the annual increase in the reserve (the Provision in col. 3), the decrease in the reserve due to write-off, and the Balance in the reserve (col.5). The percentage of the reserve is shown in column 6 to the total balance sheet account receivable amount in column 7.

The total provision must be reasonably related to the actual write-offs to support the tax deductibility of the Provision, giving effect to that portion of the remaining doubtful accounts which may be expected to be written-off. These numbers should be viewed on an aggregate basis, over the years.

The percent figure (col. 6), studied together with the previous exhibit, will prove helpful in establishing a current monthly provision for bad debts to be used as an interim financial accrual.

i. Receivable Analysis-Product Line A (Exhibit 3-n)—used by the Treasurer, Collection Manager, and Product Line marketing managers. This report is also summarized for the entire company, all product lines. The same analysis may be done by territories, as desired. The report gives sales, turnover in days, total receivables, aging of receivables in two columns—current to 60 days past due, and 61 days plus past due, with percents of each to total receivables, and, in the last two columns, total collections, aged the same as the receivables, and with per cents collected.

As a monthly running report, it permits of ready monitoring of turnover, and past dues by percent of receivables and of cash collected. The trends are thus visually established in one report.

j. Credit Analysis (Exhibit 3-o)—used by operating managers, department heads, product line managers, to analyze the reasons for the issuance of credits to customers. Each credit memo is coded with a reason for the credit, as listed in the exhibit. Credits are then sorted, by dollar amount, by product line, and the report is run. Corrective action may be taken for excessive credit issuance as indicated by the code. The report may indicate the necessity for changes in the very system, itself. For example, excessive tax credits, code C, may indicate an improper procedure for obtaining and recording tax exemption certificates from users.

PRACTICAL POINTERS FOR SUCCESSFUL CREDIT GRANTING AND ACCOUNTS RECEIVABLE COLLECTIONS:

Success in these areas requires an integrated system, starting with order-writing and credit granting procedures, continuing on to routinized collection procedures involving field personnel, with built-in features for internal security controls, and with timely reports designed to monitor performance by exception. A feature of the integrated system should be special credit arrangements for special types of customers and for special marketing programs.

CHAPTER 4

Providing Insurance Coverage As Needed

THE Treasurer is responsible for providing insurance coverage for the company. This obligation is a defined Treasurership Function in the FEI official statement of responsibilities of the Treasurer and Controller which may be found in "Treasurer's and Controller's Functions."

Insurance, by definition, is the indemnification of one by a third party against loss from a specified contingency or peril. The definition is key to an understanding of the Treasurer's obligations in this area. The peril should be contingent, meaning unpredictable, and, inherently, infrequent. Frequent and predictable perils or losses should be self-insured on an accrual basis as a continuing operating expense.

Some perils, though infrequent, may be self-insured if they are predictable. Similarly, self-insurance is often a good idea for unpredictable losses which recur with some frequency, that is, on a spasmodic basis. Insurance, then, is the safeguard against the unknown, the unpredictable, the infrequent, the unanticipated, the unaccrued for or unprovided for expense.

The definition above, however, does not encompass the overall insurance philosophy which the Treasurer should bring to the company. If there is any conceivable type of peril which, if it struck, would impair the ability of the company to continue in existence, it should be provided for through insurance coverage. The type and amount of insurance will vary for every company, it being dependent on the nature and individuality of each company. Exhibit 4-a is an actual Insurance Record for a typical company. It lists every policy, policy dates, premium amount per year, and gives a summary of the coverage. To put this in perspective, this Insurance Record is typical for a company in the $50,000,000 to $200,000,000 annual revenues range, with 40 branch office locations and approximately 3000 employees. Each type of policy is discussed below, seriatim, as listed in the "coverage" column of the exhibit:

Commercial Property Policy

This is discussed in a separate summary of the policy on pages 4 through 7 of the exhibit. Most business claims will be placed under this policy. It will, therefore, be discussed in a separate section.

Umbrella Excess Liability Policy

This is sometimes called a "blanket" policy, in that it insures against all risks which are not otherwise covered. Specific amounts of liability coverage are provided in the Commercial Property Policy. For example, $1,000,000 is provided for Personal Injury Liability. The umbrella provides coverage in excess of that, up to $10,000,000, at a small cost of only $2,991 per year. This is true catastrophe insurance. It insures against the infrequent and absolutely unpredictable. Since it is an "excess coverage" policy, coming into play only after another policy has reached its limit, and then being subject to a $10,000 deductible, it carries a very small premium cost. This type of policy, the umbrella excess liability, is an absolute requirement for any complete insurance program. At one time, the illustrated company carried a $5,000,000 umbrella, which was adequate for its needs. The courts, however, began to grant personal injury awards in excess of $5,000,000. In keeping with the Treasurer's philosophy of protecting the company against the utmost catastrophes, the coverage was increased to its present limits.

Automobile Insurance

This company has only a few owned vehicles for specific managers. Its other cars are leased with monthly rentals to include insurance. This policy includes $100,000/300,000 bodily injury coverage, per person/occurrence, as a requirement of its Umbrella Excess Liability Policy. The latter policy must always be considered in establishing any other liability limits. Another feature of this policy is uninsured motorist coverage, to provide protection in the event of an accident with an uncovered driver.

Contingent Business Interruption

A basic ingredient of any catastrophe coverage is this type of business interruption insurance. In the present case, the company is covering manufacturing facilities in a foreign location against the unpredictable, infrequent hazard, to include earthquakes, volcanoes, fire and vandalism, any of which would cause an interruption or cessation in business. Such policies are sometimes called Use and Occupancy Insurance. They all indemnify for loss of net profits during the shutdown, for continuing fixed charges, for extra expenses to replace equipment, overtime, or having the product manufactured elsewhere. The insurance coverage may be obtained in connection with riots, civil commotion, fire, sprinkler leakage, flood, water damage, tornado, boiler explosion. When one company depends on another for a continuous, uninterrupted supply of goods, it obtains "contingent" U & O insurance against the loss which it would sustain as a result of the supplier's inability to deliver. A form of business interruption insurance is often attached to an ordinary "all-risk" policy, like the Commercial Property Policy, and provides additional expense or "extra expense" coverage to defray costs incurred as a result of the loss. In the Insurance Record illustrated, there are two Contingent Business Interruption Policies, with two different companies. The reason, the carrier prefers to spread his risk of loss and has requested the company to use two carriers, each carrying $2,450,000 of risk.

Marine Open Cargo Policy

The illustrated company imports some of its product and prefers to order it FOB shipping point. Since it assumes title on shipment, it must provide its own insurance coverage. Exporters will often provide FAS shipping terms, or CIF, (Freight alongside, or Cost, insurance and freight), wherein the exporter provides the insurance coverage and includes its cost in his price. In this case, each shipment is covered separately. A report is supplied to the insurance company monthly, listing each shipment, and enclosing a check for the premium coverage, in arrears. The premium is based on the value attributed to each shipment. Coverage is to the recipient warehouse dock, at which point the Commercial Property Policy picks up coverage.

Workmen's Compensation

These policies cover the employer for his entire liability under the various state laws, usually including occupational diseases among the covered hazards. The same policy often covers employers' liability insurance against common-law suits brought by employees to obtain damages for personal injuries. Premiums are based on payroll dollars, with a deposit being made using previous payroll periods as a basis. A subsequent audit determines the actual payroll. The audit is made by accountants for the insurance carrier. As a part of this audit, they classify the payroll by class of employee (that is, functions performed, as clerical, salesman, manufacturing) and a separate premium rate is charged for each class of employee.

> **Try This Helpful Hint:** Organize your payroll records by class of employee to conform to the workmen's compensation policy requirements. You, rather than the insurance company auditors, will select the appropriate class, and you can often designate a lower rate class than the auditor would, at a significant premium saving. Moreover, at audit time, have your representative present to overview the classifications established by the auditor. Remember, the auditor may not understand the nuances of your operation and may mis-classify payroll functions.

> **Avoid This Pitfall:** Each state has different requirements for coverage. A blanket policy will not cover you in every state. Some states, in fact, require that coverage be carried with the state, itself. Contact the state labor department in every state to determine their requirements in this area.

New York State Disability

Many states provide for mandatory insurance coverage for employees with regard to accidents and disabilities incurred off the job. This insurance, in combination with Workmen's Compensation which covers on the job accidents, provides complete coverage for all employees. The amount of the premium is set by law and is paid for by the employee through payroll deductions. The employer often elects to bear the full premium cost. The laws in each state must be checked carefully for coverage requirements. Private insurance is available in states without disability laws.

Aircraft Insurance

The illustrated company operates a corporate aircraft. In addition to normal property damage insurance, called Hull, the company is covered for $10 million of liability insurance. This, considered with its Umbrella Excess Liability Policy, gives the company $20 million of liability coverage, considered to be an adequate catastrophe amount, based on court awards for liability to injured parties in aircraft cases. The pilots are specifically named, they having previously been safety rated.

Comprehensive Bond

This is basic employees fidelity coverage, without the necessity for each employee to complete a fidelity bond application. Each is automatically covered, subject to the limits shown, and the deductibles set forth. In this illustration, 2,000 employees are covered for a premium of $6,050 per year. Coverage includes protection against inventory (subject to a high $10,000 deductible, since the product is bulky, not easily stolen, there are many locations, and the system of internal control is strong), cash defalcations up to $250,000, all other thefts up to $500,000 subject to a $2,500 deductible, and blanket coverage for the loss of company issued credit cards.

> **Helpful Hint**: The Comprehensive Bond is inexpensive catastrophe insurance, covering a variety of dishonesty risks, at a low annual premium cost.

General Term Bond for Entry of Merchandise

This special policy, together with the Marine Open Cargo Policy, provides complete coverage for all importations of product. The Marine policy covers insurance in transit. The General Term Bond covers landed merchandise while it passes through customs and brokers' hands.

Miscellaneous Bid and Performance Bonds

These bonds may be required by municipal agencies who purchase products or services from the company. The Bid Bond is often in lieu of a certified check which must accompany government bids. The bond is inexpensive, may be continuous, and does not tie up cash while the bid is being negotiated or awarded. The Performance Bond, Franchise Tax Bond, Service Undertaking Bond, and Concessionaire Bond are all similar, meeting the specific requirements of various governments or agencies, insuring against the company's failure to perform under the specific contract. The Appeal Bond is a legal court requirement, which in this case, insures against an appeal of $5,595.06 for only $112, a cost of 2% per year. The appeal refers to an appeal from a previous legal verdict in a law suit.

Commercial Property Policy

This is an "all-risk" policy covering inventory in warehouses, in transit, buildings and equipment, fire damage liability on rented premises, personal injuries, property damage, product liability claims, non-owned auto liability and property damage, personal property damage, advertisers liability coverage, loss of valuable papers and records, and earthquake and flood damage. It excludes coverage of cash and securities, precious metals, aircraft, property sold under installments, and imports or exports—all of which are covered under previously described policies. To this extent, the policy is quite similar to the very familiar personal property floater which many individuals carry as part of their homeowner's policy. Everything you can think of is covered, except the specific excluded items.

This is the principal company policy, and most insurance claims will be placed under this all-risk policy. Losses in excess of the coverages set forth will be covered by the Umbrella Excess Liability Policy. Note that deductibles of $1,000 to $10,000 for various parts of the policy serve to reduce the premium cost.

> **Helpful Hint:** A claims analysis should be made, each year, to determine the type and dollar amount of claims. It is possible that the deductible amounts under the policy may be raised, and the reduction in premium will more than offset the loss in insurance reimbursement of excluded claims. In the case of the illustrated company, this analysis caused the company to raise its deductibles to $2,500.

The policy carries Additional Expense Coverage which pays for the extra costs involved as a direct result of a loss, as described under the Contingent Business Interruption policy.

A premium analysis of the Commercial Property Policy is attached, which indicates that approximately $22,000 of the premium is subject to monthly reports of values carried. The balance of $23,000 is fixed in amount, the major portions being attributable to premises liability, products liability, and transit coverage. This being the major discretionary policy, from a cost standpoint, (Workmen's Compensation cost is determined by the classifications of the various states) a Premium Summary follows the Premium Analysis sheet. The summary contains a breakdown of the premium over a five-year period and allows a rapid visual review of the components of the premium and the effect of the variable deposit premium on the total.

Other Types of Insurance

Life Insurance—usually "key man" insurance, to provide funds to the company covering the loss of services of the key man. This type of insurance may also provide cash for the purchase of the deceased's shares in a close corporation or to buy out his capital interest in a partnership.

> **Remember This:** If the business is the beneficiary, the premiums are not deductible
> for tax purposes, nor are the proceeds on death included in income. Premiums are,
> however, deductible for financial accounting purposes.

There are some other accounting considerations involved with life insurance. Dividends may be applied as a reduction of premiums or may be left with the insurance company to increase the amount of insurance and, hence, the cash surrender and loan values. The loan value may be classified as a current asset unless a lending agreement or indenture requires it to be shown as an investment or other asset.

Extended Coverage—one of the risks insured against in Contingent Business Interruption or Use and Occupancy policies. This provides for coverage from damages due to Windstorm, Hail, Smoke, Aircraft, Vehicle, Explosion and Riot, whether originating on your premises or elsewhere. It does not cover war, loss caused by foreign military forces, damage done at the direction of civil or governmental authorities, or explosions or fires caused by boilers which are separately coverable.

Sprinkler Leakage—This covers loss due to such leakage, but not loss to the sprinkler system, itself. Moreover, separate coverage is required for valuable papers and cash and securities, of the type provided under the Commercial Property Policy.

Boiler Explosion—This covers losses to the property insured and to others caused by the explosion. It does not cover explosions caused by fire, or fire from any cause. Once again, the Commercial Property Policy covers that type of loss.

Plate Glass—This policy covers not only the glass, but attached signs, lettering and ornaments. Not covered is damage due to fire, earthquake, or workers involved in repairs or construction, all of which must be separately covered.

Selling Price or Profit Insurance—This may be included as part of the Business Interruption policy, or to cover inventory loss under the Commercial Property Policy. Normal coverage pays for the actual cash value of the merchandise destroyed. For an additional premium, the profit which would have been made in a normal sale is also covered.

Co-insurance

Many policies contain a co-insurance clause. The purpose of such a clause, from the insurance company's standpoint, is to offset the tendency of insureds to insure for only a small part of the total value of the property. This is often done since most losses are only partial losses. In the co-insurance clause, the insured agrees to carry insurance in an amount equal to a specific per cent of the value. The most common is an 80% co-insurance clause. If, under an 80% co-insurance policy, the insured carries insurance equal to only 70% of the property's value, he becomes a co-insurer for 10%. He, thus, bears 1/8 of any loss, and the insurance company bears 7/8—but in no case is the insurance company liable for more than the face amount of the policy. These principles are demonstrated in this:

Helpful Formula—for Computation of Claim Against Insurance Company:

$$\text{Claim Against Insurance Co.} = \frac{\text{Face of Policy}}{80\% \text{ of Value of Property at Time of Loss}} \times \text{Loss}$$

Formula applies if: Policy is Less Than 80% of Value of Property—if the policy is 80% or greater of the Value of the Property, the formula does not apply and is not needed.

Remember These Limitations to the Claim:

1. The Face of the Policy

2. The Actual Loss

Example: Value of Property is $100,000
    Policy is for $70,000
    Property is completely destroyed in fire—loss is $100,000

$$\text{Claim} = \frac{\$70,000}{80\% \times \$100,000} \times \$100,000 = \$87,500$$

Claim is limited to Face Value or $70,000

Under the same assumptions, had the property been 50% destroyed, or a loss of $50,000, the formula would result in:

$$\text{Claim} = \frac{\$70,000}{80\% \times \$100,000} \times \$50,000 = \$43,750$$

Claim is limited to computed amount.
Actual Loss exceeds the computed amount.

Co-insurance, then, of 80% means that on *partial* losses, you recover only partially, if you are covered for less than 80% of the actual value of the property.

Avoid This Pitfall: Value of the Property at the Time of the Loss is its "cash value" or "sound value", which generally means what the property was worth on the open market, had you offered it for sale. This can be a costly trap during inflationary times. A $50,000 store, 80% insured for $40,000, could have doubled in value to $100.000 at the time of the fire. By formula, the policy would pay only its face, a total of $40,000 despite having a cost to replace if of $100,000. Your insurance coverage must be constantly reviewed in times of inflation to ascertain that coverage equals 80% current cash value.

Freight Claims

Claims for loss or damage in transit may arise from shipments via common carrier, UPS, parcel post, or special delivery services. These claims require special handling as they are generally small in dollar amount and frequent in occurrence, involving a great many different carriers. Consider self-insurance for this type of frequent risk.

Thorough procedure dictates that these types of claims be logged-in, as a prelude to handling. The log should carry notations for:

Date of claim.

Carrier.

Pro number (if any).

Bill of lading number.

Our invoice number.

Date of loss.

Type of loss (fire, missing, damage, etc.).

Date of 2nd. follow-up.

Date of 3rd. follow-up.

Date placed with our broker.

Date paid.

The log is a handy device to permit:

- accrual of dollar amount of claims for accounting entries (inventory, cost of sales, and insurance claims receivable)
- follow-up on receipt of payments from carrier or broker

The log is supported by an alphabetical file of back-up documents, filed in order by name of carrier. The file, in itself, is not sufficient to permit accurate handling of claims, without the log. Documents are misplaced or misfiled; it is inconvenient to have to pull and read each file for follow-up purposes.

The log may be referred to, at a glance, to determine whether the date paid has been completed on each line, or whether the second or third follow-up notice has been mailed. If not, the detailed file may then be pulled for action.

The procedure at Exhibit 4-b, Freight Claims, details the method to be used by branch offices for placing claims. Insurance, being a headquarters function, all such claims are placed with the home office. The home office purchasing department, in Step 2, provides the branch office with written notice that the claim has been placed. The branch may then discontinue its follow-up. The Claims Procedures, at Exhibit 4-c, detail the steps taken by the home office purchasing department in placing these claims. These claims are considered a purchasing responsibility as the loss or damage usually requires the initiation of a replacement purchase order.

Point of Information: The claims log and follow-up procedures are readily handled by 1/5 of a person, less than 2 hours a day, in a company making 20,000 shipments per month. Claims historically run at 1/4 of 1% per month of the total number of shipments and take up to 6 months to settle. There can, therefore, be as many as 300 outstanding claims for follow-up.

Second Point of Information: you will observe that the Claims' Procedures allows the shipper two chances to collect. The initial claim is placed with the common carrier. If unpaid for any reason, the claim is formally placed with the company's insurance broker for payment under its Commercial Property Policy, subject, of course, to its usual deductibles.

Medical Insurance

Employee medical insurance programs generally are the responsibility of the personnel section. In some companies, particularly where these employee benefits are non-contributory (the company pays 100% of the premium charges), the administration of this function falls within the purview of the Treasurer, he being responsible for all other types of insurance. In such event, the Treasurer should, as a minimum, provide for catastrophe coverage for employees, in the form of a Major Medical policy (usually paying 75-80% of hospital charges above a high deductible or on top of employee paid Blue Cross/Shield coverage) or, perhaps, through a Comprehensive Medical Policy. The Comprehensive policy combines major medical coverage with basic hospital/medical coverage.

For example, the Comprehensive policy may provide for a $100 deductible for doctors' bills and drugs and then pays 75% of all remaining charges up to $50,000. Such a policy may be expected to protect the employee and his dependents in the most extreme cases and so qualifies as a catastrophe policy. Variants allow for the first $2,000 in charges to be paid in full, without co-insurance, for an increased premium, which the employee may be asked to bear—making a portion of the policy contributory. Another variant, the employee may be required to carry his own Blue Cross/Shield policy whereas the company will supply the excess coverage on top of that. Should the employee not carry his own insurance, there would then be a $750 deductible before the major medical program came in to play. This device, effectively then, has become a sharing of the risk of loss between three parties—the company, the employee, and the insurance company.

The Annual Insurance Review

The company changes from year to year. It may grow, contract, change products, locations, methods of distribution. Each affects the type and amount of insurance coverage it carries. The Treasurer should conduct an annual review of the Insurance Record (Exhibit 4-a) with the Insurance Manager or the company's general agent, adding or reducing coverage as conditions require it. This would include a review and consideration of each policy, its limits and deductibles. Factors to be considered in this review would be:

- Retirement of fixed assets; additions to fixed assets.
- Premises additions or reductions.
- Inventory levels at various locations
- Cash valuation of all properties (inflation effect).
- Channels of product distribution.
- Pertinent legal cases affecting insurance awards.
- New contingent risks (new suppliers).
- New coverage requirements per check list (boiler, glass, sprinkler).

This review will keep the insurance coverage current with the company's changing posture, avoiding uninsured catastrophe losses.

Claims Handling

Freight claims are processed in the Purchasing Department, as described in detail, previously. All other claims should be processed by the Accounting Department under the aegis of the Controller, subject to final review and approval of the Treasurer. Most claims involve loss or damage to inventory, fixed assets, or cash or securities. The Controller maintains the records which provide the history of the acquisition, use or disposition of these assets. Support and documentation for claims may be prepared by internal auditors or general accounting personnel. These records should be complete accounting workpapers, following all the tenets for the proper preparation of such papers. This means properly dated, reviewed, approved, indexed and scheduled, with appropriate trails for the insurance company's reviewers.

Product liability claims, being non-asset oriented claims, may be processed by the Legal Department, or if none, by a staff assistant to the Treasurer. Where these involve loss of customer's property, he should be required to submit documented proof of loss, and depreciation should be applied to the customer's asset to obtain current sound value. These claims, if small in dollar amount, may be self-insured through the use of high deductibles on the Commercial Property Policy.

> **Take This Precaution:** Do not pay undocumented or unsupported claims. Establish a working procedure delineating the support required before a claim will be paid. Such a procedure is at Exhibit 4-d, Insurance Claims-Liability on Property Damage. This procedure avoids the payment of fraudulent claims.

Practical Approach to Insurance Coverages

Every possible loss should not be insured against. The best approach is to insure against potential catastrophes which could impair the ability of the enterprise to continue to operate. For lesser losses, an analysis of claims should be made and deductibles established at premiums savings which just exceed the deductible losses. New companies would do best to carry higher deductibles until a track record of claims is established.

Procedures should be documented and implemented for the placing and pursuing of claims. An annual review of the company's needs in the insurance area should be conducted to avoid uninsured losses.

CHAPTER 5

Forecasting Cash Requirements

As a Basis for

Maintaining Adequate Funds

THE Provision of Capital is a job function of the Treasurer, defined by FEI. The Treasurer provides for both the short-and long-term capital required by the business, and the methods to accomplish this have been examined in Chapters 1 and 2. The Controller, however, is responsible for Planning for Control, and this responsibility embodies forecasting cash requirements.

Operations are controlled through budgets. This is described in Chapter 6. The following budgets must be prepared before cash is forecasted:

- Operating budgets
- Administrative/Financial budgets
- Capital expenditure budgets

Data from these budgets is then used to complete the cash forecast. We may use the term "budget" to imply the total control plan, be it an operating plan for profits, or a cash budget or plan to control the in and outflows of cash. The word "forecast" is less extensive, merely being a prediction of cash position at a certain point in time. The cash forecast, then, is the end result of the cash budget—the final cash position resulting from the carefully controlled plan. The budget spawns the forecast.

PURPOSES OF THE CASH BUDGET

1. Analyzes other budgets as to feasibility before they are approved. Can we afford them?

2. Minimizes the element of surprise as to climbing inventories, accounts receivables, investment in fixed assets, or income taxes. The budget shows the source and uses of cash as it relates to these items.

3. Monthly comparisons of budget to actual allow for a monitoring of performance and constant corrections in the cash forecast.

PRESENTATION OF THE CASH BUDGET

The presentation of reports under the complete Operating Control Plan, as described in Chapter 6, will include the following statements:

- Income Statement.
- Balance Sheet.
- Statement of Retained Earnings.
- Statement of Changes in Financial Position.
- Supplementary Financial Data.

In short, everything which would be included in a published Annual Report for stockholders, and in the same format. The Statement of Changes in Financial Position was, at one time, called the Source and Application of Funds, in slightly different format. It is merely a reclassification of a standard Cash Requirement Statement, regroupings to fit the accepted format. An example of it is shown at Exhibit 5-a.

The Supplementary Financial Data could include the Projected Cash Requirements Statement (See it at Exhibit 5-b). In reviewing the exhibit, it is obvious the report has been prepared from other budgets—Operating (sales, cost of sales, expenses of operations), Financial/Administrative (interest expenses, R & D expenses, depreciation schedules, subsidiary operations), and Capital Expenditures.

Observe these helpful hints in preparing the report:

1. Start with receipts from operations.

2. Add other income.

3. Deduct all budgeted expenses.

4. Show non-cash items separately, amortization and depreciation.

5. Come down to a final "cash required" balance and a cumulative figure

6. Add a section at the bottom showing how you will meet your requirements, in this exhibit, through bank debt.

The Supplementary Financial Data should also include one other report which is closely related to the Cash Requirement Statement. The report provides Projected Ratios (Exhibit 5-c) of profitability, turnovers to sales, and liquidity of position. Just as the Cash Budget determines whether the other budgets are feasible, so, too, does the

Projected Ratios. There may be sufficient cash to meet the company's operating objectives, but the ratio analysis may indicate that the company's financial position is impaired, or that percentage returns which would be acceptable to shareholders are not being met.

BUDGETING STEPS

Having seen the final reports and format, how do we get here? The following are the required steps to preare the cash budget:

1. Estimate account and note receivable collections

    a. Consider the affect of of seasonal or cyclical variations.

    b. Develop a collection pattern and lag relationships.

       1) Age accounts receivable.

       2) Age cash collections.

       3) Develop the lag between sales and collections, for example:

Days' sales in net receivables

	Collected in month	Balance at end of month
Month of sale	4 days	24 days
Month after sale	12 days	12 days
Second month after sale	9 days	3 days
Third month after sale	3 days	0 days
	30 days	

       4) Provide for the allowance for uncollectible items against sales.

       5) Analyse receipts by class of goods and customers' geographical areas.

       6) Consider cash discounts, returns and allowances, as a percent of sales each month.

    c. Prepare a schedule showing Projected Collections of Accounts Receivable (see Exhibit 5-d) and ending cash.

2. Estimate cash payments for cost of sales

Use either a percentage estimate, based on historic gross profit ratios, or prepare a detailed purchase budget to include:

    a. Estimate of materials to be purchased.

    b. Purchase discounts to be taken.

    c. Seasonal or cyclical factors which will affect purchases.

d. Consider vendor payment requirements. Prepare Projected Payments for Material Purchases as seen at Exhibit 5-e.

3. Prepare a schedule of projected Payments for Operating Expenses (Exhibit 5-f).

This schedule may or may not include interest, research and development. and financial management expenses, depending on the company's reporting format. Consider the following factors in preparing this schedule:

a. Various payroll periods, such as bi-weekly for managers weekly for office personnel, monthly for salesmen.

b. Non-cash charges included in expenses, such as depreciation, accrued expenses for taxes, insurance, or legal and professional fees.

4. Prepare a schedule of Miscellaneous Cash Requirements (as in Exhibit 5-g).

This to include non-operating payments of the following type:

a. Note payments.

b. Taxes.

c. Loan repayments.

d. Various non-operating coded expenditures, such as:
   1) dividends.
   2) capital expenditures.

The capital expenditures estimate is often prepared as a separate budget. For this purpose, the Capital Expenditures Requisition described in Chapter 6 provides the basic support.

5. Prepare the Cash Budget (shown in Exhibit 5-i)

This is a simpler format than the Cash Requirements Statement seen at Exhibit 5-b. The former is merely a summary of the various schedules supporting the cash budget, and its purpose is to have a preliminary look at the ending cash balances, as well as:

a. The Balance Sheet

b. Projected Ratios (Exh. 5-c)

both of which may now be prepared.

If a review of the ending cash, financial position, and ratios indicates that more cash is required, adjustments can be made to factor in additional cash (through short term bank debt, for example), or to defer payments on trade accounts payable to a later period.

The Cash Budget is now "locked-in" and transcribed to the Cash Requirements Statement.

LONG-RANGE FORECASTS (SHORTCUT TECHNIQUE)

The long-range forecast for cash, considered to be anything over three months, is concerned with sales, profits, and balance sheet presentation. It, therefore, follows the five basic budgeting steps just described. There are some useful shortcuts, however, which may be used to generate the Cash Requirements Statement. These are particularly good for the smaller company that does not budget on a formal basis. The basic budgeting steps are re-examined below, in this light:

1. Estimate account and note receivables collections

Total sales will continue to be obtained from the Projected Income Statement. Turnover on sales is now calculated, and receipts from sales are lagged into the Cash Requirements Statement.

> **Avoid This Pitfall**: In calculating turnover, there may not be an even flow of sales or a uniformity of collectibility during the year. Uneven flows will distort the turnover figure. Resolve this by calculating turnover on a quarterly basis.

Turnover may be calculated simply:

Sales per quarter	$6,000 (a)
Receivables at end of quarter	$4,000 (b)
Per cent of quarter's sales uncollected at end of quarter (b ÷ a)	66.67% (c)
Average number of days' sales uncollected (91* x c)	61

*Use actual number of days in the quarter.

This could be further generalized, and it would be accurate enough for a long range forecast, by assuming three months in the quarter. Then 3 x c equals 2 months as the average number of months' sales uncollected. November sales may then be lagged into the January forecast as cash receipts, December as February receipts, and so on.

Assumptions using the lagging technique must be adjusted by company. In the example just given, it was assumed that sales were equal in each month of the quarter, and relatively steady throughout each month. A further refinement, unnecessary under these assumptions, would be that November sales have an average date of November 15th. and are collected by an average of January 15th.

2. Estimate cash payments for cost of sales

Broad assumptions may be made as to the month when the cash is expended, based on current paying habits:

a. Payrolls are paid in the same month as the incurred expense.

b. Vendors' invoices are paid in the following month.

Obviously, some adjustments will have to be made for major vendors who require payment in the current month or who extend terms into the second following month. But these are minor manual adjustments which do not affect the facility of the simplified calculation. Moreover, payrolls are always a separate and readily accessible figure from the total cost of sales, making the application of the assumptions uncomplicated.

Given these assumptions, the total Cost of Sales from the Projected Income Statement may be divided between payrolls and vendor cost and applied to the proper month in the cash Requirements Statement.

3. Prepare a schedule of projected Payments for Operating Expenses

The total should be adjusted downward for non-cash items included in Total Operating Expenses, such as depreciation, amortization, accruals for taxes, insurance, and legal fees. This done, a further assumption must be made as to method of payment, based on current practice—usually current expenses being paid in the following month. The Projected Income Statement's operating expenses may, thus, be lagged for one month.

4. Prepare a schedule of Miscellaneous Cash Requirements

There are no shortcuts possible, here. A review must be made of projected cash payments which are outside of operations as reflected in the Projected Income Statement. These, though, are usually few and readily anticipated. Once again, they would include note payments, taxes, loan repayments, dividends, capital expenditures, and, perhaps, contingent payments from pending litigation.

The Income projection will not reflect financial management policies to include efforts to:

a. Improve inventory turnover.

b. Improve accounts receivable collections.

c. Dispose of segments of a business.

d. Invest excess cash.

Therefore, the Miscellaneous Cash Requirements schedule should be a net schedule, showing cash inflows and outflows for these purposes. Broad assumptions can be made as to the cash effect of these financial programs, based on management's goals—for example, a 10% reduction in the dollar value of parts inventories over the next 12 months; or, a five-day improvement in days' sales uncollected, hence an 8% improvement (5/60th.).

5. Prepare the Cash Budget

This may be quickly prepared from the shortcut assumptions in the four previous steps. As before, the Balance Sheet and Projected Ratios must be reviewed to determine whether the results are acceptable.

Helpful Hint: The entire short cut budgeting process allows for several mid-stream budgeting changes to be made before the final Cash Requirements Statement is prepared.

SHORT-RANGE FORECASTS

The short-range forecast is for three months or less. This, in most companies, is prepared every month by the Controller's department for the Treasurer's review.

Using this forecast, each month of the year is forecast *three* times:

1. At the end of December, forecast January, February, and *March.*

2. At the end of January, forecast February, *March,* and April.

3. At the end of February, forecast *March,* April, and May.

This device enables us to compare plans three separate times and to determine why our plans change and the magnitude of changes from forecast to forecast.

In addition, three separate quarterly forecasts are made. The three quarterlies, plus the detailed three-month forecast are added together to give a one-year projection on cash. This is compared to the annual (long-range) forecast and an explanation of differences if obtained.

This exercise focuses on aspects of cash flow which may have been missed in the broad annual forecast.

The techniques for short-range forecasts are:

1. The same as a long-range, using the basic budgeting steps, if formal budgets are prepared, subject to near-term adjustments which are not always visible at the time long-range forecasts are made.

2. Estimate each line item on the Cash Requirements Statement, if no previous budgets have been prepared, as follows:

a. Estimate the average number of months' sales uncollected as done on page 81, and lag sales into collections for the next two or three months.

b. Obtain marketing estimates of sales for nine or ten months forward, sufficient to permit you to estimate collections into the twelfth month of your projection. These estimates may consist of a sales projection for the next three quarters, without monthly detail.

c. Estimate cost of sales from the sales projections in b. Lag payments based on current payment methods, for example, in the month following the expense. Payrolls can be separated out for payment in the current month, if manning tables are available, or based on a percentage of current payrolls as related to the increase in budgeted sales.

d. Estimate operating expenses as a percentage of current sales, based on the new marketing forecasts of sales. Assume these expenses are disbursed in the following month.

e. Estimate miscellaneous cash requirements, using the technique on page 80. There are no short cuts here. In the short run, all sources of cash receipts should also be taken in to consideration. Usual sources of such receipts are:

> Accounts and notes receivable collections.
> Cash sales.
> Sales of fixed assets.
> Sales of investments—stock or securities.
> Sales of miscellaneous supply items.
> Income from rent, royalties, services.
> Dividend income.
> Interest income from investments.
> Recoveries from doubtful trade accounts.
> Borrowings.
> Insurance recoveries.
> Law suit recoveries.
> Return of advance payments or deposits.
> Sale of capital stock or exercise of options.

3. Prepare the Projected Cash Requirements Statement as shown in Exhibit 5-b.

RAPID HANDLING OF CASH

It is evident from the previous discussion on both short- and long-range cash forecasts that mid-budget adjustments must be made. The technique illustrated provides for an interim look at the cash budget, Exhibit 5-i, to determine whether the pieces fit together—is there enough cash to implement the profit plan; does the balance sheet look all right in terms of the requirements of the owners, banks, the public; do the Projected Ratios meet the various requirements? If not, corrections must be made to the operating plan which generated the supporting budgets for the Cash Budget. As a minimum, this may require finding more cash (accelerating receipts or borrowing more), or deferring payables to the next period.

Deferring payments is, at best, a temporary measure and may adversely affect the company's credit rating; borrowing may not be possible or may be too costly; sales and operating expense budgets may already be strained to their maximums. The best response is to accelerate cash receipts into the bank by rapid handling at all phases of your system. This will require:

1. A knowledge of the entire operating system, available from:

a. a systems study, or

b. one strategically placed individual, say the Controller, VP/Administration, Management Information Systems Manager, or

c. a committee of knowledgeable managers, say managers of billing, credit and collection, data processing, accounting, field administration.

2. Implementation of techniques for handling cash rapidly through the system. This could result in one or more of the following actions being utilized:

a. Centralized handling and management of cash.

b. Little or no decentralization.

c. The use of fewer banks—less banks mean less balances.

d. Cash forecasts received from decentralized locations, if any.

e. Analysis of bank services being rendered and charges made.

f. Credit terms changed, discounts considered.

g. Speed billing as to time and errors.
    1) examine time lag from decentralized shipping points to the billing office.
    2) consider decentralized billing, or systems changes to speed billing to centralized points:
        a) TWX or Telex.
        b) Terminals.
        c) Time sharing devices to a central computer.
        d) off-line data transmission devices.

h. analyze customer needs in accounting procedures.

i. record sales net of discounts offered.
    1) lapsed discount are income and should be reported on separately.
    2) discounts offered may be deducted from balance sheet accounts receivables for proper tracking.

j. lock box handling of cash to avoid in-house clerical delays in posting and depositing cash (see page 20).

k. decentralize collections and use sales office support.

l. dispose of surplus equipment.

m. prepare a laundry list of surplus supplies to be sold.

n. publish close-out inventory lists or hold warehouse sales.

o. liquidate low yield investments.

p. settle outstanding insurance or legal claims.

q. call in security deposits and don't place new ones.

r. re-examine purchasing and manufacturing schedules to improve inventory turnover.

s. consider tax options:
    1) Expense certain items for tax purposes which are deferred for books—software expenses, insurance, parts and supplies, fixed assets, tools.
    2) Defer for tax purposes certain book income items—advance payments for goods or services.

  3) Depreciation base and methods—tax and book need not be the same.

  4) Lease and installment sales may be reported on an operating lease or installment sale basis for tax reporting.

  5) Lease instead of buy.

 t. requisitions for funds by divisions or suppliers:

  1) Telex or telephone delays disbursement.

  2) Examine use of sight drafts for salesmen's expense reimbursements.

  3) Consider sight drafts for vendors, such as frequent freight charges.

  4) Record purchases net of discounts. Lost discounts are an expense.

  5) Study "float" to carry minimum bank balances.

 u. Study and plan disbursements.

  1) Don't pay early (see discussion at page 23)

  2) Use sight drafts

  3) Use imprest and zero balance bank accounts (see page 21).

INTERNAL CONTROLS ON CASH RECEIPTS

The Controller has not only the responsibility for planning and budgeting cash, an adjunct of which is the rapid handling of cash as just discussed, but also for the control of cash. This is control against losses through fraud, negligence, incompetence, or inept systems. No budget can be planned outside the framework of a rigid control system. Otherwise, there could be no assurance, with any degree of confidence, that the forecasted numbers would be attained.

> **Key Procedural Point**: As with any internal control system, cash control requires a separation of responsibilities in the actual handling of cash from the cash record keeping. When such a separation exists, fraud will require collusion, which, by definition, restricts the number of opportunities for such fraud.

1. Types of Cash Misappropriations

a. Outright theft without regard to controls or records.

b. Lapping—misappropriating checks and reporting the cash received sometime later by misappropriating a check from another account.

c. Overstating sales allowances or cash discounts allowed.

d. Not reporting cash received from cash sales, unreported sales, accounts in the hands of third-party collection agencies, bad debt recoveries, refunds of deposits, down-payments, collection of unrecorded items such as insurance claims, damage suits.

e. Reporting part of the cash collected in d, and holding back the excess.

f. Undercharging accounts and holding back the difference when paid.

g. Mis-posting records with amounts that disagree with the amounts collected, including falsifying totals.

h. Falsifying records.

It is apparent that these misappropriations will not continue uncovered, over a period of time, unless collusion exists.

2. Checklist for internal control of cash

    a. Authorization for check writing should be separate from check signing authority.

    b. Two check signers should be required.

    c. Separate the responsibilty for receiving cash and for depositing it, fixing the definite responsibilities.

    d. Separate cash handling from the record keeping.

    e. Cross-check cash sales amounts from inventory records.

    f. Divide responsibilities for receiving cash and paying cash, preferably in separate departments.

    g. Cash receivers, appliers or handlers should not have access to cash receipts books or records.

    h. Bank reconciliations should be performed by personnel who have no other cash record keeping responsibility.

    i. Summary totals of monthly cash receipts and disbursements records should be prepared by others than the daily posting clerks. Where there is a separate data processing function, batch totals of daily items should be prepared by the accounts receivable section for control over-run listings from data processing.

    j. In a retail or cash sales business, use protective equipment—cash register, duplicate sales ticket. Read registers frequently, using separate personnel.

    k. Mail receipts and checks should be tape controlled by accounting people, photocopies made of checks, and other accounting people should deposit the funds. Copies of checks should then be sent to accounts receivable application clerks for posting.

    l. Store notes and post-dated checks separate from the accounts receivable posting function.

    m. Deposit all cash and checks daily.

    n. Company representatives selling for cash should be required to give receipts and retain a duplicate for future audit.

    o. Internal audit should be conducted by an auditor reporting outside the accounting or collection departments. Audits should be made of all sources of receipts.

    p. Personnel should be required to take annual vacations (rather than working through vacation periods), and shifts in jobs should be made frequently to prevent collusion.

    q. Personnel handling cash and checks and cash records should be bonded through Employee Fidelity Insurance (see Chapter 4).

    r. In small companies, the division of internal control above is not possible due to so few employees. Then, the owner or manager must maintain close supervision over the cash responsibilities and provide for frequent independent audits.

PRACTICAL CASH FORECASTING POINTERS

1. The cash budget proves the feasibility of the overall profit plan and all other budgets.

2. Short- and long-range cash forecasts need to be prepared and compared to actual results. This enables constant corrective action.

3. Rapid handling of cash procedures may be established to provide for slack periods and to assure meeting projections.

4. Internal cash control procedures are built around close supervision and a division of responsibility. Such procedures contribute to the validity of the cash forecasts.

CHAPTER 6

Establishing the Plan for the

Control of Operations

THIS is the first controllership function in the FEI definition: "To establish, coordinate and administer, as an integral part of management, an adequate plan for the control of operations. Such a plan would provide, to the extent required in the business, profit planning, programs for capital investing and for financing, sales forecasts, expense budgets and cost standards, together with the necessary procedures to effectuate the plan."

This, then, is alternately called the Profit Plan, the Budget, the Operating Control Plan, the Operating Plan, or, simply, the Plan.

TERMINOLOGY

We shall use the following definitions in Establishing the Plan for the Control of Operations:

   a. Budget—The quantified plan of operations for given fiscal periods, expressed in the form of financial statements with sufficient supporting schedules to enable measurement of actual performance to budget.

   b. Forecast—This is less extensive than the budget, being a prediction of one aspect of the budget at a specific point or over a period of time, such as sales for the year, or cash balance at the end. As the term is used here, it does not refer to "financial forecasts," which may be the same as budgets, but usually refer to an objective, logical, supported statement of the most probable financial results. A financial forecast differs from a budget as the latter involves motivational, control, and performance evaluation considerations as principal elements.

   c. Estimate or Projection—An estimate based on assumptions that are not necessarily the most likely. A projection is often developed in answer to "What would happen if . . . ?" The assumptions of the budget result in estimated or projected financial statements.

    d. Operating Plan—The Budget, as defined above.

    e. Profit Plan—The initial profit target as expressed by the Chief Executive Officer and as reflected in the bottom-line of the Budget. This, therefore, becomes the Forecast of a number, stated either pre-tax or after-tax.

THE BUDGETING CONCEPT

Even the small businessman or retail store owner practices budgeting. The candy store owner estimates his sales every day—they depend on the weather, is it raining or too cold, and is it a school day, will the kids be in? He expects $50 in candy sales, knows his candy cost to be 20% or $10, and his daily operating costs to be $10 for rent, electric, heat, insurance, accounting, cleaning ($3,650 per year ÷ 365 days). He expects to net $30 for the day. In fact, he needs it. That's his minimum. He's got to clear $180 for six days work to provide enought take home cash to meet his own family needs. During the day, sales are slow. He doubts he'll exceed $45 for the full day. He immediately reacts and offers the next customers 2 for 1 specials (increasing his cost of sales to 40%). He completes the day and tallies up to $52 for the day. His candy cost was $11.80, his operating expenses $10, and his net $30.20. He makes the day!

This example embodies all of the basic budgeting techniques:

1. The Profit Plan—was established by the Chief Executive Officer at $30 per day.

2. A Budget—or operating plan was established reflecting a 20% cost of sales and $10 in daily operating expenses—and a bottom line net of $30 a day as proposed by the CEO.

3. Communication—was established with his wife and family in determining that his daily home needs were $30.

4. Budget vs. actual (BVA) performance—was measured during the budgeted period, during the day, to allow for corrective action to be taken, thereby assuring that the budget for the week or the year would be met.

The Budgeting Concept is embellished in the corporate world with some additional frills, mostly related to the extended span of control found in most larger companies—but the steps are the same. Let us examine them:

THE PROFIT PLAN

The Profit Plan for the enterprise is implicitly determined by the stockholders and is reflected in the price/earnings ratio for the Company's stock as determined by the marketplace.

These marketplace expectations are signaled to the Board of Directors and the

President who react to them, refine them and examine them in light of their long-range goals. The profit objective is set and passed on to subordinates for implementation—to the VP/Finance, the VP/Marketing, the Controller, and responsible officers for manufacturing, research and development, and personnel and administration.

The profit objective is usually tied to sales growth and is quantified with one or more of the following yardsticks:

- Sales Growth, and

- Gross Profit Margin.

- Operating Expenses to Sales.

- Pre-Tax Margin.

- After-Tax Margin.

- Return on Average Net Worth.

- Return on Total Assets.

- Return Before Interest and Taxes to Total Assets.

The President may, further, specify certain minimum standards for liquidity and turnover of assets (see Exhibit 5-c for Projected Ratios).

The Controller is expected to interface with the other advised officers and translate these objectives into a formal Budget.

THE BUDGET

The Controller takes the following steps to "establish, coordinate and administer" the Budget:

1. A Budget Committee—is established to give final Budget approval. This may be a committee of one, consisting of the President, but usually involves three to five corporate officers. It is preferrably chaired by the President or VP/Finance, who can best interpret the financial goals established in the Profit Plan by the Board or the President. Other members can be division heads and marketing and manufacturing officers. The rule to follow, as to membership, is that every arm of the organization must be represented, either by the directly responsible manager or his superior. For example, if the President is on the committee, no one else must be on it, as the President has the ultimate responsibility for all areas. If the President is not a member, then all officers reporting to him should have membership.

   The Controller, himself, need not be a committee member. He will be at every Budget meeting, anyway, to present, analyse and interpret the Budget for members of the committee.

2. A Budget Calendar—is established and published, circulated to concerned managers, to establish the time-table and chronology of the Budget. See Exhibit 6-a for a Budget Calendar.

This particular calendar allows approximately 60 days for completion of the budget, from start to finish. It is important not to start the budget too far in advance, in order to obtain the latest inputs and changes which will affect the advance planning which goes in to the Budget.

Helpful Hint: Stable companies, without seasonal aspects to their operation, may allow up to 120 days in their Budget Calendar. Volatile companies should focus on a 60 to 90 day advance period.

Another Helpful Hint: In the illustrated calendar, certain dates are fixed (steps 5 through 10), and no variance in completion dates is permitted. These comprise the mechanical, accounting and data processing steps which begin after the line departments submit their budget data.

The initial issuance of the Budget forms to departments, in step 1 of Exhibit 6-a, includes the transmission of corporate goals, as to sales and expenses. This transmission may be in a memo that accompanies the forms, or it may be on the forms, themselves. This is discussed, further, in the next section on Communication.

3. Communication—of the President's profit objectives is made, initially, to officers responsible for sales, manufacturing, administration, distribution, and finance. The Profit Plan, as described on page 90, is tied to sales growth and is expressed in the form of yardsticks, relating profits to a percentage of sales, net worth, or assets, as seen at Exhibit 5-c.

The question often arises as to whether budgets should be submitted, first, by the various departments or divisions who are responsible and, then, be compared to the Profit Plan—or whether the Profit Plan should be submitted to the departments with instructions to budget so as to achieve the Profit Plan. In other words, do we budget from the bottom, up, or from the top, down?

The answer is a little of both. Successful budgeting requires total involvement of the people who are expected to achieve the forecasted results. If a plan is submitted for these people, the operating personnel, and if their performance is to be measured against this plan, they should cooperate in setting the goals by which they will be measured.

This philosophy of employee involvement cannot be overdone.

A Word of Caution: Setting performance goals for employees without their concurrence in the attainment of these goals is certain to result in failure.

However, employees should not be permitted to set goals which are not consonant with corporate objectives.

In other words—enlightened management, sensitive to stockholders needs, through the Board of Directors and the President, is in a position to determine the most likely attainable Profit Plan. This is imparted to officers who distribute the plan to subordinates, sometimes explaining, exhorting, selling, demanding—some of each—as to the total soundness of the Profit Plan. The plan is then passed down to the lowest level manager who has profit responsibility, with similar exhortations.

The Communication process follows this chronology:

a. Explaining to all managers "why we budget."

b. Communicating the Profit Plan, distributing forms and the Budget Calendar, explaining corporate goals.

c. Reviewing submitted budgets in the Budget Committee and re-communicating the need for revisions to tie-in to corporate goals.

d. Submitting an approved Budget to all levels of "responsibility," with periodic progress reports to compare actual performance to Budget and to explain variances.

The Communication process is examined in detail below.

COMMUNICATION

a. **Why Do We Budget?**—This is the most common question. The budget, they say, takes a good deal of time to prepare, it is only a guess, and probably is used as a yardstick to nail a manager with bad performance. Training classes and seminars are necessary to inculcate managers with the reasons and needs for budgeting. The following may serve as a checklist of points to be raised in the training session:

- The Budget is an estimate of anticipated costs and expenses. A study of this helps us to understand our business better, to coordinate the efforts of all divisions, to provide top management with overall visibility of operations, and to avoid surprises.

- The Budget is not restrictive. It allows for flexibility and improvement. It provides estimates of costs and expenses if goals are exceeded and, similarly, provides for reductions in expenses if goals cannot be met.

- The Profit Plan or objective is the sole important goal to be achieved. Failures to attain the stated goal are analysed each period to determine the necessary corrective actions and to permit us to achieve the required goals in the future.

- Bad habits and poor management are eliminated. Errors are corrected, at once.

- Every management decision is directed toward achievement of the Profit Plan as expressed by the Budget.

- Forecasts of sales and expenses are based on past performance, plus planned changes and expected level of business activity. These forecasts recognize population trends, indicators of business activity, employment trends, personal income levels. They are not guesses but intelligent estimates of future activity.

- The Budget is a Statement of Policy, expressed in an overall profit objective. It is not a working guide or a tool for managing. Its objectives may be quantified into useful "rule-of-thumb" guides, such as the ratios in Exhibit 5-c.

- The Budget is the tool which provides additional profits by using the processes of analysis and advance planning.

- Additional profits result because the key to successful operations lies only in the analysis and advance planning by all division managers before final Budget approval.

- Large businesses have an attenuated span of control, and it is difficult to properly communicate corporate goals. The Budget compresses the communication process into the quantified expression of a Profit Plan. Small businesses profit, equally, by an intensive study of past operations and future prospects.
- Day-to-day decisions are avoided as decisions are pre-assessed through budgetary planning as to their effect on the entire business.
- Budgetary planning requires that plans be written and that the manager be held responsible for their execution. This instills the habit of analysis and advance planning.
- Participation by managers in the budgeting procedure creates thorough familiarity with the overall objectives of the enterprise, and thorough involvement. No one is left out or by-passed. Each manager can suggest and obtain the benefit of others' counsel. The final Budget represents the combined judgment of all managers in the best ways to attain the Profit Plan.
- The Budget not only coordinates efforts along the most profitable lines but helps in controlling operations through the issuance of periodic comparison reports of Budget to Actual performance.
- The Budget uses "responsibility" accounting. It is as improper, however, to over-budget as it is to underbudget. For example, if each manager under-budgeted in order to look better in actual performance, the Company would not have enough cash budgeted to meet its attainable goals.
- The Budget uses the direct cost concept, with each manager being responsible only for those costs which he can control. There are no allocations or corporate pool charged in to any profit center.

b. Communicating the Profit Plan, distributing forms, the Budget Calendar, and explaining corporate goals—This can become an easy task when managers have been pre-trained as described in **a.** above. This part of Communication requires that each manager understand the "responsibility accounting" concept, which embodies the use of "direct costs" in the "profit center." The individual manager may then construct his own profit plan which will become a part of the overall Profit Plan.

The distribution of the forms, the calendar, and the imparting of the corporate objectives is best done in a general meeting with immediate subordinate managers who, in turn, will hold similar meetings with their immediate subordinate managers. In this way, the importance of the budget—its timing and its goals—is given a personal touch with each immediate manager. It is not relegated to a written directive. These meetings will stress the concepts mentioned above:

1. *Responsibility Accounting*—requires the creation of Profit Centers at decentralized locations where costs may be controlled by a responsible manager. The local manager becomes responsible for the sales and administration at his office, as well as the generation of costs and profits. He is, therefore, "responsible" and he, himself, creates the operating plan for his office and is responsible for its results. The Budget Department merely supplies the manager with a print-out of his own budget, set up in a readable format, and then reports the results of actual operations to the manager,

together with a statement of variances from the budget. The manager must explain and comment on these variances to his superior who, in turn, is held accountable for his subordinate's performance. The system of responsibility, thus, channels up from the lowest level of managerial control to the highest.

2. *The Profit Center*—is the lowest level on the organizational chart at which the manager exercises control over revenues and expenses. Exhibit 6-b, Organization and Operations, is a chart for a marketing division. Each box on the chart represents a Profit Center, presided over by a manager who controls its expenses and is responsible for its revenues.

3. *Direct Costs*—are used in attributing expenses to the Profit Center. A Direct Cost is defined, for Budget Purposes, as "any cost which would be eliminated if the Profit Center, itself, were eliminated." This definition is necessary as there often are costs endemic to the operation of the Profit Center which are not necessarily immediately controllable by the manager. They are, though, ultimately controllable.

> **Case in Point**—Rent expense in a remote sales office, say with a five-year lease, may not appear to be under the control of the branch manager. It is, though, ultimately, as the office could be sub-let, if necessary, and salesmen could travel from their homes.

The Direct Cost definition must be communicated to all managers to avoid arguments over what costs are charged into their Profit Center. This definition implies a degree of ultimate control which relates to the very existence of the Profit Center and is, thus, not an arguable concept as it relates to charging expenses into the cost center.

Stated another way, remove a box from the organizational chart and any costs that follow it are Direct.

> **Helpful Hint**—Avoid arguments. Do not allocate, apportion, or charge-in to the Profit Center any costs which are not Direct Costs.
>
> **Case in Point**—In one company, a Branch Manager was charged for a portion of Home Office Accounting services. He obtained a fee quotation from a local accounting firm to provide all tax and accounting services at half of the apportioned amout. It is difficult to assail his logic due to the artificial allocation of corporate charges.

4. *Intercompany Transfer Price*—is the concept used to charge corporate pool and home office expenses to Profit Centers, without the necessity of allocations. Under this concept, the Profit Center is charged for merchandise purchases at lowest dealer price. This price includes a normal mark-up and element of profit for the home office, but is the same price at which an independent, non-company owned, dealer would purchase. The Field Manager cannot argue the logic of this charge, since if he cannot operate profitably on this basis, the Company would be better off to close the field office (which is now a Loss Center, rather than a Profit Center) and franchise an independent dealer. All Profit Centers are compared on the same basis, using the published dealer price list, permitting gross profit margins to be compared against each other.

For corporate purposes, the artificial mark-up is easily eliminated to determine true gross profits.

> **Helpful Hint**: If no published dealer price list exists, or if the Company does not distribute through any secondary distribution level, a flat 40% discount from list price may be used to establish the transfer price. This is a Wholesale Concept which is equally understandable by departmental managers.

5. *The Position Description*—described in Chapter 7 as a tool necessary in Administering the Plan for the Control of Operations, is shown in the "Treasurer's and Controller's Functions" for both the Treasurer and the Controller. Likewise, there is a Position Description for each box on the Organizational Chart. Each Manager of a Profit Center is so described.

This is an essential ingredient of Communication in the budgeting process. Each manager must know where he fits in the organization and what his duties and responsibilities are, as they relate to his profit objectives. These tools set the parameters for the job, avoid duplications by other managers and fix responsibility for broad areas. I have often been asked why you can't merely tell a manager he is responsible for profits in his area, and that's it. Why do you need to go to the trouble and expense of the Position Description? The comment has merit. Profits are the goal, but where there is more than one responsible manager, more than one profit center, these corporate goals become interwoven, and each manager has functional responsibility to each other manager. Corporate policy in the form of social consciousness, anti-trust adherence, corporate image, and overall corporate posture are ingredients in attaining overall profits. Each manager may achieve his profit goal, but the corporation may lose a damaging patent infringement suit which could destroy its profits. The Position Description approaches all these ends from a corporate, not an individual standpoint.

6. *The Chart of Accounts*—is the key accounting device used in fixing responsibility at the Profit Center level. An expandable Chart of Accounts is shown at Exhibit 6-c. It is vital that responsible managers understand that expenses and vendors' invoices must be properly coded to provide accurate information. Looking at the exhibit, you will observe that a simple numbering system is used which may be expanded on an almost unlimited basis, to permit a computer to generate the data required by cost centers (Profit Centers).

This Chart of Accounts allows you to "source code" each document, with a view to charging the cost involved into the originating cost center (using the Direct Cost concept set out in 3 above). As an example, Advertising expense for direct mailing by a branch office would be coded 71XXXX. The first digit, 7, represents operating expenses; the second digit, 1, represents selling expenses; the third and fourth digits represent major descriptions of selling expenses, such as direct mailings, telephone canvassing, local advertising, etc. The fifth and sixth digits are encoded to identify each Profit Center or branch office. While this is a highly technical tool, and, perhaps, beyond the purview of the non-accounting manager, I cannot stress enough the importance of proper source coding in generating accurate information.

In this regard, I refer you to the copy of the "Accounts Payable Voucher" at Exhibit 6-d, which form is used to prepare every vendor's invoice for input to the data processing or accounting system.

> **Key Point**: Note the box "Coding Approval, if $500 and Code 3." This indicates that an accounting officer must approve every expense item of $500 or more, so that the originating document is coded properly and results in an accurate report.

7. *Divided or Functional Responsibility*—is the concept of "dotted-line," rather then direct responsibility. Communicating the Profit Plan and corporate goals requires an appreciation that *every* manager has dotted line responsibility to every other manager. In a sense, each serves the other and reports to the other, both up and down and across the organizational ladder. The Position Description shows specific Organizational Relationships, but inherent in each manager's job are the unwritten relationships to all other managers. This is the concept of cooperation by which corporate goals are attained.

> **Helpful Hint**: Every Organizational Chart should never show two direct-lines upward for one manager. Each manager should have only one superior. But every Chart, likewise, should not skimp on showing dotted lines from field managers to home office staff managers. For example, the Sales and Service Administrator in Exhibit 6-b reports directly to the Western Zone Manager. However, the Home Office National Adminstrator, who reports to the Controller (as seen in the Position Description in "Treasurer's and Controller's Functions"), carries a dotted line of authority to each Sales and Service Administrator.

There is another important communications concept illustrated by this Organizational Chart—that of divided responsibility. The basic Responsibility Accounting concept requires that a manager be responsible for all costs which are "direct" to his profit center. In Exhibit 6-b, however, the branch office manager (called the Sales and Service Center Administrator) does not report in to the local branch manager, but rather reports directly to the Zone Manager. The shibboleth of "direct cost" control by the responsible manager is shattered. But every rule needs to be flexible to permit the organization to adapt to changing situations. In this situation, we find this—

> **Case in Point**: The illustrated company was in its first stages of direct distribution through sales offices. The local managers were primarily salesmen who had been promoted to branch managers. A concentrated Branch Manager training program had not yet been instituted. It was determined that each manager should concentrate on sales results and be provided with an office manager specialist to control expenses, until his training was completed. Since the achievement of high sales could be accomplished without the proper profit perspective, it was felt the Administration Manager would more properly report to the Zone Manager. Branch Manager training programs have now been completed and sales managers are profit-oriented, as well as sales-oriented. Organizational responsibilities have been changed and Administration Managers now report directly to the Branch Manager. Through organizational flexibility, and divided responsibility, the Company was able to accomplish its Profit Plan during a period of change.

The point is—don't etch responsibility concepts in concrete. Change them to meet changing conditions, but keep the Organizational Chart and Position Descriptions current!

c. **Reviewing Submitted Budgets** and Re-communicating the Need for Revisions—is another vital part of the budgetary communicating process. The Budget Committee, as stated earlier, is composed of the President and/or key Officers of the corporation. When individually submitted budgets are viewed in total perspective by the Committee, they may not meet the corporate stated Profit Plan. It is no easy task to have to go back to managers who have labored over their budgets for weeks and convince them that revised estimates are required to meet the overall corporate goals. If, however, the communication process has carefully included the "Why Do We Budget?" checklist on page 93 as part of the training sessions, managers will understand the concept of overall profit objectivity. They can be readily convinced to make a revised contribution to the accomplishment of the Profit Plan. This may mean that one division manager may have to make a disproportionate effort, for which he obviously will expect to be rewarded.

> **Case-in-Point:** A retail outlet, in a major city, belonging to one of our largest retail chains, was a losing operation. A new manager was moved in and asked to budget a profit to permit the corporation to meet its stated return on invested assets objectives. The profits were earned and the manager subsequently was promoted to President of the chain.

This art of re-communicating budgeted objectives is best accomplished by employing the following:

1. Management training—see checklist on page 212.

2. Management by Objectives—setting performance goals; see discussion on page 206.

3. Personal Negotiation—personal motivation by superiors with the promise of reward in the future, as in the Case in Point, above.

4. Top Management Involvement—Officers may hold splinter meetings with lower level managers, personally imparting corporate goals. Higher management involvement lends a personal touch to lower management involvement, boosts morale, and creates a team atmosphere.

d. **Submitting an Approved Budget** to All Levels of Responsibility, with Periodic Comparisons of Actual Performance to Budget—is an essential ingredient of any formal budgeting system. This allows for mid-stream corrective action which assures that the organization will reach its Profit Objective. This subject will be treated fully in Chapter 7 "Administering the Plan for the Control of Operations." It deals with the Budget review techniques to measure performance up to Plan, describing how major variances are accounted for and controlled.

BUDGET VS. ACTUAL (BVA) PERFORMANCE

As just indicated, above, the reporting of actual performance as compared to Budget is reserved for the next chapter. It is important, however, as basic to establishing the Budget, that the finally approved Budget be presented to the responsible managers in a readable format which will permit future comparisons to be done quickly and easily.

A complete Budget is presented at Exhibit 6-e, to include:

Profit and Loss Budget.

Sales Budget.

Cost of Sales Budget.

Expense Budget.

Employee Forecast.

Standard Branch Profit & Loss Statement.

P & L Explanations.

General Budgeting Instructions.

The Profit and Loss Budget—is the lead schedule to which are posted the results of the following *Sales Budget, Cost of Sales Budget,* and *Expense Budget.*

Each Budget has, in common, a format which shows six months in detail, and six months in total, to make up the year.

The P & L Budget computes cost of sales at an intercompany transfer price as described on page 95, and only Direct Costs are included as expenses. Some expenses within the area are allocated (several branches sharing the same facilities or services), but no headquarters or home office corporate pool expenses are included.

The Standard Branch P & L Statement—is presented in two formats, one to conform to the same format used in the Budget, the other, listing expenses in straight alphabetical order, for ease in comparison.

The P & L Explanations—are part of the communication and training process, explaining the nature of each item on the Budget.

The General Budgeting Instructions—are used to explain how each Budget form is filled out. The instructions are complete and detailed to avoid error.

In total, these forms embody the previously discussed concepts of Direct Costing through Responsibility Accounting using Profit Centers. Planning operations, in addition, may require the expenditure of large sums of money for capital items which will benefit more than the budgeted period.

CAPITAL BUDGETING

This chapter has been concerned with budgeting for profits, and previous chapters have dealt with obtaining short-range and long-range funds with which to operate. However, funds are needed only if they can be invested profitably, and profits are a measure of the return on assets. The Company, therefore, must determine whether an investment is acceptable, before making it. Four common methods of determining acceptability may be used:

1. Payback—measures the net cash inflows against the initial cost to determine how many years of inflows are needed to obtain payback of the initial investment. This is usually expressed as a "two year payback." The method has disadvantages in that it ignores cash inflows after the payback period, and it also ignores the decrease in the value of money due to inflation and the timing of its receipt, that is, its present value. Nevertheless, the method is simple and can be an acceptable yardstick.

2. Return on Investment—is a measure of the percentage of the annual net cash inflows of the original investment. A $10,000 inflow per year, requiring an original cash outlay of $50,000 results in a 20% ROI. This method does not work well if cash flows are unequal over the useful life, nor does it give consideration to the expected duration of the cash inflows. A 30% ROI for 10 years is obviously more desirable than a 30% ROI for a shorter period, but the simple percentage figure does not express that advantage.

3. Present Value—relates the cash inflows, for each year and for all years, adjusted for the time value of the money, to the original cash investment. The cash inflows are "discounted" back to the present. The method is difficult to compute manually, but any standard book of accounting tables contains Present Value tables which make the computation easy. Some electronic portable calculators, Hewlett Packard or Texas Instruments, for two, contain pre-programmed systems to permit Present Value calculations at your desk. Time-sharing terminals of companies specializing in financial applications commonly offer Present Value programs. This method is the best of all, but it requires the use of the proper discount rate and determining the useful life of the project, both key to the calculations.

4. Internal Rate of Return—is similar to the Present Value or discounted cash flow method in 3 above. However, it finds a discount rate for the expected cash inflows, using a trial and error method, which exactly equals the original investment. This rate of return is then compared to the company's standard or required rate of return to determine whether the project is acceptable.

Due to the sophistication required to reach a capital budget decision, field offices and divisions normally complete a Capital Expenditures Authorization (Exhibit 5-h) which describes the project, setting forth complete reasons for the expenditure. From this, the Treasurer's office estimates the cash inflows and useful life with which to calculate acceptability.

BUDGETING POINTERS

Establishing the Control Plan for operations requires the formulation of a Profit Plan by the Board and the President. This Plan is translated into an operating program called a Budget which results in projected financial statements and forecasts of sales, expenses, and capital requirements. The techniques for budgeting are communicated to all levels of management through careful training, and the Operating Plan is prepared with each key manager being responsible for a Profit Center, exercising control over his direct costs of operation. This technique utilizes source coding of documents to enable proper charges to be made into cost centers; the preparation of plans or budgets for successive six-month periods; the comparison of budget to actual operations with reports of variances, and a series of reports in line with defined organizational charts. This control program involves the broad management concept of planning corporate moves in advance, and then comparing performance to the plan. It is not concerned with the details of every transaction but only with the end result—profits. Budgeting is management accounting of the highest order, not based on the output of a green-eye-shaded Uriah Heep, but, rather, on the planned performance of the management group in setting goals and realizing them, utilizing the sophisticated planning tools of responsibility and budgetary accounting in achieving them.

CHAPTER 7

Administering the Plan for the

Control of Operations

IN the previous chapter, we discussed the first Controllership function, involved with establishing the plan for the control of operations. Inherent in Planning for the Control function is the "coordination and administration" of the previously established Plan. You've got the plan. Now make it fly! This means you need an organizational framework to be sure people receive the plan, read it, understand it, are involved in it, and perform up to it. You'll want to establish Budget review techniques to measure performance against the Plan. This will involve the use of variance reports which will be discussed in the next chapter. But, first you need the framework. The framework necessary to Administer the Plan for the Control of Operations requires the following:

Organizational Charts.

Position Descriptions.

Standard Operating Procedures.

Operating Policies.

Personnel Policies.

Publication Control.

Exercise of Authority.

These devices are available to even the smallest company. They are quickly and easily constructed and once completed, they attest to the internal control which is exerted by responsible management. They also make the Plan work!

ORGANIZATIONAL CHARTS

It is a business axiom that a company's success depends on having a sound organization plan. An organization chart serves to define:

Responsibility.

Delegation of authority.

Span of control.

Job functions.

Reporting relationships.

Profit centers.

Cost centers.

Decentralized/centralized philosophy.

This is an amazing list, yet every organization chart denotes these items, either specifically or inherently. The responsible positions are indicated. The lines leading from the top boxes indicate delegation of authority and span of control. The placement of the boxes, in relation to other boxes, implies the job function and reporting relationship. Each responsible box becomes a profit or cost center and the flow of the lines will tell a good deal about the operating philosophy of the company.

Moreover if a current organization chart is maintained with identifying names, a picture is painted for every employee which associates the individual with the job—and it is worth a thousand words.

One would suppose (as would your independent auditor), the lack of even a simple and updated organization chart would indicate that there are unresolved questions of responsibility, authority, and reporting relationships—and if this be so, the organization, obviously, is unable to perform up to its promise.

In constructing an organization chart, the following principles should be considered:

1. Each person should report to only one superior.

2. Responsibility for performance of assigned duties must be accompanied by corresponding authority.

3. Each person's responsibilities should be clearly defined.

4. Charts must start at the lowest level which determines expenses and/or revenues.

5. Charts should top out with the recipients of profits, be they owners, stockholders, or trustees—not with the President.

6. Functional (dotted line) relationships should be drawn.

7. Only a few subordinates (usually no more than six) should report to each superior (unless the subordinates all perform essentially the same job).

8. All essential functions should be charted.

9. Adequate checks and balances must be provided.

10. Committees should be identified and charted.

11. Names of individuals should be slotted and kept current.

These principles are evident in Exhibit 7-a, Organization Manual, which excerpts five pages from a manual, showing:

Page 1. Contents—consisting of charts, titles and names, and committee pro-files.

Page 2. Introduction—giving a brief statement of purpose, and providing for update and change. (Note the "replaces" box at the bottom of the page.)

Page 3. Company Chart—The top chart, starting with the stockholders and Board of Directors.

Page 4. Controller's Chart—showing six persons reporting, and cross-reference at the bottom to titles and names.

Page 5. Titles and Names—the cross reference from the Controller's chart.

The responsibility for maintaining the Organizational Manual in a current and up-dated position is that of the Administrative Planning Department which reports to the Director of Administrative Operations (see page 4 of Exhibit 7-a) in the Controller's area. This is the first step in the administration of the Control Plan.

POSITION DESCRIPTIONS

The position of each box on the Organization Chart is an indication of the character of the job, shows the reporting relationships and, generally, summarizes the details which are found in the Position or Job Description. Just as every procedural narrative has a flow chart to affirm its logic, so, too, does the Organization Chart affirm the logic of the Position Description. One does not exist without the other.

A Job description Format is shown at Exhibit 7-b, and a detailed Position Description for the Treasurer and the Controller may be found in the "Treasurer's and Controller's functions." Guidelines for Writing Job Descriptions are given at Exhibit 7-c.

It is necessary to distinguish between Job Descriptions, as defined above, which are broad statements of duties and responsibilities, from the detailed job descriptions or Work Duties which should be prepared for each job in each department. Work Duties spell out in specific detail just how a job should be performed. Each department head should maintain a Work Duties sheet for each job under his aegis, with a copy in the Personnel Department.

Position Descriptions should be:

1. Current.

2. Prepared for each box on the Organization Chart.

3. Reviewed by immediate superiors.

4. Filed in a Position Description Manual for ready reference by all managers.

5. Prepared in a uniform manner using published guidelines.

The dotted line—on the Organization Chart is supported in the Job Writing Guidelines under the caption Organizational Relationships. While we have said previously that each manager has a dotted line relationship to every other manager, in theory, the specific relationships and interfacing of one department with another are set forth here.

> **Helpful Hint**: Show the dotted line on Organization charts and carefully consider these relationships in constructing the Position Description. This relates key managers to each other and is the cement in the organizational building blocks.

STANDARD OPERATING PROCEDURES

We have seen that each employee, within the department, has a detailed Work Guide prepared for his job, and his superior has a Job Description which broadly states his responsibilities. To effectuate the duties set out in Work Guides and Job Descriptions, the Director of Administrative Operations, under the aegis of the Controller, will prepare the Standard Operating Procedures for the Company.

The following guidelines should be followed in writing Standard Operating Procedures:

- Codify all procedures in a manual.
- Use a simple numbering system for identification. For example, the first Accounting procedure is A-1, the second is A-2. Purchasing is P-1, P-2, etc.
- Use a Table of Contents, divided in sections by major area, such as Accounting, Purchasing, Order/Billing, Data Processing, Office Services, Personnel.
- Index all procedures.
- Exhibit all forms as part of procedures, and prepare a Forms Index.
- Cross-reference "Procedures Applicable to Other Departments" with a Contents listing which shows, for each department, those procedures which are not primary to it, but which involve this department. For example, an Accounting procedure involving Accounts Payable is primary to the Accounting Department but secondary to Purchasing which must send a copy of a Purchase Order to the Accounting Department.
- If the manual becomes too bulky, divide it into separate binders for ease in handling, using the categories in the basic numbering system.
- Always separate field procedures from home office procedures. Use separate manuals.
- Require the Controller to approve all procedures before publication and for him to obtain other necessary approvals where other divisions are involved.
- Keep procedures current.

Helpful Hint: A change in a very detailed procedure may mean a re-write of the entire procedure. This takes time and could delay the publication of the change. Speed this up by using a special form titled "Procedures Change Order" (referred to as a PCO). This looks like a simple interoffice memo but uses a special PCO masthead. The change is described and a printed legend on the bottom of form states that the Procedure No. XXX will be up-dated soon.

- Use a special form for all procedures, to enable all personnel to identify them, immediately, as procedures. Forms may be color-coded, for emphasis, by category or department.
- Use the Correction Checklist (described below) to up-date the Procedures Manual.
- Always start the procedure with a Purpose, a General Narrative, and show its Applicability. See this illustrated in a Branch Office Procedure at Exhibit 7-d.

Helpful Hint—Summarizing the Purpose, Narrative, and Applicability makes it unnecessary for every employee to take the time to read every procedure (some procedures run 10 to 20 pages). Only the first few paragraphs need be read to ascertain whether one is involved.

- Give extensive and detailed instructions on how to complete forms properly, supporting these with an illustration, cross-referenced to the detailed instructions. This is shown at Exhibit 7-d page 2, which is a cross-referenced Exhibit to the instructions on the previous page.

The Correction Checklist, seen at Exhibit 7-e, is used to make changes in any type of numbered manual. It may be used for the:

Procedures Manual.

Position Descriptions.

Organizational Charts.

Policy Manual.

Personnel Manual.

Other Manuals—Price Lists, Service Manuals, Marketing Memos, Training Memos, Sales Slants

Every manual is originally published with a Correction Checklist as the first page inside the front cover. Thereafter, every new procedure or correction to an original procedure is given a correction number, in sequence. This correction number appears on the procedure, itself. The recipient merely crosses off the correction number on the Correction Checklist, ascertaining that it is in sequence. If it is not, an inquiry may be made of the Systems and Procedures Department requesting a duplicate of the missing correction number procedure. To illustrate this, see Exhibit 11-d which is a Standard Operating Procedure form. At the bottom left, it will be seen that this is Correction No. 253 and it will be seen to supersede Correction No. 246 (found at the upper left of the form). Number 253 must be crossed off the appropriate Correction Checklist and the procedure with No. 246 is simply thrown away, to be replaced by Correction No. 253.

Internal Auditors check Correction Checklist sequences on their periodic audits to determine that manuals are current and contain the latest changes. This is particularly important when there is a personnel change in a particular job. The old employee may be doing the job right, with an out-dated manual. The new employee may very well pick up the obsolete procedure because the manual is not current.

OPERATING POLICIES

Standard Operating Procedures are the blueprints which are behind the broad statement of duties set forth in the Position Descriptions. These procedures may be said to be the steps in the "how to" of the job. The Company needs to augment these SOP's with a Policy manual.

Each Policy is not a "how to" but, rather, a statement of the prudence or wisdom which should be exercised in certain of the organization's affairs, consonant with the broad and overall philosophy of its management. This statement of management's material interest is expressed in the form of policies which may run the gamut from anti-political activities to zero defects in performance.

The Policy Manual is the highest authority for conduct in the corporation. It takes precedence over all other publications. An introduction to the Policy Manual is shown at Exhibit 7-f page 1.

This manual is best arranged by subject matter which conforms to the company's structure (sales, service, finance, administration), with sub-sets for broad categories, as seen at Exhibit 7-f page 2.

A typical policy, this one on Alcoholism–Drugs, is at Exhibit 7-f, page 3.

Other subjects often covered in policies are listed below:

Anti-political activities.	Legal review of contracts.
Anti-trust.	Machine service and sales of parts.
Contributions.	Maintenance agreements.
Credit terms.	Meeting minutes.
Employee stock options.	New Products.
Equal opportunity employment.	Promotions.
Exercise of authority.	Public Relations.
Extension of credit and pricing.	Responsibility to auditors.
Gifts.	Stockholder and broker releases.
Gifts from suppliers.	Supplies non-company.
Labor charges.	Technical opportunities.
Law suits.	Zero defects.

As indicated before, the statement of Policy represents management's expression of the prudent way to conduct its affairs in the particular matter addressed in the Policy. However, the saying and the doing are not always the same.

Case in Point: A company had a published Policy directing its employees not to down-grade its competitor's products. The Policy was intended to avoid anti-trust actions. Unknown to the management, its salesmen persisted in stating that the use of competitor's supplies in its equipment caused malfunctions—not borne out by the facts. The company was sued by the competitor, lost on a treble-damage judgment with a cost running into the millions of dollars. The solution—training should have been conducted for field managers in the very good reasons for this policy to encourage continuing adherence.

PERSONNEL POLICIES

Some companies separate policy matters relating to their personnel from the standard Policy Manual and publish these policies in the form of a Personnel Policy Manual or a Personnel Handbook.

This type of manual is to be distinguished from operating procedures involving personnel which are printed in the SOP Manual. Such a procedure might involve the steps and paperwork in giving an employee a raise—an operating procedure. However, the prudence or wisdom in giving overall raises would become a matter of Personnel Policy. This is sometimes expressed in a Wage Administration Program which establishes wage levels for all classes of employees and determines when raises may be given. Other subjects which could be included in a Personnel Handbook would serve as orientation (for new employees), as well as to sketch prevalent policies. A Table of Contents for a personnel manual would include:

Letter from the President.

History.

Objectives.

Organization and Operations.

    A. Domestic Organization.
    B. Officers & Board of Directors.
    C. World-wide Organization.

Products.

Personnel and Progress.

    A. Your Work.
    B. Your Responsibilities.
    C. Your Pay and Advancement.

Security Programs.

    A. Income Protection.
    B. Medical Benefits.
    C. Retirement Benefits.
    D. Death Benefits.

The Company and You.

PUBLICATION CONTROL

There are a variety of other manuals which a business may issue. These have the force of procedures or policy manuals and, so, affect the administration of the Operating Plan. Consequently, the Controller must exercise jursidiction over their publication—if only to insure that they are kept current and are properly circulated to all concerned managers.

Typical of these manuals are:

Accounting Manuals	Service and Parts Manuals
Price Lists	Marketing Directives
Sales Programs	

As with any Policy Manual, the basic decision regarding the issuance of the Policy may not be the Controller's, but the responsibility for publication and circulation is his. More importantly, the lack of publication could be a serious omission which could adversely affect the successful administration of the Operating Plan.

The Controller should require that, despite the source of authorship, the distribution and mechanics of publication of all manuals remain within his jurisdiction, possibly through the Manager of Office Services or the Systems and Procedures Department. This would enable controlled publication to those who need to know, would verify that overall policies are considered and adhered to, that proper approvals have been obtained for new policies, and that circulation is timely.

Of the manuals listed above, only the Accounting Manual comes under the direct determination of the Controller. It should therefore be reviewed as a Controllership responsibility.

The Accounting Manual

Advantages:

1. Insures adherence to company policy where alternative coding situations exist.

2. Prevents variable practice regarding the coding of alternatives.

3. Helps train new employees.

4. Provides a basis for audit by both internal and independent auditors.

5. Identifies alternative situations, in advance, by the act of codifying all accounting situations in a manual.

6. Creates a uniform systems for all personnel and all offices.

7. Provides documented advice to all manual users that these are policies of top corporate management.

Format:

A page from an Accounting Manual, showing the Salaries and Wages account, is shown at Exhibit 7-g. This provides:

- A Definition—of the account
- Inclusions—the nature of items to be included
- Exclusions—specific alternative situations to be avoided.
- Classification—instructions for coding to the Chart of Accounts.

There should, of course, be a Table of Contents and Index to facilitate use by accounting personnel, as well as introductory instructions on how the material is arranged, whether by subject matter or Chart of Accounts, the former being preferable. In addition to the description of each account, as shown at Exhibit 7-g, the Accounting Manual may also have a section on Policies (for example, what is the basis and life used for depreciation?) and Procedures (such as, how to inventory fixed assets and what book entries are to be made).
Be sure the Manual is:

- Indexed and cross-indexed.
- Loose-leaf bound.
- Has a Correction Checklist (Exhibit 7-e).
- Contains a section on:
  Forms—illustrating each.
  Policies—(what to do and when to do it).
  Procedures—(how to do it).
- Has tabs and sub-dividers for easy reference.

Finally, the Format of the Accounting Manual should be based on an outline presentation, showing main headings and sub-paragraphs, for easy reading. Use charts, graphs, and diagrams, where possible.

Avoid These Pitfalls:
1. Don't use individual names. Use titles. Otherwise you'll have to correct a page every time an employee turns over.
2. Do not squirrel the manual with the Chief Accountant. Distribute it to everyone who needs it and should use it.
   a. Keep a log of users for distribution of corrections.
   b. Number and log in each copy so you can retrieve it on employee terminations.

EXERCISE OF AUTHORITY

Whether operations are conducted on a centralized or decentralized basis, decision-making authority must be vested in subordinates, to avoid higher managers having to examine every piece of paper. To this end, a Standard Operating Procedure should be established which sets decision-making limits—limits of authority.

> **Helpful Hint**: Psychologically, these limits are better received by employees if they are not titled Limits of Authority, but, rather, Exercise of Authority, to connote the employees's judicious use of his delegated authority.

These constraints should be observed in preparing the limits:

- Every possible expenditure should be listed.

- All decision makers should be included, in columnar form.

- Functional (dotted-line) authority should be shown as necessary approvers or endorsers.

- Use titles, not names, to avoid repeated corrections.

- Procedures and policies which relate to these expenditures should be cross-referenced as footnotes.

- Specifically prohibited authority should, also, be listed, such as Pricing Policies, Credit Terms, Compensation Plans.

- A catch-all category, with low limits, should be provided to catch forgotten or omitted authority. Title it Miscellaneous or Various.

A sample page from such a procedure is shown at Exhibit 7-h. This is one of nine pages of all possible authority for expenditure. The items to be included would vary based on the nature of each company.

The procedure includes several pages of footnotes, referring to procedures and policies which govern these expenditures, as set forth in other publications. The procedure also includes an explanatory page which refers to the previously listed constraints, describes the use of the procedure in administering the Plan for the Control of Operations, and further advises that each limit is a monthly amount per invoice, or series of invoices related to the same transaction.

PRACTICAL POINTERS FOR ADMINISTERING THE CONTROL PLAN

Today's management accountant and financial executive operates in concepts, not details. These concepts are dynamic, in that they consist of continuous productive activity which is necessary to implement the Operating Plan. The Controller provides a framework for the operating structure of the enterprise. He provides for Organizational Charts, so everyone knows where he belongs, and for Position Descriptions, so everyone knows what to do. Codified Standard Operating Procedures provide the "how to," and Operating Policies are published to direct individual or group activities in line with higher management's overall philosophies. Ancillary publications such as Price Lists, Accounting Manuals, and Marketing Directives are used to augment Standard Operating Procedures, and Limits of Authority are established to permit subordinates to exercise judgment in making expenditures. These devices enable the Budget to be administered by the Controller. They provide for the free flow of reports which enable us to monitor actual performance against the Plan.

CHAPTER 8

Systematic, Simplified Financial

Reporting: Monitoring and

High-lighting Results of Operations

REPORTING and Interpreting is the second Controllership function listed in the FEI Controller's definition, as exhibited in "Treasurer's and Controller's Functions." That function is "To compare performance with operating plans and standards, and to report and interpret the results of operations to all levels of management and to the owners of the business. It includes the formulation of accounting policy, the coordination of systems and procedures, the preparation of operating data and of special reports as required."

Acquitting this responsibility requires that the Controller develop a reporting philosophy which will accomodate all users of reports (a part of which philosophy includes the definition of who shall be a user). We shall examine this further.

This chapter will be concerned with the presentation of reports on the Budget (as defined at page 89) (otherwise known as the Operating Plan), and schedules or reports which support that Budget. Various other special reports are covered in other chapters and are shown as exhibits to the related subjects—such as Cash Forecasts in Chapter 5, or Insurance Coverage in Chapter 4. Moreover, no attempt will be made to list or exhibit all the reports which might apply to every department of a typical business. Companies are so varied in their styles and operation that reports must be individually designed after a thorough study of each department's operations. For example, the Credit and Collection Department would have some reports prepared within the department, others by the accounting department. The following information would be presented:

1. Aged trial balance.

2. Analysis of bad debt losses by type of account, territory, size.

3. Collections from bad or doubtful accounts.

4. Credit held orders, by volume and prior period.

5. Loss percentage to sales.

6. Actual losses compared to reserve, by month and year.

7. Collections compared to budget.

8. Turnover of receivables, by month and quarter, by class.

9. Collections as a percentage of sales, by age.

10. Percentage of monthly collections, by age, to outstanding receivable, by age.

11. Collection costs as a percentage of sales.

12. Analysis of slow accounts by reason for slowness.

13. Bad account write-offs, by quarter and years.

14. Contacts made per collector.

15. Collection cost, per collector, related to collections.

Instead of presenting the detail of each such report, and there could be thousands, we shall examine only those reports which demonstrate the theory and philosophy of effective management reporting.

A complete set of financial statements are the ultimate reports which flow from any budgetary system. These reports are described in Chapter 5, in connection with cash budgeting and include:

- Income Statement.
- Balance Sheet.
- Statement of Retained Earnings.
- Statement of Changes in Financial Position.
- Supplementary Financial Data.

Accordingly, our study will be concerned with:

I. A Reporting Philosophy

II. How to Prepare Reports

III. Budget versus Actual Comparison (BVA)

IV. Staff Meetings

V. The Monthly Report

VI. Operating Reports
    A. Exception Reports
    B. Trend Reports
    C. Detailed Reports
    D. Flash Reports

I. A REPORTING PHILOSOPHY

The Controller must design a complete accounting system to enable him to perform the Controllership functions defined by the Financial Executives Institute and as delineated in his Position Description (see "Treasurer's and Controller's Functions"). He has a responsibility to the owners, top management, industry associations, the SEC, stock exchanges, employees, and the public. His accounting system will result in the financial statements listed above. But he must design that system to permit the generation of reports which will serve the other users to whom he is responsible.

> **For example:** A cash Receipts Journal may be kept with a single total column and posted to the General Ledger. This is certainly sufficient to generate a balance sheet but not to perform some of the credit and collection analyses listed above. Columns could be added for type of account, age of cash, product line, and territory, thereby enabling any of the previous analyses to be accomplished.

Essential to the proper systems design is a study of the data structure of the company. Data inputs, processing, and reports are carefully examined as described in Chapter 14 under the section Organization-Evaluation on page 202. After this study is completed, users of reports will be defined and their needs established. The reporting system may then be developed using the following caveats:

1. *Do not copy someone else's reports.* Reports are not tailor made. They must meet the needs of your organization as developed by your own evaluation.

2. Financial reports will be required for publication and for top management. But most reports are non-financial and must meet the needs of operating managers. The accounting system must *provide for* the generation of *both types of reports.*

3. Operating reports should *compare performance to plan,* should highlight deviations, suggest action, and relate current position to the ultimate goal.

4. The report format influences its usefulness. Hence, *show summary information* only, not details; determine whether last month or last year comparisons are the more meaningful; do not flood the user with masses of data or too many pages; show percentage relationships; show exceptions to Plan as highlights.

5. *Use graphs and charts* frequently to add sauce to your presentation.

6. *Use acronyms* for report titles to create enthusiasm and facilitate familiarity by the user:

   For example: PABST = Product Analysis by Sales Territories
   SST   = Sales Statistical Tables

   The acronyms are familiar to every user. Calling for the report by acronym avoids receiving a wrong report with a similar title.

7. *Show the Distribution* on all reports, so each reader will know who else received it, without having to look it up. Don't waste the user's time.

8. *Show major assumptions* on the face, or attached to each report. Avoid the reader's having to ask questions or research the underlying assumptions. Facts change with different assumptions.

9. *Publish only necessary and key reports.* Don't flood the company with unneeded reports. Don't distribute the report to anyone who doesn't need it.

10. *Reports must be issued on a timely basis* to be useful. Daily reports on the following day; weekly reports within three days, and monthly reports within ten days of the close.

11. Some *reports can create problems,* in addition to providing information:

    a. Reports are costly—to print, distribute, forms design, systems study, programming, to prepare.

    Avoid this Pitfall: Due to the high cost of reports, design the report for broad distribution, not just for one or two individuals.

    b. Temporary reports often become permanent, at continued cost, and obsolete reports continue to be used.

    Helpful Hint: A frequent report study by the systems department will avoid the cost of obsolete reports as well as the issuance of misinformation.

    c. Effective use of reports requires teaching, explanation and understanding by the recipient. This is costly but prevents the reports from degenerating into useless masses of data.

II. HOW TO PREPARE REPORTS

The following checklist has been used by a large public accounting firm in its consulting work, and it has general applicability to most internal financial and operating reports:

Reporting Level:

1. Make results identifiable with responsible executive.

2. Prepare for each executive a statement reflecting only results for which he is responsible.

3. Integrate individual statements in a pattern that clearly follows the organization chart—so that, for example, net profit can be "exploded" like a bill of materials.

4. Ignore subsidiary corporate entities for management reports when such corporate structure does not coincide with the management organization.

5. Design report structure so that statements for lower management levels can be added without altering existing statements.

Content:

1. Present only one set of results—avoid estimates that are subsequently connected to actual.

2. Compare results with expected performance.

3. Present results on an exception basis that only emphasizes good and bad performance.

4. Segregate controllable from non-controllable expense.

5. Establish pre-determined amounts for allocated expenses over which the charged department has no control.

6. Use standards for transferring costs that "flow" with production between departments.

Timing:

1. Issue statements immediately after end of month—preferrable within five working days.

    a. Use control totals. Do not wait for detail distributions.

    b. Accumulate "totals to date" as month progresses.

    c. Do not cut off before end of month any item significantly affecting profits.

    d. Decrease monthly report load by issuing daily and weekly reports on items like sales, production, etc.

2. Stagger release of statements where necessary to ease digestion of contents.

Form:

1. Present information in the same manner that executives plan and think about their operations.

2. Let statements highlight results; do not try to present all the answers; leave exhausting details in the books to be used only for special statements and analyses when required.

3. Express results in one figure at the bottom of the statements; make the figure easily traceable to a single figure on the next "higher" statement.

4. Make statements easy to read.

    a. Use 8 1/2″ x 11″ paper.

    b. Limit columns of figures to not more than three columns in a group.

    c. Leave plenty of white space on page.

    d. Omit all cents; omit thousands of dollars where possible.

    e. Segregate only significant expenses, group remainder.

    f. Use operating terminology, but make items understandable to uninformed third party.

    g. Clearly caption each statement and use informative headings.

    h. Show "year-to-date" figures to the left of account description.

5. Provide sufficient space on each statement for statistics and interpretive comments.

Helpful Hint: The maker should date and initial all reports. Date should show year, not just month and day. This permits intelligent review and later research, even though years have passed.

Another Hint: Provide binders for repetitive, important reports. This allows the user to retrieve the report more quickly, assures you that all reports are filed and current (this may be audited periodically).

III. BUDGET VERSUS ACTUAL COMPARISON (BVA)

The crux of the budgetary system is the comparison of planned operations to actual results. These reports should follow the tenets previously described. They will then show results against plan, show percentage relationships, and will highlight variances. In this manner, they fulfill the Controllership function of interpretation. They are related to financial statements since the Operating Plan is presented in the format of a P & L Statement. A Budget Report is prepared for each of the budgets shown at Exhibit 6-e. Only the P & L Statement is exhibited below:

Exhibit 8-a; Profit & Loss BVA—The report shows the current month in the left columns, with year to date on the right. Each line is numbered for easy reference. The percent column lists percents of each line to Total Net Sales. Lines 10-18 represent budgeted expences only, meaning controllable items. Lines 19-22 are allocated expenses, but not corporate allocations. They represent commonly shared expenses in an area, all of which are controllable. Line 24 shows the Contribution to Non-Budgeted Expenses. Line 25 deducts non-budgeted expenses, none of which are controlled by this profit center, but which are directly attributed to it. Cost of Sales on line 5 is at an intercompany transfer price which precludes corporate allocations. Certain lines are cross-referenced to detailed schedules which follow.

The BVA's below, while not exhibited follow the format of the budget at Exhibit 6-e.

Sales BVA— This is Schedule 1 of the P & L BVA. The format is the same as the P & L's. The report shows each significant product in units and dollars, net of returns and allowances. The final total of this report is carried forward to P & L BVA line 3.

Cost of Sales BVA—This is Schedule II of the P & L BVA. It follows the same format. The cost is shown for the same sales items in Schedule I. The final total is carried to P & L BVA line 5. Cost is at dealer list price.

Expense BVA—This is Schedule III of P & L BVA. Again, the same format is followed. Eight items of significant, controllable expenses are detailed. Some common area expenses are allocated on line 32 (not corporate allocations). The final total of budgeted expenses is carried forward to P & L BVA line 23.

Non-Budgeted Expenses BVA—This is Schedule VI of the P & L BVA. These are expenses considered to be non-controllable by the profit center's manager, even though they are direct costs to his operation. For example, Rent is direct but not readily controllable in the immediate budget period, due to a lease running for several years. The items, however, are listed, as they could become controllable at any time (The manager could elect to sub-let the premises and seek less expensive quarters). These expenses, therefore, while significant in amount, are listed separately as requiring less scrutiny and control in any budgeted period. The total is carried to line 25 of the P & L BVA.

Employee Forecast BVA—This Schedule IV is a head count of employees, actual to budget. It is simply an informative report and is not posted to any lead schedule.

> **Helpful Hint**: Reports are more valuable when reduced to units. A dollar amount payroll report would not be adjusted for payroll dollar increases. This unit head count report readily identifies every job category with an increased work count.

Variances of over 5% on sales and 10% on expenses are marked with an asterisk. The Budget Department obtains an explanation for such items for the Budget Committee.

> **Helpful Budget Hint**: The Controller or Treasurer, either of whom is present at most high-level staff meetings, should advise the Budget Manager of situations which will affect the budget and explain variances. This will speed up the process of communicating the final BVA figures, with explanations of variances, for the budget period.

> **Avoid This Pitfall**: The Current Budget columns should not be changed during the year. The Budget, as established (see Chapter 6) represents the Operating Plan for the year. Differences to Plan will appear as variances. Managers, including top management, should continue to observe these differences all during the budgeted period.

> **Exception**: If a permanent change is made in the profit objective, as approved by the Board, this may be reflected in a revised Budget which is, by definition, a bottom-line reflection of the Profit Plan.

> **Word of Caution**: Budget versus actual comparisons do not control operations. They only aid in control. Managers make decisions, not reports. Therefore, the BVA must be interpreted by the Controller to managers, hence the explanation of variances, with suggestions for corrective action.

IV. STAFF MEETINGS

Staff meetings belong under any discussion of Reporting the Results of Operations. In this context, staff meetings mean any meetings involving managers concerned with attaining budgeted objectives. Thus, a line department, like a branch office, may have a staff meeting with the Branch Manager, Office Manager, and Service Manager, representing all of the concerned managers. Or, a headquarters staff manager, say a Field Administrative Manager, may hold a staff meeting with line Office Managers for Budget review purposes.

These meetings may be planning meetings (to work on submission of a new

Budget) or action meetings (to discuss budget versus actual, BVA, results, to discuss variances, and to plan corrective action).

The Budget Reports previously exhibited should be discussed at a monthly staff meeting to be held immediately after their issuance. If the reports need interpretation (usually they are self-evident, particularly with an explanation of variances), a Budget Department representative, or Field Accounting Manager, or Controller's representative should be invited to be present.

> **Helpful Hint**: Staff Meetings with subordinate managers serve to involve these managers in attaining the desired Budget goal—make them feel a part of the team.

> **Actual Company Example**: One company was losing top department heads to other companies. The turnover seemed to be unrelated to any division or any particular senior manager. The Controller instituted monthly or "sooner as needed" staff meetings, between managers of various departments, related to budgetary interpretations and corrective policies. Minutes were drawn and called to the President's attention. The President began to call his own monthly staff meetings to examine these minutes. This technique caused total involvement of middle-line managers in company policy, with the result that middle-manager turnover disappeared completely.

> **Try This**: Minutes should be taken, typed, and circulated to any other concerned manager and to the immediate superior. This allows your superior to coordinate your mid-stream actions with those of other departments.

> **Avoid This Pitfall**: Meetings should consist of three to five persons. Under three is not a meeting—it's a discussion between the manager and a subordinate and will not produce a free exchange of ideas. More than five can cause the meeting to break down into a forum, everyone trying to get a message in, just to make points.

> **Use These Tools**: Meetings are more effective if you use flip charts or an overhead projector to view transparencies. The act of preparing these tools in advance of the meeting leads to a well-thought-out agenda and a better meeting. Photocopies of the items on the chart or the projector should always be made for 8½″ x 11″ distribution to the attendees, in advance. This avoids wasting everyone's time copying key information.

Staff meetings should be chaired by the responsible manager of each box on the Organization Chart. Where organizational lines are crossed, there will still be a key profit center being discussed and that manager should chair.

V. THE MONTHLY REPORT

To augment the BVA reports and staff meeting minutes previously described, as well as the standard reports and graphs to be outlined in the next Section VI on Operating Reports, a monthly narrative reporting system should be used throughout the company. These fulfill the interpretive function.

Branch Managers file a monthly report with their District Manager, District Managers report, monthly, to the Zone Manager; Zone Managers report, monthly, to the National Sales Manager; he reports, monthly, to the VP/Marketing who, in turn, reports, monthly, to the Executive VP. Similarly, in the administrative area, Branch Administrators report monthly, to the Zone Manager (to whom they report directly, see page 97), with copies of all reports being sent to the Controller to monitor the reporting system. Reports flow up the Organization Chart, are summarized by the immediate superior in his report to his superior, so on to the President.

> **Useful Control**: Field operational audits are made during the month at various branch offices. These serve, in part, as the basis for the Controller's own monthly report.

> **Helpful Hint**: The Monthly Narrative Report should be not less than 1/2 page nor more than two pages long. Less than 1/2 page is not informative enough. More than two pages tends to be verbose and full of excuses for poor performance.

> **Crux of Monthly Reports**: These monthly reports are broad summarizations of results of operations and plans for corrective actions for the various profit centers which are abridged further by top management, into broad Company outlines. They are, thus, "exception reports" which permit management to make the necessary corporate decisions.

A variant on the monthly reports are quarterly earnings reports released to stockholders and regulatory agencies and the Board of Directors by the President. These generally contain a President's letter or comments which synthesize the monthly narrative reports, interpreting them for the users.

VI. OPERATING REPORTS

Financial Statements, Budget versus Actual reports, and their supporting reports have been discussed in Chapter 5 and Section III of this chapter, respectively. Other chapters have exhibited reports which are pertinent to the subject matter of those chapters. This Section will examine reports in general which are unique in form or style and present the message to management in a particularly effective way. They are the results of a reporting philosophy developed in Section I and follow the dicta of report preparation set out in Section II.

A. Exception Reports

Exhibit 8-b; Back Order Information Report—This report contains the interesting elements of which orders cannot be completed, gives estimated time of arrival of components to complete the orders (ETA), and presents pertinent comments. It is a weekly report, distributed to those concerned with filling parts orders.

Exhibit 8-c Shipping Survey—This is a narrative report to monitor shipping efficacy. It is short, clear, a summary, explains failures and suggests improvement.

Exhibit 8-d; Credit Analysis (CRAN)—This report, through prior coding of credit memos by reason for issuance, analyzes such reasons in summary form, by location of branch office which issued the credit, and in summary for the entire company.

Exhibit 8-e; Call Back Report (Cabare)—Using a familiar acronym for easy identification, this summarizes orders received from customers, by branch office location, and lists total customers who have not ordered a key product in 3 months or over, up to one year. Detailed names to support totals are sent to each location for follow-up action. Results for the previous five months are at the bottom of the form, thus giving a full six-months look. If numbers in previous months decrease, from the bottom up, it means lost accounts are being regained. Looking at the 8 mos. column, there were 555 accounts on 7/31 which were 3 months old: on 8/31, 423 of them still had not ordered and were now 4 months old, and so on up to the current month, 12/31, which indicated 199 of these accounts are now 8 mos. without having ordered.

Exhibit 8-f Keyvolume Report (Keyvol)—Here is an exception report for marketing which supplies the local sales office with the names of each "key" account which contributed more than 1% to total sales volume in the previous 3 months. The names, units of product and percentage of volume are given. You know who your customers are! This report is prepared monthly with rolling quarters. Next month April will be dropped, May added, and the quarter will end July 31.

Exhibit 8-g; Retail Paper Report (Repap)—This illustrates the use of exception reporting against standards on a continuing basis. The standard is established in the fifth column from the right, representing 3 times the number of machines in the field each month. The quarters roll. Next month March will drop off the left side and this year's March will be added to the right side. The average number of rolls for each quarter on the page are computed, subtracted from the standard, and if less than standard, an asterisk (*) is printed next to the result. The report shows an assumption under the heading caption which is important to an understanding of this report.

B. Trend Reports

Exhibit 8-h is a graph summary of some of the data in Exhibit 8-i. This data is prepared by the National Service Department from an analysis of Service Call Reports which are completed by Field Engineers after each service call. These exhibits are part of a total report for all products called the Rainbow Report. Each product exhibits its data on a different color paper. This aids reader identification and makes for easier reading. The cover page supplies dates, assumptions and distribution information.

Exhibit 8-h Travel & Response Time—Here are two bar graphs representing the number of miles traveled to reach each call, and the second graph, the percentage of calls which took less than four hours to respond.

Thus, four hours is a standard against which the company is measured!
The Bar Graph allows for easy comparison!

Exhibit 8-i; Service Analysis Product A—This is the summary data from which the previous graph is prepared. It is not presented in graph or trend line format but is simply presented, in tabular form, to support the bar graphs.

> **Helpful Hint:** In constructing bar graphs, note that each graph shows the required numerical information at the top of each column. Thus, the eye does not have to scan to the margin to identify the number related to the top of the bar.

In addition to the Trend Report type of graph, covering a period of months, many trend graphs cover years, showing performance year to year, or comparing one company against another:

Exhibit 8-j Industry Comparison graph (Incom)—This graph compares our company against another company which releases data, as well as against an industry study which represents a standard. Sales are compared for each month of the year. Our company takes a look at three separate years. The inset graph on the upper left smooths out the months and presents quarters only for the current year, thus simplifying the graph. The inset at the right shows only the current year for our company, again simplifying the presentation.

Exhibit 8-k Revenue and Income graph (Rain)—Here is a summary of Sales and Income, for two years, by months. The trends are thus developed and seasonal or cyclical factors may be evaluated. The graph also indicates number of salesmen at the bottom, a significant determinant of the level of sales.

> **Word of Caution:** In constructing graphs, be careful of the scale used. It must be such as to present meaningful information. For example, if you show sales at $50 million, and a 10% increase to $55 million, the graph will not show a sharp increase. If the same graph were used to compare the movement of expenses against sales, an increase from $500 to $1000 would be a 100% increase which would appear disproportionate on the same sales scale. To avoid this disparity, use semi-log paper to show expenses with a smaller slope to the line. If your purpose is to highlight and aggravate the expense increase, then, by all means, use standard graph paper.

Exhibit 8-1; Break-Even Analysis—This graph uses normal direct costing techniques to construct the break-even graph. The graph, however, is not fuzzed up with masses of data which might confound the reader. The graph shows a $37,000 break-even volume, with fixed or period costs at the $16,200 level.

> **Helpful Hint:** In constructing the graph, unit sales information is presented which serves as the underlying assumption for the $37,000 break-even volume. Units indicate that with 5 sales, 18 rentals, and 1 sale which is converted from a prior rental, the break-even volume is attained.

> **Assumption:** The construction of this graph presupposes a definition of direct costs, which is in line with that on page 95.

Exhibit 8-m; Box Score—This is a Trend Report, in columnar form. Important operating data is listed in each row. Months are compared in the columns. It is an exception report to the extent that all key data has been extracted and summarized on this report.

> **Key Point:** A branch manager, or a travelling headquarters officer, armed with this

report, and comparing it to other branches of similar size, can quickly identify adverse trends and trouble areas.

Page 2 of the report illustrates a legend which is used to identify the source from which each piece of data is extracted. The legend serves to avoid repetitive questions about the report's source data.

C. Detailed Reports

Not all reports need to be, nor should they be, exception reports, summaries, comparisons, or trend reports. Too much data suffocates, but, often, a good deal of data is needed on a timely basis to permit a quick look-in to facilitate making fast decisions. There is not always time to summarize each month's data, to compare it to prior months, to chart it or graph it. The cost of doing this must be weighed against the need for such summaries.

The detailed report, and the flash reports described in the next section, can fulfill the manager's immediate need for information. If the reports are carefully constructed, in line with the reporting philosophy described on page 114, the overall reporting cost can be reduced, with little or no reduction in the efficacy of these reports:

Exhibit 8-n; Payroll Distribution—This is a payroll summary which lists key areas of the company, giving payroll dollars, head-counts of employees, and a further head-count breakdown by each product line. While there is a good deal of information on each page, and no comparative information, the Controller can use this report to quickly compare the broad summary totals to last week's report. If a headcount has increased, he can identify it for immediate review or follow-up if there is a further increase next week. The reports are hole-punched and filed in a loose leaf book in order. He can flip back to last month or last year for instant comparative information. This would take days or weeks to accomplish through the computer every time he had a question. Even a time-sharing terminal would not supply the same speed as these visual, detailed comparisons.

Exhibit 8-o; Salesman Support Report—This detailed report is provided to National Sales Managers with supporting detailed reports to individual Field Managers. The report indicates the degree of national or headquarters support for field offices. Page 2 of the report gives a narrative explanation of the column headings. The report is exploded downward on subsequent pages (not exhibited), to show support for other than salemen—that is, service technicians, customer relations representatives. Pages 4 and 5 analyze the types of calls made, and pages 6 and 7 provide details for each "supporter." There is a wealth of support information presented, but it is broken down into segments so that each manager can work with the detailed information that concerns only him. The entire report enforces management's philosophy of providing headquarter's assistance to its field managers and salesmen.

Exhibit 8-p; Cumulative Retail Paper Report—This is a format for a report showing number of rolls of paper sold for each field office. The offices are listed on both the left and right hand edges so the numbers can be traced more easily. The first 4 columns show number of salesmen, and number of machines in the field (which determines the number of rolls of paper which might be consumed) by machine model number. Two prior months' and the current month's figures are then presented. The report is prepared daily. The source of the data is shown at the bottom of the report, as well as the distribution. A few key managers are, thus, able to track daily progress on supply sales, by branch, compared to prior months. Trends are quickly spotted and the daily monitoring enables immediate corrective action to be taken.

Exhibit 8-q; Cost/Pricing Product Sheet—This informational form is prepared for each product. The right-hand section shows all costs. The left-hand side shows prices for each level of distribution, percent of gross profit and mark-up, percent and dollars of commission. A control product (standard pricing) is shown, and subsequent columns supply recommendations of accounting and marketing departments and then the final approved pricing column. At the bottom of the page, boxes are provided for all necessary pricing approvals, as well as for cost approvals on the right. These boxes assure that no key manager has been by-passed in obtaining approvals.

> **Word of Advice**: Use detailed reports. If you depend only on exception reports, you'll lose much of the feel and flavor of the business and you'll probably receive many reports too late for decision making purposes.

D. Flash Reports

Any of the previously described reports may be a flash report. The flash report is supplied early in the reporting period, before compete or closed information is available. Often, therefore, the source data for the flash report is obtained off-line or outside the regular data system. For example, billings or shipments reports usually are generated from invoices. But final totals go through edit checks, proof readings, bursting, mailing, corrections, sorting, key punching, and data processing. This takes time and usually involves an end-of-the-month crunch with overtime for processing closing billing. The problem is simply handled by phoning, telexing results, or picking up totals from order logs, even before the invoice has been processed. See the Instructions at the bottom of Exhibit 8-w, Cumulative Retail Paper Report. This detailed, daily report is, thus, a Flash Report.

The most common Flash Report is the quick P & L Statement at month end. It is prepared between one and seven days from the end of the month, usually using actual sales data and estimates of gross profits and expenses. As experience is gained in its preparation, the report can become quite accurate. At any rate, while the given month may present some problems, it is best presented on a cumulative basis, showing previous actual P & L's, plus this one month's flash. The cumulative result, as the year draws closer to the end, is extremely accurate. If the assumptions used in the monthly flash are carefully worked out, the few inaccuracies in the report are more than offset by the speed with which it is delivered.

Application-in-an-Actual-Company: A large, public company continued to be late in its publication of monthly financial statements and quarterly releases of earnings. As it grew and acquired other companies, its reporting problems became further aggravated. Each quarter, its listed stock price declined as the public attributed the possibility of bad news to the delayed earnings. Utilization of flash P & L reporting was implemented, using standard journal entries to summarize the monthly close. Reports are now available on the seventh working day of each month. The result is more stable quarterly stock prices and added investor confidence in the management of the company.

Exhibit 8-r; Flash Cost Change Report—This is an example of a report prepared on the same day a vendor notifies of a price increase. Rather than waiting for circulation of Exhibit 8-x, which is the Cost/Pricing Product Sheet and which shows mark-ups, gross profits, commissions, and optimum pricing, this Flash Report is prepared at once to show the annual cost increase, it being $109,760, a 26.57% change. This is further broken down between the amount of increase by distribution channel, retail or dealer customer. In this case, the increase is equal for each class of customer. This Flash Report instantly identifies the effect on profits and permits management to react, today, if need be.

Application-in-an-Actual-Company: In a period of sharply rising, inflationary prices, one Controller instituted the Flash Cost Change Report in anticipation of inflationary price rises. This enabled his company to react more quickly than competitors and to pass-through immediate price rises to customers, as the necessity was indicated by the magnitude of the annual cost increase on the flash report. His company maintained its gross profit margins for the year while competitors, due to their slower reaction time, suffered a decline in earnings.

Flash Reports should be prepared using the features of other reports:

a. Present them so they can be studied by exception, not too much detail. Show trends and percentages.

b. Summarize data and present only top line information on the flash. Use narrative where necessary to make the point. The monthly narrative report described in Section V, page 119, is a Flash Report.

c. Circulate reports timely. Don't let the time of month throw you off. Flash Reports may be daily, Monday, Wednesday, and Friday, Weekly, semi-monthly, and even monthly.

d. Don't worry about 100% accuracy. If you explain your assumptions, the report will be close enough. Too many accounting reports show pennies, hundreds, and even thousands of dollars, when this amount of accuracy has no meaning.

Helpful Hint: With all these reports flowing in from all departments, how do you keep track of them? Use a calendar as in Exhibit 8-s, Departmental Reports. This shows each non-accounting generated report, where it comes from, the due date, and the actual date received. A schedule of Accounting Department Reports is also show at Exhibit 14-e, using the same format.

Another Reporting Hint: From time to time, prepare a report but hold back its distribution. If you don't get follow-up complaints, the report may not be being used. Perhaps it can be eliminated.

REPORTING CONCLUSIONS

The Controller needs to develop a complete reporting philosophy to satisfy the needs of management, the owners, and government. This means designing reports which suit your particular type of company, which compare performance to Plan, which summarize and show trends through exception—reports which are key and necessary, timely, contain distribution listings and major assumptions, and are zestfully formated. Budget Reports should be presented and discussed at Staff Meetings, and a Monthly Report, in narrative form is the ultimate Flash Report to apprise superiors of the results of operations. Specific reports should be presented in a variety of forms to maintain interest and to supply information—trend reports, graphs and charts, and timely flash reports. Detailed reports are not to be omitted, either. They may contain summary information, but, principally, they provide a storehouse of quickly accessed information, useful in making immediate decisions.

CHAPTER 9

Implementing and Administering

Tax Policies and Procedures

THE fourth Controllership function defined by the Financial Executives Institute, as listed in the "Treasurer's and Controller's Functions," and in the Controller's Position Description is "To establish and administer tax policies and procedures."

We may define a "policy" as "prudence or wisdom in the management of affairs" (a dictionary definition), or another, "a definite course or method of action selected from alternatives."

Once the alternatives are prudently selected, the "procedure" sets limits and controls on "how to do it."

This chapter will consider the following tax-related topics:

1. Information on Alternatives—the source of tax information; where do you learn about it?

2. The Philosophy of Responsibility—Who selects the alternatives and why.

3. Alternatives—What are the choices?

4. Procedures—the administration of selected alternatives.

INFORMATION ON ALTERNATIVES

Not only are there tax alternatives in company management, but there are course alternatives in college accounting programs. Tax study is not a required course, but is a required foundation for any Controller's job. If a study of federal taxes was one of many skipped electives in college, you can make it up with a night school course in a community college. Many CPA coach courses offer special Saturday tax classes, and local state CPA societies offer evening lectures. Seminars are held by the American Management Association (New York City based, but with meetings held in major cities across the country) and by the Continuing Professional Education department of the

American Institute of Certified Public Accountants. Often, public accounting firms invite clients to in-house training courses for orientation to changes in the tax laws, and all of these offer tape cassettes for home study on particular areas of taxation. There are also legal associations and societies which offer tax lectures pointed toward lawyers, but these tend to be somewhat more technical than is required for the selection of alternative courses of action.

The best of these suggestions is the complete college night course, usually consisting of 45 class hours, and offered in either 8-week or 15-week programs. Time not permitting, a series of evening lectures in different areas of taxation, augmented by a home cassette general course, will provide the required basics.

Helpful Hint: For those who commute to work by car, a tape cassette lesson can fill in unproductive time while driving.

Once the foundation is acquired in general federal taxation (State courses are unnecessary; the laws are too diverse and the dollar tax impact is usually not great; The computation of income mostly follows federal laws), all that is required, as in any good diet, is a modicum of lip-service and some attention to the regimen—that is, an overview of tax law changes. This overview is available to the Controller or Tax Manager from a variety of sources:

- The Executive Report—published by Prentice-Hall, Inc., is a weekly management letter which also contains several pages of pertinent tax developments. The advantage to the busy manager is that it highlights only major areas of concern. A more detailed 8-page weekly tax bulletin is also available from this publisher.

- The RIA Tax Report—published by the Research Institute of America, is a "Weekly Alert," usually about 8 pages, offering information on law changes and court cases.

- Commerce Clearing House (CCH)—offers a similar report.

- Federal Tax Guides—are offered by all three of the publishers above. Prentice-Hall offers a complete summary of federal tax laws in one book, annotated with pertinent references to the code. The detailed code is available in another complete service, if required. The Tax Guide is an annual service, not very expensive, which provides Weekly Report Bulletins covering changes in the law, the results of tax cases, and latest developments. In general, it contains more detail than the Executive Report but may be easily scanned for important areas.

- Journal of Accountancy—published by the AICPA monthly, contains a tax practitioners' section and highlights significant tax areas which may be overviewed for pertinence.

- Journal of Taxation—is a lawyers-oriented magazine which summarizes current tax cases and it, too, may be scanned for related cases and information.

- Independent Accounting Firms and Corporate Counsel—Your lawyer or accounting firm will usually publish releases for internal use (and often for dissemination to clients) and will place you on his distribution list, on request. The larger firms publish monthly newsletters for clients which are often concerned with tax developments.

The Controller may sample all or any of these sources, selecting one or more for continued use with which he is most comfortable. While two sources may supply repetitive information, one acting as a backstop for the other, I would recommend it. The second source is quickly scanned for only new information.

> **The Point Is:** A solid tax background, obtained through a thorough federal tax course, is sharply honed by weekly or monthly reports which are quickly overviewed for areas that relate to your business.

THE PHILOSOPHY OF RESPONSIBILITY

Or, who selects the alternatives, and why.

The introduction to this chapter noted that the FEI has defined the tax responsibility as being within the Controller's purview. But we can't all be experts in everything. And taxes really are such a specialized area that they really need the deft touch of the tax accountant or attorney. So let's leave this area of responsibility to the experts and stick to controlling operations.

Right? Wrong!

The nuances of taxation are no more esoteric than those of data processing, budgeting, auditing, or accounting—all of which are Controllership functions. The Controller is a generalist and needs to have a functioning knowledge of all these subjects. He need not be an expert in any of them.

The overall knowledge about the operations of the enterprise places the Controller in a unique vantage point which the tax expert does not enjoy. The important tax decisions which affect the business do and should come from the Controller, not the tax specialist.

Supported by a basic knowledge of taxation and kept current through weekly and monthly overviews of tax literature, the Controller will spot tax law changes which affect his business. The lawyer, outside consultant or tax accountant has many clients and is apt to miss the connection between a specific event and your business.

Once the Controller has identified a feasible alternative, from his vantage point, the tax expert should be consulted for sophisticated advice as to whether the policy may be implemented.

> **Truism:** The good tax ideas come from the Controller who keeps current on his tax developments, not from the tax experts.

Every company, of course, works to optimize cash flow and to pay the lowest taxes required by the law, but not if the company objectives require a different result. One company, with a high price/earnings ratio on its stock, may be striving to build an earnings record to permit it to raise equity through common stock issuance. Taxes are then secondary. Depreciation methods would be selected which resulted in the most income and highest tax in the early years. Another company may have available operating loss carry forwards which would permit the sheltering of gain on a sale and lease back transaction, the funds from which would be used to reduce short-term debt.

Truism: Tax policies attuned to defined corporate goals make these goals more readily attainable.

Don't abdicate this area of responsibility to the outside tax experts. They'll give you some good ideas and alternatives, but you'll miss a lot of others by not doing it yourself or within your department.

A proper approach to company taxation will be based on corporate goals, as expressed by the President through the Budget (see Chapter 6) and reflected in the Profit Plan. This will be further depicted by the financial ratios shown at Exhibit 5-c. The company's tax posture will be devoted to the attainment of these quantified corporate objectives. The alternatives selected will be those which are consonant with the Profit Plan over the projected period.

ALTERNATIVES

What are the choices? Why are there choices?

Most of the alternatives arise because general accounting precepts, as promulgated by the Financial Accounting Standards Board, and its predecessor, the American Institute of CPA's, differ from accounting as required by the Internal Revenue Code. In other cases, the Code, itself, permits a variety of treatments. Listed below are the most common alternatives available to most businesses and a brief description of each. Details as to proper accounting treatment, for reporting purposes, may be found in APB's (Opinions of the Accounting Principles Board of the AICPA), and in FASB Statements and Interpretations. For tax purposes, the Federal Tax Guide or Regulations of the IRS should be reviewed:

a. *Advance Revenues*—Examples are service contracts, for one year in advance, usually paid up front (for example, a television service contract), or coupon sales (used in the carbon paper industry to sell a one-year supply of carbon paper, paid in advance, future deliveries made against coupons, each of which provides for no charge delivery of a specific number of packages). For accounting purposes, these are generally unearned income items, until shipped, at which time sales and income are recognized.

Prepayments received for services in one taxable year to be performed in the next may be included in gross income as earned by an accrual taxpayer. However, if the inclusion in income is deferred until the year succeeding the year of receipt and services are not performed by the end of the the succeeding year, the income will be recognized in such succeeding year. This procedure is not applicable to amounts received under warranty or guarantee contracts, nor to prepaid rent or to prepaid interest. This requirement may cause a difference between accounting and tax treatment, as the accounting income is recognized when the service is performed, regardless of the tax year. (See Revenue Procedure 70-21 and Regulations Section 1.451-5). There is a further requirement that the books of account (the booking rule) shall not reflect more income than the tax books (in other words, tax and accounting records must agree). Under some circumstances, the company could report this income when paid for, but only if it did the same for tax purposes.

Prepayments received for merchandise, such as the sale of coupons redeemable for carbon paper or other supplies, may be deferred for tax purposes until delivery is made. There is no booking requirement similar to that with prepayments for services. A company, thus, might recognize the gross profit on such sales, under certain conditions, while it deferred the tax until delivery is made.

b. *Bad Debts*—Most accrual basis taxpayers record a provision for bad debts to a reserve for doubtful accounts.

The accounting provision, however, provides for more than just bad debts. It recognizes the reserve needed for billing adjustments and allowances and future merchandise returns which will be credited. It also recognizes the provision, based on an estimate, for accounts which will go bad in the future. The reserve for tax purposes, however, must be supported by write-offs against the reserve as proof of the reasonableness of the provision for bad debts. The two situations are dichotomous. The accounting reserve, generally, tends not to be large enough. The independent accountants will strive to see that the company maintains a conservative, or large reserve. The tax people, on the other hand, will attempt to prove that the reserve is overstated, that bad debts are actually less than the amount provided. The tax provision arises only from bad accounts, the accounting provisions from returns and allowances.

> **Helpful Hint**: Always clean out and write-off accounts against the reserve, before the end of each tax year, to support the charge to the provision for bad debts. This should be done, even though collection activity will continue to recover these accounts. These accounts receivable, if still being collected, should be recorded in a separate trial balance, for control purposes.

c. *Capital Gains*—Financial accounting does not recognize the capital gains concept. Therefore, business transactions which result in income should be structured, where possible, to result in capital gains at the lower associated tax rates. These opportunities do not readily exist in the ordinary course of business but may be available in sale and lease back transactions, sale of capital equipment and royalty contracts. These are discussed in the paragraphs below.

d. *Captive Finance Subsidiaries*—The captive finance company is discussed on pages 46 and 59. From a tax viewpoint, the captive sub offers the alternatives of using finance lease (sale treatment) or operating lease (recognition of rental income as received) accounting. It may also be a cash basis taxpayer, allowing for deductions from income for unpaid leases receibable. The sub. may utilize accelerated depreciation benefits and retain the investment tax credit. Consolidated tax returns may be filed with the parent, despite non-consolidation for accounting reasons. The result is usually losses for tax purposes and profits for accounting reporting. This provides immediate cash benefits which, of themselves, produce profits.

> **Case In Point**: One equipment manufacturer, earning about $1 million in profits a year, obtained cash flow benefits of $5 million over a three-year period, in addition to its regular earnings, through a captive finance subsidiary.

e. *Cash Basis*—The opportunity exists to report on an accrual basis for financial accounting reporting and on a cash basis for tax reporting. This is a decided benefit when receivables are an important factor, as in the captive finance subsidiary. A similar advantage exists when purchases must be made on a cash basis from suppliers.

f. *Contingency Reserves*—Generally-accepted accounting properly indicates the establishing of contingency reserves if it is "probable" that an asset has been impaired or a liability incurred; an event is reasonably expected to occur to confirm the fact and amount of the loss; and the amount of the loss can be reasonably estimated. Thus, the financial statements may include an expense for a contingency reserve which is not an acceptable tax deduction.

g. *Depreciation*—A choice of methods is permitted for tax as well as accounting purposes. Methods may be selected to accelerate or slow down deductions in early years. Proper depreciation planning will depend on the existence of carry forward operating losses and the expectation of future profits.

Exhibit 9-a Depreciation, illustrates the differences in available deductions for depreciation under the straight-line, declining-balance and sum-of-the-digits methods. The exhibit is a reprinted page from the P-H Federal Tax Guide.

Exhibit 9-b, Depreciation Methods, outlines the assorted types of depreciation which are available for accounting and/or tax purposes. In item 2a) of the exhibit, DD means double-declining method. Item 2c) gives the formula for the sum-of-the digits as:

$$\frac{n \times (n + 1)}{2} = \text{sum-of-the-digits}$$

For example, the sum-of-the-years-digits for 5 years is 15 (5 + 4 + 3 + 2 + 1). By formula, where n = the number of years:

$$\frac{5 \times (5 + 1)}{2} = 15$$

Depreciation alternatives present a marvelous opportunity for tax and accounting benefits.

Try This: If maximum deductions are desired in the early years, use double-declining depreciation for the first three years of a five-year asset. Switch to straight-line for the last two years. No special election is required. Your use of the new method in the tax return is your election. Cumulative deductions, under this method, will exceed those under any other method.

For example: Assume a $100 asset, 5-year life, and compare straight-line, double-declining, and double-declining for 3 years with straight-line for the last 2 years.

	Deductions		
	S-L	D-D	D-D/S-L
	$ 20	$40	$ 40
	20	24	24
	20	14	14
	20	9	11 Switch to S-L
	20	5	11
Totals	$100	$92	$100

h. *Foreign Currency Translation*—Foreign currency transactions and foreign currency financial statements (those prepared in a currency other than U.S. dollars and consolidated with or accounted for on the equity basis in the U.S. company's financial, statements) should be treated for accounting purposes by translating foreign currency cash and amounts receivable or payable into dollars at the current rate of exchange in effect at the balance sheet date. For other accounts, the temporal method described in Accounting Research Study No. 12 of the AICPA, which is similar to the monetary-nonmonetary methods, should be used.

Exchange gains or losses may result and will be included in accounting statements net income. In addition, changes in market value of unperformed forward exchange contracts would be accrued and included in net income.

For tax purposes, no gain need be recognized if income is sheltered or deferred in a foreign subsidiary. See the next paragraph on ways to accomplish this.

i. *Foreign Subsidiaries*—There are a great many foreign subsidiary alternatives, as delineated on Exhibit 9-c.

Before establishing a subsidiary or making a decision as to the form of the overseas organization, Information should be obtained in the form of the tax treaty from the country being examined. Contact should also be made with the local embassy and trade offices to determine business and tax conditions. Accounting and legal firms may be helpful in obtaining such information. Many large public accounting firms publish accounting manuals and maintain offices in most foreign countries.

An accountant or attorney in the foreign country should be contacted to discuss local tax problems (in addition to the U.S. tax considerations) and to review any non-tax factors which could affect a decision. For example, there may be an unstable political situation which would obviate the formation of a new company.

The form of organization would greatly depend on the income projections which have been made. If early losses are expected, a Branch Office will prove to be simple, with no tax problems, and will provide a complete tax deduction for these losses.

When profits result, the corporate form would be considered.

• The Western Hemisphere Trade Corporation (WHTC) provides a 30% tax saving for a corporation which does most of its business in this hemisphere, with 95% of its gross income from outside the U.S. and 90% from an active business. It may be consolidated with its parent for tax purposes, allows for tax-free property transfers between it and the parent and for capital gain on liquidation or sale of its shares. The only disadvantage is that there is no deferral of tax, it is payable now, although at the lower rate. Intercompany pricing must have a realistic basis and withstand tax scrutiny. The WHTC tax benefits are phased out from 1976 through 1979, under the Tax Reform Act of 1976.

• A U.S. Possessions Corporation (USPC) must derive 80% of its gross income from a U.S. possession, although the Virgin Islands does not qualify. 50% of gross income must be from an active business. Any tax due on income earned in the possession is offset by a special foreign tax credit. There is also a dividends-received deduction for dividends from a qualifying PC. There are special tax benefits offered by Puerto Rico. Like the WHTC, there is a capital gain on liquidation or sale of shares and if the shares are owned by an individual, rather than a corporation, a double tax is avoided.

• The Controlled Foreign Corporation (CFC) requires that the parent have over 50% stock control. Any tax deferral advantages will be lost if the foreign country has a high tax rate, since the foreign tax paid will result in a foreign tax credit which may be greater than the U.S. tax. If manufacturing is done abroad, there will be no tax due. The CFC may establish its own subsidiaries which will be tax free. A maximum of 30% of the sub's gross income may be sub-part F type income without it being taxed. A CFC's sub-part F income would include passive income such as dividends, rents, royalties, stock sales, income from services rendered outside the CFC's country to a related person, and income from the CFC's purchase and sale of goods to a related person where the goods are both produced and sold for use outside the CFC's country. Under the minimum distribution provisions of Subpart F, a corporate U.S. shareholder of a CFC pays no tax on the CFC's undistributed sub-part F income for any year if 43% of the CFC's entire income for that year is distributed.

If the CFC buys U.S. components and finishes them off abroad, as opposed to the complete manufacturing above, the CFC pays no U.S. tax until dividends are paid. However, if the CFC buys from the U.S. corporation and merely sells abroad, its income is a deemed paid dividend and there is no tax benefit.

• The Domestic International Sales Corp. (DISC) is a U.S. corporation which receives a tax benefit by having the tax on 50% of its profits postponed for 10 years. There is a good likelihood that the postponement will be made permanent, at the end of the ten-year period. The DISC must have 95% of its gross receipts from exports, which could include sales to another DISC, or to a broker for shipment abroad. While there are liberal intercompany pricing rules and the DISC is exempt from taxation, its profits are taxed to its stockholders or parent. There is no WHTC tax rate reduction permitted for a DISC, and consolidated returns may not be filed with the parent.

j. *General Purchasing Power Financial Statements*—These represent financial reporting in units of general purchasing power. Many companies disclose supplemental accounting information restated for changes in the general purchasing power of the dollar, by applying the GNP Implicit Price Deflator. At present, there is no provision in the tax laws for recognition of any gains or losses which result from these restatements, and they do not offer a possibility for alternative tax planning.

k. *Imputed Interest*—Financial accounting may impute interest to transactions which are essentially interest free loans. The borrower may have taxable interest income, and the lender a tax deduction (See example on page 135).

l. *Interim Financial Statements*—Cumulative-effect type accounting changes made after the first quarter are included in restated net income of the first quarter and in any year to date financial reports that include the first interim period. Whenever financial information that includes those pre-change interim periods is presented, it is to be presented on a restated basis. Such accounting changes will create differences to taxable income and may require tax allocation. The tax effect of such changes may appear as a extraordinary item and should be considered as they relate to financial statement presentation.

m. *Inventory*—The opportunity for tax planning related to inventories is exceptional.

During times of increasing costs of materials, a change in the method of valuing inventories from FIFO to LIFO will result in reduced profits and increased cash flow from reduced taxes.

There are some disadvantages, however, to such a change, and the method should be carefully evaluated. Exhibit 9-d, Lifo Method of Inventory Costing, presents the advantages and disadvantages.

The SEC has placed restrictions on the references to and the type of disclosure made regarding the change.

In the state tax area, many states impose inventory taxes or personal property taxes, annually. Inventories may be planned to be in transit or at their lowest level on the imposition date.

> **Helpful Hint**: Review the state laws carefully. In many states, inventory of product
> in original cases is not taxable. It is presumed to be held for transshipment.

n. *Investment Tax Credits*—The company may recognize tax credits on investment in equipment over the life of the equipment, for accounting purposes. The credit may be flowed through, in the year of purchase, for tax reporting.

o. *Leases*—If capitalized, equipment under lease will be treated as fixed assets and depreciated over the useful life. This accounting treatment may result in a charge for depreciation which may be more or less than the deduction for taxes resulting from not capitalizing the lease and treating the rental payments as an operating expense.

Capitalization of leases should be determined on the basis of whether the lease is, in substance, an installment purchase. Generally, the lease should be capitalized if the lessee builds up material equity, or the lease term equals at least 75% of the useful life, or the lessee guarantees the lessor's debt, or the lessee assumes the risks and rewards of ownership, or the residual value at the end of the lease is nominal, or the lease provides the lessor with recovery of his investment plus a fair return.

The need for careful tax planning on leasing contracts has often been demonstrated through cases in which both parties have lost important tax benefits because the IRS has refused to recognize the agreements as leases for tax purposes. The IRS has treated these as sale contracts or as forms of financing. The IRS may take the position that a sale has transpired because ownership has in reality passed to the lessee. In sale and leaseback arrangements, the IRS has held this to be a form of financing, because ownership remains with the intended lessee—the reasoning being that the contract lessee did not sell the property but simply mortgaged it to the contract lessor.

In these cases, if the contract is regarded by IRS as a sale, there are these consequences: The monied party or contract lessor is taxed on any gain realized over an imputed sale price, which price would be the total present value of the required payments. He would also lose the depreciation allowance and any investment tax credit. Moreover, his entire gain would be reportable in the year the contract become effective, unless the installment method were permitted. As to the contract lessee, or borrower, he would lose the deduction for periodic payments, except for the interest portion, and since IRS deems him to be the owner, he would take a deduction for depreciation and the ITC.

If the lease were considered by IRS to be a financing arrangement, the imputed mortgage is arrived at as the totaling of the present value of the future payments. The lessee may deduct only the interest portion of his rental payments, which is the excess of his actual payment over the payment's discounted value in the year of the contract. The remainder of each payment, as well as the price of any purchase option, is treated as repayment of the loan.

The IRS considers certain guidelines, prepared from its rulings and policy statements, to arrive at a favorable presumption that a transaction is a lease:

- If there is a purchase option, the purchase price is not less than the fair market value of the property at the time the option is exercised.
- If there is a renewal option, the renewal charge will not be less than the fair rental value of the property at the time of renewal.
- If the lease term is 18 years or less, the residual value should be 15% or more. If the lease term is over 18 years, the residual value must be at least 5% of original cost if discounted at 6% to the year of the agreement.
- The estimated economic useful life of the property exceeds the original term by at least 2 years or 10% of the original term, whichever is greater.
- The lessor's equity is 20% or more of the property's cost, that is, he cannot finance more than 80% of the purchase price.
- If an involuntary conversion of the property results, the excess proceeds of the conversion belong to the contract lessor.

Helpful Hint: Independent appraisals which determine fair market value, residual value, fair rental value, and useful life, if timely made, may prevent adverse decisions by the IRS on audit.

The sale and lease back of owned fixed assets is often used to raise long-term funds (See discussion on page 45). When depreciable equipment is sold and leased back, if it is over 6 months old it qualifies as a Section 1231 asset and a capital gain results on the sale for that portion of the gain which exceeds the amount of depreciation taken in prior years. Prior year's depreciation is recaptured at ordinary income rates.

Helpful Hint: A sale and lease back may be accomplished by selling at cost to a subsidiary on the cash basis for tax purposes. The sub. will then execute the sale and lease back. The gain may then be recognized on the cost recovery basis, that is, as cash is received (usually over a period of years through payment of principal on notes), the first cash is applied to a recovery of cost and the balance is recognized as gain.

p. *Marketable Securities*—Persuasive evidence is needed to retain the cost basis for securities classified as a current asset when the market value is lower than cost. Generally, such evidence would be limited to substantial recovery subsequent to the year end. Failing this, the financial statements could reflect a charge to income which would not be allowed for tax purposes, no sale or exchange having taken place.

q. *Revenue Recognition with Right of Return*—When the right of return exists, the financial statements may not recognize the sale. For taxes, under most cases, the sale would be recognized with no tax deferral.

For accounting purposes, the sale is analysed to determine its economic substance. If the seller is exposed to risks of ownership through return of the property, the transaction should not be recorded as a sale—unless the price to buyer is fixed, and payment is not deferred until resale, and the buyer's obligations would not be changed due to theft, destruction, or damage to the property, and the buyer is not a straw party or conduit, and the seller has no significant obligations for future performance to bring about resale of the property by the buyer, and future loss to the seller from future returns can be predicted. In such case, the recorded sale should be reduced by estimated returns to a net sales basis—again causing a revenue difference for tax acccounting.

r. *Royalties*—The receipt of royalties from patent-licensing arrangements may, under carefully considered conditions, be capital gains income. In general, these requirements should be met:

- Rights to patents should be transferred, in substantial measure.

- Territorial limitations have been held not to invalidate the substantial transfer of rights. Licensing rights need not be world-wide to be considered sales for capital gains purposes.

- Cancellation rights retained by the seller, if based on default or other reasonable grounds, should not affect the "sale" nature of an agreement.

- Sub-licensing restrictions have been repeatedly held by the courts not to be a substantial limitation with regard to a "sale" transaction.

- Exclusivity of use need not necessarily be granted. As stated above, territorial divisions do not affect the substantiality of a a sale of patent rights with regard to capital gains treatment. Moreover, the existence of a previously granted limited license would not obviate sale treatment. However, no consequential rights to use the patent for itself should be retained by the licensor. Courts have held, though, that the reservation of a license to itself by the grantor does not obviate the sale treatment.

- When "know-how" is part of a bundle of rights transferred, consisting of patents and engineering information, the "know-how" takes on the nature of property for capital gains purposes and proceeds from "know-how" transfers should be taxable as capital gains.

Caution: Structuring such contracts is not for amateurs or Controllers. Suffice it for the Controller to suggest the application of capital gains and to obtain professional tax and contract advice in structuring the agreement.

Royalty income of a Controlled Foreign Subsidiary (CFC) must be derived from the active conduct of a business of the CFC in order not to be considered "effectively connected" to the parent and subject to inclusion of its profits as sub-part F income in the U.S. parent. The CFC must conduct business in the foreign country through a fixed place of business and the CFC must 1) be engaged in the development creation, improvement or production of and licensing of property (patents, etc. which it has developed or substantially improved, or 2) must, through its own staff, be engaged in the business of marketing licenses of its property. The U.S. corporation must not 1) actively participate in soliciting or performing other activities required to arrange the license, or 2) perform significant services incident to such licenses.

> **Key Point**: Under these circumstances, then, patents could be sold to a CFC for improvement by it and the execution of licenses abroad, which would not be taxable sub-part F U.S. income! (see IRC Sec. 864 (c) (4) (b), IRC Sec. 862 (a) (4), Sec. 882 of the Code (1966 Act), Regulations 1.954-2(d) (1), and Income Tax Regulations 1.954-2(d) (1) (iii), also S.Rep. No. 1707, 89th. Cong. 2nd. Sess. 20-21 and H-Rep. 1450, 89th. Cong. 2nd. Sess., 65).

s. *Special or Extraordinary Items*—The accounting concept of extraordinary item treatment is based on the infrequent and unusual nature of the item. The item may not meet the extraordinary concept but may still be considered for special item status because of its unusual nature or materiality. There is no similar concept in taxation. Financial statement planning will recognize this desparity.

t. *State Taxes*—Because of the diverse nature of the state tax laws, state tax planning cannot be considered here, except as the broad planning moves would relate to the creating of a deductible state tax for federal purposes.

The most frequent state tax considerations are:

- Whether or not to incorporate in a state—Consider whether you have offices, assets, write orders or contracts, travel salesmen or need to collect money in the state. Most state tax services, including Prentice-Hall, publish schedules or check lists showing whether these activities are considered doing business in the state. Incorporation requires the filing of an Annual Report or Franchise Tax Return. An alternative is to file sales or use tax returns as a foreign corporation.

> **Helpful Hint**: Creating sales and accounts receivable in a state, together with the possibility of having to institute legal collection actions, does not always mean you must incorporate and receive a license to do business in the state. Collection claims, in most states, may be assigned to collection attorneys who can bring actions in their own names, for the benefit of the assignor.

- Which taxes to pay—The state taxes to be paid will depend on whether or not you are franchised, in which case the Annual Report or Franchise Tax is due. If not, personal property or inventory taxes will, in any event be payable, in most states.

> **Interesting Sidelight**: Most states do not assess a penalty for failure of foreign corporations to file personal property tax returns. An assessor will file for the state on property which he can locate, at lower values than the company might file.

> **Helpful Sales Tax Hint**: When sales taxes are normally paid based on invoices billed to customers, do not neglect the opportunity to obtain a rebate of previously paid taxes when accounts receivable are written off as uncollectable against the reserve for bad debts. The same would apply to allowances and billing adjustments—tax-effect credits offered to customers.

PROCEDURES

How to control the payment of taxes and administration of tax policies:

1. Establish tax calendars, tax files, and ticklers.

2. Use Authorization for Payment and Narrative.

3. List payments on Control Sheet and calendar.

4. File documentation in Tax File.

5. Reconcile taxes payable to general ledger, quarterly.

6. Procedure before the IRS.

1. Calendars, Tax Files, and Ticklers

Any tax service publishes federal and state tax calendars. The Prentice-Hall Tax Calendar for fixed and recurring monthly dates is shown at Exhibits 9-e and 9-f. The fixed date calendar will change annually, as some taxes are due not on a specific date, but, for example, on a third Monday. The recurring monthly date calendar will change as state tax laws are revised.

Most large banks publish complete federal tax calendars. Exhibit 9-g is a Timetable for Federal Taxes published by Manufacturers Hanover Trust Co. and copyrighted by Motivational Systems, Inc., NYC, NY. It gives both dates and general rules for filing, and is available from many banks.

Payroll taxes present a special problem and are not included in the regular state tax calendars, However, Payroll Guides are also published by most taxes services. These guides explain the state payroll tax laws and will give due dates for state withholding tax, unemployment insurance tax, and disability tax.

As an alternative to use of the state tax guides, corporate representatives for legal service, such as Corporation Trust Co. or Prentice-Hall, supply weekly bulletins, tax reminders, and advices of tax law changes.

If the company is represented in only a few states, the same information may be obtained directly from state agencies—labor department, income tax bureau, or Secretary of State. Since this type of contact requires direct contact, and since the state agency does not provide mailing services for changes in the law, the use of tax guides and services is recommended where the company files in many states.

Having obtained the published tax calendars from the selected source, the company should establish its own calendar each month. A page from the company Tax Calendar is at Exhibit 9-h. The Date Due is obtained from the published tax calendar; the Date Submitted refers to the date the tax return was completed by the tax accountant and submitted for payment. The Date Mailed is subsequently entered to provide a record evidencing payment. It is easily scanned for open boxes.

Helpful Hint: If a penalty for late filing is assessed, the tax department would usually accept this calendar, showing date mailed, as satisfactory evidence that the tax was paid timely.

The company Tax Calendar illustrated will have separate pages for:

Sales tax,

Personal Property Tax,

Payroll tax,

Other taxes (occupancy, excise),

or for any other tax commonly imposed by most states due to the nature of the company's business. County or city taxes are listed within the appropriate state.

Having set up the calendars, which reflect due date:

a. A file is created for each tax.

b. The return to be filed is set up in a tickler file, approximately 15 days prior to the due date. The tickler file is merely a desk calendar.

c. On the tickled date, the return is removed from the tax file, completed, submitted for payment, and the Date Submitted is completed on the Tax Calendar.

2. The Authorization for Payment and Narrative

When the tax return is submitted (step 1.c., above), an Authorization for Payment (Exhibit 9-i) is completed by the tax return preparer, who approves the authorization and draws the check (from a separate pegboard tax account). The authorization, return, and check are submitted for approval by the Accounting Service Manager. After his approval on the authorization, the entire package is submitted to the check signatory.

If the payment is unusual in nature (a special assessment, a tax audit deficiency, interest or penalty, a new tax, over a pre-specified limit for each kind of tax), a narrative explanation should be attached to the authorization. The Narrative is a hand written document explaining the reason for the unusual payment and relating the details of any audit deficiency.

Key Point: Tax returns are detailed, complex, and routine. The narrative becomes an Exception Report which saves you reading every return. It provides you with an overview of the unusual situation and allows you to form a judgment as to whether the proper steps have been taken.

Helpful Hint: Run the "tax account" on an imprest basis—make deposits only in the amount of the total of the daily checks you write. This prevents fraud (your balance is just enough to cover authorized checks written), saves on the cost of carrying idle balances, and makes checkbook reconciliations unnecessary. It may be operated on a zero balance or minimum balance basis.

3. List Payments on Control Sheet and calendar

Signed checks are returned to the disbursing section (a separate person from the check drawer or return preparer) for mailing and entry on the company Tax Calendar in the Date Mailed column (see Exhibit 9-h). Concurrently, the dollar amount of the payment is entered on a Control Sheet for each class of tax—a separate sheet for payroll taxes, sales taxes, or personal property taxes. This sheet is illustrated at Exhibit 9-j. Line 37 of that sheet shows the entry of $597.46 of the Hartford, Conn. tax listed on the Authorization for Payment at Exhibit 9-i. This Control Sheet is used for the quarterly reconciliation in step 5.

4. File Documentation

After mailing by the disbursing section, the entire package (tax return, any invoice, Authorization, Narrative) is filed in the Tax File (which was opened in step 1).

The file is best retained in the tax department, rather than the disbursements section, as the file is frequently consulted, certainly each month or quarter to file the next tax return.

5. Reconciliation

Quarterly, the general ledger is examined and each account to which tax payments are charged is traced back to the Control Sheet (Exhibit 9-j). Every item reflected on the general ledger as a tax payment must be accounted for on the Control Sheet. The internal audit section conducts this review.

Unlisted items are investigated for proper authorization for payment and back-up documentation and are entered on the Control Sheet. Items listed on the Control Sheet but not found through the ledger are investigated for improper posting or coding errors.

6. Procedure before the IRS

What do you do when the tax man comes to call? The steps are these:

a. Returns are checked for form and accuracy and classified for audit by the district or regional director's office. Mathematical errors are corrected, overpayments refunded, and demand made for additional tax.

b. A field audit on your premises is scheduled. You should have your tax attorney or accountant present.

c. Technical advice from the Washington National Office of IRS may be requested by either the taxpayer or the district director, to resolve thorny procedural or technical questions.

d. After audit, adjustments are proposed to the taxpayer's liability. These may be agreed to, or contested by requesting a conference.

e. You will then receive a 30-day letter and a copy of the examining officer's report. This letter outlines your appeal right and protest requirements. If you do not appeal, IRS will institute whatever they consider to be appropriate enforcement actions. If you appeal, you may request district and Appellate Division conferences. No protest is required in cases involving $2,500 or less, but you may submit a written statement of facts.

f. District conferences are held by the Conference Staff without the examining officer. Matters under $2,500 can be settled by the Conference Staff Chief. In matters over $2,500, the taxpayer is encouraged to bypass the district conference and go directly to the Appellate Division.

g. At the Appellate conference, you may agree to any proposed decisions, and if you do not, you will receive a 90-day letter.

h. You may then pay the tax and apply for a refund or appeal to the Tax Court, usually without paying in advance. If you fail to pay or appeal, IRS will start any appropriate enforcement action.

i. After the case is docketed, you may call for a further conference with the Appellate Division to attempt to compromise or settle.

j. No appeal is permitted from Tax Court in cases handled under the Small Tax Case Procedure. Otherwise, appeal may be made to the Court of Appeals and then to the U.S. Supreme Court.

Caution: Always appear at a conference, at any level, with your qualified agent or attorney. Don't do it yourself. The laws are too complex and you may give evidence which can damage your position.

Further Caution: Always have your tax agent present when a field agent questions your employees or accounting personnel. Instruct your people to have no conversation with the agent, without your tax professional being present, other than to produce books and records for him. Don't take a chance on wrong information being given to the field agent by an employee who is trying to show how smart he is.

TAX TIPS

The canny Controller may have a limited foundation in taxes but maintains a stream of information on taxes to apprise him of alternative tax courses. The Controller conceives the proper tax moves for the company, aided by, not led by, his outside tax consultants. Proper tax planning is integrated with corporate goals as expressed by higher management. Often, the alternatives chosen will be treated differently from financial statements for tax purposes. Both effects need to be considered carefully. Administration of tax policies requires timely payments through the use of tax calendars, tickling due dates, and establishing separate tax files. As with other responsibilities, control is achieved through division of responsibilities, exception reports (the Narrative), and review of results through audit and reconciliation.

CHAPTER 10

Organizing the Operational Audit

AUDITING, financial or operational, is not a defined function of the Controller or Treasurer in the official EFI statement of responsibilities as exhibited in "Treasurer's and Controller's Functions." The Controller, however, has the official duty for Evaluating and Consulting ". . . . as it relates to the attainment of objectives and the effectiveness of policies, organization structure and procedures." Another defined duty is Protection of Assets " . . . . through internal control, internal auditing . . . ."

Inferentially, therefore, the FEI definition provides the authority for operational auditing—for the evaluation of the efficacy of the operating policies and procedures. It explicitly provides authority for the protection of assets, generally intended to mean through financial auditing, and, again, inferentially, through the Operational Audit of the system which spawns these assets.

The Controllers Position Description in "Treasurer's and Controller's Functions" accordingly, provides under Organizational Relationships that Auditors will report to him. He is responsible for the Operating Plan (see page 89) and should have the opportunity to review, check, edit, criticize and validate the performance of that Plan. There are those who will maintain that managers responsible for performance should not evaluate themselves, that this responsibility should be divided and undertaken by others as a performance check on any given manager. This is a valid argument as it relates to financial audits (concerned with preparation of financial statements), but it cannot apply to operational audits (reviews of operating systems and procedures). There is a point beyond which responsibility should not be divided. The "buck" has to stop here. The Controller has established and implemented the Operating Plan and needs the tools to review its efficiency—the internal audit of operations. The comparison of the actual results of operations to the Budget is a "measure" of performance—a quantification of results. The operational audit is an "evaluation" of the Plan—a statement of its effectiveness. Both are necessary!

This chapter will not consider financial audits, which are sometimes the responsibility of the President, the Treasurer, the Controller, or even the Board of Directors. The subject will be considered in Chapter 11, Supervising Special Administrative Areas of Responsibility.

These pages will consider the operational audit as to:

• Purpose (why is it needed?)

• Nature (what should be audited?)

• Organization (how should it be audited?)

• Review (how and by whom should audit reports be reviewed?)

PURPOSE

The operational audit is an internal procedure, performed by company personnel, which is philosophically oriented toward monitoring the possibility of attainment of the Operating Plan's bottom-line objective.

It does this, not through measuring and comparing actual results to the budgeted figures, but through evaluating personnel, operations, plans, policies, systems, procedures, and even the tools of management (Procedures Manuals, Organizational Charts, Position Descriptions and the multitude of other devices described in Chapter 7).

Operational audits are specific engagements by auditors to review specific areas of the business. These audits are augmented by a system of internal check and control, sometimes called automatic auditing, which provides for a system of internal checking on each and every transaction being processed regularly during the daily operations. Internal checking is a Controllership responsibility which, together with the outside audit function, will be discussed more fully in the next chapter, Supervising Special Administrative Areas of Responsibility.

The outside audit, often called the external audit as opposed to the internal operational audit, is performed by independent public accountants. It is not oriented to the attainment of Plan objectives but serves as the vehicle wherein the outside auditors express an opinion on the fairness, consistency and conformity with accepted accounting principals of the company's published financial statements. Whatever the results of the Operating Plan, the outside audit reviews these results and expresses an opinion on them.

The differences between outside audits and operational, inside audits are:

1. Outside, independent audits are required by public agencies, financing institutions, stock exchanges and stockholders, contracting parties, creditors, directors, and top management. Inside audits are used by individual department heads and other management as a control tool to evaluate conformity to internal procedures.

2. The outside audit produces a formal report, supported by a body of accounting rules and dicta, which tells the recipients above whether the financial statements are fair, consistent, and in conformity with accounting principals. The inside audit report is less formal, and its format varies with the nature of the job being audited. It is designed for internal company use, only.

3. Outside audits are performed by independent professionals, either managment consultants, certified public accounting firms, or independent specialists in specific areas such as traffic, distribution, data processing, plant management, administration or engineering, for a fee. Inside audits are done by company employees.

4. Outside audits review financial statements and the broader aspects of the internal control system. Inside audits may also review the internal control system but, generally, are concerned with individual segments of that system and a variety of reports, forms, and operating departments, rather than the financial statements in themselves.

5. Outside audits are usually conducted at the end of fiscal quarters or the year. Inside audits are performed on a continuing basis throughout the year.

6. Outside audits may be the responsibility of an officer other than the Controller. Inside audits are the Controller's responsibility in that they evaluate the soundness of the Operating Plan.

The objectives of internal operational audits may, thus, be said to be:

1. Evaluating actual operations (as opposed to budgeting which measures results vs. a plan, and as opposed to outside auditing, which merely looks at the financial statements which result from these operations).

2. Controlling operations, through corrective action taken as a result of the audit evaluation.

3. Integration with outside auditors in determining the validity of the system of internal check and control.

4. Improving operations through the evaluation process, in that it identifies personnel, policies, and procedures which may be improved in the future, thereby permitting the more ready attainment of future Profit Plans.

5. Providing for the protection of company assets.

6. Preventing and uncovering defalcations or other fraud.

NATURE

The operational audit, being concerned by definition with the evaluation of company operations, may evoke as its performance sphere any area or segment of the business. There should be no prohibitions on the divisions, segments, departments, committees, policies, procedures, personnel, or plans which the auditor may approach.

This authority should come down from the President in a stated Policy Manual release and be explicit in the Position Description for the auditor. Obviously, the one exception is the outside audit function, which would not be reviewed or audited by the inside audit group, it being performed by independent outside accountants on a fee-paid basis.

Avoid This Pitfall: Don't conduct nit-picking audits. Since everything may be audited, a sense of proportion needs to be employed in determining what to audit.

Nit-picking audits are divisive and contribute nothing to the over-all achievement of company goals.

The following areas should be audited:

- Profit centers—areas that generate revenues and expenses, such as a branch office.
- Cost centers—areas that generate costs and expenses without revenue, such as a data processing department (assuming such charges are not allocated to users).
- Vertical systems—procedures which cause the generation of data to emanate from a profit or cost center and to cross departmental lines, such as a billing system which starts in a branch office and ends with a home office posting to an accounts receivable trial balance; or areas of an accounting department which generate reports for other departments.
- Internal check systems—areas of internal control and division of responsibility within one or many departments. This also includes over-all policies.

Obviously, the audit of profit or cost centers will be for the purpose of improving profits or controlling costs through an evaluation of the operating systems being employed. The audit of a vertical system is merely a way to trace the practicability of a system across divisional lines, which would not otherwise be accomplished in the single audit of a profit or cost center. Audits or internal check systems will protect company assets and guard against fraud.

This list precludes the audit of:

- Personnel—as a specific function. We do not set out to evaluate personnel. Our audit may reveal excellence or incompetence and the audit report provides for such comment.

  A Word of Caution: Some chief executive officers require an audit of company personnel, with a view to evaluating an upgrading in weak areas. This is not an audit function, other than through audit report comment. Such an audit, if conducted, should be done by specially assigned people or the personnel department. An internal auditor cannot function or obtain the cooperation of employees if they believe he is constantly auditing them, rather than their departmental systems and procedures.

- Intra-departmental procedures—unless a question of internal control or security is involved. We do not need to review the detailed mechanics and work responsibilities within the department. This is the function of the department's manager. We review only those procedures which emanate from one department and affect another.

  For example: The internal auditor does not review the methods employed by the switchboard operator to answer telephone calls. That is the function of the Office Service Manager. The auditor does review the method employed by the operator in taking and transmitting messages for absent personnel, as these affect other departments.

- Repetitive functions—such as bank reconciliations, vendor accounts payable statements, taking physical inventories, or accounts receivable confirmation. Such repetitive functions are operating responsibilities of department heads. The assumption of these duties by auditors tends to swell the auditing staff and turn it into an operating department, rather than a reviewing and evaluating section. The argument is made that the audit of these functions, by auditors, is a repetition of the work already being performed by the department, hence at greater cost. The argument is valid, but the conclusion is not. The purpose of the audit function is not to cut costs. Certainly that is an ultimate goal, but its purpose, as defined previously, is oriented toward the attainment of the Operating Plan's bottom-line objective. The cost of auditing, of this review function, is a budgeted cost. Any attempt to cut costs elsewhere, using the services of auditors, will impugn the stated objectives of this function.

To the extent that these functions affect other departments, and they all do, they should be the subject of internal audits, on an occasional basis, but not on a continuing, operational basis.

ORGANIZATION

The "how do we audit operations?" facet of internal auditing includes:

1. *Overseeing the internal Audit Function*—Exhibit 10-a is a checklist for executives and directors which embodies the principals of Purpose and Nature set forth in the pages above. This list was prepared by a large, independent accounting firm, Coopers and Lybrand, and circulated in a Newsletter to all of their clients. It is a minimum checklist of internal audit procedures.

2. *A Position Description*—prepared along the lines indicated in Chapter 7, defines the funcitons and responsibilities of auditors. If separate auditors are used for home office and field offices, a separate description should be prepared for each auditor. Exhibit 10-b is a Position Description for a Field Auditor.

> **Helpful Hint:** Note that the field auditor assists in interviewing, training, and maintaining field levels of administrative performance, in addition to straight auditing work. These are non-repetitive functions, related to the field auditing work, and they are consonant with the attainment of the corporate Operating Plan objectives.

3. *Internal Audit Programs*—should be prepared for profit and cost centers, vertical systems, and internal check systems, as described under the Nature of Audits, above. Exhibit 10-c, Field Audit Announcement, is directed to field managers at profit centers which will be audited. It includes the auditor's Position Description, the actual audit programs, and a format of the reports which will follow.

> **Auditing Assist:** Don't be afraid to circulate your audit program. The corporate goal is to achieve systems that work. If managers know what will be audited, the areas which you stress and consider important, you are more apt to obtain conformity to procedures.
> Don't fear that disclosure of your programs will allow someone to construct a fraud, to circumvent the system. The audit program is designed to test for lack of

internal control, lack of divison of duties, fraud. The very publication of the audit program is a deterrent to fraud.

Absolute Auditing Requirement: The last paragraph of the Field Audit Announcement Exhibit provides for the submission by the field office of a memo on corrective action which must be taken within 30 days of the audit. The Regional Administrator will then comment on this in the monthly Narrative Report (page 119), which then flows up the management ladder in successive higher monthly reports, and the Field Auditor will review this deficiency on his next audit.

A detailed Internal Audit Program for a Branch Office is shown at Exhibit 10-d, e, and f:

10-d—Audit Procedures at the Home Office. These procedures are performed at headquarters, prior to conducting the field audit, in preparation for the field visit. The procedure takes about 2½ days. The auditor will generally pre-audit two branches, in this manner, preparatory for a two week field trip to audit two branches.

10-e—Audit Procedures at the Branch Office. These procedures follow-on and stem from the work previously done at the Home Office. Both financial and procedural areas are examined. This review consumes one week per branch.

10-f—Audit Questionnaire for Branch Offices. This is a "walk-through" review of the branch office. It is comprehensive, covers all facets of the profit center's operations, is directed to determining conformity to company procedures and policies, does not require detailed work papers, and consumes one day out of the five required by 10-e. This walk-through is usually performed after cash is counted upon arrival at the branch office.

Time Saving Suggestion: If there are many branch offices and it is determined that 7½ days is too much to spend on each branch audit, an abbreviated 2½-to 3-day audit program may be conducted. This is shown at Exhibits 10-g, h, and i which are extracted highlights from the longer audit programs.

Similar audit programs may be prepared for any profit or cost center. To construct such a program, the inside auditor should review:

1. The Organization Chart to determine reporting responsibilities.

2. Position Description for the manager and Work Duties sheets for each employee in the department.

3. The Data Processing Evaluation study, described on page 202, which lists all input and output reports and gives an overview of the entire system.

4. Work processing flow charts for the department, which if not prepared in 3 above, would be prepared by the department manager. If not on hand, the auditor should prepare it. This should be augmented by 5.

5. A narrative summary of the general nature of the work prepared by this department. This gives the manager's version of what he thinks the work is.

6. Every input and output form used by this department.

7. Every report generated by this department.

8. Manuals and procedures used intra-departmentally.

Helpful Hint: If a formal Systems and Procedures Department exists, the audit need merely be a review of existing procedures as documented in the Procedures Manual. *For Example:* The Systems group could establish the typical (usable by any company which ships product) Warehouse Security and Procedures shown at Exhibit 10-j. The audit program is a review of each point, by observation and examination of records and files, to determine adherence to the procedure. The audit report is keyed to the procedure and reports on only those numbers which are not in conformity.

4. *Training and Conduct of Inside Auditors*—is a necessary ingredient of a successful audit program. It is important that the auditor have accounting training, though a CPA certificate may not be necessary for anyone except the Audit Manager. While many audits are operational and not accounting-oriented, many others are. One Day Field Audits like those in Exhibits 10-g, h, and i may be performed by non-accounting auditors, perhaps former field administrative people who have been successful in their positions and promoted.

Information on training is available from the Institute of Internal Auditors, and an excellent Course for Staff Auditors is offered regularly by the American Management Association. Public accounting firms are not too helpful with literature for internal auditors, but business publishers like Prentice-Hall offer a variety of specialized books on the subject.

Auditors should be trained to:

1. Maintain objectivity during audits.

2. Refrain from establishing excessively close personal relationships with personnel in offices being audited, to assure continued objectivity on audits.

Case in Point: A traveling auditor consistently gave high marks to a field office which management, from observation from its vantage point, knew was not performing up to the auditor's reports. It was determined that the auditor, a bachelor, was squiring the office manager, an unmarried young woman. The manager rotated auditors and instituted rules of conduct which specifically limited this action.

3. Not establish policy or procedures.

4. Refrain from debating or arguing the propriety of extant policies or procedures.

5. Rotate between jobs, if staff permits, every two or three years.

6. Maintain a pleasant face and helpful, constructive attitude during audits and report reviews.

5. *Whether to Have a Separate Audit Department*—is a decision which varies by company. The question is not whether to conduct inside audits—these must be performed, even if by the owner in a small company, or a manager in a slightly larger company who divides his regular duties with an audit function. But should the company utilize one or more operational auditors, preparing formal Position Descriptions, Internal Audit Programs, and Training, as just discussed?

These factors should be considered in reaching a decision:

a. Are there many locations involved in operations?

b. Are there many employees, and in many locations?

c. Is the system of internal check incomplete?

d. Do the independent accountants comment unfavorably on the internal control systems?

e. Are there a variety of products and services?

f. Are inventories composed of many small items?

g. Are there a great many invoices to customers each month?

h. Can the independent accountant's work be reduced through internal audit?

i. Do competitors of similar size use operational auditors?

j. Have the outside auditors made major year-end accounting adjustments each year?

k. Are the Profit Plans being missed each budget period?

While the significance of an affirmative response to each question would vary with different companies, a positive answer to any one of the questions would indicate the propriety of establishing a separate operational audit function.

REVIEW

The end result of the operational audit is the Report. It may be presented orally in the small company but should be written when a separate audit function has been established. The report should be oriented toward all concerned levels of management and be suitable for follow-up.

Helpful Hint: Restudy How to Prepare Reports on page 115, as to reporting level, content, timing, and form. This all applies.

There are five basic reports generated by the Audit Department:

1. *Summary Audit Report,* Exhibit 10-k—This is a brief report, only a few lines, addressed (in this case) to the EVP who is responsible for operations, and to the VP/Marketing who has overall responsibility, at the corporate level, for the branch being audited. Both officers report directly to the President. The report is prepared by the manager of the Audit Department (not the auditor, since he is addressing high corporate officers), and the Controller (to whom the Audit Manager reports) is copied.

While the detailed report (see the next exhibit) covers many items, this report extracts only those which are significant and should be called to top management's attention, to insure that corrective action is taken. These officers, thus, are not burdened with offensive detail and may concentrate on the important areas. The summary, therefore, becomes an Exception Report. Further, copies of this summary are not sent to lower managers who receive the detailed report; the impression is thereby created that higher managers and officers also received the detailed report and that all items listed on it are significant and worthy of attention.

Note that the branch being audited is graded (see Exhibit 10-m).

2. *Audit Report,* Exhibit 10-l—This is the detailed Audit Report which supports the previous Summary Audit Report.

It is generally two or three pages, never longer, the first page being a cover page showing the subject of the audit and the distribution of the report. In this exhibit, a branch is being audited and the report is sent to the Branch Administrator (the office manager) and the Branch Manager (the general manager directly responsible). His immediate superior is the Regional Manager who reports, in turn, to a Zone Manager. In this company, there are 40 branches, 8 regions, and 3 zones. Thus, all of the directly concerned operating managers receive a copy of the detailed Audit Report. The Controller is copied since he has direct responsibility for the Audit Department. The Audit Manager, if the department is large enough to have one other than the Controller, is automatically copied but need not be shown on the distribution listing. Names, rather than titles, are copied, to insure receipt.

The use of the cover page, with lots of white space and a precise delineation of names and date, sets the tone for the precision of the report to follow.

The second page of the report lists the principle items in A, gives more detail in B about one of the principal items (item A.2., warehouse security, indicated that inventory was not being controlled), and items C or more would list secondary items for comment. The branch rating is at D.

The report format includes an opening paragraph showing the period covered and closes with a courteous expression.

The key items are briefly summarized and carried forward to the Summary Audit Report.

> **Helpful Hint**: Other than the cover page, there should be one or one and a half
> additional pages. More than that would be picayune and officious. We are seeking
> to report on major items, only, whose failure would affect the Operating Plan.

3. *Audit Appraisals,* Exhibit 10-m—This is a semi-annual summary of the grades on the detailed Audit Reports.

Each letter grade is simply defined, and the name of each office is listed under the appropriate column. Summary Audit Report copies are enclosed for ready reference, and the Appraisal is directed to the officer directly responsible for operations under the President, in this case the EVP. Copies are sent to the VP Marketing, as he is responsible to the EVP for field operations, and to the Controller, as the report emanates from one of his departments.

Some criticism of this type report, using letter grades, will arise from the branches being judged. The report may be called school-boyish and the assignment of grades, arbitrary, without due consideration to other factors such as attainment of sales objectives, motivation of personnel, or performance up to budget standards. This report, though, is a review of operating systems and procedures, only, and the assigned grade is concerned only with evaluating those procedures, and no other factors. The use of the grade provides a quick, incisive, recognizable standard for judging performance within operating areas, only.

Audit Reports and Appraisals are used by reviewers in evaluating managers for salary increases. Their primary purpose, of course, is to attain Profit Plan objectives.

4. *Individual Systems Report,* Exhibit 10-n—This report, called the ISR, is a detailed review of a specific system within an operating department. In this case, a Freight Prepayment Plan procedure with the Accounting Department is being audited.

The familiar cover page sets forth the time period and type of audit, showing distribution. Since only one department is involved, the auditor reports to the department head, the Manager of Accounting Services, and his superior, the Controller. In this company, the audit department also reports to the Controller who would be copied were another department, not his responsibility, being reviewed.

This report shows deficiencies in performance and recommends corrections.

If the report is long or the system complex, the list of deficiencies could be keyed to the item number in the procedure and the procedure attached for easy reference.

5. *Audit Program,* Exhibit 10-o—This is not a report as such, but belongs in any listing of audit reports. This Audit Program is used by inside auditors for performing financial audits (not operational) of wholly owned subsidiaries. The reports which are generated (not exhibited here) are the usual financial statements—balance sheet, income statement and statement of retained earnings, statement of changes in financial position, statement of additional paid-in capital, and notes to financial statements. Included, too, would be an internal audit opinion as to scope, consistency and conformity to generally accepted accounting principles, quite similar to the opinion of an outside auditor.

This Audit Program is a good example of a complete financial audit program which may be used when independent public accountants are not retained to conduct the audit of the subsidiary.

While operational audits of the sub. may be performed, the financial audit is more usual. The sub usually operates outside of the parent's normal systems and procedures, with its own Profit Plan. It generally supplies its own monthly financial statements which are the ultimate measure of its effectiveness to Plan.

AUDIT AFFIRMATIONS

The operational audit is a defined Controllership responsibility, its purpose being the evaluation, control, and improvement of actual operations. It examines internal checks and controls and supports the examination by independent, outside auditors. It differs from outside audits by examining the details of individual systems, rather than the financial statements themselves. Operational audits are conducted of profit and cost centers, vertical systems and procedures, and internal check systems. Auditors utilize written audit programs and reports. Their reports keep all concerned managers advised of the effectiveness of operating procedures and provide a control tool to aid the manager in achieving his profit objectives. Every company, large or small, should utilize an audit capability, even if assigned individuals must perform it on a part-time basis.

CHAPTER **11**

Supervising Special Administrative

Areas of Responsibility

THE term "administrative" in the title refers to executive or management performance of duties. The FEI definition of Controllership and Treasurership Functions in "Treasurer's and Controller's Functions" explains the broad areas of responsibility. The elements of these broad areas have been treated in other chapters of this book. However, inherent in these overall functions are specific management tasks which may be said to be sub-sets of the larger functions—hence, "special administrative areas of responsibility."

Moreover, in many companies, usually below the $50 million sales range, the Controller or Treasurer is asked to accept responsibility for areas which are not normally associated with his office. For example, Customer Relations is generally a marketing department, reporting to a general sales manager. In some companies, though, since the Controller supervises the order/billing function, and since customer complaints are related to credits and billing adjustments arising out of the order/billing function, the Controller's assumption of the customer relations responsibility is a natural process.

Furthermore, while the assignment of major functions to the Treasurer or Controller is clear, for a few functions, no clear-cut assignment is evident. There may be other financial or administrative officers who divide up functions. The National Conference Board, in a study on The Duties of Financial Executives, reports that the following are Functions of Indefinite Responsibility:

- Cash budget preparation.

- Formulation of disbursing procedures for pension plan payments and interest.

- Accounts payable disbursement.

- Annual report preparation for stockholders.

- Contracts review for financial and tax provisions.

- Confidential payroll handling.

Many functions, too, are frequently reassigned from the Treasurer to the Controller and vice-versa. Exhibit 11-a lists some of these as reported in actual business practice by the Conference Board. It is important, therefore, that a clear, current organizational chart exists (see Chapter 7) and that Position Descriptions are consulted for the exact determination of special areas of responsibilities in each company.

This chapter will examine each of these "special" areas, in alphabetical order, citing the authority for the responsibility by reference to the FEI definition or the Position Descriptions for the Treasurer or Controller in "Treasurer's and Controller's Functions."

ACCOUNTING CALENDAR

Various calendars have been exhibited elsewhere, as they relate to overall responsibilities—the Budget Calendar at Exhibit 6-a; the Departmental Reports calendar at Exhibit 8-s; various Tax Calendars at Exhibits 9-e through h; and Data Processing Report and Accounting Department Report calendars at Exhibits 14-d and e. In addition, the Controller should personally maintain an Accounting Calendar as seen at Exhibit 11-b. The authority in the FEI definition is Planning for Control and Reporting and Interpreting. The tool to be sure that nothing slips through the cracks is the Accounting Calendar.

> **Helpful Hint**: Prepare this on a monthly basis, as exhibited, rather than using a repetitive tickler file calendar. This saves you the trouble of re-tickling the same items each month. Instead, consult the accounting calendar daily.
> **Caution**: Do not assign the perusal of this calendar to subordinates. They are not expected to have the same sense of responsibility that you have. They forget; there are terminations—Do It Yourself! It insures that *all* major areas of responsibility will be handled on time.

ANNUAL REPORT AND MEETING

The second Treasurership FEI function is Investor Relations. This specifies the responsibility for invesmtent bankers, financial analysts and shareholder liaison. The Proxy Statement, Notice of Annual Meeting and Annual Report are specific to the acquittal of that responsibility.

The Treasurer, while directly in charge, may work with or through the company's advertising agency, legal staff, outside counsel, or internal advertising department in preparing the Annual Report, and with the Office Services Department in arranging a well-planned annual meeting.

> **Helpful Hint**: If time and economy in preparation are key, a financial printer will provide a better payoff than a commercial printer. They will do layout and advise on the legal requirement for size of type.
> **Annual Report Tip**: The SEC's requirements for publication of reports and filing with

the SEC are found in SEC Regulations 14a and 14c under the Securities Exchange Act of 1934.

AUDITS, EXTERNAL

The Controller is the fulcrum between the independent auditors and the company. This responsibility is derived from the FEI defined functions of Planning for Control and Reporting and Interpreting.

The differences between the inside or operational audit and the outside or external audit are explained in Chapter 10. Despite the differences, the Controller is responsible for both audits. Many people, investors and the public, may believe that the independent auditor's certificate is a guarantee that the independent auditor's certificate is a guarantee that the auditor has found the financial statements to be correct and reliable. Not so! The audit establishes fairness, consistency and adherence to principles, not correctness. Moreover, management, through the Controller's staff, is fully responsible for the company's financial statements, not the outside accountants.

> **Note This Difference**: The outside auditor will use care, diligence and training in his audit. However, it is an audit of the Controller's internally generated statements, reflecting the efficacy of the systems, procedures, internal auditing, and internal control established by the company Controller.

In his relationship to the outside accountants, the Controller should:

- Be friendly and cooperative.

- Provide complete access to all books, data, contracts, reports.

- Explain the system of internal check and control.

- Present an overview of operating systems and procedures.

- Establish a chain of communication between the auditors and his staff.

- Never question the reasons or motives for the auditor's review of any records.

- Maintain a cordial but aloof social relationship, to avoid impugning the auditor's independence.

Audits of public companies are required by stock exchanges, the SEC, regulatory agencies, banks and other creditors. Even where there is no legal need for an external audit, the company should have one. Try this. . . .

> **Helpful Hint**: Well-managed companies, no matter how small, would do well to have an annual, independent audit. This may prevent fraud, will verify the actual reported income, will confirm the values of the major assets such as inventory and receivables, and will give banks, lenders, major stockholders, and prospective buyers of the business (you may someday decide to sell out) confidence in the management and accuracy of the reported figures. The cost of the outside audit is a small cost compared to the benefit of the confidence level obtained.

An adjunct to the external audit is the formation of an Audit Committee within the company. If possible, this should be composed of, or at least chaired by, outside directors. The Controller should not be a part of the committee but will be invited to comment at most meetings. The duties of the committee are:

1. Meet with independent CPA's before the annual audit to discuss the general scope of the audit and to firm up the audit engagement memorandum.

2. Meet with independent CPA's after the annual audit to review the certified financial statements and their management internal control letter.

3. Meet with independent CPA's at periodic intervals, to discuss interim quarterly reviews and FASB statements, interpretations, and proposals. Review the quality and depth of the company's accounting and financial departments.

4. Monitor the company's internal control systems through:
   a. Meetings with the internal audit manager to discuss his programs and findings.
   b. Visit branches or other locations to discuss accounting and internal controls.
   c. Meet with the Controller to discuss internal controls, recommendations of the independent CPA's in their management control letter, and alternative accounting policies.

5. Recommend the independent auditors for submission to voting approval by stockholders at the annual meeting.

6. Select among alternative accounting policies.

7. Review officers' expense account reimbursements.

8. Review and approve bank account signatories, or recommend such approvals to the banking committee.

9. Provide ready access to the board of directors for the company's independent CPA's and its internal auditors.

10. Report to the board of directors concerning the work of the committee and its findings.

11. Keep the size of the committee at three members to prevent it from becoming unwieldy, and rotate one member every two or three years to bring a fresh approach to the committee.

BENEFIT PROGRAMS

Where there is no company personnel department, the administration of employee insurance and benefit programs may fall to the Treasurer or Controller. The Treasurer's authority derives from the broad Insurance function in the FEI definition, although that responsibility for insurance coverage is usually identified with corporate assets or casualty protection. The Controller, likewise, has an insurance responsibility under the Protection of Assets function. The organization, the employees, are certainly the company's most valuable asset. The Treasurer has further involvement through his broad Investment function, when funds from pension trusts are invested.

The usual types of employee benefit programs are:

1. *Employee Stock Ownership Trusts*—The trust borrows funds from a bank to invest in company stock. The company makes contributions to the trust which are used to repay the bank loans. The company's contributions are tax deductible and are not taxed to the trust. The company receives an additional 1% investment tax credit on its trust investment. Up to 15% of payrolls may be contributed. Some companies use this device to refinance existing bank loans, thereby obtaining a tax deduction for the loan repayment. It is a good device where the company has no objection to earnings dilution through stock give-aways.

2. *Employee Stock Purchase Plans*—The employee subscribes to company stock up to 10% of his wages, payable through payroll deductions over a two-year period. The price he pays may be as low as 85% of the market value on the date he subscribes or at the end of the payroll deduction period. There is no tax effect to the company or the employee on the up to 15% spread. He may withdraw from the plan at any time and receive the return of his payroll deductions, with interest. This type of plan is usually one with high employee participation since it is practically risk-free. It provides a built-in profit or a certain return on savings. The plans are Qualified under the Internal Revenue Code.

3. *Executive Compensation*—This includes non-salaried benefits to high-tax-bracket executives. The benefits include educational trusts, company cars, life insurance (over $50,000 under Sec. 79 of the Code), medical programs, investment and financial advisory services and liberal expense accounts.

4. *Options*—Both Qualified and Non-Qualified Options are discussed at Chapter 15.

5. *Payroll Deduction Plans*—These include non-contributory plans (no company participation) for employee Credit Unions (employees save, lend money to themselves at interest, and pay dividends to shareholders, all under federal and state regulation), treasury bonds purchase, or savings bank deposit. The company may contribute on a *pari passu* or some lesser basis.

6. *Profit Sharing Plans*—These plans represent one of the oldest types of benefit programs. They may include key managers or all employees. Payments may be in cash, stock, or in deferred compensation after retirement. Pension Plan contributions by the company may be geared to profits.

CUSTOMER RELATIONS

This marketing function may be assigned to the Controller when customer complaints and problems arise out of billing, issuance of credits, or processing of orders. The administration of the Order/Billing function is part of the FEI Planning for Control responsibility of the Controller and, in this case, the Controller might well assume the customer relations responsibility. Similarly, the Treasurer could assume it, if the major associated customer related problems arose from the Credit and Collection function.

> **Helpful Hint**: Where there are a great many customer complaints, solve the problem by logging in phone calls and letters, log them out to various departments for corrective action, and log in the ultimate response to the customer. Establish a standard time for correction, say 48 hours, and follow-up each logged entry for conformity to standard.

ENVIRONMENTAL ASPECTS

The affect on the business of economic, governmental and social forces, in short, the environment in which the company operates, should be appraised and interpreted by the Controller as a major FEI responsibility. The Treasurer, too, will find that these factors influence his performance with respect to Provision of Capital, Investor Relations, and Short-Term Financing.

A sub-set of this major function is *Compliance with Federal Regulations,* to include:

- Anti-discrimination.
- Fair-employment.
- Consumer protection.
- Federal aid.
- Occupational safety and health.
- Pollution Control.
- SEC disclosure.
- Truth in lending.
- Various state and federal laws on loans to officers and employees, directors' liability and officers' responsibilities.

> **Helpful Hint**: Prentice-Hall publishes an excellent booklet on *How to Get Help in Complying with New Federal Laws,* which covers most of these areas. Man & Manager of Plainview, N.Y. 11803 publishes two newsletters, twice a month: *The Businessman & the Law* (a timely report on actual legal cases and their effect on your day-to-day business decisions) and *Marketing and the Law* (a newsletter that reports and interprets court and government rulings affecting sales, promotion, advertising and the protection of your products and services).

A question will often arise as to what extent compliance or reporting is necessary to governmental agencies, when such reporting is for informational purposes only—in other words, the agency has no legal mandate requiring compliance. Typical are governmental studies on exports, imports, purchase order levels, manufacturing, capital expenditures and debt financing. Obviously, the studies are conducted to enable the agency to garner useful statistical information which will assist private industry and government for planning purposes. Each company must evaluate the validity of these requests in terms of its own posture and the cost involved in generating such reports. As in many types of circularizations, once you respond, you're on the list and will be solicited continuously.

> **Helpful Hint:** When responding to voluntary agency report requests, estimates are time-saving and are, in fact, encouraged by the agencies. A broad, ball-park response, on time, is considered better than none at all.

A second sub-set of this major function is *social disclosure.* The SEC is considering the extent to which corporations should be required, in Annual Reports, to report on employment conditions, environmental impacts and various other social consequences to their operations. Techniques for gathering and reporting information concerning the social impact of business on consumers, employees, and the general public should be encouraged by both the SEC and corporations. A special AICPA task force, studying social impacts, has recommended that such disclosures should be permitted, but not required, in sections of reports not covered by an auditor's opinion.

> **Helpful Hint:** Stockholders can be advised that considerable information on some areas of business performance relating to pollution and employment practices already exists as a result of government requirements, without the necessity of characterizing this in published financial reports.

The task force's comments were directed at measurement areas, attestation and presentation, rather than to the broad implications of social policy. The AICPA's accounting standards division will supply copies of the task force study on request.

Industry studies and comparative interpretations are an aspect of economic affects on the business. The Industry Comparison Graph at Exhibit 8-q is a typical result of such studies. Helpful in these areas are the publications of business services companies. Dun & Bradstreet offers a series of weekly, monthly, and some quarterly publications on the following trends and outlooks:

Business failures—comment and analysis.

Wholesale commodity prices—noting changes in 30 basic ones.

Wholesale food prices—comment on costs of 31 primary foods.

Bank clearings—volume changes in 26 major cities.

Trade review—interpreting retail, wholesale, manufacturing developments.

New business incorporations—comparative, by states.

Building permit values—totals from major cities.

Business men's expectations—summary of nationwide interviews.

These, augmented by industry-wide studies, can provide the Treasurer and Controller with a sufficient base for economic interpretation. Industry statistics are available from:

> Prentice-Hall: *Almanac of Business and Industrial Financial Ratios,* by Leo Troy.

Dun & Bradstreet: *Key Business Ratios* (from 125 lines of retailing, whole-saling, manufacturing and construction).

and from many banks, who supply comparative ratio studies on specific industries. The Bank of New York, for example, has available an excellent study on the Sales Finance Company, giving pertinent ratios for that industry, particularly related to percentages of receivables and outstandings. The more general industry studies offer percentages on:

- Cost of goods sold.
- Gross margin.
- Compensation of officers.
- Rent paid on business property.
- Repairs.
- Bad debts.
- Interest paid.
- Taxes paid.
- Amortization, depletion and depreciation.
- Advertising.
- Pension and other employee benefit plans.

Carrying industry aspects one step further, the Treasurer and Controller should study the *macroeconomics* effect of current situations on the business. A knowledge of:

- The level of economic activity
- Consumption versus savings
- Level of Investment.
- The supply of money
- Federal monetary control
- Fiscal and budgetary policies
- Economic fluctuations and growth
- Effects of overseas trade
- Economic forecasting
- Forecasting product demand

can be related to your industry and business to aid in effective short- and long-range planning. The AICPA has published a 20-24 hour self-study course to help one understand these factors and thus improve financial planning, called *Macroeconomics and Company Planning.*

INTERNAL CONTROL

The Controller, through the Protection of Assets FEI function, has the overall internal control responsibility, and the Treasurer, through the Banking and Custody function, the responsiblity for cash control.

Internal check and control, sometimes called automatic auditing, augments the internal, operational audit described in the previous chapter. The efficacy of the system of internal control is measured and reported on by the external auditors (See page 144.

The techniques of internal check and control are as varied as there are businesses. The following steps, however, are inherent in most good internal control systems:

1. Accounts receivable controls—include order entry, billing, credit adjustment, and application of cash receipts (see Chapter 3 for details).

2. Division of Responsibility—consists of subdividing work so that no single individual has complete control over the physical asset, recording, or summarizing of the account involved.

3. Work Flow Verification—provides that one employee, usually in a different department, or acting independently, carries forward the work of the previous employee and, in so doing, automatically verifies it, without duplicating it.

For Example: Individual cash receipts from customers are posted by one employee; all checks are totaled and deposited by a second employee, and a third verifies that the individual totals of all customers posted by the first, equal the deposit of the second.

4. Protection of Work—means providing mechanical aids to deter fraud (a check writer to prevent check raising), as well as physical facilities (a locked computer room to prevent tampering with program controls).

Case in Point: A company did not lock up its customer files each evening. An employee photocopied customer names and sold them to a former, disgruntled salesman who contacted each customer, cut prices and succeeded in poaching most of the accounts. A simple locked file could have avoided a disaster.

5. Supervision—is indigenous to good internal control. The best system of internal check will fail unless properly supervised.

6. Work Duty Specification—the written requirements and the "how-to" of each job should be prepared and kept current for each job. Internal control cautions should be a part of such specifications.

7. Vacations and Job Rotation—should be a requirement. Do not offer pay in lieu of vacation. Frauds are discovered during absences or job changes.

Helpful Hint: Job rotation also provides additional trained employees, to help out during sickness, strikes, or terminations—prevents shut-downs.

8. Internal Audit—described in Chapter 10, the Operational Audit, verifies that the systems and procedures comprising the internal control system are working.

9. Outside Audit—serves as an independent appraisal of the efficacy of the system of internal control, helps to detect and prevent fraud, and is almost the only deterrent to fraud at higher level, by officers and executives.

10. Bonding—when all else fails, provides protections against most business frauds, including theft, embezzlement, and valuable records. Small losses need not be covered, but catastrophes can be averted (See page 66).

INVENTORY TAKING AND CONTROL

Physical inventories are taken to:

• Prevent fraud.

• Verify the accuracy of perpetual inventories.

• Verify shrinkage percentages and computed gross profit margins.

The Controller's authority for inventory taking is derived from the FEI functions of Reporting and Interpreting and the Protection of Assets.

Inventory taking is an element of internal control, and like systems of internal control, the methods for inventory taking vary with the type of business. The following characteristics are essential to good inventory taking:

1. Cycle count—where possible, to avoid having to take one massive inventory at year end.

2. Count twice—whether on cycle or periodically. Once a year is too long to wait to determine whether recorded profits are accurate, to ascertain that there is no fraud or inventory loss.

3. Announce in advance—30 to 45 days, to allow locations time to schedule and plan, arrange stock and employ counters.

4. Send written instructions—on the techniques to be used, with the advance announcement, to provide for a uniform inventory taking. Include uniform forms and schedules.

5. Train and send observers—to key locations. This will assure that the proper techniques are used and an accurate inventory is taken.

6. Pre-print items to be taken—rather than leaving it up to each location to determine whether something is inventory.

   For example: Are tools inventory or assets; do we count shipping supplies?

7. Count twice—or verify all high value items.

8. Log in—inventory schedules from all locations, to be sure none are missing, and log out all costed and extended completed schedules, for the same reason.

9. Establish verification edits—to recheck specified quantities, costs, extensions and footings.

Inventory Control is further gained through inventory analysis which, in the case of many items, requires a computerized assist. Reports should be prepared to:

- Analyze inventory investment through usage distribution reports.
- Identify imbalances in the inventory through inventory turnovers.
- Evaluate the levels of customer service at each inventory segment.
- Examine both direct and indirect inventory costs.

The technique to accomplish this control is as follows:

- Survey inventory records and determine the adequacy of of available data and the probability of obtaining useful results.
- If adequate data does not exist, begin to create it and to accumulate meaningful information for future analysis.
- Take into effect abnormalities as to lead time, cyclical patterns of demand, unusual cost.
- Select random samples and gather data as follows:

  a. Classify by dollar value of usage and level carried.
  b. Obtain amount of investment in slow-moving stock and turnover times.
  c. Evaluate inventory controls, ordering techniques, and and areas of improvement.
  d. Obtain space requirements and how well they are utilized.

After analyzing the resultant reports, the following gains can be expected:

a. The size of the inventory investment can be reduced.

b. The balance of inventories can be improved.

c. Customers will receive better service.

d. Costs, both direct and indirect, can be reduced.

e. Better inventory control procedures will be established.

LEGAL LIAISON

The responsibility for the interrelationships between the company and corporate counsel is not specific to the FEI financial definitions. Where house counsel does not exist, these relationships are often assigned to a specific officer, most usually the Treasurer or the Controller. The Controller's authority derives from the Evaluating and Consulting function ". . . . concerning any phase of the operation of the business as it relates to the attainment of objectives. . . ." The Treasurer's authority is related to his Investor Relations function, in that his maintainance of a market for the company's securities and ". . . . adequate liaison with investment bankers, financial analysts and shareholders," carries with it the need for legal liaison.

The Corporate Policy Manual (see page 107) should specify the responsibility for legal liaison under the caption Law Suits or Legal Review. This should clearly indicate:

- Who initiates legal contacts.

- Who responds to summonses or legal letters.

- Who signs contracts (and contracts need to be defined).

Such a statement of policy is necessary to avoid unauthorized and continuing legal expenses. These legal actions sometimes take years to develop and some legal firms bill only at the end of the case. More important, legal action results in counter-actions and the effect on the corporation can be significant. This should be controlled, therefore, on the higher management levels.

LOANS TO EMPLOYEES

Loans to officers and employees may be subject to state, federal, corporate charter, banking, SEC, and accounting rules and principles. They should not, therefore, be handled through normal disbursing channels as with travel advances or expense reimbursements. A travel advance, not supported quickly by an expense report, becomes, in effect, a loan to the employee which should become the Treasurer's responsibility. The Treasurer's authority is defined by the FEI under the Banking and Custody and Credit and Collections functions.

Each employee's loan should be supported by a demand note receivable, and a Loan Agreement Letter, shown as Exhibit 11-c. The terms of the letter agreement will be such to protect the company in terms of the various rules and principles cited above. The exhibited letter contains the following features:

- The loan is payable on demand.

- The purpose of the loan is personal and not for stock purchases.

- Stock owned or to be purchased will be held as collateral.

- A repayment schedule is specified, subject to call on demand by the company, at any time.

- A non-usurious interest rate is specified.

- Authorization for repayment through payroll deduction is given.

MANAGING PEOPLE

Every manager, whatever his position with the company, has a responsibility to the people he manages—to bring out the best in them, to permit them to fulfill the requirements of their jobs with maximum effectiveness, to recognize their potential for promotion—all with a view toward simplifying attainment of the corporate profit objectives..

Managing people requires structuring a proper operational framework, through the use of Position Descriptions, Organizational Charts, Standard Operating Procedures, Policy Manuals and other administrative aids as described in Chapter 7. Everyone must know what his job is, to whom he reports, and what is expected of him.

Personnel Management is discussed in some detail in Chapter 14 under Controlling the Data Processing Function. The principles set forth, a management philosophy, setting a management example, and management by objectives, are applicable, equally, to the Treasurer's and Controller's management of other departments and people reporting to them.

MANAGEMENT PHILOSOPHY

While the development of a management philosophy is an element of managing people, it is of concomitant importance in the Controller's functions of Planning for Control and Reporting and Interpreting. The Plan for control and the formulation of reporting policies should be shaped, in tone and style, by the Controller's philosophy of management which will be attuned to that of the corporate hegemony, as it relates to his own field of control. There are three rudimentary requirements to developing a management philosophy:

1. *Artistry*—The Controller must acquire, possess, and demonstrate a superb command of his craft. He will bring to his profession an educational background in accounting, finance, taxes, and management. He will hone this with continuing professional educatational courses given by local chapters of his state CPA society or the National Association of Accountants. He will maintain proficiency by extensive reading of:

    a. *The Journal of Accountancy*—published by the AICPA and oriented to an overview of the profession.

    b. *Management Accounting*—published by the NAA, and pointed to specific technical accounting areas.

    c. FASB releases—published by the Financial Accounting Standards Board, consisting of exposure drafts of discussion memoranda, interpretations and pronouncements relating to accounting principles.

    Helpful Hint: The FASB publishes a periodic Status Report, and the AICPA, *The CPA Letter,* a semi-monthly news report for members of the AICPA. Each is in pamphlet form, approximately four pages, and deals with current and projected studies, SEC trends in accounting, auditing standards, management advisory service issues and other current developments.

    d. *The Accounting Review*—a quarterly publication of the American Accounting

Association, consisting of academic treatments of theoretical problems in accounting—presenting a thorough analysis of current issues in the profession.

e. *The Financial Executive*—published by the Financial Executives Institute, dealing with current issues of interest to the financial manager, and augmented with position papers on SEC and accounting proposals by the profession or other regulatory agencies.

f. SEC Releases—distributed to registered companies, directly by the SEC. These releases are proposals for changes and Accounting Series Releases, ASR's, initiating changes.

g. Monthly business magazines—Any one of several business monthlies will keep the Controller abreast of current business developments and practices, will demonstrate the applicability of the technical positions previously studied in a through f. Typical are *Forbes, Business Week, Dun's Review, U.S. News* and *World Report, Finance.*

h. Business dailies—*The Wall Street Journal* or *Journal of Commerce* provide on-the-spot information on current trends and developments.

This would appear to be a massive amount of reading, but it is not. Each publication need only be scanned for special articles of interest and those often can be scanned or sight-read for pertinent matter. See page 128 for tax literature sources.

This reading will be put to good use in thousands of ways—during the conduct of the year-end audit, in formulating interim accounting policies, in creating new operating techniques and evaluating old ones. They are the colors on the Controller's palette with which he appoints the operating picture.

2. *Creativity*—The artistry of the Controller must express itself, not in a me-too approach to management, but with originality. One cannot copy systems, procedures, forms and operating techniques from other companies, even competitors. Every business is different, and every organization, composed of individuals, is different. The successful Controller will use his artistry as a departure point from which to create a Plan of operations which is unique and suitable to his company.

3. *Excitement*—The artistic and creative Controller will almost certainly, without trying, engender an enthusiasm and excitement in his company which breeds success. The Controller or Treasurer, using the management accounting techniques described in these chapters, is surely as innovative and original in his planning and fruition of the corporate Plan as any novelist, painter, or film-maker.

> **Helpful Hint**: Hold monthly staff meetings with your people to apprise them of plans and current developments, to keep them enthused and excited about the job everyone is doing. One-on-one meetings during the month aren't as good. They're usually too concerned with specific operating details and exigencies of the moment.

PRODUCT PRICING CONTROL

The pricing responsibility for products is found in the FEI Controllership functions definitions under the Planning for Control heading, "cost standards," and in the Evaluating and Consulting function, as costs relate to pricing policies.

Inherent in this responsibility are the interrelationships between accounting, marketing, and selling divisions. Procedures must be designed to coordinate all these areas of the business, to supply them with proper costing information and to obtain the necessary approvals before publishing any prices.

One such procedure is shown at Exhibit 11-d. It is characterized by a smooth flow of information from the Purchasing Department, which initiates the cost change, to Order/Billing Department, which codes the product for data processing purposes, to the Accounting Department, which establishes pricing at standard mark-ups, to Marketing Product Managers who review and recommend prices, to appropriate officers who review the recommendations of marketing and accounting in light of corporate objectives, back to Accounting for distribution of approved prices to all departments, to Data Processing Department to revise related DP files, to Customer Service Department for Price Book issuance, to Product Managers for marketing circularization, and to customers.

Product pricing control is the "top-line" in generating profits. A coordinated procedure, administered by the Controller, is essential to assuring that these top-line profits are brought home.

PROFIT IMPROVEMENT PROGRAMS

Sometimes called PIP, cost reduction, cost control, or plain cost cutting, these programs are continuous with some companies, explosions with others. The determination as to whether they are ongoing or sporadic will depend on the company and its officers' philosophy of management.

The best program is probably a compromise between the two methods. Cost controls need to be maintained on a continuing basis. But there is slippage in every system, and a periodic tightening of controls will always produce savings.

The origination, implementation, control, and reporting of these profit improvement programs is usually assigned to the Controller and should, in fact, be initiated by him independently. Most of the FEI defined functions serve as the authority for the Controller's role in PIP—Planning for Control (procedures to effectuate the plan), Reporting and Interpreting (the coordination of systems and procedures), Evaluating and Consulting (the attainment of objectives and the effectiveness of policies), and the Protection of Assets (through internal control, internal auditing).

The following areas should be reviewed in cost control programs:

1. Advertising and promotion—may be discontinued with no deleterious effects for brief periods of time. Promotional work in the securities and investor relation area may also be curtailed.

2. Branch offices—or decentralized independent operations may be discontinued if they are direct loss operations. These are sometimes maintained for marketing purposes, to hold a national posture or provide a network of offices, which may be unnecessary in a short-run period.

3. Cafeteria operations—are usually provided for employees at a loss. These can be closed, sandwich machines substituted, or the operation of the cafeteria may be

contracted-out to an independent service on a fixed-fee basis, thereby eliminating the loss. Problems such as food shortages and employee turnover are eliminated.

4. Centralized purchasing—may be employeed where the company has many locations. A low limit, say $100, could be established and only items under that limit may be purchased in the local office. This procedure submits the over $100 purchase order to closer centralized (and less involved) scrutiny. Quantities and even need can be independently evaluated. There may be a personnel savings—a central office can do the same job with fewer people than many independent offices.

5. Collections—of accounts receivable may usually be decentralized without adding people. Most such work is done on the phone, at a significant saving in the telephone cost, if done through the local office. Collection staff need not be added since regular order takers may be trained to check credit lists or aged trial balances, and to obtain collections, on the same phone call in which the order is placed.

6. Commissions—for salesmen, may be restructured, raising them, and eliminating base salary or guaranteed draw. This will tend to shake out the unproductive salesmen more quickly and to compensate the big producers more highly. Unit selling cost per man will be reduced.

7. Compensation policy—should be reviewed with regard to having quotas or bonus programs for salesmen and their managers. These programs work better in an expanding economy, but then, so do any programs. Quotas and bonuses can be eliminated at all levels and, instead, profit sharing can be substituted to give salesmen and managers a share in profits which equals last year's bonus (if the same level of profits is at least achieved), and also gives them 50% of the increase in net income (or any desired percentage), before such profit sharing. This type of program, if properly structured, should eliminate bonuses and extra commissions during periods when the company's profits are declining, due to disparities in product mix sales.

8. Contests—for salesmen or classes of customers may be eliminated with no short-run effect. Or, national contests (at high cost) may be eliminated in favor of less expensive local contests.

9. Demonstration materials—and free give-aways used by salesmen may be eliminated, or more carefully doled out by supervisors. Total amounts should be budgeted at lower levels.

10. District offices—and zone or outlying staff offices may be closed and operated out of other local sales offices. Some managers try to become empire builders, creating their own sphere of control—separate staff and offices which often duplicate other corporate functions.

11. Freight charges—may be raised to more than offset the increase in freight costs. In many cases, freight and delivery charges are intended to be borne by the customer but they are not, due to creeping increases in freight costs which are accepted at lower levels and not called to management's attention. Freight companies do not send out formal notices of rate increases—they just happen.

12. Inventory controls—are a continuous and on-going program, as discussed on

page 162. Costs are controlled and profits improved by good inventory taking and good inventory management. However, some immediate steps can be taken if there are inventory losses. A watchman can be hired for sensitive areas during working hours and alarm systems connected to detective services installed for night hours. One watchman can watch a vast inventory area using in-house television monitoring. If necessary, undercover men can be used to staff working crews to protect against mysterious disappearances of inventory. An immediate warehouse security system should be installed—see Exhibit 10-j, to prevent mysterious disappearance. Establish an immediate perpetual inventory control, a manual procedure, wherein the inventory clerk reports not to the warehouse manager, but to the accounting manager. He should control the location and picking of each order and spot-check and cycle-count inventories.

13. Legal costs—may be reduced by negotiating issues instead of litigating them. Settle, don't sue, in the short-run to keep costs down. Hold off new issues until a later time—patent infringement suits and anti-trust issues. Institute a legal liaison procedure and policy as described at page 164.

14. Study the size of the product line. Reduce it by eliminating loss items and leaders, which may not be necessary in the near term.

15. Mail and messenger service—may be curtailed with no loss in revenues. Mail once a day instead of picking up several times in the morning and afternoon. Eliminate messengers, limousines, and special delivery services.

16. Office machines—should be examined for effective utilization. Word processing units (automatic editing typewriters) can save 25% of a secretary's time. Photo copy machines can replace carbon paper and duplicate typing at less cost. Dictating machines, even inexpensive portable tape recorders, can save the substantial time spent by an author and secretary in personal dictation.

17. Office temporaries—should not be authorized and should be eliminated in interim periods of cost reduction. Regular staff will handle the work if it needs to be done.

18. Order handling—can be streamlined to eliminate main office edits and reviews. Just give the order a cursory check and process it. Put teeth in this by penalizing salesmen for errors they make on the order. This can save personnel.

19. Office services—may be curtailed in central locations. Eliminate private secretaries in favor of a secretarial and typing pool.

Helpful Hint: This saves having to hire a new secretary every time a new managerial job is created. You simply don't have secretaries, using the pool instead.

Failing this extreme, double-up or quadruple-up on the use of secretaries, several managers sharing. Share by location of office, rather than division or type of work.

Other office service areas—clean and maintain premises twice weekly, instead of daily; have individual department heads do their own interviewing for new hires, by-passing personnel; examine dial 9 or centrex telephone systems to save on phone operators.

20. Payroll costs—may be reduced by simplifying payroll systems (see Zero Balance

Accounts and Imprest and Color-coded Accounts in Chapter I). Reduce payroll taxes by considering payments as consulting fees instead of payroll. Also, determine that portion of a salesman's pay and earnings which is attributable to travel expenses, and therefore not subject to withholding or payroll taxes as wages. Consider your cost of handling payroll check writing and record keeping. Perhaps an outside payroll service will be more economical. This should be reviewed periodically, as the cost effectiveness will change with the type and amount of payrolls and number of people.

Other payroll saving steps: Freeze wages over a limit, say $12,500 per year; grant wage increases under that limit only once each year, whether from merit, annual, or promotion, and then subject to a percentage limit, say a range of 5% to 10%; Reduce salaries of key managers and officers by 10% to 20% if over $25,000 per year.

Helpful Hint: Partially offset payroll reductions with company paid insurance benefits. Under Sec. 79 of the IRC company paid term insurance in amounts over $50,000 a year is taxable to the employee, but at substantially lower than regular income tax rates. This may be tied to insurance with a cash surrender value which will exceed the employee's income tax. The company, thus, will obtain a tax deductible expense, in full, and the employee will pay less tax. This makes it possible to reduce his salary and offset it, partially, with an insurance benefit increase.

Helpful Hint: Avoid personnel recruitment costs on hiring new or replacement employees by advancing agency fees and then recovering this from the employee over a six-month period, through payroll reductions. Caution—some states do not permit such deductions unless they are an employee loan being repaid. Exhibit 11-e, Authorization for Repayment of Employee Loans will satisfy this requirement in most states.

Freeze new hires; require two approvals on any replacements; Review each individual job with his superior and determine the necessity for that job (there is probably 10% to 20% inefficiency built into every organization that does not practice continuing cost control); eliminate all overtime.

21. Petty cash—may be reduced in outlying offices by scheduling prompt central payments. The reduced fund results in reduced expenditures.

22. Postage—can be budgeted at 80% of the previous run rate. Discontinue the use of air mail or special delivery. Batch mail to repetitive locations; mail only once a day; defer direct mail programs.

23. Price increases—should be effected, selectively, to pass on appropriate cost increases to customers. This requires good Product Pricing Control as evidenced by the procedure at Exhibit 11-d, to avoid cost increases creeping through without pricing actions.

24. Relocations—of company personnel from one location to another should be avoided. Relocation policy includes personnel benefits such as air fare to search for a home, home closing costs, fixing up costs, costs and losses of moving from the old home, and interim hotel expenses. These far exceed the cost of hiring someone new in the immediate location. The benefit of the experienced employee in the relocated job is a short-lived one (in six months the new

employee is experienced) and may be considerably offset by hiring someone experienced in the same industry.

25. Reports—which no one wants are often generated. See the report study evaluation discussed on page 114 and detailed on page 202. With such a study, many reports may be eliminated.

Reporting Hint: Discontinue distribution of some reports which you suspect are not needed. See whether you get any complaints after two successive periods of non-distribution. If not, write the recipients and "tell them" you have discontinued the report due to lack of need. Always give an alternate source of the information, perhaps in another format.

26. Second source—should be considered from suppliers. This may result in lower prices or reduced quantity ordering requirements. If quantities are large enough, purchases can be made from two sources, with the original vendor reducing his price to meet the second source. Alternatively, single sourcing may result in savings when two sources are being used to divide up insufficient quantities.

27. Service support functions—may be discontinued. This may include goodwill ambassadors, institutional showrooms, public relations personnel and services, or customer relations people who follow-up on the salesmen. All will result in short-run savings, but the cost of discontinuing these services and then restarting them may obviate their discontinuance.

28. Severance policy—should be defined, in writing, for terminated employees, particularly at times of lay-offs. Superiors tend to soften the blow with extra severance pay.

Helpful Hint: Many companies pay one week of severance for each year of service, with a minimum of one week and a maximum of two months. Severance is a company option, not an employee right, and its grant should depend on the employee's cooperation and attitude.

29. Shipping and distribution costs—should be studied by qualified in-house people or outside professionals, every several years or when the company changes its distribution methods. Outside consulting firms will perform the initial analysis and teach future analyses to company personnel so that distribution costs may be monitored internally. Methods of shipping, routing, and warehousing are studied, together with effective space utilization for various types of inventories. In short, the "logistics" of shipping and distribution are studied. The result may be a shifting of inventories, storage in different locations, shipping in carload lots or containers, drop-shipping from vendors to customers, storage in bonded warehouses, shifting to consignment sales—but whatever the change, it will be cost-effective.

30. Staff functions—much like service support functions, may be reviewed and reduced or eliminated. These would include levels of administrative or marketing management which are not direct to the operation. For example, four salesmen may have a team leader; four team leaders may report to a sales manager; two sales managers may report to a general manager. All levels between salesman and general manager could be eliminated for limited periods

without reducing sales effectiveness. Many headquarters functions such as staff assistants, liaison managers, administrative assistants, secretaries, assistant supervisors, product managers, assistants to, are performing functions which could be reduced or discontinued without affecting the profit objective in the near term, and many of them are probably doing work which their superiors should be doing, or could be doing in tight times.

31. Sundry expenses—are a catch-all category in any business used to record those expenses which are not able to be classified in the chart of accounts, as it presently exists. Sundry expenses are hard to analyze and control when they are improperly recorded this way. Eliminate the caption. When an item arises that does not fit the chart of accounts, add a caption to the chart which does fit. Provide for numbering expansion in the chart of accounts as shown in Exhibit 6-c and discussed on page 96.

32. Telephone and Telex expenses—are one of the most fruitful areas for cost control. Telex messenges should be typed in advance and sent, using tapes, at maximum speeds. Telexes may be eliminated by using telephone (WATS lines), facsimile devices, or magnetic tape transmission over dial-up phone lines to central switching terminals. The efficacy of these systems depends on the volume of transmissions and the need for speed and accuracy.

Magnetic tape transmissions off word-processing equipment may offer side benefits of being able to store correspondence on tape, rather than in traditional files, as described in Chapter 13 on records retention.

Special self-dial systems may be used in place of operator assisted telephone service. These are dial 7 or 9 systems, and Centrex systems, which completely by-pass the operator. Long-distance calls are blocked out on these systems. Using a central in-house operator, only, for long-distance keeps better control. Use a long-distance log and have the employee's supervisor initial every call; budget long-distance calls at 80% of prior levels; charge department heads 25¢ on each dollar in excess of the budgeted levels (do it as a contest to get cooperation, with the winner getting all contributions from the losers); eliminate inter-branch phone calls; when calls must be made, direct dial to save 30% of the cost of the call if operator assisted; require messages to be written, not phoned, to outlying offices; use the telex in lieu of the phone; remove instruments from every desk—keep only one or two in a department; eliminate private wires and telephone numbers unless they fit in to the phone system being used. Managers and executives abuse private numbers more than anyone; use WATS lines if you have many short calls in specific covered areas; require supervisors to personally sign every telex message before it is sent.

The phone company is a regulated utility. It makes a guaranteed profit. You don't!

33. Training expenses—may be curtailed or eliminated for brief periods, both in the selling and administrative areas. As a substitute, use on-the-job training. Have new salesmen trail experienced ones. Have administrative, technical and service personnel instructed in one step at a time, on-line, before proceeding to the next. Eliminate the costly travel and hotel expenses of central training courses; substitute cassette tape training programs augmented with on-location in-house

television or film projectors; design programmed learning courses, consisting of successive question and answer steps.

Helpful Hint: Develop a competent salary level and benefits program to eliminate most employee turnover. This will keep training costs down for new employees and permit them to be trained on-the-job.

34. Travel expenses—require special control. Employees often like to travel, create trips, and end up visiting friends and family, and as a side benefit, making a profit on their per-diem expenses.

    Try These Steps: Budget travel at 80% of previous levels; require a Travel Authorization (Exhibit 11-f) from all employees who do not customarily travel as a part of their jobs; require two levels of approval on employees who do customarily travel, one of which must be the division manager; do not permit approvers to delegate approving authority to secretaries or subordinates; discontinue all credit cards; do not pay meal expenses unless the travel is overnight; specify by title only those who are permitted to entertain; do not authorize or reimburse company employees who entertain other company employees—thus, eliminate working lunches or dinners; use a uniform Statement of Reimbursable Expenses form (Exhibit 11-g), which sets out some of the rules and limitations, and back these up with a written travel procedure.

35. Typing—of reports, interoffice memos and schedules can be reduced substantially, to take the load off the typing pool. Require: interoffice memos to be hand written; reports are not typed unless for external or Board submission; all schedules are to be hand written. Save the time to prepare, type, and proofread, when a single preparation will achieve the same result.

    Answer correspondence by replying directly on the same letter, photocopying it, and returning the original, or use snap-out carbon type speed memos. The degree of clarity and formality obtained on typewritten letters, for unimportant purposes, is unnecessary and costly.

SECURITY ANALYSTS AND STOCKHOLDERS

The Treasurer, through his FEI function of Investor Relations, has the responsibility to maintain an adequate market in his company's securities. Contacts with analysts and shareholders, however, are subject to disclosure rules and insider information rules as set forth by the SEC. In general, projections of sales and profits should not be released to anyone unless they are released to everyone. Analysts, however, and this may include bankers, investors or shareholders, may require detailed information about the company's operations before making substantial investments in its stock. Specific information may be given as to production and selling levels in units, but no total volume or profit projections should be made unless you are prepared to disseminate these to the entire financial community (and face the embarrassment and possible consequences of not meeting these projections). For your protection, keep a written record of everything you say to an analyst and file it as a permanent record.

The record may be maintained simply on the Security Analysts Report shown at Exhibit 11-h.

UNREASONABLE ACCUMULATION OF EARNINGS

The IRS imposes an accumulated earnings tax, really a heavy penalty, on a corporation, with high cost to its key people, for allowing earnings to accumulate beyond the "reasonable needs" of the business. This is a punitive tax of up to 38½% on the corporation, with additional penalities to its officer and director shareholders. The penalty is often imposed and most often accepted by the corporation, without litigation. Most corporations do not have a defense and prefer to keep minority shareholders from suing officers and directors to reimburse the corporation out of their own funds for these penalties. There is no immunity to any corporation, but smaller and close-held ones are particularly exposed, these being the ones which try to avoid paying out dividends to save the principal shareholders income taxes.

The Controller is responsible for Tax Administration as a major FEI function. This includes establishing tax policy and thus, legitimate avoidance of paying undue taxes. He has the additional responsibility of Protection of Assets, which would be dissipated through this penalty tax. The Treasurer, on his part, has the Investment responsibility, to invest the company's funds as required. It is surely a requirement to invest funds in a manner to avoid this punitive result.

The IRS has further ruled that the penalty tax is a Subtitle A tax on which the 5% negligence penalty can be imposed. More woe! But whether there is negligence will depend on the facts of each case.

In general, if you do not distribute retained earnings, you should have a written plan for their utilization, a back-up plan, written evidence why plans were not implemented (Board Meeting minutes are good), information that you tried to execute the plan, that retention was required by competition or banking money requirements, and that tax avoidance was not the principal consideration in retention.

The "Bardahl" business cycle formula defense has been effective for businesses with inventories. This formula has, similarly, been used to determine the operating capital needs during one business cycle of a service industry, in the motor freight business, without inventories. Exhibit 11-i demonstrates the Operating Capital Determination using the "Bardahl" formula defense against the penalty tax. Average receivables were used in the formula, rather than peak receivables, since it took no longer to collect larger receivables. Amounts due from officers, employees and shareholders could be included in the receivables if they are a legitimate business activity. Time allowance for payment of accounts payable must be taken into account.

BOTTOM-LINE BOOSTERS

The Treasurer, and mostly the Controller, are responsible for overseeing special administrative areas which are not specific to their defined functions. Juxtaposed to

SUPERVISING SPECIAL ADMINSTRATIVE AREAS

these specific duties are inherent responsibilities for the proper management of timed events through the use of the accounting calendar, the annual report and meeting, the coordination of external audits, the origination and administration of benefit programs, the possible assumption of even the customer relations function, and the evaluation of environmental, economic and social forces on the business.

The Treasurer must provide for automatic auditing through internal check and control and must protect the bottom-line through proper periodic inventory taking the control procedures. His contribution to corporate profits is expressed through control of legal matters, loans to employees, and, mostly, through his management of people and development of a management philosophy which will set the tone for operations, directly reflecting his artistry, creativity and excitement.

The Controller will establish product pricing control to prevent cost increases from slipping through the cracks, and he will examine the 35 ways to assure profit improvement through expense reduction programs. The Treasurer will deal with security analysts and stockholders to provide a ready market for the company's securities, without making inadequate disclosures, and both financial officers will protect the corporation against penalties for unreasonable accumulations of earnings through the use of written plans for earnings utilization, supported by proper documentary evidence as to their implementation and augmented by a formula calculation of the operating capital needed in the company.

Thus, the Controller and Treasurer will look beyond their specified tasks to determine the intrinsic responsibilities of their jobs. They will grasp those implied responsibilities with fervor and devotion, thereby assuring that even the less apparent facets of the business are under control and contribute to profits.

CHAPTER 12

The Art of Handling Mergers

and Acquisitions

THE Position Description of the Treasurer in "Treasurer's and Controller's Functions," provides under Organizational Relationships, that the Treasurer "Analyzes and (is) primarily responsible for negotiating the acquisition of companies brought to the Corporation's attention by the Executive Vice President." The definition of the Controller's and Treasurer's functions published by the FEI includes as a Treasurer's function the Provision of Capital and Investments, both of which embrace the acquisitions act.

Handling mergers and acquisitions is a special area of responsibility which would be properly included under that caption in the previous chapter. Due to its significance, however, the amount of dollars involved and the potential impact on future earnings, it is best treated as a separate subject. Every company, at some time in its history, either acquires or sells a company. Any evaluation of acquisitions relates, equally, to your company being the acquirer or acquiree. When an acquisition or divestiture does occur, the responsibility for its artful handling falls to the Treasurer or the Controller.

TAX CONSIDERATIONS

> **Rule of Thumb**: Never make an acquisition solely for tax reasons. There must always be a good business purpose. But always consider the tax effects to obtain the lowest present and future cost. Adverse tax implications need not negate a deal if the business purpose is met.
> **Seller's Rule of Thumb**: No deal can be made without a careful evaluation of tax considerations in determining net profit on the sale.

Inherent in these rules are opposite goals for the buyer and seller. What is tax deductible to the buyer is usually taxable to the seller and vice-versa. Since the buyer is usually the dominant party, larger than the seller, he must bring to the negotiations a delicate understanding of the seller's tax problems.

As discussed in Chapter 9 under the Philosophy of Responsibility as it relates to taxes, the Controller needs to have an overview of the entire tax situation and to spawn the good tax ideas. The experts can then structure the contract to achieve the desired tax result.

> **Avoid This Pitfall**: Do not structure the contract without expert tax advice. The Controller's tax knowledge is expected to be general, not specific in these areas. Tax laws require that T's be crossed and I's dotted. An inept contract can cause horrendous tax consequences.

Exhibit 12-a, Provisions of the Tax Law, lists those sections of the Code which relate to acquisitions and mergers. Each of these sections is discussed in the Prentice-Hall Federal Tax Service. The total reading consists of 70 pages for the 27 sections. A good course in home study would be to read a section a night, perhaps 2 to 3 pages. In 10 or 15 minutes a night, all pertinent areas of the Internal Revenue Code relating to acquisitions could be reviewed in a month.

REASONS FOR ACQUISITIONS

Companies acquire other companies for as many reasons as there are companies. A few of the most common reasons, and a brief discussion of each, follows:

1. New Products—Instead of developing your own new products through research and development, a company can be bought which has already developed the desired product.

2. Vertical or Horizontal Integration—Vertical integration is the purchase of companies from whom you buy or sell, thereby saving the profit which others normally make on your company. Horizontal integration involves companies making a different product but selling it within your industry, usually to the same customers. Cost savings are explicit in horizontal integration.

3. Personnel—A company may seek to buy a marketing force, a research capability, manufacturing expertise, or top management through an acquisition.

4. Profits—Acquisitions are often made of companies which have a good earnings track record or the potential for good earnings. The trick, here, obviously, is to discount those earnings at a yield which makes the acquisition feasible. You can't overpay for future earnings.

5. Tax Benefits—Under some circumstances, companies can be acquired which have net operating loss carry-forwards which can be utilized by the acquirer. This cannot be done if the primary purpose is the utilization of the tax losses, but given other benefits, the tax considerations could sweeten the purchase price and make for an easier acquisition. Exhibit 12-b lists the conditions in which tax losses may be utilized.

6. The Seller Must Sell—The death of an owner, with improper tax planning, may

force the sale by the deceased's estate. There are, often, time considerations which impel the estate to make a quick sale. The buyer may be getting a bargain purchase.

7. Realization of Goals—The buyer may simply be in a position to acquire a company in a field in which he has always wanted to be. This may be nothing more than the realization of early dreams.

8. Fixed Assets—As with personnel, a company may seek to buy the assets, physical plant or manufacturing facilities of the acquiree. This may be done because the assets cannot be built or purchased elsewhere for the equivalent cost, or because assets of this excellence cannot otherwise be obtained. This would pertain to the acquisition of a retail store with a preferred location, or a factory in a highly skilled labor area.

9. Listed Stock—A private company may desire to go public. One of the routes is acquisition of a smaller company, already listed. Similarly, "going private" may be accomplished through merger.

10. Diversification—While this may be accomplished to a limited degree through integration, the company may desire to protect future earnings by diversification of markets, product lines, and technology.

11. Future Benefit—Long-range planning may indicate a change in marketing effort to an industry which will grow at a greater rate than ours.

12. Balance Sheet Advantages—The seller may have a strong current ratio which, when consolidated with ours, would improve our position. Similarly, it may have a debt to equity ratio which, in consolidation, would improve ours.

13. Liquidity—Related to the balance sheet advantages, the seller may have cash, high receivables and inventory, a segment of the business which could be sold off—all of which he will sell to us for stock. This liquidity may be obtained at less cost than through the issuance of new stock or debt.

14. Source of Supply Maintenance—Related to integration, but usually done because of a supplier's weak financial condition. The company may acquire a supplier in distress. Or, a supplier may be acquired to prevent a competitor from obtaining it.

15. Market Protection—A distributor or dealer may decide to sell out. The new buyer might not buy our product and an acquisition might be indicated.

Word of Caution: Consider anti-trust regulations and restraint of trade. Obtain legal advice in these areas before acquiring any company.

EVALUATION OF ACQUISITIONS

The acquisition-minded company should, first, evaluate the above enumerated reasons and reduce to writing its acquisition goals. Through this technique, time will not be wasted on reviewing candidates which do not meet the corporate criteria.

The acquisition goals will vary for every company, but once established, they provide a quick checklist for evaluating a potential acquiree. If these broad goals are met, the acquisition evaluation may proceed. Exhibit 12-c, Acquisition Goals, is an example of a broad corporate statement in this area.

Having met the Acquisitions Goals requirement, a preliminary financial evaluation may then be prepared. This is a Schedule of Merger Analyses shown at Exhibit 12-d. The data is filled in based on an expectation of the type of agreement which would be reached. The schedule permits a quick determination of book value, earnings, working capital, return on investment, and market value increase after the merger. If the analysis indicates continuing dominance and increases in the other components, the evaluation may continue. During the course of negotiations, this schedule will again be completed, each time a new acquisition price is proposed during the course of the negotiations.

The conformity to Acquisition Goals and the Schedule of Merger Analyses may be completed without any contact with the seller. If these preliminary tests are passed, initial contact may then be made with the seller and the Acquisition Evaluation Checklist at Exhibit 12-e should be completed. This will present, on four brief pages, a summary of the acquisition for higher management review. It, together with the financial review in the Schedule of Merger Analyses, will enable top management to quickly determine whether to proceed with negotiations.

If the acquisition is to be pursued, a Financial-Operations Review should be initiated. A complete audit is performed by our independent accountants (sometimes our internal auditors). An operations review is performed by company personnel. Company personnel may be a corporate development department, an internal auditor, the Treasurer, Controller, or the manager of each of the departments being reviewed. All such reviews are evaluated by the Treasurer and Controller and the previously estimated purchase price is firmed up and presented to the seller.

DETERMINATION OF THE PRICE

A business is bought for future profits! All of the reasons for acquisitions propounded on page 177 have at their core the ultimate goal of increased profits.

Therefore, an attempt must be made to project future earnings and the rate of growth of these future earnings before a purchase price is determined.

> **Helpful Hint:** Since the purchase price depends on future earnings, and since the business is usually "new" to the purchaser, you should require the old owners to continue to manage the business for several years. Their continued management will minimize the risk of low earnings. The lower your risk, the more you can pay for the purchase.
>
> **Case in Point:** The owner of one business rejected a cash offer of $1 million in favor of receiving a payment of 5 times his annual profits, above a base, for 3 years. The former owner continued to manage the company during this "earn-out" period and ultimately received $2 million for his company via the earnings route.

The rationale for purchases based on an earn-out formula is an acceptable concept to most sellers. They can obtain a higher selling price for their company as a result of minimizing the buyer's risk and deferring a portion of the payment until earnings have been attained, earnings which they are in a position to control through their continued management of the operation.

Future earnings may be determined by:

1. Forecasting—using standard techniques to project earnings out for several years to be covered by the earn-out.

2. Projecting out prior years—this being a study of past earnings, with adjustments being made for known changes. In short, it assumes that future earnings will be the same as average past earnings. It is less accurate than the first method which takes into consideration future plans, the economy, new products, and the changing business environment.

Helpful Hint: The AICPA has prepared and published Guidelines for Systems for the Preparation of Financial Forecasts. It defines the differences between budgets, plans, goals, objectives, projections and forecasts and tells how to construct and monitor forecasts. A summary of these Guidelines is shown at Exhibit 12-f.

Once the forecasted or projected future profits are determined, Six Methods of Determining the Purchase Price are available. These are shown at Exhibit 12-g. Methods 4 and 6 of the exhibit are the same, showing 5 years of average profits, less a deduction for a normal return on the investment in net assets, assumed here to be 12½%. The remaining amount is the excess profits of the business over the normal return required on the investment in net assets. These excess profits are capitalized at 3 years and 4 years, respectively, in the examples. The purchase price would, therefore, be the $100,000 for the net assets, plus the goodwill, as determined in the examples.

Method 3 is a variant on 4 and 6, producing essentially the same result but averaging only the last 3 years of profits, instead of the last 5. In actual practice, the seller is often able to negotiate the use of only the most recent year of earnings which, during a period of an inflationary economy, would be most apt to be the highest of the last 5 years.

Methods 1 and 2 are commonly used to calculate the goodwill of a company, but they suffer the disadvantage of providing for no return on the $100,000 of invested assets. As a result, the computation produces a higher goodwill amount.

Helpful Hint: The use of a higher goodwill amount may produce a desired psychological result when breaking down the purchase price between hard assets and goodwill for future earnings. The seller will think he's getting more on futures. An offset can be made by reducing net assets for an obsolescense factor, thereby resulting in the same purchase price offer as using methods 4 or 6.

Method 5 capitalizes average profits 8 times (100% ÷ 12-1/2%) and then deducts the average net assets. It results in a higher goodwill figure by assuming profits should be capitalized at the same normal rate of return, 12-1/2%, used for the investment in net assets. Actually, profits are more tenuous than assets and the payback should be over a much shorter period, using capitalization rates of 33-1/3% or 50%.

Helpful Hint: A public company, with a quoted price/earnings ratio of say, 20 times (earnings at $1 per share, stock selling at $20) may use a capitalization rate based on anything up to 20 years and may pay for the acquisition in stock without suffering dilution of earnings. *Caution*—discount the 20 to some lesser number based on the expectation of lower market-generated p/e ratios, or the possibility of a down-turn in the economy which could depress stock prices. Your acquisition would then turn dilutive if the rate were not discounted.

DETERMINING THE METHOD OF PAYMENT

Having determined the price, the method of payment will depend on:

1. The tax consequences to the seller.

2. The buyer's financial position.

3. Liquidity and p/e ratio of the buyer's stock.

4. The earn-out contract.

1. The seller may be seeking a tax-free sale or may desire to receive stock in exchange for his business which he can hold for appreciation and subsequent disposal at capital gains rates. In this event, the various Provisions of the Tax Law at Exhibit 12-a would come into play. The goal is to structure a *Tax-Free Reorganization*. The seller exchanges his shares for ours, and we pick up his assets at his tax basis. Convertible securities, if given, must not be converted for five years, to retain the tax-free status.

The IRS Code allows for a tax-free Statutory Merger or Consolidation. In a merger, A is merged into B and B survives. In a consolidation, A and B combine to create a new C, which is the consolidated company. There are three types of Tax-Free Reorganizations:

Type A—Cash. The shareholder gets cash, up to 50%, and stock. The cash received is taxable as a capital gain.

Type B—Stock swap or tender offer—The buyer must issue only voting stock and receive an 80% minimum of the acquired company, and a parent-subsidiary relationship is then established. You cannot buy shares for cash even shortly before the tender offer. You cannot give a guaranty as to the future value of your stock, and you may not pay the finder's fees of the selling company or the non-taxability of the reorganization will be destroyed.

Type C—Acquisition of of assets—The buyer must acquire substantially all of the assets of the seller corporation and must give only voting stock. Some or all of the liabilities may be assumed, but you must obtain at least 90% of the net assets (assets minus liabilities). Thus, the selling company may retain only 10% of net assets to pay off any dissenting stockholders.

The issuance of *contingent stock* (all shares not being issued presently) may destroy the tax-free reorganization, as the seller is receiving something other than voting stock. This would defeat a stock swap, Type B, or acquisition of assets, Type C. But the IRS will allow contingent shares to be issued if:

a. The maximum number of shares to be issued is pre-determined.

b. At least 50% of the maximum shares are issued at closing.

c. The contingent share payout does not exceed five years.

d. There is a contract (not a certificate or warrant).

e. There is a good business reason for the contingent issuance, such as not being able to determine the value of the purchase and needing future earnings as a guide.

When contingent shares are issued, the imputed interest rules on deferred payments may come into play. Section 483 imputes a higher interest rate, giving the seller an interest deduction, but:

Beware this Pitfall: it causes taxable interest income to you, the buyer.

Avoid this Pitfall by: 1) specifying a 6% interest charge, the minimum prescribed amount, which will result in lower taxable income for the buyer, or 2) issuing the shares into escrow, pending their possible return if the future earnings level is not met, thus completely avoiding the interest income imputation. While in escrow, the seller must have voting rights to the shares, and dividend rights.

A *spin-off* may be accomplished prior to the tax-free merger or acquisition. This is the disposal of unwanted assets or a segment of the business. Usually, if the business is over five-years old and there is a business purpose for disposal, a spin-off will be tax-free.

But Use Caution: If the merger follows too closely on the spin-off, it may be taxable. It would be best to go for an IRS ruling, prior to spin-off.

A variety of *types of security* may be given to effect the merger, as long as they are voting securities. Warrants are not stock, however, and if given with voting stock, they must be valued and would be dividend income to the seller, not capital gain.

Voting preferred stock is also acceptable. Class A preferred, paying a cash dividend, or Class B preferred, paying a stock dividend, may be used, and the dividends would be taxable dividend income to the holder. A convertible preferred is sometimes used, convertible into common in increasing amounts, say 4% each year, in lieu of the cash dividends. The increments of 4% would be a taxable dividend to the holder. There are advantages and disadvantages to convertible preferred which are discussed below.

2. The buyer's financial position may be such that he needs immediate cash, even more than the 50% in a Type A Merger. In this event, a *taxable acquisition* may need to be structured. The buyer may acquire stock, or any of the assets, but instead of giving voting stock, you give more than 50% in cash or other securities, with the following tax considerations:

a) The seller has capital gain—but he may use the installment sale method and pay less than 30% in the year of sale, thus postponing 70% of the tax. No contingent payout is permitted on the installment method.

Beware This Pitfall: In computing the 30%, allow for imputed interest which IRS will apply on any deferred payment. This could make the entire sale taxable at once.

Helpful Hint: Use a convertible debenture. This is taxable to seller, but it carries a lower interest rate to the buyer and does not dilute earnings until conversion. If the buyer puts certain restrictions on the bonds, such as making them non-negotiable for a period of time, they may not be taxable until the restrictions lapse. The gain to the seller is locked-in until conversion.

Another Pitfall: The conversion feature on bonds creates a contingent aspect, as the value of the bond fluctuates based on its conversion feature. As a consequence, the installment sale method may not be used.

b)   If the seller sells assets—he will effectively lose his capital gain treatment on that portion of the assets (put into service after 1961) which have depreciated. Thus, he must recapture depreciation as ordinary taxable income. Similarly, he would have an Investment Credit Recapture, which would have to be paid, whether or not he had any taxable income.

c)   A Calendar Year Reorganization (Section 337)—may be undertaken by seller, with usually no tax to his corporation. Inventory or assets may be sold with no gain being recognized, except for the ordinary income, taxed at the corporate level, as a result of recapture of depreciation, described above.

d)   If the seller is willing to be taxed on the sale, and the buyer wants a higher, or stepped-up tax basis, you must buy assets, rather than capital stock.

e)   Finder's Fees and SEC Registration Costs—are deductible to the acquiring corporation, and the IRS has ruled that they are not taxable to the selling corporation.

Avoid This Pitfall: Non-taxability applies only to finder's fees and registration costs, nothing else. If you pay the seller's accounting or legal fees, it can make the entire sale taxable in an otherwise tax-free reorganization.

The *Cash Tender Offer*—fully taxed to the seller, is often used where there are numerous stockholders, or where the buyer is not negotiating directly with management but approaches the stockholders. It has these advantages:

• You need not make SEC disclosure of the offer unless you have $1 million in assets and 500 or more shareholders, but this disclosure is less burdensome than the disclosure on a merger or stock swap, which may need stockholder approvals and 20 days advance notice on exchange. This needs disclosure, but only at the time of the tender, and the SEC will not usually examine the offer until you exercise the tender.

• The disclosure does not need independent public accounting audits and certifications of financial statements.

• The disclosure does not need extensive information as to the nature of your business. You are, thus, less vulnerable to attack or resistance by a recalcitrant management group.

• Your total investment can be much less than in a merger. You do not need to acquire "all" of the stock, or even the 80% minimum for a stock swap.

- You may withdraw within 7 to 60 days for any reason.

- You need not name the exact source of your funds, such as the bank who makes the loan for purposes of the tender.

- You need not disclose your "ideas" to manage the newly acquired company nor tell of the "minor" changes you plan.

It has these disadvantages:

- Under SEC 16, a 10% holder must file with the SEC in 10 days, just as if you had taken the company over in a tender. You must give ten years of information, the source of your funds, the amount of shares held, name of your partners or group or syndicate. The 10 days begin on the date of your option, contract or committment, not on actual receipt of the stock.

- You must accept, pro-rata, during the first 10 days when you get more stock than you desire. This gives management more time to fight the tender—up to 10 days.

- If a complete disclosure is not made, the SEC or management may sue. This obviates the blind tender offer.

- The disclosure must relate your plans to sell, merge, liquidate or change the corporate structure. If you do not so disclose and you later do a merger, even though not intended to be done at the time of the cash tender offer, you expose yourself to litigation.

- The offer is subject to the 1967 "corporate takeover bill" and to the SEC rules which followed that bill.

These management defenses are available:

a. The Buy-In. The tenderee can use its own funds to buy-in its own stock on the open market, The courts will allow this if management shows that the tenderer will hurt the company. Management normally cannot buy-in after notice of the tender, unless it files the number of shares it will buy and its source of funds, in a notice to all shareholders and the SEC.

b. Management may advertise, say the price offered is too low, tells plans, makes promises. The SEC will look at the offer to be sure it is not false or misleading. The SEC may, in fact, sue the tenderer, which will prejudice the stockholders.

c. The tax consequences may be adverse to stockholders, who may not be prepared to be taxed on their gain.

d. Management may quickly merge with another company.

e. Management may alert the Justice Department which has been taking a more active advance role in acquisitions.

f. Alert management is sensitive to the possibility of a takeover and may even have boiler-plate press releases prepared, mailings to shareholders, and signed and sealed documents (undated, already in Washington), to be completed for quick SEC filing, charging anti-trust violations by the tenderer.

g. Stock held by employees in Employee Stock Option Plans, the Employee Stock Ownership Trust, the hands of management, can be marshalled for a solid block. Loans may be made to employees to exercise large blocks of key employee stock options, or stock may be given away, free to employees, in amounts based on seniority. These all provide excellent employee benefits in return for which management is assured of employee support in the takeover fight.

h. Large blocks of stock may be held by friendly institutions, known to the alert company. The company may have held many meetings, over the years, with these institutions.

i. The company may enlist the aid of its national union to resist the tender. If labor resists, on a national basis, the tenderer may withdraw.

j. Management, with shareholder approval, can raise the percentage of votes required to approve a merger, to call a special stockholders' meeting, to remove a director, from the usual 51% to 70% or 75%.

k. Long-term employment contracts with top executives will present the tenderer with the problem of managing the company as it will be bound by the contracts.

l. The company may stagger the board of directors, for example with 3 out of 9 directors due up for election in any year. Using this device, the acquirer would need at least 2 years to gain control of the board.

m. The certificate of incorporation may be amended to require 5 to 8 directors for a quorum, with chairman having the tie-breaking vote.

n. Standby directors can be named in advance, and voted on at the annual meeting, who would fill any vacancy, automatically, in proscribed order.

o. The company may reorganize itself into a different state, like Delaware, which makes corporate takeovers more difficult. In fact, ten states have anti-takeover statutes which, in general, provide that the target company may call for a state securities hearing on the fairness of the proposal, providing for an automatic 30-day delay. The states are Virginia, Idaho, Indiana, Ohio, South Dakota, Kansas, Minnesota, Nevada, Wisconsin, and Hawaii.

p. Litigation on anti-trust arguments, securities regulations, or other regulatory agencies is a common defense. Even if ineffective, the suit allows time to counteract the offer.

Convertible Preferred Stock, if voting, may be used in a tax-free reorganization and if non-voting, in a taxable purchase. In general, like convertible bonds, it carries a low equivalent interest rate (dividend) but may be more attractive than bonds. It has these advantages:

• You postpone dilution of earnings.

• The conversion price may be above the common based on the fact of the preferred dividend.

• The seller receives income, via the dividend, over a period of years (which may be a strong psychological point in making the purchase), without the necessity of giving income to all common stock holders.

• The seller is protected against the volatility of the buyer's stock. The preferred dividend gives him down-side protection.

• Earnings per share should be increased. You will earn more on the preferred (on the seller's business which you bought for your preferred), than you pay out to the seller in preferred dividends. The leverage should increase EPS and the market value of the buyer's stock.

It has these disadvantages:

- Pro-forma earnings per share, giving effect to conversion, must be shown in the Form 10-K and in the Annual Report, if the conversion price is below market value.

- If a major portion of the value of the preferred is attributed to the common stock, the preferred may be considered a residual security, not a senior security. Moreover, since the common stock may fluctuate, then the value of the conversion feature may fluctuate, and the preferred may be considered as a residual security one year and not the next. If considered as a residual security, earnings would be reduced by the amount attributable to the residual security, further reducing pro-forma EPS.

- The convertible preferred, if not registered, has no market and provides no down-side protection. Registration is expensive.

- It may be hard to buy back convertible preferred later, especially if you divest yourself of the acquisition.

- The risk is greater, as you are committed to an after-tax dividend, which you cannot convert to debt. Some preference stock may circumvent this risk by 1) paying no cash dividends. 2) setting a convertible feature which compounds annually at over 3% (meaning you get 3% more common, compounded, each year). 3) setting a conversion price that compounds equal to the amount above, thus, 1 : 1 in year 1, then 1.03 : 1, in year 2, etc. 4) redeeming up to 3% of the total issue each year at par. The IRS has ruled that the yield to the seller is ordinary income, but this is no worse than any dividend he might receive. On the other hand, the buyer does not reduce EPS (as the redemption is not an expense but a capital transaction).

- If the dividend is too low, and less than 75% of its value is in the preferred stock itself, its issuance may not be attractive to the seller.

3. The liquidity of the buyer (or lack of it), coupled with a high price/earnings ratio on his own stock may dictate that a common stock, or convertible into common, purchase be made. By completing the worksheet at Exhibit 12-d, the buyer may determine that he can offer far more than a competitive bidder, and still not dilute his earnings or book value per share.

In this case, the determined purchase price could be paid through a Pooling of Interests, rather than a Purchase. The pooling would be tax-free or taxable, based on the same considerations as any purchase.

Pooling and Purchase accounting is governed by the Accounting Principles Board Opinion No. 16, Business Combinations and Opinion No. 17, Intangibles (referring to the goodwill element in the purchase). These two opinions, in general, limit the use of poolings; in purchases, provide rules and guidelines for allocating fair value to the assets and liabilities purchased; provide for amortization of goodwill (the excess of fair value of the purchase price over the fair value of the assets and liabilities) over the period to be benefited, but not over 40 years. Prior to this opinion, goodwill need not have been written off at all.

The pooling method accounts for a business combination as a joining of companies which exchange their equity securities. It is not considered an acquisition or purchase since the union takes place without anything being disbursed. The former ownership interests must continue; the old bases of accounting are kept; each carries forward his assets and liabilities to the combined company at their recorded amounts, and new goodwill does not arise. The combined company's income is that of the constituents for the entire fiscal period in which the union occurred. This means a pooling in the last month of your fiscal year is effective back to the start of the year. Previously reported income of both companies for prior years is combined and restated as income of the pooled company.

The purchase method, previously described, accounts for the business combination as an acquisition of one company by the other. The buyer records, at cost, assets acquired and liabilities assumed. Goodwill is recorded for any difference between the cost (purchase price paid) and the sum of the fair values of the tangible and identifiable intangible assets minus liabilities. The goodwill must be amortized as charges to earnings, not exceeding 40 years, and the future income of the buyer includes the seller's income, only after the date of acquisition, based on the cost to the acquirer.

> **Word of Caution**: It is obvious that the determination of fair values of assets and liabilities requires careful study and detailed consideration, as these will be recorded on the books to affect future earnings, through amortization of goodwill which will arise, depreciation of assets, or interest charges arising from the present value of future liabilities.

Warrants may be used in lieu of stock. The warrants may trade at 25% of the price of the common stock. Their issuance, thus, creates value. Warrants are not considered an underlying security since they are not stock and, therefore, do not dilute EPS. Warrants may also be used together with debentures. This creates fixed interest charges and makes the company more vulnerable to cyclical downturns.

> **Helpful Hint**: The high fixed interest charges could be offset by acquiring a company with large cash flow, say an insurance company, despite its low earnings. It might be bought for below book value (if you offer a good growth stock in exchange). In this case, purchase, don't pool. This creates negative goodwill which can be written-up to book value over the years, thereby creating income.
> **Another Hint**: Having served the above purpose, the low income, high cash flow company may then be spun-off, tax-free. It is probably worth more as a separate entity than in consolidation. The price for which it is sold is then plowed back into new, future earnings.

Don't neglect *Cash*. In times of a depressed stock market and low p/e ratios, stocks lose appeal and the seller may prefer cash. Many buyers, with high liquidity, during depressed markets, make the most advantageous acquisitions.

When liquidity problems do not permit the luxury of cash acquisitions, a good technique is to buy assets for preferred stock, and earnings (minus the preferred dividend) for common stock.

> **Helpful Hint:** Exhibit 12-h illustrates the method of allotting the purchase price to preferred stock and common stock, respectively. The method is to issue preferred for the net assets and to issue common for the earnings, after deduction of the preferred dividend, based on a reasonable capitalization rate. The preferred dividends, obviously, may not exceed the earnings of either company.

A study of Exhibit 12-h indicates that a 6% dividend on preferred and 20% on the common provides the same income after dividends, whichever is computed first. Once the preferred dividends of 6% have been deducted, it does not matter what capitalization rate is used for the remaining average income, since the two remain in the same proportion.

4. The earn-out contract, being a key motivator for the seller, in arriving at a higher price than he would otherwise receive, also determines the method of payment.

The earn-out contract, as well as all the negotiated details, need to be set out in a memorandum which will memorialize the agreement, prior to going to actual legal contracts. The memorandum should be in letter form, should tell the details of the purchase, and, in fact, should have a brief reference to every clause which will ultimately be in the contract—down to the minutiae of assignability of the contract, which state law will prevail, whom the old owner will report to.

> **Helpful Hint:** The guideline for preparing the memorandum should be an actual contract. If none is available from a prior acquisition, make one up for this purchase, but don't allow the seller to see it until after the memorandum is prepared and agreed to. Changes to the memorandum may be quickly incorporated into the actual contract, and you are much more likely to get quick approval on the contract when the seller later tells his lawyer he has already agreed to a specific point.

A sample letter memorandum is seen at Exhibit 12-i. Attached to it is a detailed schedule showing earn-out examples under many different performance levels. The seller can see exactly how many shares he will receive under differing circumstances.

If there is any misconception on either the acquirer's or the acquiree's part, this will surface in the memorandum. Sometimes, in fact, the seller may seem to have been very amenable and anxious to sell, during the verbal negotiations. But when the memorandum arrives, shock sets in! He suddenly realizes he is selling his business, his life's work. He may have second thoughts or even try to strike a better deal. Better to face these now than have him walk out of the closing. Therefore, the memorandum should be direct and to the point, covering all points, but not so severe and rigid (as in a contract) that it will scare him off.

> **Important Point:** Observe that the earn-out formula sets a base for earnings. This is what we are capitalizing and paying 5 times for. He gets paid more only for increases over the base.
>
> **Avoid This Pitfall:** Insist that the seller use an attorney, for his own protection, not

only in reviewing the contract, but in assuring that he conforms to SEC regulations on the sale of his securities.

ACQUISITION RULES OF THUMB

The acquisition goals of the organization are worked out as seen at Exhibit 12-c. These goals vary from company to company. Listed below are some of the rules of thumb used by companies in evaluating acquisition candidates:

- Don't acquire companies unless you are a growth company, that is: a) successive increases in earnings at a rate greater than the GNP.; b) you use conservative accounting techniques; c) you already have high quality of management.
- Always use an earn-out formula.
- Your return on investment should be at least 15%.
- Pay not more than 1½ times net worth.
- The seller should have a 50% gross profit margin on his sales.
- Seller's pre-tax profits should be 10% or more.
- Seller must have had required earnings for the past three years.
- Pay no more than 8 times the earnings average.
- Don't try to make a "bargain" purchase.
- You must "sell" the prospective seller on your company.
- If no earn-out, give the old owner other incentives.
- The seller must have competent management.
- Don't expect miracle future earnings from the seller.
- The buyer's EPS must increase in the year of acquisition.
- There must be synergy—a real business fit or purpose.

ARTFUL ACQUISITIONS

The mergers and acquisitions responsibility rests with the Treasurer. Tax considerations, while inherent in the acquisitions process, are never a reason for making an acquisition. There are, on the contrary, a variety of good and solid business reasons for making acquisitions. Goals must be carefully set in approaching target companies and the price should be determined by projecting out prior years' profits or forecasting future earnings using formal forecasting techniques. The method of payment may be artfully constructed, depending on whether the seller has a tax-free reorganization or a taxable exchange. A variety of securities may be given by the buyer—even cash may be used! The combination of the business interests may be treated, for accounting purposes, as a purchase, or as a pooling of interests, depending on the method of payment and type of agreement. A memorandum agreement is used to reduce the agreements to writing, before contract, and this should always include an earn-out formula. Pin-point acquisitions—develop rules of thumb in considering candidates. Be an artful acquisitor.

CHAPTER 13

Establishing and Administering a

Records Retention Program

THE Controller's functions of Planning, Reporting, Consulting and Protection of Assets encompass the records retention responsibility. Records need to be filed, sorted, stored, and retrieved for a variety of reasons—for historical reviews, tax audits, litigation, vendor and employee claims. This function logically falls under the aegis of the principal operational manager, the Controller.

WHAT IS IT?

The name, Records Retention Program, is universally used to define a program which has a great many more aspects than mere retention of records. A complete records program embraces the following features:

1. A current filing system—concerned with day-to-day operations, and located close to the user departments.

2. A long-range filing system—in a permanent storage facility, properly arranged for quick retrieval.

3. A definition of which records to retain—and, therefore, which records to destroy.

4. A systematic records destruction procedure—to allow for retention of records defined in No. 3.

5. A security system—to protect the integrity of both current and long-range records.

WHAT ARE THE NEEDS AND BENEFITS?

The needs and benefits of a Records Retention Program vary with the record to be retrieved, and the need to retrieve that record. Assume, for example, that our company signs a manufacturing agreement with another company, licensing them to use our patents and know-how to manufacture a product for us and others, with an annual ten-year licensing fee paid to us, which we take into income on a capital gains basis. That contract needs to be filed in a safe place for three years after the filing of the last tax return at the end of the tenth year. The last tax return is filed in April of the eleventh year (assuming there is no extension of the time to file) and the record may not be destroyed until the fourteenth year. During this extended period of retention, in addition to the IRS, others may want to examine the contract: our independent accountants, to review the basis for accrual of income and capital gains treatment; the Federal Trade Commission, to determine that we are not in restraint of trade or, perhaps, in connection with an industry-wide anti-trust review; the SEC, in the event the contract is material and requires public disclosure (through the filing of a Form 8K or as an exhibit to a Registration Statement); various department heads—to check on cost formulas, termination clauses, purchase order requirements and payment terms; and, of course, corporate officers, with regard to contract disputes arising with the licensee. The need to retrieve in this particular circumstance, and the benefits, by definition, arise out of the solution to the need. Obviously, the cost and impediment to a successful solution can be severe if the contract, or a key document related to it, cannot be located.

Perhaps the most frequent example of the frustrations involved in not being able to locate a record is found at income tax audit time. The revenue agents are voracious in their need for documents and to "show me." Your argument is half lost if you cannot turn up that 4-year-old canceled check or March 5, years ago, petty cash voucher. But even more important than a casual record, you may need every book of original entry for any specific year.

In summary, the needs are as varied as the records being sought, and the benefits are as many and varied as the needs giving rise to them. Business is built around the written word and proper control requires that the related document be made available on command.

HOW IS THE PROGRAM ESTABLISHED?

A Records Rentention Program is established by the Controller identifying and defining the 5 features set out on page 191. This requires setting up rules or a procedure to handle each feature. The method of codifying these procedures is set forth in Chapter 7, describing the Procedures Manual. An outline of the components of each of the 5 features follows:

1. A current filing system

a. Locate it close to the user departments to save steps.

b. Do not allow entry into the file department by anyone except the File Department. Manager and his people. This is necessary solely to prevent disruption of the basic filing system.

c. Establish written rules on where to file each type of document. The way you file is not important, only that you are consistent, your method is written down, and the record can be retrieved based on a knowledge of your filing system. A few helpful filing hints are:
   1) Never file by person's name (senders or receivers leave the company and people can't recall who wrote what).
   2) File by broadest possible category. For example, memos to salesmen may be filed under "salesmen's memos," broken down into subsets for training memos, pricing memos, competitors' equipment, sales slants, procedures, sales contests, performance reports, and so on.

d. Do not permit individual managers to maintain their own desk files or departmental files, unless these are used in daily operations. Next year, move even daily files out of the department and in to the central file department.

e. Files, whether central or working departmental, should be retained only by the sender, never the receiver (to cut down on duplicate and unnecessary file retention).

f. Individual files maintained by corporate officers should be summarized by broad category (1.c.2. above), and a listing of these broad categories must be sent to central files for available reference by key managers and other officers.

g. Department Heads should require a quarterly desk inspection by all employees (every drawer and file is opened and reviewed) to determine that no key records are being squirreled.

h. Managers should personally inspect the desk of every terminated employee to determine that an orderly transition of work is made to the replacement employee and that pertinent records are sent to central files.

i. Organizationally, the central file manager should report directly to, or on a line to, the corporate Controller.

j. Central files must be revolved yearly, with transfers being made to permanent files, to allow room for this year's current filing. Working files should usually include 16 months of records; that is; December's files are not transferred to permanent file room until the end of April.

k. Originals should not leave the files unless legally required. In such a case, a photocopy is made, dated, and marked with the name of the recipient, to be removed and destroyed when the original is returned.

2. A long-range filing system

a. A permanent, locked storage facility is required. This presupposes adequate space in a secure area, sprinklered for fire protection. Files may be cardboard transfiles.

b. The storage area should be reasonably close to the main facility, even if facsimile transmission of documents is used. This allows for ready access without each request requiring a major expenditure in time, effort and dollars.

c. Entry into the secure area must be limited to the area manager or the central file manager.

d. Written rules on filing are required and may be the same as used for the current filing system in l.c.

e. The area file manager should report to the central file manager in the Controller's division.

f. Every file or transfile must be numbered within an area location.

g. The general contents of each file must be labeled on the front of each carton.

h. A listing is made of each carton number and its contents, such listing organized by subject matter in l.c.

i. A cross-reference locater listing is maintained by carton number, showing the location by subject matter.

j. Originals should not leave the files unless legally required. In such a case, a photocopy is made, dated, and marked with the name of the recipient, to be removed and destroyed when the original is returned.

3. A definition of which records to retain

This subject is covered in considerable detail in a publication by Prentice-Hall, *Your Business Records—A Simplified Guide to What Records You Must Keep and How Long You Must Keep Them* and in another publication by William E. Mitchell, titled *Records Retention,* published by Ellsworth Publishing Company, Evansville, Indiana. The American Society of Corporate Secretaries, Inc., has completed a *Survey on Records Retention Practices.*

These publications list the gamut of corporate and business records, the legal and business reasons for holding them for certain periods of time, and the authority for these decisions. There are generally minimum holding periods which may be adapted or lengthened for each particular company, depending on its own requirements.

The list of records to be reviewed for holding period is complete and concerned with every phase of the operation of the enterprise. An example of the detail provided in the Prentice-Hall publication is shown on a typical page exhibited at Exhibit 13-a. The list below is not intended as a substitute for a thorough review of the cited publications. It lists, however, the most common business records which take up the most space and gives the minimum retention period:

Document	Holding Period in Years
Accounts Payable (Vouchers & Invoices)	6
Bank Statements and Reconciliations	6
Canceled Voucher Checks	6
Cash Receipts Books	permanent

Claim Files—Against us	6
Claim Files—By us	3
Employee Travel Expense Reports	6
Financial Statements—internal	5
General Books—all journals	permanent
Physical Inventory Records	6
Payroll Registers	6
Payments and Reports to Government Agencies	6
Cancelled Stock Certificates	permanent
Contracts, Agreements, and Leases	permanent
Basic Scientific Records	permanent
Correspondence with Vendors	2
Orders Filled	2
Sales Correspondence	2
Sales Invoices	6
General Correspondence	permanent

4. A systematic records destruction procedure

a. The Records Retention listing in No. 3 should be published and made available to all managers of departments.

b. A Standard Operating Procedure should be circulated giving the times of records destruction, the authority and the responsibility (central files manager) for such destruction. The destruction date, each year, should be the day following the filing of the tax return for the appropriate year. Extensions in filing should be taken into consideration. For example, a company on an April 30th, fiscal year normally files its tax return on July 15th. Thus, a record dated December 1, 1973, on 3-year retention, is scheduled for destruction after July 15, 1977. If an annual destruction date of the first Tuesday of each February is established, this record would be slated for destruction in February 1978.

c. A listing of cartons and records to be destroyed should be circulated to all key managers, 30 days before destruction, with *positive* confirmation required that no listed records need be retained.

d. Notations of destroyed cartons should be made on the listing in 2.h., with the date of destruction. This, itself, is retained as a permanent record, to prove destruction in any future litigation on proceedings.

e. Prior to each destruction, the listing of records to be destroyed is approved by the Controller, after the receipt of all positive confirmations from key managers. The controller retains this listing in his working file as a back-up for the central file original listing.

f. The retention period, as adjusted from the Prentice-Hall or Corporate Secretaries listing, should be reviewed for changes every second year. These changes should relate to up-dates in the general listing as provided by the appropriate publica-tion, based on changes in the existing law, as well as changes required in the adjusted dates used by the company, based on changes within the company's own procedures.

5. A security system

a. A File Retrieval procedure is necessary to insure control over the transmittal, storage and retrieval of all current and historical filed documents. This procedure is detailed at Exhibit 13-b, together with supporting forms to administer the procedure.

b. Records destruction should be accomplished either by sale to a responsible scrap dealer (who will promptly shred and bale the material) or by burning under observation by a responsible company representative.
  1) Records should not be left, untended, at a municipal dump to be destroyed at some later date.
  2) Purchasing and operating a paper shredder or baler is costly and not recommended unless there is considerable volume, in which case it may be cost justified.
  3) Destruction may be integrated with a trash or garbage disposal system utilizing a compacter and baler.

c. No personnel should be permitted in the records room except file department personnel. This includes other department heads, officers, and auditors.
  1) As an exception, file units may be assigned to specific departments, and personnel from such departments may have free access to such records.
  2) The balance of the records room should be fenced off from the free access area.

d. The records room should be clean, dry, and well lighted.
  1) Avoid dampness and excessive dryness.
  2) Do not use sprinkler protection because water damages more records than actual fire. Tightly packed records in metal files will usually not be damaged irreparably by fire.
  3) Metal, interlocking files are better than cardboard as they are more fire resistant.

e. File papers away when not in use, and clear all office desks at night.

f. Use special, fireproof metal files for irreplaceable, important records.

g. Provide for duplicate copies of important records and store them in a separate location, away from your place of business. This would include all data necessary to reconstruct accounts receivable records and a trial balance:
  1) Last month's Aged Trial Balance.
  2) Copies of daily billings to customers.
  3) Last month's cash disbursements journal.
  4) Capital asset records.
  5) Copies of current month's journal entries.
  6) Copies of important contracts.
  7) Summary individual earnings payroll records, quarterly.
  8) Last month's data processing tapes.
  9) Microfilm copies of important computer programs.

STORAGE AND RETRIEVAL SYSTEMS

Storage of records is the phrase used for inactive records. Retrieval most often applies to current, working records. Most inactive records are retained for a period of years, or permanently, in accord with the established records retention program. Many permanent or long retention period documents need to be retrieved frequently. Examples would be installment contracts payable over a period of years, standing customer orders, working contracts, cost records, and tax returns. Inactive records simply need be filed in the records room under the records retention procedures described previously. Active records require a current filing system as described on page 193. There are degrees of sophistication to both the active and inactive filing systems contemplated. Filing systems can include the manual systems previously described, or:

1. Computer tape storage
2. Word processing magnetic tape storage
3. Microfilm storage

The overall features of each concept are discussed below:

COMPUTER TAPE STORAGE

Words, numbers, statistics and data may be computer inputted and stored on computer tape. Since the computer reads tape sequentially, the method is best for chronological storage. A variant may include the use of disk storage devices for random access retrieval.

The limitation of such a system is that most file copies need to be put into computer readable form. This means key punching or preparation of computer tape through a keyboard input device. In some cases, when paper tape or magnetic tape is prepared as a by-product of another operation, these tapes can be "pooled" (run through a black box that converts it into computer readable tape).

As a consequence of the input difficulties, computer tape storage is used in limited applications. Where the application is suitable, however, computer tape storage is fast, economical, and desirable.

An example of an application using computer tape storage of an office document is to be found in an automated billing system. The invoice is typed for mailing to the customer. A by-product of this typing is a punched card, paper tape, or a magnetic tape cassette. The by-product is then mailed or passed through a terminal, then over telephone lines, into the computer. It is processed by the computer's central processing unit and outputted onto tape or disk for storage and future retrieval.

Obviously, the cost of setting up such a system, utilizing a computer, terminals, and input devices would be prohibitive, except for the largest systems. Nevertheless, the computers and terminals are often on hand for typical data processing operations. These may be easily interfaced with word processing equipment to create a billing system of the type above, at very little cost. Storage and retrieval, in such a case, become available at practically no cost as a by-product of the system itself.

WORD PROCESSING MAGNETIC TAPE STORAGE

As used here, word processing is intended to mean typewritten words which can be edited, corrected, deleted, added and manipulated through the use of word processing machines. These are, in effect, nothing more than typewriters tied in to mini-computers. Examples are the IBM MT/ST or the Savin #900 Word Master systems.

The Word Master creates a small magnetic tape cassette, the same kind as used in your home tape recorder, as a by-product of typing the letter. This cassette may be run through a terminal, over direct dial telephone lines, into a receiving terminal. It may then be outputted immediately on a typewriter tied to the terminal, or may be stored on computer tape, subsequently recalled and run back onto magnetic tape cassettes for retyping. This is a unique feature. You actually receive a typewritten document in exactly the same format as originally inputted. It is, thus, possible to type all ordinary correspondence on a Word Master, store it on computer tape, recall it to tape cassettes, and retype it on demand. It could similarly be used for the billing application described in the Computer Tape Storage section above.

Like computer tape storage systems, and this really is an adjunct to such systems, word processing storage and retrieval can be expensive as a stand alone device. But when it is already in use for normal office typing operations, file storage, billing and other similar applications are able to be added on at very little cost.

MICROFILM STORAGE

Other than manual systems, perhaps the most well known storage and retrieval systems are microfilm. As a rule of thumb, however, microfilm systems are not the most economical for straight storage purposes. Manual systems are usually less costly and safer. When tied to a timely retrieval system, though, microfilm can offer many advantages. Some advantages are:

1. 98% of needed storage space can be saved by reducing hard copy to microfilm.

2. Microfilm copies are acceptable to federal and state agencies.

3. Records can be retrieved more quickly.

4. Records may be copied, automatically, at the time of retrieval, for delivery to the user.

5. Refiling of the microfilm is automatic and less time-consuming than refiling a manual record.

6. Microfilm records need to be indexed to be retrieved, whereas manual file records are usually not indexed, thereby providing greater knowledge and control of the contents of the record room.

7. Large documents or voluminous files which require absolute protection and permanent storage are better handled through microfilm.

Microfilm systems, despite some advantages, are not the end-all of storage and retrieval systems. On the contrary, there may be some disadvantages:

1. The cost may be prohibitive. Some elements of cost to set up a microfilm system are:
    a. Labor is required to prepare files for filming, consisting of proofreading, indexing, unstapling copies, reviewing developed film and reshooting where necessary.
    b. Camera cost to buy ($1800 to $2500) or rent ($3.50 to $5.00 per day).
    c. Film cost and developing cost (approximately $2.50 per thousand documents).
    d. Floor space for camera, file cabinet and copier.

2. The run-rate may be too time-consuming. Approximately 2,000 documents a day can be processed. It may take too long to get into the system.

3. Files must be rearranged for filming, including unbinding and unfastening and unstapling.

4. Some colors and carbon copies do not copy well. Where credit balances or losses are in red, they will not show up differently on film and may need to be circled.

5. Only one person can use the reader at a time.

6. It may take longer to retrieve a microfilm copy than a hard copy, depending on the type of indexing system used.

7. Loss of film through accident or theft is not readily detectable and is more likely to happen than to a large file of hard copy records.

8. Internal Revenue Service may require transcription of photographic copies to hard copy.

One of the best uses of microfilm is to interface it with a manual system, instead of making a complete conversion to microfilm. This will allow one to avail himself of most of the advantages, at the same time avoiding the obvious disadvantages of microfilm. The following items could be microfilmed within the manual system:

1. Customer invoice copies, which are voluminous, sequential, and usually permanent as to retention may be filmed without much initial preparation and with no indexing.

2. Large, permanent documents, such as books of original entry, may be filmed and kept safe in locked, fireproof files.

The above two categories encompass all of the large, bulky, permanent files which are not actively used. Microfilming in these categories should begin after the completion of the federal tax audit or six years, whichever is later. There is no point in microfilming these records during their active periods, unless the entire filing system is set up on microfilm. Under the type of system proposed, microfilm is used for storage purposes, primarily, not retrieval.

Such a system requires the rental of a camera, once a year, an inexpensive reader and photocopier. The cost would be between $3000 to $5000 and is the type of equipment which the manufacturers finance on three- to five-year full payout leases, with monthly costs running about $100 on a five-year lease.

SUMMARY

The Records Retention Program is the responsibility of the corporate Controller. Such a program envisages a controlled current filing system, a long-range filing system, a well defined list of which records to retain for how long, a systematic records destruction program, and an overall security system to protect these files. There are a variety of programs available to the user, including manual systems, computer storage, word processing, or microfilm storage. These can be integrated into manual systems, in part, depending on the size of the system and the amount of data.

CHAPTER **14**

Controlling the

Data Processing Function

THE controllership function of Reporting and Interpreting and that of Evaluating and Consulting, as set forth in the FEI definition, includes the coordination of systems and procedures, the preparation of operating data and reports, and the evaluation of organization structures and procedures. This is, logically, a Controller's responsibility, since the generation of financial statements and supporting reports is a by-product of the flow of data through the organization. Management of this function requires:

1. Organization—a proper organizational structure within the data processing department, and proper interfacing with other departments.

2. Personnel management—establishing standards of work performance, monitoring performance, cross-training, educational advancement, and integration into the entire organization.

3. Control—control and monitoring of the work flow, systems and procedures work, and operations input and output.

4. Security—development of suitable security procedures for hardware, forms, and software.

ORGANIZATION

Two organizational problems exist in the data processing area; that of the organizational structure of the department itself, and the location of the department within the overall corporate organization. A proper evaluation of the data structure is required before the organizational chart can be implemented.

a. Evaluation

This is the process wherein the entire company is examined as to the data inputs, processing, and output or reports. This is an overview of the enterprise and leads to a decision as to whether or not to automate, the type of equipment to use, and to whom the department will report. The results of this study will vary within every company, and the scope and amount of detail in the study will often depend on the size of the company and its data processing expertise. This study includes:

1. A listing of all output reports and data contained in them.

2. A cross-listing of reports containing duplicate output data.

3. A similar listing of input data.

4. Interviews with top management to obtain their impressions of the present reporting system and what they really want.

5. Work counts associated with all listings, such as number of vendors, checks written, invoices to customers, statements mailed, credits issued, employees, commission checks written, journal entries, total number of customers per period, items of inventory, frequency of shipments.

While the results of this study vary by company, the study, itself, creates a better understanding of the company, shatters some myths about volumes of work, and permits the Controller to determine the data processing needs of the company.

A typical result of such a study might reveal that the present system is providing voluminous information in tremendous detail—too much, and too late. Top management might prefer more timely flash reports with fewer numbers, to give a fast status report on overall operations. This could mean a requirement for faster automation of initial input (for example, every credit card sale in a gas station is run through a charge plate which puts it in machine readable format, suitable for optical scanning). Or, it could mean a requirement to completely by-pass machine handling of data (for example, branch managers telex to headquarters, daily, with orders written information).

This study will be quite useful, as we shall see in the Control section, in establishing edit control to provide more correct output (for example, the highest commission on any product is $600 and the computer may be programmed to identify for review any higher amount). The volume of data will also identify the proper type of equipment to use in the data processing department, or whether to use any, at all. A daily newspaper, for example, must meet a daily deadline of publication, or it will soon be out of business. This requires daily processing of data to its culmination, daily, and so the computer must be used. A trading stamp company, on the other hand, processes a great many books of stamps, but the urgency of meeting a deadline is not present, and most trading stamp companies rely on manual work, rather than the computer, to handle the requirements of the business.

In evaluating the need for a machine system, advantages and disadvantages of automation may readily be set forth, but the advantages are manifest and the disadvantages easily resolved:

1. Machines are not sick and absent from work. When they break down, the manufacturers maintain 24-hour repair staffing.

2. Typewritten or written data may be machine-oriented free, as a by-product of the typing or writing.

3. The same data is used for many types of reports, and only the computer can process and reprocess it without further repetitive writing.

4. The machine will not make errors of transcription, under proper control, nor will it make arithmetic errors.

5. Security with machines is better. They don't quit and go to work for competitors.

6. The computer can perform processing and arithmetic functions far more quickly than persons, and in more depth.

7. Machine output reports are more readable than hand-written.

8. Storage of information and security are better by machine.

The most commonly mentioned disadvantages, and their solution, are:

1. The cost of hardware and software is enormous. (The system must be cost-justified in terms of the results achieved.)

2. The staffing for the data processing organization is a problem, difficult to find, high-salaried, high turnover to competitors. (Data processing personnel must be properly motivated within the company, as must any employee, and their salaries are consistent with those of any corporate high technology people.)

3. The responsibility for processing functions, like payrolls and monthly financial statements, rests with a few, key, difficult to control people. (The responsibility rests with the Controller and the Data Processing Manager, who, hopefully, are no more difficult to control than any other managers. Adequate cross-training and back-up personnel are available on every job.)

4. The time required to hire the right people and to implement the programs, systems and procedures is prohibitive. (Time is a major consideration, but the results to be achieved must justify the advance planning and expenditures. See No. 1, above. Like any capital expenditure, cost justification is required.)

Having evaluated the data processing system, a decision to implement a data processing department may now be made.

b. Implementation

This requires, as a first step, identifying, hiring, and training the data processing staff. Staff may be obtained from:

1. Company personnel files.

2. Personnel agencies specializing in DP personnel.

3. Management advisory staffs of independent accounting firms.

4. Recommendations from peers, banks, consultants, associates.

5. Advertising in national papers, local area papers, and DP magazines.

For the company new to data processing, interviewing and identification of the right personnel may be done by the company's outside consultants or accounting firm, although this should not be necessary. The same techniques should be brought to interviewing and hiring the DP manager as any other management people. You may not have the ability to judge his technical competence, but you can evaluate him for his management ability, and proper reference checks can verify the former. Once you have identified, hired, and trained the new DP manager in the standard corporate training program, which may simply involve time spent with other managers, he is ready to take his place in the organization and to establish the structure of his own department:

1. Corporate Organization—The Data Processing Manager may report directly to the Controller, or through an Operations Manager, Administrative Control Manager, Management Information Systems Manager, or Director of Administration and then to the Controller. Regardless of the type and size of company, the data processing control function is a controllership responsibility.

2. Departmental Organization—An average organizational chart for a data processing department is shown at Exhibit 14-a. This includes Systems and Programming & Operations (Computer and Key Punch).

   In this chart, key punch operations reports to the Operations Manager, as does the actual Computer Room and the Input/Output staff, which is a control function, responsible for balancing all reports.

   Systems analysts and programmers report to the Systems and Programming Manager, and both he and the Operations Manager report to the head of the department, who, in turn, reports to the Controller.

   There are no dotted lines of interface on this chart, showing the functional relationships of one department head to another. In the company illustrated, the Data Processing Manager has full department head status, and as shown on page 237 of the Controller's Position Description in the "Treasurer's and Controller's Functions," he interfaces with the auditors, manager of accounting services department, the national administrator (responsible for branch office administrative operations), and the order/billing manager. These key managers, together are responsible for the administrative operations of the company. All report to the Vice-President/Controller.

PERSONNEL MANAGEMENT

The need to manage personnel is a key ingredient of every manager's job, including the Treasurer or Controller. There seems to be a certain mystique, however, surrounding data processing personnel, perhaps because the discipline of data processing (as it relates to the computer) is only twenty-years old, which fills the manager with trepidation.

Standard personnel management techniques apply, no less, to data processing people. These include:

1. A Management Philosophy

This is first and foremost and relates to the manager's own attitude and approach to his people. It means proper training of the manager (in this case the Controller), and his immediate subordinates (the Operations Manager or Data Processing Manager), leading to identification with corporate goals. This may be done formally, through management training courses within or without the company, or informally, through conversations with higher management or by a project of personal education in management by the Controller. The vital point is that the Controller be aware and proceed to develop a corporate philosophy which he imparts to his personnel as a continuing and on-going part of their jobs.

2. A Management Example

Once the corporate philosophy has been adopted, as described above, the Controller proceeds to implement this by setting an example of a manager in action. This requires the adoption of traits which he must express, on the job, even though they are not characteristic of his nature. Through attention and effort, they become second nature. Only the rare manager is endowed with all these appearances. The rest of us must develop them and can be equally successful.

These traits are leadership, integrity, and sensitivity. There are others, but these are the ones needed to succeed.

Leadership—encompasses the marks of management with which personnel will identify. It may simply mean the proper appearance in front of subordinates (from not too many drinks at the Christmas party to leaving your tie knotted on a hot summer day) (although the standard needs to apply to the particular circumstance—no tie may be appropriate for the manufacturer of sport shirts). Or it may mean taking the lead in cutting his own departmental budget, selling this to and obtaining the support of his people.

> **A Case in Point**: One company had a desperate need to reduce corporate payrolls by 5%. The Controller took the lead by instructing the payroll department to reduce his salary by 10%. The manager of the data processing department immediately volunteered to take a 5% pay cut. His section managers, the data processing operations manager and the systems and programming manager, agreed to reassign work tasks, to absorb some of the tasks themselves, and not to replace attrited employees for the next 60 days. Result, within two months, the data processing department had fully achieved the 5% payroll cut and set the tone for the entire company. The two managers who took pay cuts more than made these back on the next round of payroll increases.

Integrity—is the adoption of a standard of moral value which is seen by subordinates as a chalk mark to a sense of conscience and respect for duty. The manager's expression of this morality is seen and sensed by his subordinates who will respond in kind. To this extent, it is another form of leadership.

> **Another Case in Point**: A DP manager had evaluated and cost-justified a new, more powerful computer. The project received higher management approval and, on the strength of this, five programmers and analysts were hired to take the company into the new machine. The company, in a cost reduction move, subsequently raised its return on investment objectives and reevaluated the ROI on the new computer. The DP manager responded by selling the changed decision to his new personnel and offered them two alternatives—he would find room in his training budget to give them advanced educational training in the new machine in anticipation of eventually being able to cost–justify it under the newer ROI standards, or he would use his best efforts to relocate them to another company which was currently using the new machine. One accepted the latter alternative and was immediately relocated, at the same salary, using a data processing personnel agency which had, in the past, worked closely with the DP manager. The other four employees, seeing the sincerity of the proposal, elected to remain with the company and eventually were rewarded by seeing the company reselect the larger computer. The DP manager's integrity in either training his people in the new machine or in actually transferring them to a company using it, in the face of a corporate decision to abandon the computer, was a commitment to the conditions of their hire. His action won the respect of his people and maintained a cadre of trained people, prepared to take the company into the next higher phase of its computer operations when conditions permitted it.

Sensitivity—is the ability to be receptive to and respond to the feelings of employees, to enable the manager to exercise the traits of leadership and integrity which command the respect and cooperation of those employees.

This management attribute connotes a perception of the employee as an individual. It means observation of his performance and questioning the reasons for lack of it, or equally important, determining how to maintain consistently high performance.

The manager who is sensitive to the feelings of his employees, enabling him to react in the company's best interest, sets a management example which encourages all employees to attain the overall corporate goals. But the manager should:

> **Avoid This Pitfall**: Do not set up a climate which encourages invalid complaints. That's like "sick call" in the army. Any malingerer can avail himself of it to avoid his duty. Repetitive invalid complaints will identify the exaggerator who should be firmly upbraided.

3. Management by Objectives

Having developed a philosophy and proceded to set an example, of management using leadership, integrity and sensitivity, the manager sets objectives for his personnel and measures their performance against these objectives.

In some companies, Management by Objectives is a corporate program, administered by the Personnel Manager, utilizing specialized forms designed for this purpose. Exhibit 14-b depicts a Management by Objectives form which is part of a formal program.

A formal Management by Objectives program starts with top management's (the Board of Directors and/or President) goal or objective for the coming year, usually expressed in X dollars of sales and earnings. This may be quantified by product line or class of sale, such as wholesale or retail, but does not usually go beyond that degree. This objective is passed down to those reporting directly to the President. They set their broad objectives, consonant with the President's goals. The Treasurer, for example, may establish a goal of improving accounts receivable turnover by 5 days, thereby increasing cash flow and decreasing interest costs on short-term borrowings by X dollars. These goals, in turn, are passed down to the next level. Second-level managers then set their objectives within the framework of their superiors; the Credit and Collection Manager, for example, to support his Treasurer's goal, may set his object of reducing 90-day past due accounts receivable by 20% or X dollars. Each manager also identifies trouble areas in his department which improve overall performance. An example, to reduce departmental turnover by x%, thereby saving X dollars in personnel recruitment costs. The department manager imparts his goals to his employees, receives back their suggestions, and creates his final objectives which have the input and support of his people. The entire company is thus involved in the attainment of the corporate objectives. Bi-monthly or quarterly reviews of progress are a part of the program, to monitor progress and allow for mid-stream correction. Annual evaluations give consideration to the success in meeting objectives.

> **An Obvious Pitfall**: Avoid permitting managers to set objectives which are too easily attained, thereby restricting corporate growth.

An informal Management by Objectives program may be implemented quite simply, using the same techniques above, merely dispensing with the use of special forms, with each manager being responsible for the attainment of objectives of those in his department. There is no formal measurement process by the Personnel Department.

> **The Key Point Is**: Given the dignity of a formal procedure, each manager should set objectives for personnel reporting to him and measure their performance against these objectives.
> **Helpful Hint**: A prerequisite to any Management by Objectives system is the definition of the basic responsibilities of each employee. There must be a Position Description (see Chapter 7) for each job. Standards of Performance should be established, to augment the functions described in the Position Description. Exhibit 14-c is the first page of a 21-point list of typical standards for programmers. Addended to it is an 8-point standard for programming trainees.

Whether or not there is a formal Management by Objectives program, following are:

GUIDES TO BE USED IN SETTING OBJECTIVES

When setting objectives for any individual's job, it is important to remember that the objective should not simply be a restatement of all the aspects of the individual's job description. The purpose of setting objectives is to pick 5 to 7 key goals or results to achieve within a specified time.

The objectives or goals or results desired should be stated as precisely as possible. The best way of achieving precise descriptions is to quantify the objectives. For example, the objective to "lower production costs" should be defined as "lower the cost of producing model 250 by 7% by September 1st." Unless the goal or objective is specifically defined, it will be difficult to determine to what degree it has been reached at the end of the specified period. Non-specific goals also result in a failure to properly appraise the magnitude of the job necessary to meet that goal.

For example, in discussing decreasing costs it is obvious that if you are producing three different items, you should be talking about three separate cost reduction goals rather than one. Additionally, with non-specfic goals or objectives, all the variables related to achieving those goals are not investigated by the managers who have to do the job to achieve them. For example, in one company a computer operations manager set a goal "to reduce the total time for processing customer statements by 10%." Not only did the manager fail to meet this goal, but he was barely able to hold his time down to the previous level. The fact that had been overlooked was the sales manager's goal. He had reached his goal of increasing volume with many new accounts, so the billing increased. If more effort were devoted to identifying the specific objective, it would have been related to "average time per statement" rather than the general way in which it was described. This is a very common error.

Results or objectives may be stated in dates for completion when no other measurement seems appropriate. For example, "complete a study of alternate life insurance programs by August 1 and recommend a new program to the President by November 1." This could even be restated as "recommend to the President by November 1 a new program that will provide benefits to match or exceed those offered in this area, but with no increase in cost for employees or the company." The more precise statement not only provides guidelines for evaluating the adequacy of the program, but provides considerable guidance to the man who has to accomplish the work. Below are some criteria in helping you to analyze your objectives to determine whether or not they are specific.

Criteria for Judging Objectives

"Good" Commitments are:

1. Stated in terms of end results.

2. Achievable in definite time period.

3. Definite as to the form of accomplishment.

4. Related to management of the business.

5. Important to success of the business.

6. Precisely stated in terms of quantities, where possible.

7. Each limited to one important commitment to a statement.

8. Those which require stretch to improve results or personal effectiveness.

"Poor" Commitments are:

1. Stated in terms of processes or activities.

2. Never fully achievable; no specific target date.

3. Ambiguous in defining what is expected.

4. Theoretical or "idealistic."

5. Not of real consequence.

6. Either too brief, indefinite, long or complex.

7. Compound, covering two or more commitments to a statement.

8. Lacking requirement for improvement. Following established routines and procedures will assure the commitment.

Although the objectives you list should not cover your entire job, they should cover those important or critical areas that will probably require your major efforts during the specified period. Do not list routine duties which are normal functions, and which do not require major efforts to bring about changes or up-grading. If your statement of objectives end up describing the maintenance of normal performance in your area of responsibility, do not bother writing them.

Attached are possible objectives which may be written for a plant superintendent.

OBJECTIVES

Prepared by a Plant Superintendent

1. Reduce plant operating costs to $0.94 per M units produced, by January 1.

2. Speed increase in #53 grade in the range of 100 fpm or more, by June 30.

3. Set up Central Planning Office where orders will be accumulated, by April 1.

4. Late orders not to exceed 10% of all orders shipped, by June 30.

5. Reduce budget $450.00 per month (3.5%), by January 1.

6. Analyze, develop drawings, and submit recommendations to determine feasibility of relocating Printing and Cutting Sections, by December 1.

7. Reduce exempt and non-exempt factory payroll $1,500.00 per month, by October 1.

8. All first level foremen attend in-plant training program stressing leadership techniques and communication, by June 30.

9. Obtain closer cooperation and communication between departmental foremen, by December 31.

10. Plan and carry out specified reading program in area of Production Management, by October 15.

11. Attend AMA Workshop Seminars on Production and Inventory Control, by March 31.

Giving due consideration to these guides, the following pages present a formal outline for implementing the Objectives program, showing, step by step, how the objectives are communicated to all company employees:

OUTLINE FOR
COMMUNICATING COMPANY OBJECTIVES

1. The President communicated his objectives to managers answering to him.

2. These managers draft specific objectives relating to the performance of the unit under their responsibility.

3. These managers meet with the President separately to discuss and mutually agree upon that manager's objectives, for the current fiscal year.

4. Each of these managers will then take the agreed-upon objectives and expose them in a group discussion with the next level managers reporting to them. The purpose of the meeting will be twofold, as follows:
   a. To explain our interest in the steps we will be taking to increase our communications regarding objectives.
   b. To fully explain the objectives of that division and to involve the lower level department heads in an open discussion covering ways they may develop objectives in their own areas of responsibility to meet the greater team objectives of that division. Each of these department heads will then be required to return within five working days with a draft of their specific objectives and will meet separately with the division head to discuss and mutually establish objectives for that department.

5. Department heads will then meet with a group of managers answering directly to them to carry on the same type of meeting as was conducted by the division head. (The Director of Personnel may meet with department heads either as a group or individually to provide guidance in wording or identifying objectives as well as to provide guidance in conducting the fact-to-face meetings between the department head and his subordinate managers.)

6. Attached is a form for recording objectives and recording due dates or anticipated review dates. Expected completion dates should be either the date on which a project must be completed or the end of the period; such as, the end of the fiscal year. The form also includes a section for review notes concerning the progress on each of the objectives, but there is no "evaluation" section per se. Results can be written in at the follow-up sessions between a manager and his superior. Our aim in this program is to achieve management participation without introducing a concept of a new or different evaluation procedure, or another way to pressure a manager.
   The Personnel Department will, in addition, develop a "performance evaluation guide" to be used by managers in reviewing and evaluating their subordinate managers, no less frequently than annually. (There is no formalized program at present.)

OBJECTIVES PLANNING

Job Title _____ Name _____ Date _____

Priority	Objectives	Expected Completion Date	Results
1.			
2.			
3.			
4.			
5.			
6.			
7.			

7. It is understood that the establishing of certain objectives for one particular department or division may require the cooperation and a similar objective on the part of another division or department. For example, should the Marketing Division desire to establish a program of collection and analysis of certain sales data, it may be necessary for discussion and a mutual agreement between Marketing and Data Processing to establish due dates when such a program would be available from the computer. Data Processing would also have as one of their objectives the related due dates for the revision or creation of necessary programs to provide the data needed by Marketing.

FOLLOW-UP

1. The President would maintain a file of the objectives as stated by the managers reporting to him.

2. These managers would, in turn, maintain a complete file of objectives for all of the managers or supervisors under their responsibility.

3. The President and each manager will meet individually with his subordinate

managers for the purpose of reviewing objectives, no less than quarterly. However, when an objective of any manager involves a completion date which is not consistent with a quarterly review, that specific objective may be reviewed by the two appropriate managers on a frequency as desired by the senior manager.

4. In the event that due either to conditions beyond the corporation's control or because of decisions made by the corporation, it is necessary to revise or eliminate objectives within a division, the changes may be accomplished only with the approval of the President. Changes in objectives at any level within a division would require the approval of the head of that division prior to the change.

5. Within 90 days of the date of introduction of the program, the President will meet with managers answering to him to evaluate the program's progress.

In summary, management of the personnel of the data processing department is no mystery. It involves the same techniques that the good manager brings to managing people in any department.

The key is:

Employees are individuals and different things motivate each one. How can we reach each person when everyone is so different? Does a common denominator exist? It does—it is INVOLVEMENT. All people are more productive when they experience *pride* and a *sense of accomplishment* in their work. People need to be *recognized* for their efforts, not only financially, but with *praise, status,* and even constructive criticism.

Involvement is the key to productivity. When you involve an individual, you are actually telling him, "I feel you have something to offer; you are a responsible individual who has an important role in our company. I recognize your ability and seek your help with this project."

The steps to take are these:

1. Fully communicate goals and objectives of both your job and their own, role of the department, general targets of the company, etc.

2. Through discussion get them to spell out specific job duties and responsibilities.

3. Let each man set objectives to be reached for each responsibility in terms of time, dollars, number of pieces produced, etc.

4. Help each man write an operating plan as to *how* the objectives will be reached.

5. Measure the progress and discuss problem areas along the way.

6. Help each man develop his strengths and correct any limitations blocking his effectiveness.

7. Reset goals and objectives for the next time period.

Through this technique, not only do we have a highly motivated, responsive work cadre, but we also have developed independent, capable workers whose personal desires more nearly align themselves with the desires of the company.

CONTROL

The third aspect of the managment of the data processing function, preceded by Organization and Personnel Management, is Control. This insures that the DP manager will not become the tool of the department, the machine, or the system; that he will not need to accept excuses that the machine is down, the program doesn't work, the key punch operator didn't show up to work, the input hasn't come in from another department . . . . and on and on. Control involves direction, regulation, verification, and planning. In short—no surprises.

> **Case in Point:** The Equity Funding insurance scandal, perhaps the biggest insurance fraud in history, was based on the recording, by the computer, of non-existent insurance policies. With proper input-output controls in the DP department, and the tieing-out of report totals, one to the other, the scheme could not have succeeded. It would have had to involve too many lower echelon personnel. It succeeded with the involvement of only a few key people, simply because quality controls were omitted in the DP department.

The fulcrum for this control system is the Input/Output Staff (see Exhibit 14-a for Organizational Chart position), sometimes called the Quality Control Staff, reporting directly to the Manager of Data Processing Operations. It is set apart from keypunching or other inputting services as well as from systems and programming. It cannot, thus, be manipulated by other sections of the department but is concerned only with proper, quality-controlled operations.

Let us see how Control works.

It starts with the formal implementation of a Systems and Procedures Department. The may consist of one man and, at first, is not concerned only with computer documentation, but rather with the flow of data, paperwork, and reports which are manually generated. The work study used in the evaluation process, described on page 202, is the first task of the new Systems and Procedures Department. Not only is this fundamental to the decision on whether and how to automate, but it is equally fundamental to the management of the company which functions under manual control. These are the steps taken by the Systems group:

1. Evaluate the reporting system (See page 202).

2. Establish major business categories which will require system control, such as: accounting, order/billing, purchasing, data processing, office services, personnel, production, sales, research. Use the Organizational Chart to help in this.

3. Establish Position Descriptions for each job (Chapter 7) in a management capacity, and work standards (Exhibit 14-c) for each employee reporting to a manager.

4. Write down the operating procedures for each department if they involve the transmission of data outside the department—that is, the procedures are inter-departmental.

5. Record these procedures in a Procedures Manual, organized by major business

categories, containing an index, and with provision for up-date and correction through a Correction Checklist (Chapter 7).

6. Require, through one of the inter-departmental procedures in the Procedures Manual, that all intra-departmental procedures and work rules be written down, kept current, expanded to fit new jobs, and kept under the control of the department head.

The duties and responsibilities of every employee have now been written down and circulated; the flow of paper work has been delineated in the procedures; inter-departmental relationships have been established, and the framework for a Control system is in place.

The performance within this framework must now be measured and monitored. Monitoring measures progress, avoids surprises, allows corrective action, and provides that deadlines will be met. The entire system is monitored through the Data Processing Report Schedule shown in Exhibit 14-d. This records and tracks each machine-generated report, comparing delivery dates to due dates and input delivery dates to input due dates. Tracking of input data provides an early warning that output reports may be late. This schedule is up-dated and recirculated for every new date or change listed therein. Each department head examines the schedule for those items which effect his area, taking corrective action necessary to meet the due dates.

Similarly, various departments receive reports from data processing which are used as a basis for generating various manual reports. Most of these are accounting-department generated. Others come from Purchasing or Production departments. A report schedule, for monitoring purposes, is shown at Exhibit 14-e. This shows each manually generated accounting department report. the due date, and the actually delivered date for each of three months. The Accounting Manager uses this to monitor the production of his own department, and other recipient managers use it to plan reports and work which they, in turn, generate off these reports.

We have just examined how finished report production is monitored. This involves circulation of status reports inter-departmentally. However, the work-in-progress needs, also, to be monitored within each department. Such reports are mainly for the department head's use but may be circulated to other department managers who have an interest in the work. A Systems and Programming Department Status report is shown at Exhibit 14-f. This lists open projects and compares actual to budgeted hours, dates, people and man days, shows the percent complete and any comments.

> **Note of Caution:** This is not an exception report, but rather contains a great deal of detail about each job. Each line must be scrutinized carefully to get the full benefit of the report. If this report is simply scanned or only one column is monitored, important warning signals may be missed, such as the actual start date.

In addition to monitoring the overall activities of the department, that is, all their tasks, in Exhibit 14-f through the Department Status report, each specific project is tracked, in detail, by the project manager. Exhibit 14-g through m is a series of forms to meet this need:

Exhibit 14-g — New Project Request, or

      14-h — Program Change Request   — to define the job.

      14-i — Project Status Notice   — to the user department head, to keep him informed of project progress.

      14-j — Implementation Schedule — prepared by the project manager for assignment of tasks to his people.

      14-k — Program Assignment Form — to define the specific program and assign it to a specific programmer.

      14-l — Trouble Scan Request   — to identify programming problems and correct them.

      14-m — Gantt Chart   — to establish scheduling.

The skillful utilization of these monitoring tools will provide all the controls necessary to have a smoothly functioning data processing department. The final aspect of control to be considered is that of security.

SECURITY

Data processing security involves not only safeguards to prevent theft, fire, power failure, or negligence, but also to provide for the proper and accurate generation of data.

The Input/Output staff, described on page 204, has the responsibility to tie-out and sign-off on all reports before they are released. Where control totals are not a part of the program, this staff strikes manual totals to verify the program result. All related reports are cross-checked and tied-out. Batch totals and counts are verified. The end result provides assurance that:

1. All input data has been key-punched or otherwise processed.

2. The correct program and report has been run.

3. The data has been processed without error.

4. Proof totals have been checked and the report is not at variance with any other report.

5. The totals of this report are/will be carried forward to other appropriate reports.

For example, all customers' invoices are batch-totaled, with hash totals by invoice number and totals of dollar amounts. Invoices are run through the Invoice Register program. The totals are carried forward to the Sales program, Accounts Receivable program, Sales Taxes Payable program, Freight Billable program, Product Line Sales program, Average Pricing program, Credit Analysis program, and Product Line Analysis by Sales Territories program. The output of the Invoice Register program is the input for each of the other listed programs. There is no possibility for undetected fraud or error.

The detailed work performance standards for the Input/Output Staff clearly delineate the cross-checking controls to be effected for each program. These, of course, will vary with each particular company, but it is essential that proper planning and effort be put into this part of the control system. In this regard, the Systems Department plays a vital role in designing, analysing, programming, and "running" the system. It uses a Check List, shown at Exhibit 14-n to be sure that every aspect of the system is controlled. This begins with the Assignment of the job and ends with the Run Book Instructions, shown in Exhibit 14-o. The operation run book contains complete instructions to run each program within each system. It insures that the program will be run in the proper sequence, that proper edits will be performed and control routines utilized.

Try These Other Helpful Security Hints:

- Lock up money-oriented forms—checks, invoices, credit memos, accounts receivable statements—to avoid stealing and substitution of a falsified document.
- Divide responsibilities—programmers have no access to the computer; computer personnel have no access to programs; operations personnel have no access to money-oriented forms; other departments have no access to the computer room, to programming records, to forms; decollation and distribution of reports is performed by another department; accounts receivable and collection functions are separate; the authority to issue credits to customers is part of the collection function, not that of accounts receivable.

In addition to the security against incorrect reports and fraud, steps must be taken to provide for the basic protection against catastrophe—fire, theft, bombing, earthquake, flood. No amount of insurance can compensate you for the difficulties involved in recreating your files and records. Security against catastrophe basically involves storing duplicate records off-premises and replacing them with updates, each month. In that way, only the current month's transactions must be restructured in the event of a disaster. Storage can be done in a vault at a local bank, or in a safe on other company owned premises.

The following vital files should be duplicated off-premises:

- Daily Billing
- Monthly Accounts Receivable
- Customer Name/Address Master File
- Year to Date Payroll

The billing file should be updated daily to include daily billing. The accounts receivable file should be updated to include the daily transaction register of cash and journal entries.

This daily updating means that files must be run and delivered to the vault, daily. Timely, and a bother, but well worth the effort in the event of a fire. These files are the only ones necessary to enable the company to continue operating without sustaining any losses. It will not be necessary to so control accounts payable, as these can be reconstructed from bank records.

The Systems Department should further review the paperwork flow of the business to determine what additional security is needed in this particular company. For example, orders in the process of being shipped are pre-data entry, but they should be controlled off premises to avoid much customer dissatisfaction.

Try This Helpful Security Device for Orders:

Copies of all orders written by the Order/Billing department are mailed on a daily basis to one of two Post Office boxes rented at the local post office. The boxes are used alternately, month to month. On the first of each month, one box is emptied and that empty box is the one to which orders are then sent for the current month. The contents of the emptied box are put through a shredder under the supervision of the Order/Billing Department manager. In the event of a fire, pertinent batches of orders are easily retrieved, since they are still in their original post marked envelopes.

This system will allow the company to fill all orders, collect all accounts receivable, continue to pay and account for all employee payrolls, and, effectively, to generate financial statements from the end of the preceeding month. The only remaining requirement is to safeguard the data processing programs, themselves.

Accomplish the Security of Data This Way:

- Duplicate and store off-premises all source decks.

- Duplicate program documentation and sotre off-premises.

- Run cumulative files onto tape and store off-premises.

- Microfilm the run book and store off-premises.

- Microfilm unaudited tax year general ledgers and store off-premises.

- Microfilm posting copies of invoices for permanent off-premises storage.

Case in Point: A distribution company sustained a $2 million warehouse fire—a total loss. The cumulative perpetual inventory file had been duplicated and retained off-premises, at the end of each month. Current month's usage was easily recreated from the daily billing update file, also retained off the premises. Receipts were built up from proofs of delivery supplied by vendors and common carriers. Within a month the entire perpetual inventory at the time of the loss was reconstructed and submitted to the insurance company for full payment.

These additional security devices can be provided for hardware. The computer manufacturer will lend assistance and advice in each area:

1. Sprinkler protection (in specific areas).

2. Fireproof and explosion proof window guards.

3. Humidity control.

4. By-pass electrical generator.

Bear in mind these Practical Pointers: The Data Processing Function, whether manual or automated, is vital to the success of every operation. It must have proper organization within the corporate structure; its personnel should set objectives, consonant with corporate goals; all phases of the input and output of the department should be monitored and controlled, and positive security procedures should be instituted against fraud or other disasters.

CHAPTER **15**

Administering Stock Option

and Incentive Plans

S TOCK option and incentive plans, regardless of the verbiage with which they are varnished, are nothing more than profit-sharing plans and, as such, they represent the best way to motivate and retain employees, from the lowest ranks to the most key. Current income tax treatment is a determinant of the amount of after-tax benefits to be retained, but this is of significant interest only to the highest-paid employee group. Tax treatment notwithstanding, these profit-sharing devices work in any tax climate to perform their basic function, that of increasing the profits of the enterprise through employee motivation. These plans are variously known as Qualified Stock Option Plans and Non-qualified Stock Option Plans. The features of each and means of administering and controlling them, their accounting and tax aspects are discussed in this chapter.

QUALIFIED STOCK OPTIONS

Features

Qualified Stock Options are options granted to individual employees to buy stock in their employer corporation. There is usually no income realized by the employee on receipt of the grant nor on exercise of the option, though the exercise may subject him to a minimum tax preference under the Internal Revenue Code. Gain on sale of the stock is usually long-term capital gain. The obvious advantage to the employee is one of leverage. He receives the right to buy the stock at today's price, for years to come, with no cash outlay required. In effect, he has a "call" on the corporation's stock, without having had to pay for it. The right to exercise is generally spread out over a period of years. Thus, if the company's stock appreciates, the employee is induced to remain with the company until he completes the exercise of all available options. In order to be "qualified" and enjoy this favored tax treatment, a stock option must meet all of the following requirements:

1. The option must be granted within 12 months before or after adoption of the plan approved by shareholders. The plan may not run for over 10 years, must state total shares available for option and the classes or employees covered by the plan.

2. The option may not be exercised later than 5 years after grant; only the employee himself may exercise it while he lives, and there are restrictions on transfer at death; no option may be exercised while there is a prior outstanding option at a higher price for each employee.

3. The option price at the time of grant may not be less than the fair market value of the stock (usually the average of the high and low traded prices for a public company, or the average of the high bid and low asked prices for over-the-counter stocks).

4. Options may not be granted to persons owning more than 5% of the company's stock. This may be increased to 10%, by formula, for companies with equity capital up to $2 million.

Tax Treatment and Accounting

For tax years ending after 12/31/69, the difference between the exercise price and the fair market value of the stock on the date of exercise is a tax preference item, subject to minimum tax. One-half of any net long-term capital gain on sale of the stock is also a tax preference item. The Tax Reform Act of 1976 imposed the minimum tax on tax preference items. Briefly, it is a 5% tax, or one-half of the regular income taxes imposed for the tax year, whichever is greater. With proper planning of stock sales over a period of years, the minimum tax can gererally be avoided except in the case of enormous gains.

> **Word of Caution:** The Tax Reform Act of 1976 permits Qualified Option Treatment only for options granted from Plans in effect prior to May 20, 1976, provided that such options are exercised by May 21, 1976.

The Qualified Stock Option Plan, like all other option plans, is a profit-sharing device, to the extent that the optionee, once he purchases the shares, participates in the profits of the corporation like any other shareholder, receiving dividends and, presumably, if there are profits, a higher stock price as reflected in the fair market value of the shares as determined with reference to the company's price/earnings ratio.

A Qualified Plan, like any of the other plans discussed in this chapter, is applicable to the public and private company, alike. Because most option plans have a market value feature, they are generally thought to be useful only to the public company with a readily ascertainable market for its shares. All that is needed, however, is a relatively simple formula to determine stock price, consistently applied from year to year, and a stock option program may become a viable profit-sharing device for the privately owned company.

> **Helpful Hint:** Valuation of closely held stock, aside from arriving at an option grant

price, should be a continuing thing. Tremendous tax payments may depend on the outcome of IRS disputes over the stock's value. Even the continuity of the business may be at stake if a liquidation at sacrifice price is necessary to pay for estate taxes. Particularly in a declining market, an owner may find an excellent tax planning opportunity, since the value of a close-held company is related to the value of equivalent publicly traded companies.

The Plan will meet the requirement of the Code even if the employee must first offer the stock to the corporation before selling it, and the corporation may pay the employee to cancel the option. This makes it possible for the close-held corporation to offer options to its employees as an "incentifying" device, without actually losing control of any of its shares. Payments received by the employee for cancellation of the option are taxed to him as ordinary income and are likewise tax deductible by the corporation. If stock acquired under an option is not held the required time (3 years), any gain on disposition is ordinary income, and the corporation can also tax-deduct the same amount as compensation paid to the employee. No deduction is given the corporation when it transfers the stock on exercise of an option. For financial accounting purposes, then, there is no charge against current earnings when the option is granted or exercised, nor when the stock is disposed of, whether it be an early or normal disposition. Earnings will be charged if payment is made to cancel the option. If the corporation repurchases stock from the employee at a higher than grant price, earnings are not charged. The corporation is merely buying treasury stock, and any gain or loss is deferred until eventual disposition of the treasury stock. As previously stated, however, the corporation is allowed a tax deduction for an early, under 3-year, disposition, though not a financial accounting deduction. This becomes a Schedule M-1 item on the corporation's Form 1120 tax return, to reconcile book income with taxable income. It is reflected on the company's books through a direct reduction in the current tax liability and an increase in paid in capital, in accord with APB Opinion No. 15. This handsome aspect of the Qualified Plan is generally overlooked—it can actually decrease taxable income with no effect on financial reported income, or, said another way, it can increase total net worth by the tax effect of the allowable deduction. The simplest way to monitor the availability of this benefit is to send a questionnaire, annually, to each optionee, requiring him to report, as to his sales of option stocks, the date acquired, option price, date sold and sale price. This is most easily accomplished on January 31st of each year, at which time Form 3921 must be sent to each employee who exercised stock options during the year. Form 3921 (see Exhibit 15-a) must be filed at an Internal Revenue Service Center by February 28th, with a covering summary Form 4067. The Internal Revenue Code covering Qualified Stock Options is Section 422.

Non-corporate Use of Options

A typical method for finding the market value of options granted in the stock of a non-public company is to use the price/earnings ratio of similar or competitive public companies. If this is not available, a p/e ratio may be "attributed" to the company based on offers it may have had to buy the company or which the company, itself, may have made to buy others. Failing such offers, the company may analyze its own financial position, history of earnings and future prospects to arrive at a value for the corporation which it would consider as a reasonable selling price should a buyer materialize. The option price is now discernible:

Number of shares outstanding	50,000
Net income, last fiscal year	$100,000
Price at which the company would sell	$500,000
Price/earnings ratio	5 to 1
Fair Market Value per share (option price)	$10

It is possible that the price at which the company would sell is more or less than the p/e ratio, in which case one or the other figure must be used. The p/e ratio, if readily evident, is usually more accurate since, by definition, it encompasses a fair market value price for the company that discounts all factors affecting earnings. No adjustments, therefore, need be made to the p/e ratio calculation. If the price at which the company would sell is used, then a myriad of adjustments could be made to sophisticate the calculation. Is the price payable in installments; is investment letter stock used to buy the company subject to the usual selling restrictions; what is the interest rate on the time payout; how is property paid in lieu of cash to be valued? All of these factors should be discounted or present valued to arrive at a reduced selling price in terms of cash today.

> **Helpful Hint**: Qualified options, while applicable only to corporations, can be an equally effective incentive device for employees of individual proprietorships, partnerships or non-corporate joint ventures. While the plan will not be considered "qualified" for IRS purposes, all of the features may be adopted by the enterprise to achieve the motivational aspects of the plan. The employee receives a call on the stock for 5 years at a fixed price. If the option is structured so that it may be exercised only to the extent of 25% each year after the first year, the employee is effectively wedded to the company for at least this 5-year period, particularly in a period of increasing earnings and p/e ratios, which is exactly the time when you want and need that employee. Such a plan reduces key personnel turnover, increases employee morale, and induces each optionee to be profit motivated.

A Typical Qualified Plan

A fully Qualified Stock Option Plan for key employees, containing this 25% per year exercisable feature, is shown at Exhibit 15-b. The Qualified Stock Option Contract, between the company and the employee, specifies the number of shares granted, the price, the expiration date for exercise, the 25% exercise limitation, the employee's requirement for continued employment, and certain IRS rules which prohibit exercise while there are prior outstanding options. This contract is shown in Exhibit 15-c.

> **Beware This Pitfall**: The Code requires a qualified stock option plan to be approved by the stockholders of the employer corporation. Treasury regulations amplify this,

requiring consent of a majority of the voting stock. This means an absolute majority of the outstanding stock. Thus, if stockholders holding 40% of the voting stock voted and approved the plan by 80% of the votes cast, this would be only 32% (80% x 40%) of the outstanding stock and would not constitute majority approval.

Administration of Option Plans

The administration of any type of stock option plan requires control over the number of shares granted and exercised and provision for determination of shares available for grant and calculation of unexercised shares at any given point in time. This information is required for presentation in the Notes to Financial Statements in the Capital Stock footnote to the Annual Report. It may also be required if form S-8 is filed with the Securities and Exchange Commission in the event that the option plan is registered for public trading. A typical Annual Report footnote to the Financial Statements is presented in Exhibit 15-d which illustrates the type and amount of disclosure required with regard to stock option plans of any type. The grant and exercise of options may be recorded in a Stock Option Ledger, a page of which is reproduced at Exhibit 15-e. This is used to accumulate, on one page, all the historical information that will ever be needed with reference to any option—the date of grant, number of shares, price at time of grant, date and amount of shares exercised, market value at date of exercise, number of shares terminating, and the balance of shares which may be exercised at the present time or in the future. Information can be pulled from these ledger pages to present total option information in any required format. Exhibit 15-f presents an Employee Stock Option Summary sheet which is used by the employee's supervisor as a basis to recommend the grant of additional options. It summarizes all previous grants and exercises, keying off each exercise against the original grant, to enable the reviewer to ascertain readily how many shares remain unexercised attributable to each grant and showing the cumulative unexercised shares from all grants. This record is posted concurrently with the Stock Option Ledger page to provide an instantly retrievable summary for management review.

Qualified vs. Non-qualified

In summary, then, Qualified Stock Option Plans offer certain favorable tax benefits to the corporation and the employee if the pre-set conditions under the Code are met. These benefits generally do not tax the employee at the time of grant or exercise and offer long-term capital gain treatment if the stock is held for 3 years after exercise. Subsequent grants at lower prices may not be exercised before prior grants at higher prices. This condition may make Qualified Options undesirable in times of a declining stock market. For example, an employee is granted 100 shares in year 1 at $20 a share, with the right to exercise 25% each year. He is, then, granted 100 additional shares at the end of year 1 at $10 per share. Under the IRC requirements, he may exercise 25 shares at $20 at the end of years 1 and 2 and no shares at $10 until he has bought another 50 shares at $20 in years 3 and 4. This could effectively negate any value any Qualified Option might have. No one will pay $20 when the market is $10. To counter this objection, a company may turn to the use of Non-qualified Stock Options.

NON-QUALIFIED STOCK OPTIONS

Features

The Non-qualified Stock Option Plan is any plan which is not Qualified and, therefore, not the recipient of the favorable tax treatment which accrues to Qualified plans. Non-qualified plans are diverse in their terms and conditions, each containing a somewhat different wrinkle, limited only by the imaginations of the plan designers. Their commonality is their purpose, the same as in Qualified plans, of motivating employees through profit-sharing incentive. Options in such plans are usually granted at market value or below, and in some cases, even at prices above market value. The Code provides that the difference between the grant price and exercise price is taxable income at the time of exercise, unlike the relief from this tax provided for Qualified options. This means the employee may have a tax to pay at the time he *buys* the stock. He must lay out cash to purchase and to pay tax on the grant/exercise spread. On the other hand, non-qualified option stock need be held only 6 months to obtain long-term capital gain treatment, rather than 3 years as with a Qualified option. A corporation may use both Qualified and Non-qualified plans at the same time. In fact, this is advisable in times of a declining market where Qualified options have been granted. As described just above, no Qualified option may be exercised while there is outstanding a prior option at a higher price. This does not totally obviate the use of the Qualified option, as the employee can permit the 5 years to elapse on the prior option without exercising it, at which time it automatically is canceled, and the next option in line may then be exercised. This, however, requires up to 5 years and may effectively blunt any incentive aspects of the plan. As an alternative, Non-qualified options may be granted in times of declining market values, and these may be exercised in accordance with the terms of the grant, without regard to any previously granted Qualified options. IRS Revenue Ruling 73-26 merely provides that the employer may not issue "tandem" options, consisting of a Non-qualified and a Qualified option, under terms providing that the exercise of one option reduces the number of shares for which the other option can be exercised. This ruling was effective 1/2/72 and was not retroactive. Plans which included a tandem feature could continue to be used, thereafter, provided that the Non-qualified option was no longer attached to the Qualified grant.

Tax Treatment and Accounting

Non-qualified options, further, became more attractive with the Tax Reform Act of 1969 which imposed the minimum tax on tax preference items (see page 220) and, at the same time, raised the long-term capital gains rate to 30% above $50,000. This served to narrow the gap between ordinary income and capital gains tax rates. Tax rates, then, combined with the declining stock market prices since 1969 have made the Non-gualified stock option a most attractive incentive strategy. By properly structuring their terms, such as requiring the ability to exercise at the rate of 25% each year, the same inducement can be provided for continuous employment. From the employee standpoint, moreover, the holding period for whatever long-term capital gains benefit there may be is reduced from 3 years to 6 months. As an added advantage, the Non-qualified option may be granted to holders of more than 5% of the company's stock.

From a tax standpoint, any option which does not meet all the requirements of a Qualified option is defined as a Non-qualified option. As such, the Non-qualified option is taxed when the stock option is exercised. The tax is ordinary, not capital gain, and it is based on the difference between the grant price and the market value at the time of exercise. The company receives a tax deduction in the same amount as the employee has taxable income, and, for financial accounting purposes, paid-in capital is increased, as with Qualified options (page 221). Within this framework, a variety of Non-qualified plans may be structured to meet the requirements of the company.

A Typical Non-qualified Plan

The most common Non-qualified plan is one which offers almost all of the features of the standard Qualified plan, except that one of its features is changed to make it non-qualified. For example, the option may be exercised up to 6 years after grant, rather than 5 years. If tied in with an exercise privilege of 25% per year, it provides for continuity of employment on the part of each grantee. Even more simply, the standard option plan may provide for the grant of Qualified or Non-qualified options, as long as they are not issued in "tandem." The mere designation of the grant as Non-qualified by the company makes it so, even though the terms and conditions are similar to those of the Qualified grant. The actual contract and all supporting documentation, would have to bear the words "non-qualified" in their title and terms.

A Non-qualified Plan with Option Repurchase Feature

An attractive Non-qualified plan may commonly be structured to take advantage of the tax to the employee on the difference between the fair market value of the stock purchased and the purchase (grant) price which is taxed as earned income in the year the option is exercised. Because this tax treatment may require a substantial cash outlay by the optionee at the time the option is exercised, the plan could permit the optionee to exercise less than all of his options, while the issuing company would purchase back the remaining options for the difference between the fair market value and the exercise price. To give an example, suppose Company A grants employee B a Non-qualified option to purchase 2000 shares of stock at $15 per share. The stock price then rises to $30 per share. B will then exercise his option for 1000 shares, which will require a cash payment of $15,000. In addition, B will be taxed on the difference between the fair market value of the stock and the exercise price, say at an earned income rate of 50%, bringing the total cash outlay involved to $22,500. Now, suppose at the same time A purchases B's remaining option of 1000 shares for $15,000, on which B will be taxed in the amount of $7,500. The effect of this is to bring B's total cash outlay to $30,000, of which $15,000 has been provided by A, which, in turn, will receive a tax deduction for $30,000 (B's taxable income of $15,000 on the grant/market value at purchase spread, plus the $15,000 cost of buying B's remaining option). B has paid $15,000 for stock worth $30,000 and, effectively, pays no tax on the difference. This type of arrangement may be artfully combined with an option feature like a decrease in the exercise price in proportion to an increase in the stock price, providing even more beneficial results to A and B. Such a feature is called a "variable-price" option.

A Non-qualified Plan with Variable-Price Feature

The Variable-Price Non-qualified Option is primarily directed at solving the employee's tax problem when he exercises his option (the difference between the price he pays for the option, or the grant price, and the market value at the time he exercises it will be taxed to him at the highest bracket which applies, subject to a maximum tax of 50% on earned income). In some cases, this type of option can net the optionee even more after-tax money than the usual Qualified option. In a variable-price plan, assume a market price at the time of grant of $100 and a market value at exercise time of $160. This $60 increase in the stock price is deducted, dollar for dollar, from the $100 grant price, resulting in a new exercise price of $40 per share. The optionee has ordinary income of the difference between market price at the time of exercise and his exercise price, or $120 ($160 minus $40). This $120 is earned income subject to the 50% maximum, and his tax would therefore be $60 per share. The company, similarly, has a tax deduction of $120 and an increase in paid-in capital of the tax effect, or $60. Adding the employee's tax of $60 to his purchase price of $40 gives him a cost of $100 per share. This will equate to the same cost as if he had been granted a Qualified option at the $100 market value at the time of the grant. However, the optionee has received a more favored tax position using the variable-price option. His tax basis is now $160 per share ($40 purchase price plus his ordinary income of $120), whereas his Qualified basis would be $100. If he now sells one year after exercise at say $200, his long-term capital gain would be only $40. Taxed at 25% up to $50,000 of income, he would pay a tax of $10 per share, netting $190 after tax. With an original cost of $100 ($40 purchase price plus $60 tax paid on exercise), his net after-tax income would be $90 per share. Contrasting this with the Qualified option, he could not have obtained long-term capital gain treatment unless he had held the stock for a full 3-year period. He would, thus, have had ordinary income of $100 a share ($200 sale price minus $100 exercise price), a 50% tax of $50, and net after-tax income of $50 per share, compared to $90 for the variable-price shares. If he had waited the full 3 years to avail himself of the 25% long-term capital gains rate, his tax of $25 would net him $75, still less than the $90 under the variable-price plan. There is a further advantage over the Qualified option. With a Qualified option, a tax-preference item exists for the difference between the grant price (which is the exercise price) and the market value at the time of exercise (see page 220). This amount is subject to a 15% tax and also reduces earned income which is eligible for the 50% ceiling rate above the statutory exemptions.

From an after-tax dollar standpoint, the company is in about the same position on either the variable-price or the Qualified option. It would have collected $100 from the employee in the Qualified plan, with no tax deduction. In the variable-price plan, it collects $40 and receives a tax deduction as employee compensation paid of $120, worth $60 to the company, resulting in a net of $100—about the same under either plan. From a financial accounting standpoint, neither the Qualified nor the Non-qualified plan illustrated has any affect on net income reported, since they were both granted at market value, with no discount. Paid-in Capital, and hence net worth, are increased by the tax effect of any disposition made under the Qualified Plan in less than three years, or $50 in this example. There would, also, be a corresponding reduction in the current tax liability account. In the case of the variable-price plan, the corporation would have an ordinary tax deduction as compensation paid of $120 on exercise, and the tax effect of $60 would increase paid-in capital and decrease the current tax liability.

FINANCING OPTIONS

Qualified options generally do not require any formal company financial assistance. One of their principal features is to permit the grantee to receive and hold the option for up to 5 years, subject to no tax. This permits him to observe the market and not exercise his option until the market price is significantly higher than the grant price. In this enviable position, he is usually able to obtain financing from friends, relatives, or even banks. Bank loans to purchase stock are subject to Federal Reserve Board requirements which are similar to the margin requirements established by brokerage houses. The margin rates fluctuate, tied to the money supply, but generally range from 65% to 80%, as a percentage of market value which a bank may lend. This type of loan has the disadvantage that a drop in market value will occasion a margin call by the bank which the employee may not be able to meet. Banks do not count fractions of a point in stock value, so that a 1/4 point drop could require 1 point in margin. As an example, a bank lends 80% of market value when 5000 shares of stock are selling at $4 per share—a $16,000 loan. The market value declines to $3 3/4 a share. The bank will value the stock at the nearest lower whole point or $3 a share. Their maximum loan of 80% on $15,000 can be $12,000. The margin call is, thus, $4000 on a 1/4 price drop with a total market value drop of only $1,250 on the 5000 shares. A better strategy for the employee could be personal loans over a 36-month period. This requires a uniform pay-down at standard interest rates over the loan term at the end of which, he would own the stock outright. At some point, say after a year, a small portion of the stock could be sold in an early disposition to meet future loan payments. The balance of the stock would then be held the full 3 years to obtain the favorable long-term capital gain treatment. As another alternative, some companies may make a loan to the employee for a 6-month or 1-year period, to provide a bridge financing until the first sale of stock is made. This does not require a formal loan program, but the corporation should require that the stock be held as collateral for repayment of the loan. The features of this type of loan are discussed in Chapter 11.

Non-qualified options present some special problems with regard to financing. The cash needs are usually more stringent as an immediate tax must be paid on exercise on the difference between the exercise price and the market value on the date of exercise. Of course, if this spread is large, the employee will exercise and sell the same day, going for the assured profit, despite the ordinary tax rate which attaches to that profit. In this case, no financing is needed, at least not for more than a few days. However, if he elects to go for the long-term gain after 6 months, then he may require financing to purchase the stock, and, perhaps, to pay the tax on exercise, should his tax payment date fall due prior to sale of the stock. In the case of a straight wage-earner, subject to wage withholding taxes, and filing no estimated tax returns because he has no other income, a sudden surge of income through the exercise of non-qualified options could throw him into a position where estimated income tax returns need to be filed at the next quarterly due date. This makes the need for cash urgent and imminent. The employee's company may provide financing through a formal plan, available to all key option holders. State laws must be researched first, however, as some states prohibit corporations to lend money to employees to finance stock purchases. A notable example of this is New York State. If state laws prohibit such loans by the parent corporation, a subsidiary corporation in another state without such prohibition may be used. Delaware, a common home for many corporations, has no such restrictions. This notwithstanding, Regulation G of the Federal Reserve Board established a limitation of 35% of the market value, at any time, as the maximum amount of such a loan by a corporation. This may be a benefit as the corporation can lend more money to the employee after exercise, should the market value rise. A financing plan for either Qualified or Non-qualified options is illustrated at Exhibit 15-g. Under this program, 30% of market value is loaned to the employee to provide a 5% cushion under the 35% FRB maximum loan requirement. This avoids having to call the optionee for margin due to slight fluctuations in the market value. The loan is secured by the stock and a non-recourse note. The non-recourse note means that the corporation may look only to the stock for repayment of the loan, not to any other assets the borrower may have.

The company may further assist the option holder with financing by providing introductions to banks with which it deals and making specific recommendations to bank officers for key employees. Bank accommodations for these recommendations are usually a matter of customer good-will and are done without any corporate guarantees for the employee.

OPTING FOR OPTIONS

It is possible to effectively reach and motivate the myriads of individuals involved in any company's growth. The best technique to use is some sort of profit-sharing plan. The best of these is probably the stock option plan. It is glamourous, smacking of ownership in the enterprise, simple to understand, and easy to administer. It may be adapted to any form of organizational structure and provides interesting tax benefits to both the company and the recipient. Stock option plans may be tied in to individual performance by varying the amount of shares granted, but they mainly stress overall company performance and goals, since their ultimate value over the years comes down to bottom-line performance, earnings per share after taxes. As the company is successful in its environment, so, too, may the key manager share in that success through the proper incentive option plan. The stock option plan will work in any tax climate and under any market conditions.

APPENDIX A

Treasurer's and Controller's Functions Defined by the Financial Executives Institute

THE major areas of responsibilities of Treasurers and Controllers have been defined by the Financial Executives Institute (FEI), the managing financial executives' major professional society. It is the voice of the professional manager in the business and financial community and has established rules of practice and conduct for him. These defined responsibilities, as they appeared in *Financial Executive* magazine, are reproduced below:

CONTROLLERSHIP AND TREASURERSHIP FUNCTIONS DEFINED BY FEI

The first official statement of the responsibilities of the corporate treasurership function was approved in 1962 by the Board of Directors of Financial Executives Institute (established in 1931 as Controllers Institute of America). For many years the Institute and its predecessor body had published an established list of functions of controllership. The newly approved list of treasurership functions was developed coincident with the change of scope and name of the Institute from Controllers Institute to Financial Executives Institute.

FINANCIAL MANAGEMENT

CONTROLLERSHIP	TREASURERSHIP
Planning for Control	**Provision of Capital**
To establish, coordinate and administer, as an integral part of management, an adequate plan for the control of operations. Such a plan would provide, to the extent required in the business, profit planning, programs for capital investing and for financing, sales forecasts, expense budgets and cost standards, together with the necessary procedures to effectuate the plan.	To establish and execute programs for the provision of the capital required by the business, including negotiating the procurement of capital and maintaining the required financial arrangements.
	Investor Relations
	To establish and maintain an adequate market for the company's securities and, in connection

FINANCIAL MANAGEMENT

CONTROLLERSHIP

Reporting and Interpreting

To compare performance with operating plans and standards, and to report and interpret the results of operations to all levels of management and to the owners of the business. This function includes the formulation of accounting policy, the coordination of systems and procedures, the preparation of operating data and of special reports as required.

Evaluating and Consulting

To consult with all segments of management responsible for policy or action concerning any phase of the operation of the business as it relates to the attainment of objectives and the effectiveness of policies, organization structure and procedures.

Tax Administration

To establish and administer tax policies and procedures.

Government Reporting

To supervise or coordinate the preparation of reports to government agencies.

Protection of Assets

To assure protection for the assets of the business through internal control, internal auditing and assuring proper insurance coverage.

Economic Appraisal

To continuously appraise economic and social forces and government influences, and to interpret their effect upon the business.

TREASURERSHIP

therewith, to maintain adequate liaison with investment bankers, financial analysts and shareholders.

Short-Term Financing

To maintain adequate sources for the company's current borrowings from commercial banks and other lending institutions.

Banking and Custody

To maintain banking arrangements, to receive, have custody of and disburse the company's monies and securities and to be responsible for the financial aspects of real estate transactions.

Credits and Collections

To direct the granting of credit and the collection of accounts due the company, including the supervision of required special arrangements for financing sales, such as time payment and leasing plans.

Investments

To invest the company's funds as required, and to establish and coordinate policies for investment in pension and other similar trusts.

Insurance

To provide insurance coverage as may be required.

These functions are organized into Position Descriptions which delineate the specific route to performance of the various responsibilities. A Position Description for the Treasurer and another for the Controller follow.

POSITION DESCRIPTION
(Vice President Finance and Treasurer)

Effective Date:

TITLE: Vice President Finance and
Treasurer   DIVISION: President's
                                    DEPARTMENT: N/A
President, Diversified   SECTION: N/A
  Equipment
Leasing Corporation   UNIT: N/A
  (Divisional)

REPORTS TO: The President

SUMMARY OF FUNCTIONS:

Corporate—Responsible to the President for all long-range financial matters and to establish company-wide financial and administrative objectives, policies, programs, and practices which insure the Company of a continuously sound financial structure. As Chief Financial Officer, controls the flow of cash through the organization and maintains the integrity of funds, securities and other valuable documents. A member of the Banking Committee and the Board of Directors.

Divisional—As Chief Operating Officer, conducts the affairs of the Company; interprets and applies the policies of the Board of Directors; establishes policy, controls the operations and activities of the various departments; and conducts public relations.

MAJOR DUTIES AND RESPONSIBILITIES:

Corporate—Establishes and executes programs for the provision of the capital required by the business, including negotiating the procurement of capital and maintaining the required financial arrangements.

Coordinates the long-range plans (over three months) of the Corporation, assesses the financial requirements implicit in these plans, evaluates the potential return on investment, and develops alternative ways in which financial requirements can be satisfied.

Establishes and maintains an adequate market for the Company's securities and, in connection therewith, maintains adequate liaison with investment bankers, financial analysts and shareholders (in conjunction with the President).

Maintains adequate sources for the Company's current borrowings from commercial banks and other lending institutions.

Administers banking arrangements and loan agreements, receives, has custody of and disburses the Company's monies and securities and is responsible for the financial aspects of real estate transactions, and executes bids, contracts and leases.

Analyzes financial effects of proposals for acquisition of other companies and negotiates these acquisitions on behalf of the Company.

Directs the granting of credit and the collection of accounts due the Company, including the supervision of required special arrangements for financing sales, such as time payments and leasing plans.

Invests the Company's funds as required, and establishes and coordinates policies for investment in pension and other similar trusts.

Provides insurance coverage as may be required.

Reviews and endorses or revises budget proposals received from those people reporting directly, according to Corporate policy and procedure; submits budgets for assigned activiities in accordance with the budget procedure, discusses proposed charges and significant revisions with those reporting directly.

Administers all stock option plans, incentive and pension fund programs.

Establishes, coordinates and administers as an integral part of management, an adequate plan for the provision of capital. Such a plan provides, to the extent required in the business, programs for capital investing and for financing, together with the necessary controls and procedures to effectuate the plan.

Recommends financial policy affecting budgets and the expenditure of funds.

Analyzes the Company's stockholder relations policies and recommends new or revised policies when needed.

Approves operating and administrative policies and procedures.

Compares performance with operating plans and standards, and reports and interprets the results of operations to all levels of management and to the owners of the business as they relate to his area of responsbility.

Continuously appraises economic and social forces and government influences, and interprets their effect upon the business.

Analyzes the Company's stockholder information program covering such matters as the annual and interim reports to stockholders and recommends to the President new or revised programs.

Keeps abreast of new developments in the field of stockholder relations and advises the President of significant developments.

Ensures the execution of his functions at the lowest cost consistent with effective performance.

Establishes and issues the plans, policies and procedures governing the performance of assigned activiities.

Directs, reviews and appraises the performance of the units immediately reporting, and provides the necessary coordination between the activities of such units.

Develops and presents matters requiring the decision of the President.

Provides advice on *all* matters to the President.

Provides other Company units with information required by them to carry out their assigned responsibilities.

Establishes and implements a sound plan of organization of his assigned functions.

Coordinates activities of the assigned units with those of other Company units; seeks material agreement on problems involving coordination.

Determines the necessary manpower required to perform his assigned functions; selects and maintains qualified personnel in all positions reporting directly, and recommends compensation for same.

Assists the President in the formulation of overall corporate objectives.

Keeps the President informed of the Group's performance.

Divisional—Controls and coordinates operations and activities; approves operating plans; fosters economy throughout the Company.

Ensures proper application of allotted funds, and fosters the best use of facilities in the interest of the Company.

Approves operating and administrative policies.

Acts as the principal public relations officer of the Company.

Reviews and analyzes qualitatively the Company's efforts and results at regular intervals.

With the Chairman of the Board, reviews operations to enlarge the scope of the Company through suitable acquisitions and other contractual arrangements.

Assures overall Company profitability.

Approves and enforces the organization plan of the Company and any of its components, and changes therein.

Approves the addition, elimination or alteration of management positions.

Approves salary and wage structures within Corporate budgetary guidelines.

Recommends to the Board of Directors and Stock Option Committee compensation for all officers of the Company.

Sets the compensation of those (non-officers) reporting directly.

Approves the hiring, appointing, releasing and compensation of personnel reporting directly to his staff.

Coordinates personnel policies in conjunction with Corporate Direction of Personnel.

Ensures equitable administration of wage and salary policies and structures, employee benefit plans, and personnel rating programs, within the overall Corporate policies.

Approves and submits the consolidated annual budget and proposed capital and extraordinary expenditure programs to the Corporate President for final approval, making appropriate recommendations thereon.

Approves the initiation of any legal action within his limits of authority.

Sets the moral tone of the Company by formulating policies that will govern the conduct of the business.

Promotes a climate for high motivation and dedication to corporate objectives.

ORGANIZATIONAL RELATIONSHIPS

Accountable to the President (corporate) for all phases of his activities and functions.

He is a member of the Product Development Committee.

Credit and Collection Manager is accountable for all phases of his activities and functions.

Enlists the aid and cooperation of the Vice President and Controller:

> Executes programs for the provision of the capital required by Savin. Coordinates both long and short range financial planning. Maintains adequate sources for the Company's borrowing from lending institutions.

> Analyzes the financial effects of potential acquisitions of other companies or the sale of existing ones.

Provides insurance on recommended assets.

Aids and assists the Executive Vice President/Market Planning:

> Prepares, reviews and analyzes financial projections with regard to the potential introduction of new products.

> Analyzes and primarily responsible for negotiating the acquisition of companies brought to the Corporation's attention by the Executive Vice President.

> Projections and forecasts on new products and distribution alternatives; estimates and projects royalty and licensing fees attributable to trademarks and patents; product line statistics and reports; budgets.

Aids and assists the Vice President/Marketing:

> Develops and administers third-party leasing and rental programs designed to promote the sale of the Corporation's products to the end user.
> Budgets.

> Takes part in the development of programs designed to promote the sale of the Corporation's products to dealers, distributors and licensees on a wholesale level.

Aids and assists the Director of Purchasing and Distribution:

> Financing and timing for fixed assets, capital expenditures and leasehold improvements.

POSITION DESCRIPTION
(Vice President and Controller)

Effective Date:

TITLE: Vice President and Controller

DIVISION: President's
DEPARTMENT: N/A
REPORTS TO: President.
SECTION: N/A
UNIT: N/A

SUMMARY OF FUNCTIONS:

Directs the accounting and control functions, reporting the results of operations, providing chronological systems and data processing services.

MAJOR DUTIES AND RESPONSIBILITIES:

Coordinates all matters of business between the Corporation and its stock transfer agents and registrars.

Prescribes the form of evidence and the manner of collection of loans to employees.

Forecasts short-range (3 months) cash requirements and obligations, as a basis for maintaining adequate funds.

Provides advice on *all* matters to the President.

Establishes, coordinates and administers as an integral part of management, an adequate plan for the control of operations. Such a plan provides, to the extent required in the business, profit planning; programs for capital investing and for financing, sales forecasts, expense budgets and cost standards, together with the necessary controls and procedures to effectuate the plan.

Reviews and endorses, or revises budget proposals received from those people reporting directly; submits budgets for assigned activities in accordance with the budget procedure and discusses proposed changes and significant revisions with those reporting directly.

Directs, reviews and appraises the performance of the units immediately reporting, and provides the necessary coordination between the activities of such units.

Compares performance with operating plans and standards, and reports and interprets the results of operations to all levels of management and to the owners of the business. This function includes the formulation of accounting policies, the coordination of Systems and Procedures, and the preparation of operating data and special reports as required.

Consults with all segments of management responsible for policy or action concerning any phase of the operation of the business as it relates to the attainment of objectives and the effectiveness of policies, organization structure and procedures.

236

Provides for the control and editing of all Company orders, to insure conformity to established policies and procedures, and to facilitate data control and retrieval of records generated by these orders.

Establishes and administers tax policies and procedures.

Supervises or coordinates the preparation of reports to government agencies.

Assures protection for the assets of the business through internal control, internal auditing and assuring proper insurance coverage.

Assists Marketing in establishing and maintaining product pricing policies.

Serves as liaison between Company and legal counsel, and recommends the appointment of independent public accountants and the extent and scope of their audit work.

Provides advice on *all* matters to the President.

Provides other Company units with information required by them to carry out their assigned responsibilities.

Establishes and implements a sound plan of organization of his assigned functions.

Coordinates activities of the assigned units with those of other Company units. Seeks mutual agreement on problems involving coordination.

Determines the necessary manpower required to perform his assigned functions. Selects and maintains qualified personnel in all positions reporting directly and recommends compensation for same.

Assists the President in the formulation of overall corporate objectives.

Keeps the President informed of the Groups' performance.

Performs his functions at the lowest cost, consistent with effective performance.

Establishes and issues the plans, policies and procedures governing the performance of assigned activities.

Develops and presents to the President matters requiring his decision.

Approves expense accounts of management reporting directly to him.

Coordinates plan and budget for the findings of the Product Development Committee.

ORGANIZATIONAL RELATIONSHIPS:

Accountable to the President for all phases of his activities and functions.

He is a member of the Product Development Committee.

The following are accountable for all phases of their activities and functions:

> Auditor Manager
> Manager of Accounting Services Department
> Director of Administrative Operations
>   (Data Processing)
> National Administrator (Field Administrator)
> Manager of Collection Application
> Director of Purchasing

He advises, consults with, coordinates with, and provides administrative support, as follows:

> Vice President/Treasurer-Capital programs; insurance coverage; cash procedures; financial analyses.

> Vice President/Marketing—Compensation plans; product pricing; Branch Operating Statements; control of field expenses; sales analyses by product and territory.

> President, Diversified Equipment Leasing Corporation—Reports and analyses on leases by territory and product; financial statements preparation and analysis; credit and collection procedures, budgets.

> Director of Personnel and Office Services—Reports on payrolls and fringe benefits; compensation plans; planning of fixed assets, capital expenditures and leasehold improvements (lease or buy and timing); office layout; budgets.

* * * * *

Observe that all of the FEI's defined functions appear in the Position Descriptions, in more detail to adapt them to the particular company using them. A summary of the overall function appears as the first paragraph of each Position Description and is worthy of repetition:

> Treasurer— Responsible for all long-range financial matters and to establish company-wide financial and administrative objectives, policies, programs, and practices which insure the Company of a continuously sound financial structure. As Chief Financial Officer, controls the flow of cash through the organization and maintains the integrity of funds, securities and other valuable documents.

> Controller—Directs the accounting and control functions, reporting the results of operations, providing chronological systems and data processing services.

APPENDIX B

INDEX OF WORKING AIDS (EXHIBITS)

SCHEDULE OF LIMITATIONS UNDER BANK AGREEMENT
FYE 4/30/
$000 omitted

	LIMITS	5/31/	6/30/	7/31/
Aggregate credit including L/C's	18,000	15,175	15,829	16,547
Letters of Credit	6,000	1,802	1,205	1,289
Notices of litigation required - minimum	500	--	--	--
Secured indebtedness excluding mortgage	725	291	261	249
Working capital - minimum	10,000	10,300	10,135	10,153
Tangible net worth - minimum	9,000	10,654	10,690	10,807
Debt to equity	1.5 to 1	1.44 to 1	1.50 to 1	1.49 to 1
R & D and capital expenditures (excluding rental equipment)	1,000	23	47	78
Aggregate guarantees	250	--	--	--
Lease rental payments - annual	1,500	800	800	800
Dealer acquisitions for stock	400	--	--	--
Undischarged judgments	500	--	--	--

Exhibit 1-a

Credit and Security Agreement

19

PG.	ART.	
1		Whereas (Purpose)
2	1	Defined Terms (See Schedule)
17		1.2 Use of Defined Terms
17	2	Amount and Terms of Credit
17		2.1 Commitments
20		2.2 Notice of Borrowing & Request for L/C's
20		a) 2 days notice - $250,000 multiple (except for L/C's)(oral & writing)
21		b) 2 days notice for L/C's
22		c) Officers' Certificate with Notice (Exh. F)
25		2.3 Reduction of Commitments for outstanding L/C's
25		2.4 The Notes - 1 1/2% over prime, on demand, interest quarterly
26		2.5 Letters of Credit - 1/8% to MHCC, 1/8% to each Bank
26		2.6 Fees for Letters of Credit
27		2.7 Computation of Interest - 3-6-5 day basis
28		2.8 Pro Rata Treatment & Payments
29		2.9 Borrowing Base
29	3	Use Of Proceeds
29		3.1 Proceeds of Initial Borrowing
30		3.2 Proceeds of Subsequent Borrowing
30		3.3 General Prohibitions on Use of Proceeds
30	4	Collateral Security
30		4.1 Collateral security (Initial Borrowers Certificate, Exh. B & C)
31		(As needed - Assignment - Exh. B-1)
31		(45 days monthly - Assignment - Exh. C-1)
32		4.2 Collections - Lock Boxes Named "Cash Collateral Account"
34		4.3 Application of Collections - M, W, F of each week
35		4.4 Officers' Certificate with reference to receivables -
35		15th & 30th of each month - Certificate
35		Supplement to Exh. E
36		4.5 Notation on Books of Company - on C.L. accounts
37		4.6 Information regarding collateral
38		4.7 Receivables from Government & Agencies thereof
39		4.8 Communicating with Account Debtors, etc.
40		4.9 Waiver by the Company
40		4.10 Provision with respect to collateral in event of default
43		4.11 Power of Attorney
45		4.12 Financing Statements
46		4.13 Reimbursement of Expenses
47		4.14 Agent & Banks not liable with respect to collateral
47		4.15 Agent on premises
48	5	Conditions of Borrowing
48		5.1 Conditions of Initial Loans
48		a) Note b) Assignments c) Officers Certificate
49		d) Senox Guarantee, Exh. I (e) Senox Security Agreement, Exh. J
49		f) Guarantee of Subs, Exh. K g) Guarantee of Sofax, Exh. 5
50		h) Guarantee of Savin-Canada, Exh. L i) Security Agreement
50		of Diversified, Exh. L; Security Agreement of Savin
50		World Trade, Exh. J & L; k) Notice to Equilease
51		l) Certificate of Swift, Florida, m) M. Low subordination
51		n) Ricoh subordination o) Secretary's Certificate - Savin

Exhibit 1-b

Daily Cash Summary
February, 19 __

Date	Sterling National Bank			Manufacturers Hanover Trust Co.		
	General	Accts Pay.	SBMCL	General	Accts Pay.	Lock Box
1-31	19322955	122373	<14368076>	45237460	<84046657>	9541396
2-1	19322955	122373	<14368076>	58769077	<84046657>	13600099
2-4	19322955	122373	<14397793>	36047186	<64046657>	5903451
2-5	29322955	122373	602207	47260664	<64046657>	11855010
2-6	29322955	122373	584106	49812245	<64046657>	14541090
2-7	29322955	122373	584106	60977102	<49362177>	5862009
2-8	29322955	122373	584106	68350429	<49362177>	13009276
2-11	29322955	122373	584106	50053248	637823	7505718
2-12	29293438	122373	532439	22445225	637823	3383475
2-13	29293438	122373	532439	3082461	637823	9915479
2-14	29293438	122373	532439	8379784	637823	9270865
2-15	19293438	122373	532439	135148039	637823	13181353
2-19	19293438	122373	519375	129213787	637823	7425275
2-20	30293438	122373	156884	57213787	637823	13987395
2-21	30283510	122373	90156884	83773440	637823	6996445
2-22	29415209	122373	90156884	83773440	637823	10915370
2-25	29415209	122373	156884	110006202	637823	6611420
2-26	29415209	122373	92352	78295282	637823	11274767
2-27	29372425	122373	258767	86243733	637823	16121802
2-28	29372425	122373	258767	144116148	637823	6419843

Exhibit 1-c

Schedule of Borrowing From Banks
August, September 19 __

Date	Activity Borrowed	Payments	Total Borrowed	Manufacturers+Turnover Activity 27.77%	Balance
Bal 7-30			15254959		423630194
8- 1		⟨358800⟩	14896159	⟨9963876⟩	413666318
8- 5	1000000		15896159	277700	414436318
8- 6		⟨577100⟩	15319059	⟨160260⟩	425410318
8- 8		⟨333900⟩	14985159	⟨9272403⟩	416137915
8- 9	844900		15830059	234620	439599915
8-12	1250000		17080059	347126	474312515
8-13		⟨671500⟩	16408559	⟨186476⟩	455264915
8-15	106400	⟨388600⟩	16126359	⟨78367⟩	447828215
8-19	1000000		17126359	277700	475598215
8-20		⟨517400⟩	16608959	⟨14368198⟩	461230017
8-22		⟨412900⟩	16196059	⟨11466233⟩	449763784
8-26	793700		16989759	220411	471804884
8-27		⟨432900⟩	16556859	⟨120216⟩	459783284
8-29		⟨723100⟩	15833759	⟨200794⟩	439703884
9- 3	1297300		17131059	360262	475730084
9- 4		⟨754800⟩	16376259	⟨209608⟩	454769284
9- 6		⟨274800⟩	16101459	⟨76312⟩	447138084
9- 9	752600		16854059	208997	468037784
9-10	3	⟨643300⟩	16210762	⟨178644⟩	455172384
9-12		⟨738100⟩	15472662	⟨204970⟩	429475384
9-13		⟨1417700⟩	14054962	⟨393695⟩	390305884
9-16	1052700		15107662	292335	419539384
9-17		⟨530500⟩	14577162	⟨147320⟩	404807384
9-19		⟨264900⟩	14292262	⟨79118⟩	396895584
9-23	2000000		16292262	555400	452435584
9-24		⟨357700⟩	15934562	⟨99333⟩	442502284
9-26		⟨361800⟩	15572762	⟨100472⟩	432455584
9-30	1422700		16995462	395084	471963484

Exhibit 1-d

Manufacturers Hanover TRUST Company
Lock Box A/c # _____
FEBruary 19 __

Date		Receipts		Disbursements		Balance
1-31						9541396
2-1		4058703	1-31			13600099
2-4		2533615	2-1	2-1	10230263	5903451
2-5		8470535	2-4	2-4	2518976	11855010
2-6		2686080	2-5			14541090
2-7		2478534	2-6	2-6	11157615	5862009
2-8		7147267	2-7			13009276
2-11		4122243	2-8	2-8	9625801	7505718
2-12				2-11	4122243	3383475
2-13		6532004	2-11			9915479
2-14		5887390	2-13	2-13	6532004	9270865
2-15		3910488	2-14			13181353
2-19		4040900	2-15	2-15	9796978	7425275
2-20		6562120	2-19			13987395
2-21		3612070	2-20	2-20	10514814	7084651
				—	88206	6996445
2-22		3918925	2-21			10915370
2-25		3227045	2-22	2-22	7530995	6611420
2-26		7925382	2-25	2-25	3262035	11274767
2-27		4847035	2-26	.		16121802
2-28		3070456	2-27	2-27	12772415	6419843

Exhibit 1-e

LOCKBOX IN CHICAGO   RECEIVES A TOTAL OF $ 981657 FROM THE FOLLOWING CITIES

ATLANTA	BTNROUGE	BUFFALO	CHICAGO	CINCINNA	CLVELAND	CORPCHRI	DALLAS	DENVER	DETROIT
HOUSTON	INDIANAP	JACKSON	KAN CITY	MEMPHIS	MIAMI	MINNEAPO	MOBILE	MONTGMRY	PHILADEL

LOCKBOX IN SAN FRAN   RECEIVES A TOTAL OF $ 557483 FROM THE FOLLOWING CITIES

HUNTSVIL	LOS ANGE	OAKLAND	SAN FRAN

LOCKBOX IN NEW YORK   RECEIVES A TOTAL OF $ 747764 FROM THE FOLLOWING CITIES

ALBANY	BLTIMORE	BOSTON	BRATBORO	HARTFORD	MANCHSTR	NEWARK	NEWHAVEN	NEW ORLE	NEW YORK
PROVIDEN	SPGFLDMS	SYRACUSE	WASH DC

IF DOLLAR DELAY CONSIDERS MAIL TIME + CLEARANCE TIME + CHECK PROCESSING TIME, AND CONSIDERS HOLIDAYS, THEN

DOLLAR DELAY IS   7800376.00 DOLLAR–DAYS FOR LOCKBOXES IN

                  CHICAGO   SAN FRAN   NEW YORK

DOLLAR DELAY BASED ON MAIL TIME + CLEARANCE TIME, WEIGHTED BY DOLLAR AMOUNTS IS   6337736.00 DOLLAR–DAYS

Exhibit 1-f (page 1)

SURVEY RESULTS

Total Dollars   : $2,286,904.00
Number of Cities: 41

More than half (57.5%) of the total dollar amount was

received from only 7 of the remitting areas. Totals by area

drop sharply after that.

Delays generated by one lock box city, two lock box

cities, and three lock box cities are shown below. These

are the best locations as chosen by the program. The Summary

Page shows the delay for these solutions as well as for

those which had locations pre-specified.

LOCK BOX CITY	COLUMN I DELAY (Including holidays, processing, mail & clearance time expressed in dollar days)	COLUMN II DELAY (Including mail & clearance time only, expressed in dollar days)
Chicago	8,423,028	7,576,777
Chicago, San Francisco	8,225,615	6,933,345
Chicago, San Francisco, New York	7,800,376	6,337,736

The figures which are of the most immediate interest are those

in Column II (shown again on Summary Page) which show absolute

delay based on mail and clearance time only (weekends and

holidays which fell during the survey period do not affect

this figure).

Exhibit 1-f (page 2)

September 9, 19__

Mr._____
Manufacturers Hanover Trust Company
350 Park Avenue
New York, N. Y. 10022

Dear Mr._____ :

Confirming our telephone conversation of August 30, I am enclosing a
copy of our statement and invoice, for your review.

This letter will confirm the arrangements for our use of your Lock Box
Service which we look forward to inaugurating, on receipt of this letter.
We will instruct our customers to send remittances to_____
Corporation, c/o P. O. Box_____, Church Street Station, New York,
N. Y. 10049.

You will charge our account approximately $40 annually, to cover the post
office box rental. We have not discussed this charge, but I assume it
will be in this range.

Your Lock Box Department will open the envelopes, remove contents, inspect
and process remittances, as follows:

1. Checks will be inspected for correct payee.

2. Undated checks will be dated to correspond with envelope post
    office cancellation date.

3. Postdated checks which would not reach the drawee bank on or before
    the date on the check will be processed. All other postdated checks
    will not be processed, but will be forwarded to_____without entry,
    together with the accompanying remittance data.

4. Checks with alterations and erasures and checks bearing typed or
    handwritten restrictive notations, such as, "Payment in Full," will
    not be processed and will be forwarded to _____with the attached
    envelope and all other accompanying remittance data.

5. When remittances are received and the accompanying statements and the
    check amounts differ, you will lightly rule out the statement amount
    and inscribe the check amount and process the check.

6. One copy of each check will be provided - it will accompany the
    remittance details and envelopes forwarded to_____, New York,
    attention Mr._____.

7. When an invoice accompanies a payment and the check coincides with
    the invoice total, the amount of the total will be circled. Copies of
    checks and invoices will be segregated and batched separately. All other
    payment copies and remittance details will be grouped and batched.

8. Unsigned checks will be processed with proper notification of the drawee
    bank requesting that the signature be obtained.

9. We will guarantee and process checks that reflect a difference between
    the written and numerical amounts provided the correct amount can be
    determined from any enclosed statement.

Exhibit 1-g (page 1)

Mr._____
September 9, 19__
Page Two

10. Checks which are in order for deposit will be endorsed "Credited to the Account of the Within-Named Payee. Lack of Endorsement Guaranteed."

11. All "unprocessed items," with each check's envelope and any accompanying enclosures, will be separately batched for delivery with other processed items.

12. Checks returned unpaid because of insufficient funds will automatically be re-presented. On second refusal, items will be charged back and mailed to the customer's office with advice of debit. Items returned for "no account," "account closed," or other reasons implying inability of re-presentment, will be charged back immediately. Items for $1,000 or over will be charged back with telephone and debit advice of nonpayment, to Mr._____, at the address above.

13. At the close of the processing day, posting media will be mailed to us, together with duplicate credit advices, adding machine tapes of individual items, unprocessed items batch and any miscellaneous mail, and deposit tags and duplicate checks to_____Corporation,_____,N.Y. 10595, Attention Credit/Collection Department.

14. On Monday, Wednesday and Friday of each week, any federally available funds in our account, in excess of $20,000, should be transferred to our General Account, No. _____, Manufacturers Hanover Trust Company, 530 Seventh Avenue, New York, N. Y. 10018.

    If there are any questions concerning the transfer, please contact Mr. _____, Assistant Vice President, at that office.

    A copy of the transfer advice should be sent to us on each Monday, Wednesday and Friday, at _____, New York 10595, attention Accounting Department.

15. Monthly bank statements should be sent to us at _____, New York 10595, attention Accounting Department.

16. You are directed and authorized to pick up mail from our post office box, Monday through Saturday, at frequent intervals. Enclosed is copy of our letter of authorization to the Postmaster, Church Street Station, covering Post Office Box_____.

Thank you for your cooperation in establishing this Lock Box Account.

Very truly yours,

DANIEL L. GOTTHILF
Treasurer

DLG:R

Enclosure

sc:

Exhibit 1-g (page 2)

45-604 EYE EASE
45-704 20/20 BUFF
Made in U.S.A.

Bank Loan for Dodge Van

Purchased from Eastern Dodge Motors for $5,200. Financed through
Chemical Bank, Thornwood. Garaged at Portchester warehouse.
Assigned to warehouse for local deliveries. Financed over 24 months,
after $1,000 down payment (Ch. #1872 Chemical of 2/1/ , net of
$4,200) Payments of $197.71/mo. Lease capitalized -- see JE 2-6 of
2/14/ . Original P.O. #16723 approved by RWB. Payments due 1st
of each month with coupon book receipts.

Amount financed - $197.71 x 24 months.

Declining
Balance
$4,745.04

Payment No.	Date Pd.	Amt. Pd.	Ck. No.	Bank	Approval & Remarks	
1	3-01	197.71	1920	CB	JDR	454133
2	4-01	197.71	80004	ST	DG	434962
3	5-01	197.71	2430	CB	JDR	415191
4	6-01	197.71	12006	MH	JDR	395420
5	7-01	197.71	33002	CB	JDR	375649
6	8-01	197.71	44809	CB	JDR	355878
7	9-01	197.71	81516	ST	JDR	336107
8	10-01	197.71	63922	CB	JDR	316336
9	11-01	197.71	74500	CB	DG	296565
10						
11						
12						
13						
14						
15						
16						
17						
18						
19						
20						
21						
22						
23						
24						

Exhibit 1-h

LEASED PREMISES

DESCRIPTION CODE: O - Office   W - Warehouse   T - Total   B - Combined (No Breakdown)

R - Lease in Renewal or extension period

WESTERN ZONE	DESC.	FOOTAGE	MONTHLY RENTAL	COST PER SQ. FT.	LESSOR	PERIOD	OPTIONS
1016 So. 23rd Ave. ARIZONA, PHOENIX	O W T	4500 1800 6300	$1196	$2.28	Meyer Turken Realty	8/1/ - 7/31/	8/1/ - 7/31/ $1248 per mo.
816 E. Evans Blvd. ARIZONA, TUCSON	O W T	2000 1500 3500	$ 536.02	$1.84	Vic Edelbrock	4/15/ -2/15/	
43 Park Lane CALIFORNIA, BRISBANE (San Francisco Branch)	O W T	4400 7200 11600	$2539 +40 $2579	$2.66	Hogland & Bogard/ Crocker Land Co.	3/27/ -3/26/	
13811 Artesia Blvd. CALIFORNIA, CERRITOS (Warehouse & Tech Ctr)	W B T	10032 4752 14784	$1815	$1.47	Cerritos-Pacific Development Co.	9/1/ -7/31/	5 yrs. - CPI increase in rent
19433 East Walnut Drive CALIFORNIA, CITY OF INDUSTRY	O	4158	$ 850	$2.45	L & M Plaster	12/8/ -11/30/	First refusal on additional space
3303 Harbor Blvd. CALIFORNIA, COSTA MESA (Santa Ana Branch)	O	4200	$1249.50	$3.57	Koll Income Prop.	11/15/ -7/31/ (Possession 8/1/)	5 yrs. at prevailing rate
7668 Telegraph Road CALIFORNIA, LOS ANGELES	O	5000	$1552.50	$3.73	Ruby H. Price	9/1/ -8/31/	$1606.84 effective 9/1/
731 South Main St. CALIFORNIA, SALINAS (San Jose Sub-Office)	(	225	$ 150	$8.00	Frank E. & Judith M. Cosco	7/17/ -7/16/	Thereafter mo. to mo. @ $175/mo.

Exhibit 1-i

7 1/2% Convertible Senior Subordinated Notes

General Outline of Principal Terms

Amount:	$11,000,000
Interest Rate:	7.50% per annum payable quarterly
Maturity:	15 years

Conversion: The Notes will be convertible into 637,681 shares of its Common Stock at $17.25 per share. Customary anti-dilution provisions will be included.

Fixed Sinking Fund: Level payments of $1,100,000 per annum at the end of each of the last 10 years to retire 100% of the issue by maturity. The company may make an optional pre-payment on a non-cumulative basis in the amount of $1,100,000 in any year that a principal payment is due. In all cases, the holders will have adequate opportunity to convert the amount of any principal payments.

Redemption: The Notes will be non-callable for any reason for the first three years; from the fourth year through the average life of the issue, the Notes will be callable only if the stock price is at least 200% of the conversion price for at least 45 consecutive trading days; thereafter, the Notes will be callable at the company's option at a premium of 7 1/2%, declining evenly over the remaining life of the issue to par in the final year. In all cases, ample opportunity for conversion will be afforded to the Note-holders. The Notes will be non-refundable to the average life of the issue from the proceeds of an issue having an effective interest cost of 7 1/2% or less.

Registration: Holders of not less than 40% of the Notes (including, in any event, holders of outstanding Notes convertible into not less than 100,000 shares of common stock) will have the right to request (a) a registration of the underlying stock at the company's expense where audits exist that are acceptable for purposes of the registration; and (b) an additional registration at the company's expense whether or not acceptable audits are available. In addition, Noteholders will have unlimited "piggyback" rights (subject to approval of underwriters, if any). Lenders will have one registration right at their own expense.

Exhibit 2-a (page 1)

-2-

Condition:

The company and applicable subsidiaries shall have substantially completed the contemplated sale of receivables to the Independent Finance Corporation, and Captive Finance Subsidiary Corporation shall not then be accepting the new receivables and shall accept none thereafter, except to the extent that the customer's second payment has not yet been received, as provided in the agreement with Equilease. This is in addition to other normal conditions of closing, including the absence of any material adverse change.

Permitted Current Borrowing:

Current unsecured borrowing from banks, together with letter of credit and acceptance financing (secured as customary in the trade) will be permitted in the normal course of business for the purpose of financing import transactions. Other current unsecured borrowing shall be limited to $1,000,000 provided that no such debt is outstanding for at least 60 consecutive days in each 12-month period.

Permitted Additional Funded Debt:

(a) Up to $10 million revolving credit, convertible into not less than 3-year Notes, incurred for the purpose of financing rental machines.

(b) Additional amounts of senior and subordinated debt if, after giving effect thereto, consolidated funded indebtedness does not exceed 60% of book capitalization plus deferred income taxes (if any) and provided that pro forma interest charges on all funded debt is earned at least three times on the average over the most recent three fiscal years.

Working Capital:

Consolidated working capital is to be maintained at least equal to the greater of $11 million or 100% of funded indebtedness.

Seniority:

The Convertible Senior Subordinated Notes will be subordinated in insolvency to existing senior debt and existing and future indebtedness held by banks and other senior debt (if any) held by institutions. The Notes will be senior to other junior securities, including public debenture issues, if any.

Dividends:

Dividends and net stock repurchases are to be limited to net income earned after April 30, 19__, plus $1,000,000, less any payments on indebtedness owed to First Subordinated Lender.

Exhibit 2-a (page 2)

-3-

Loans, Investments,   (a) Additional investments in Rapifax and Delco (after
Advances & Guarantees: the contemplated sale of 80% of receivables to X Corp.
                         and other non-consolidated partnerships and other persons
                         will be limited to amounts available for dividends.

                         (b) Securities or other assets received from sale of
                         Docustat.

                         (c) U. S. Government securities, prime commercial
                         paper, certificates of deposit in banks having capital
                         funds of at least $100,000,000.

Merger & Consolidation: The company may merge and consolidate provided that
                         it is the surviving corporation and that the survivor
                         is in compliance with the Note Agreement. The company
                         may not sell, lease or dispose of any substantial
                         portion of its assets.

Leases: The company will not enter into any sale-leaseback
                         transaction without the consent of the lenders, except
                         to the extent of sale-leaseback of non-revenue producing
                         assets carrying annual fixed charges not to exceed
                         $500,000.

Financial Statements: (1) Within 45 days after each of the first three
                         quarterly periods, the company will furnish comparative
                         consolidated income statements and balance sheets in
                         duplicate, accompanied by a breakdown showing sales and
                         profit contribution by product category. Also, a certi-
                         ficate from a responsible officer indicating compliance
                         with the Note Agreement will be provided.

                         (2) Within 90 days after the end of each fiscal year,
                         the company will furnish comparative consolidated income
                         statements and balance sheets certified by auditors, as
                         well as unaudited sales and profit breakdown by product
                         category. A certificate of compliance with the Note
                         Agreement signed by the auditors and responsible company
                         officers will also be provided.

Other Terms: Other terms normally included in a transaction of this
                         character will be included.

Special Counsel,   Necessary legal documents will be prepared by counsel
    etc: approved by the lenders. All legal expenses and other
                         expenses incurred in connection with this financing will
                         be paid by the_____Corporation whether or not the
                         loan is consummated.

jck   Lawrence Smith
                                      for
                              Mutual Insurance Co.

Exhibit 2-a (page 3)

Branch Office Procedure

Title		B.O.P Number: 1.01
	ORDER ACCEPTANCE	Page 1 of 11
Vol. No. 1	**Vol. Name:** Order Processing	

PURPOSE:

To provide a procedure governing the verification of the acceptability of all orders received.

GENERAL NARRATIVE:

Acceptance of orders is based on review of all information required for all new and repeat sales of machines, supplies and service.

RESPONSIBILITIES:

Sales: For the proper preparation of sales orders.
Field Engineering: Preparation of Maintenance Agreement forms and Service Call Reports.
Administration: Determines acceptability by; Verification, Credit Checking & Telephone Confirmation of Orders.

Table of Contents:

Section:

Supersedes		Orig. Code	Release No.	Effective Date
B.O.P. No.(s).	**Page No.(s).**	AP2	B-004	10/1/
Related Publications		Inquiries: Corporate Credit Manager		

Exhibit 3-a (page 1)

Branch Office Procedure

Title	B.O.P Number: 1.01
ORDER ACCEPTANCE	Page 2 of 11

Vol. No. 1	Vol. Name: Order Processing

VERIFICATION OF ORDERS

Section A

Responsibility

Administration;to insure that all required information pertaining to an order is available.

Procedure:

1. Receives orders from following sources:
    a. Sales Order Form (#0-16-7) (Exhibit A) from Sales Representative
    b. Written requests or Purchase Orders from customers
    c. Telephone Orders - from Administration or sales
    d. Service Calls & Maintenance Agreements - Field Engineering

2. Checks order forms to insure completion as follows:

    A. Sales

        1. Name and Address
        2. Purchase Order number or name of individual placing order.
            A. Purchase Order number is required and must be included on invoices for all Government Agencies, banks, utilities, hospitals and large corporations
        3. Product and quantity (clearly defined)
        4. Pricing (in accord with current marketing programs and trade-in schedules) on telephone orders, confirm current pricing with customer.
        5. Credit references (one bank, two trades) if new or inactive customer.
        6. Special terms/conditions (must comply with current Savin policy)
        7. Signature and title of individual who is authorized to make the purchase; Office Manager, Purchasing Agent, Branch Manager, Regional Director, etc.

Leases:

1. Leasee name and address
2. Product and quantity (clearly defined)

Supersedes		Orig. Code	Release No.	Effective Date
B.O.P. No.(s).	Page No.(s).	AP2	B-004	10/1/
Related Publications		Inquiries: Corporate Credit Manager		

Exhibit 3-a (page 2)

Branch Office Procedure

Title	B.O.P Number: 1.01
ORDER ACCEPTANCE	Page 3 of 11
Vol. No. 1 **Vol. Name:** Order Processing	

 3. Pricing (in accord with sales order form)
 4. Term of Lease
 5. Monthly Payment Schedule
 6. Security deposit check received
 7. Type of business
 8. Length of time in business
 9. Credit reference (See "Credit Checking Procedure)
10. If corporation in business for less than one year, must have personal quarantee and personal bank reference on guarantor.
11. Duly authorized corporate officer signature - president, vice president treasurer, corporate secretary, purchasing agent, partner, proprietor or owner.
12. If a parent company is involved, a letter of authorization or corporate quarantee is necessary.

MAINTENANCE AGREEMENTS:

1. Name and Address
2. Model & Serial Number of Equipment
3. Period covered by Agreement
4. Authorized Customer Signature
5. Pricing must be in accordance with current price schedule.

SERVICE CALL REPORTS

1. Name and Address
2. Customer Signature (Verifying receipt of service)

Supersedes		Orig. Code	Release No.	Effective Date
B.O.P. No.(s). **Page No.(s).**		AP2	B-004	10/1/
Related Publications		**Inquiries:** Corporate Credit Manager		

Exhibit 3-a (page 3)

Branch Office Procedure

Title		B.O.P Number: 1.01
ORDER ACCEPTANCE		
		Page 4 of 11
Vol. No. 1	**Vol. Name:** Order Processing	

Section B Credit Checking

PURPOSE:

Provide criteria to enable Savin to determine ability and willingness of a customer to pay for products purchased.

GENERAL NARRATIVE:

Attempt to verify criteria by using credit references provided by customer on sales order. Determination is based on information received from references.

RESPONSIBILITIES:

SALES:

Sales order submitted must provide one of the following:

1. Credit references (one bank, two trades),
2. D & B rating of DC2 or better, or
3. States present account

ADMINISTRATION:

Checks all references provided and determines acceptability.

PROCEDURE:

A. Retail Outright Sales (Non-lease) all machine placements, supplies and service.

   1. New Customers

Administration:

   a. Receives orders from sales representative or customer.
   b. Phone Orders - Administration requests by phone, required bank and trade references.

Supersedes		Orig. Code	Release No.	Effective Date
B.O.P. No.(s).	**Page No.(s).**	AP2	B-004	10/1/
Related Publications		**Inquiries:**		
		Corporate Credit Manager		

Exhibit 3-a (page 4)

Branch Office Procedure

Title	B.O.P Number: 1.01
ORDER ACCEPTANCE	Page 5 of 11
Vol. No. 1 Vol. Name: Order Processing	

    c. Calls and/or writes each reference and verifies past history and present standing (Check form based on credit Exhibits B & C) if the bank refuses to supply information, Branch Administration Manager should address a letter to the bank, attention of the officer in charge of the customers account, authorizing release of information concerning the account, and this should be signed by the customer and mailed by the BAM. A copy of the completed letter is attached to order as backup documentation.

    d. Retail Credit Bureau (contract #131593 plus branch code) may be used to gather credit info if other sources are not available.

    e. D & B rating DC2 or better automatically qualifies customer as an acceptable credit risk, except any business involved in financing or the credit field. If the digit in the rating (i.e., the 2 in DC2) is 3 or 4, in any category, then the references are to be obtained.

    f. Political orders can only be sold on a cash in advance or C.O.D. basis. Never on open account.

2. Evaluation of References

    a. Bank Reference
        1. The potential customer must have a minimum average balance of four figures unless the sale is for new products to a service type company or a funded organization and then additional payments may be required up front and the lease term shortened.
        2. Account must be open for a reasonable length of time.
        3. No overdrafts or returns.
        4. Paying habits on past loans must be satisfactory.
        5. If sales order has 30 day option to lease there must be a minimum average balance of four figures and the account must be at least one year old.

    b. Trades
        1. These should indicate applicants willingness to pay. Do not include those vendors vital for customers operation (i.e. telephone, electricity, etc.)
        2. Paying habits should be prompt. References indicating 60 days and slower are unacceptable.

Supersedes		Orig. Code	Release No.	Effective Date
B.O.P. No.(s).	Page No.(s).	AP3	B-039	2/21/
1.01	5,9,10,11			
Related Publications		Inquiries: CORPORATE CREDIT MANAGER		

Exhibit 3-a (page 5)

Branch Office Procedure

Title		B.O.P Number: 1.01
ORDER ACCEPTANCE		
		Page 6 of 11
Vol. No. 1	Vol. Name: Order Processing	

B. Leases

    1. Retail Sales - Financed on Lease thru Home Office

        a. Bank References

            1) All judgements in compliance with paragraph 2a are applicable.

            2) Check how long the applicant has been an account of the bank against how long the applicant has been in business. There must be a reasonable relationship between the two. If not, previous bank reference(s) must be obtained.

        b. Trade References

            1. All judgements in compliance with paragraph 2b are applicable..

            2. Another leasing company, or some other installment purchase would be acceptable as one reference, while the second reference should be a major supplier so that insight may be gained into the size and scope of the applicants business.

        c. Additional Requirement for Leases:

            1. Advance rentals, Security Deposits, length of lease and personal quarantees.

               -Four-year (48 month) and five year (60 month) leases must be accompanied by a check in an amount equal to three months rental; which will be applied to the first and last two months rent.

               Lease applications for four & five year leases submitted on behalf of applicants in business for less than five years, will be subject to a more intensive credit review than other shorter term leases. Based upon this review, additional advance rentals may be requested as an alternative to outright rejection.

               -Two-year (24 month) and three-year (36 month) leases must be accompanied by a check in an amount equal to two months rental; which will be applied to the first & last months rent.

               -One-year leases need only be accompanied by a check for the first months rent.

Supersedes		Orig. Code	Release No.	Effective Date
B.O.P. No.(s).	Page No.(s).			
1.01 Rel. B-004	6	AP3	B-048	4/1/
Related Publications		Inquiries: Corporate Credit Manager		

Exhibit 3-a (page 6)

Branch Office Procedure

Title	B.O.P Number: 1.01
ORDER ACCEPTANCE	Page 7 of 11
Vol. No. 1 Vol. Name: Order Processing	

These advance rental rules may be waived where the lease applicant has a D & B rating of 1A1. In this instance the purchase order must accompany the lease.

    d. The following maximum lease terms are available with regard to low dollar sales.

        1. -Where the total cost to lessor is at least $800.00, will accept a lease up to 36 months.

        2. -Where the "total cost to lessor" is less than $800.00, will accept a lease up to 24 months.

        3. -Where the "total cost to lessor" is less than $600.00, but more than $300.00,   will accept a lease for a 12 month period only.

        4. - Four & five year leases for dollar amounts under $800.00 are not acceptable under any condition.

        NOTE: A corporation in business 12 months or less, or a service type organization (selling a service with little or no investment in inventory, machinery, equipment, etc.) in business less than 3 years must provide a personal guarantee from one of the principal officers.

              Additionally, a bank reference is required from the personal guarantor.

Fiscal Funded Leases

Leases may not be written for GSA-nor for Municipal, County and State governments to whom we have generally extended GSA provisions.

    Instituional Agencies (Universities, Hospitals, etc.) may be on fiscal funded lease but under the following conditions:

    A. Price must be retail list.
    B. Maximum lease term 36 months.
    C. Only 1/3 commission to be given annually when renewal Purchase Order received.
    D. Purchase Order should be made out to Equilease covering monthly payments.

Supersedes		Orig. Code	Release No.	Effective Date
B.O.P. No.(s).	Page No.(s).			
1.01 Rel. B-004	7	AP3	B-048	4/1/
Related Publications		Inquiries: Corporate Credit Manager		

Exhibit 3-a (page 7)

Branch Office Procedure

Title		B.O.P Number: 1.01
	ORDER ACCEPTANCE	Page 8 of 11
Vol. No. 1	**Vol. Name:** Order Processing	

Funded Organizations - Neighborhood type of organizations that are primarily dependent upon government allotment or charitable contributions for existence have proven to be too vulnerable for extinction and are not acceptable.

3. Present Customer

    a. Receives the following Customer Credit Data from Home Office

       -Copies of Statement of Account for all active customers of the branch. (Exhibit "D").
       -"Turn-Over Notice" (Exhibit "E")
       -"Doubtful Account" Statements (Exhibit "F")
       -Copy of the final "Dun Letter" (L-3) (Exhibit "G").
       -Dun-Master List (Exhibit "H").

    b. Refers to the above data on all incoming orders from present customers, and checks to determine if there is a past due balance.

    c. Upon checking credit status, proceeds as follows:

      1. In all instances when the statement balance plus the order on hand exceeds $7500.00, contact Credit Department for approval.

      2. If amounts due are within 1-40 days from invoice date, Okay to ship.

      3. If amounts due are within 41-70 days from invoice date, call customer an request payment for past due amount. The order may be shipped with customer's assurance that payment will be or has been made. Notify Credit Department of the transaction.

      4. If amounts due are 71 days and over from invoice date, do not ship and advise customer that the matter has been referred to the Credit Department.

Supersedes		Orig. Code	Release No.	Effective Date
B.O.P. No.(s).	**Page No.(s).**			
1.01 Rel. B-004	8	AP3	B-048	4/1/
Related Publications		**Inquiries:**		
		Corporate Credit Manager		

Exhibit 3-a (page 8)

Branch Office Procedure

Title		B.O.P Number: 1.01
	ORDER ACCEPTANCE	Page 9 of 11
Vol. No. 1	Vol. Name: Order Processing	

5. "Doubtful Accounts" - Upon receipt of order, advises customer that their account has been placed for collection. Should shipment, or invoice, be deemed essential, the Branch Administration Manager contacts Credit Department's Third Party Collection Supervisor for approval.

6. If the customer has Savin equipment on lease at present, and wishes to lease additional equipment, all payments on existing lease must be current and a current bank reference obtained. In the event the customer has changed banks, completed new bank reference is required.

7. When a machine sale is made to a present customer a complete credit check must be performed as for New Customers. This includes conversion from rental to sale.

4. Multiple Machine Orders

    a. Total sales in amounts up to $7,500.00 may be credit approved by Branch Administration Manager.

    b. Sales in amounts over $7,500.00 must be submitted in writing to Corporate Credit Manager for final credit approval, prior to shipping the equipment.

5. Special Terms

    Any terms other than those standard terms listed below must be approved in writing in advance by the Corporate Credit Manager.

    Machines: Net 10 days
                     1/3 with order, 1/3-30, 1/3-60
                     1/2 with order, 1/2-60

    Cpn. Books: Net 10 days
                     1/3 with order, 1/3-30, 1/3-60
                     1/2 with order and 1/2-60

    When extended terms are granted, they should appear on the invoice exactly as above.

    All other billing net 10 days - no exception.

Supersedes		Orig. Code	Release No.	Effective Date
B.O.P. No.(s).	Page No.(s).	AP3	B-048	4/1/
1.01 Rel. B-039	9			
Related Publications		Inquiries:		
		CORPORATE CREDIT MANAGER		

Exhibit 3-a (page 9)

Branch Office Procedure

Title	B.O.P Number: 1.01	
ORDER ACCEPTANCE		
	Page 10 of 11	

Vol. No. 1	Vol. Name: Order Processing

6. Cash Discounts

   Equipment Sales (Non-Lease) including conversions to sale
   (Not applicable to typewriter sales)
   5% for payment in full with order.
   2% for payment in full within 10 days of the invoice date.

   Coupon Book Sales

   5% for payment in full with order.

GENERAL INFORMATION

Credit approval of orders is the Branch Administration Manager's
responsibility. If after analyzing the facts gathered about a
specific order, a credit decision cannot be made, all information
should be submitted to the Corporate Credit Manager for a final
decision.

Even though the equipment may be sold for cash, bank & trade references
are still required and should be checked. This is necessary to
establish credit for ensuing supply & service business.

In such instances, shipment should not be delayed pending completion of
the credit check.

An order accepted for future delivery should be credit checked at
delivery time.

SECTION C

Telephone Confirmations:

Purpose:

To insure validity of new orders through phone contact by Administration to each customer placing a new machine or coupon book
order to insure agreement on general terms and conditions of the order.

Supersedes		Orig. Code	Release No.	Effective Date
B.O.P. No.(s).	Page No.(s).	AP2	B-059	8/5/
B.O.P. 101 Rel. # 039	10			
Related Publications		Inquiries:		
		Corporate Credit Manager		

Exhibit 3-a (page 10)

Branch Office Procedure

Title	B.O.P Number: 1.01
ORDER ACCEPTANCE	Page 11 of 11
Vol. No. 1 **Vol. Name:** Order Processing	

Responsibility:

Administration

Procedure:

A. After receipt of the Sales Order Form for machines or coupon
   book sales, using that form for reference and with the use of
   Telephone Confirmation form (See Exhibit I) a phone call is
   made to the customer. This call is to be made only after the
   order and credit has been determined to be acceptable.
B. Speak only to the person who signed the Sales Order Form.
C. Ask all applicable questions on the Telephone Confirmation Form
   (See Exhibit I). Refer to the Sales Order Form as a cross
   reference.
D. Fill in form (See Exhibit I) as each question is discussed.
E. If any part of the confirmation is not in agreement with the
   Sales Order Form advise the customer that you will get further
   information. Then hold order and advise the Sales Manager.
   Upon advice from Sales Manager of correction, reconfirm the
   order.
F. Sign and date the Telephone Confirmation.
G. Attaches to invoice along with other backup paperwork on the
   order.

D.   APPENDIX OF EXHIBITS

Exhibit	Description
A	Sales Order Form
B	Trade Reference Letter
C	Bank Reference Letter
D	Statement of Account
E	Turnover Notice
F	Doubtful-Statement of Account
G	"Final" Dun Letter (L-3)
H	Dun Master List
I	Confirmation Telephone Call

Supersedes		Orig. Code	Release No.	Effective Date
B.O.P. No.(s).	**Page No.(s).**			
1.01	5, 9, 10, 11	AP3	B-039	2/21/
Related Publications		**Inquiries:** CORPORATE CREDIT MANAGER		

Exhibit 3-a (page 11)

STANDARD OPERATING PROCEDURE		
Subject:		Number C-4d
	CONFIRMATION PHONE CALLS	Page of 2 2
		Effective Date
Supersedes Cor. No. Page 199	Dated	Related S.O.P./H.O.P

1. Give Speech (reason for call is marketing information)
2. Check:
   a. Their Purchase Order Number
   b. Price of Machine
   c. Terms
   d. Quantity of Machines and/or Supplies
   e. Price of Supplies (first order and reorders)
   f. Price of Future Supplies from Salesman, if these are No Charge
   g. *Marketing Questions—Complete form
   h. Authority of Signer—If Not Obvious
   i. If Lease—Payments required per month terms; number of months on lease; options available on Lease/Purchase Plan; if interest-free rental:
      1. Is it clear that you have one of four options which may be exercised at the end of 36 months, but that until this option is exercised, title to the machine remains with us?
      2. Were you advised that your monthly payments will be payable to an outside Equipment Leasing Corp., but options at the end of 36 months are payable to this company.
      3. Were you handed a printed sheet showing the various options available to you? If not, we'll send it to you now.
   j. If a Trade-In-Machine request an appointment for pickup
   k. *Any Branches or Subsidiaries - Names and Addresses - Name of Contact
3. Conclude by asking "are there any other conditions I have omitted?"
4. Sign Form—Send original with Bill Only—Date it. File Duplicate with Pink awaiting Green Invoice Copy
5. Party Spoken To: _____

*Send to Home Office Marketing Division   _____

                                                                  SIGNED

                                                      _____

                                                      DATE CALL MADE

Correction No. 242
Date Prepared 4/8

Exhibit 3-b

STANDARD OPERATING PROCEDURE		
Subject:		Number HOP C-46
	COLLECTION PROCEDURES - HOME OFFICE	Page of 1 4
		Effective Date 5/5/
Supersedes Cor. No. Page	Dated	Related S.O.P./H.O.P.

PURPOSE: To provide a means for the timely processing and collection follow-up of customer statement of accounts and Dunning Notices.

METHOD: 1. Customer Statements of Account for each branch are prepared by Data Processing twice monthly—at the month end and mid-month. These aged customer statements are provided to collection correspondents; and copies mailed to Branch Administrators for order processing and collection follow-up in accordance with SOP C-25.

2. Dunning notices are prepared by Data Processing twice monthly for mailing to delinquent accounts. Each cycle provides the following requests for payment.
   a. Courtesy Notices - Accounts past due 15-30 days.
   b. D1 Form Letter - Accounts past due 31-45 days.
   c. D2 Form Letter - Accounts past due 46-60 days.
   d. D5 Form Letter - Accounts past due 61-75 days.
   e. Dun Master List - Accounts past due over 75 days.

3. Accounts with special terms (Activity Codes F-P-N-T) are excluded from the dunning cycle and appear on a dun master list when the invoice has been past due more than 60 days:
   a. If no payment has been made on (Activity Codes P-N-T), a copy of the invoice is obtained and forwarded with D7 form with follow-ups as indicated in Step 6 below, with D8 form (Intent to Charge Back) sent to Branch.
   b. If no payment on Activity Code F (leases) refer problem to Leasing Desk as to reason for non-payment.

Date Prepared: 5/5/
HOP Correction No. 168

STANDARD OPERATING PROCEDURE		
Subject:		**Number** HOP C-46
	COLLECTION PROCEDURE - HOME OFFICE	**Page of** 2 4
		Effective **Date** 5/5/
Supersedes Cor. No. **Page**	**Dated**	**Related** **S.O.P./H.O.P.**

4. After accounts have received a Courtesy Notice, D1 and D2 collection letter, the collection correspondents receive computerized copies of D5 forms for review before notifying customer of intent to place account for 3rd party collection. Earlier notices are mailed immediately without referral to the correspondents.

5. Correspondents check D5's for previous correspondence or referral to Branch for sales or service problem, etc.

6. If no prior problem, D5 is mailed and correspondent sends copy to Branch Administrator alerting him that account is in jeopardy of being litigated unless amount past due is paid within 20 days.

7. If no reply or payment within 20 days, the correspondent takes the following action:

   a. *Machine sale, Coupon book or balance over $300-*
      1. Telephones account to request payment or to determine reason for non-payment.
      2. If problem exists involving branch, follows Step (8a) below.
      3. If collection problem apparent and payment commitment cannot be obtained, customer is notified that account is being placed for collection.
      4. Submits commission charge back (S/C Branch Manager) copies of invoice, statement and collection folder to supervisor for review and placement with collection agency.
      5. Account is transferred to Doubtful trial balance.

   b. *Balances under $300-*Correspondent obtains copies of the following data and submits to supervisor for review and 3rd party collection placement.
      1. Customer invoices
      2. Customer statement
      3. D5 collection notice
      4. Commission charge back
      5. Account transferred to Doubtful trial balance.

   c. *Balances under $25.00-*Collection supervisor reviews accounts under $25.00 to determine whether to place for collection or to charge to Sales Allowance immediately.

8. Sales Disputes, Cancellations, Service Problems, *Pricing Disputes, Allowances, Lease Conversions, etc.*

When problems of this nature arise, as a result of replies to dunning notices or telephone

Date Prepared: 5/5/
HOP Correction No. 168

HOP C-46

Exhibit 3-c (page 2)

STANDARD OPERATING PROCEDURE		
Subject:		Number HOP C-46
COLLECTION PROCEDURES - HOME OFFICE		Page of 3 4
		Effective Date 5/5/
Supersedes Cor. No. Page	Dated	Related S.O.P./H.O.P.

discussions, the branch is notified immediately by memo from or by use of D8 form (Intent to Charge Back). The Branch Administrator or salesman must correct the problem within 20 days and advise the correspondent in writing what action has been taken. In the event that no reply or payment is received within the 20 day period, the following steps are taken:

a. Commission charge back initiated and forwarded to Branch Administrator and Branch Manager.

b. Branch Manager notified of problem with request to investigate and notify correspondent within 10 days.

c. If no reply or payment as indicated in Step B above, memo is sent to Zone Administrator with copies to either the District Manager or Zone General Manager for reply within 10 days.

d. If no reply or payment, as indicated in Step C above, the problem and collection folder is submitted to the Collection Supervisor for further action.

e. Manager Credit/Collections will be responsible for review of uncollected and unresolved sales problems with Vice President/Marketing.

Note: Copies of all credit adjustment correspondence will be forwarded to Branch Credit Department, if a return or billing adjustment is involved.

9. After accounts have progressed through complete dunning cycle (C/N, D1, D2, D5) or have matured beyond 60 days past due on special term codes, the names, account numbers and balances are itemized on the dun master list. Copies are provided for correspondents and branch administrators.

Correspondents utilize the list in conjunction with their collection folders to:

a. Check to make certain that each account has received collection activity.

b. Follow-up on D5 and D8 forms to charge back commission and/or refer account for third party collection.

c. Up-date collection activity on special terms (Activity Codes F-P-N-T) as detailed in Step 3 above.

10. Branch Administrators use the dun list as a ready reference to accounts which are on credit hold.

11. If details of the dun list balance require examination, the B/A should refer to copy of the customer's statement of account for clarification.

Date Prepared: 5/5/
HOP Correction No. 168

HOP C-46

Exhibit 3-c (page 3)

STANDARD OPERATING PROCEDURE		
Subject:	Number	
	HOP C-46	
COLLECTION PROCEDURE - HOME OFFICE	Page of	
	4 4	
	Effective	
	Date 5/5/	
Supersedes Cor. No. Page Dated	Related	
	S.O.P./H.O.P	

12. Under the procedures as outlined above, all past due accounts should be referred to 3rd party collection and commissions charged back within 91 to 120 days past due. Sales problems and disputes should be referred by Manager Credit/Collection to Vice President/Marketing within 151 days past due.

13. *Area Collection*-Dunning cycles proceed as outlined above. Copies of D5's and dun master lists are mailed to Regional offices and collections proceed in the manner prescribed. Third party action and sales problems are referred to the Area Credit Manager for decision and further action.

INQUIRIES: Manager Credit/Collection Department
DISTRIBUTION: List 11.0 HOP Manual Holders

Date Prepared: 5/5/
HOP Correction No. 168

HOP C-46

Exhibit 3-c (page 4)

BUY BACK AGREEMENT

AGREEMENT between **Albert Bakers**   Corporation, a New York corporation (" **ABC**") and
("Dealer").

WHEREAS, Dealer is a dealer for the sale of **ABC's #900**   Equipment ("Equipment") and is desirous of purchasing Equipment from time to time from **ABC** on the understanding that **ABC** is willing to repurchase Equipment from Dealer; and

WHEREAS, **ABC** is willing to repurchase Equipment from Dealer upon the terms and conditions hereinafter set forth,

THEREFORE, the parties hereto do hereby agree as follows:

1.   The terms and conditions of this Agreement shall relate only to units of Equipment purchased by Dealer from **ABC** at a cost of Two Thousand Five Hundred and Forty Five Dollars ($2,545) per unit of Equipment.

2.   Subject to the terms and conditions hereof, **ABC** shall repurchase units of Equipment from Dealer at the following prices during the following periods from the date of delivery of the Equipment to the Dealer:

Period	Amount	Period	Amount	Period	Amount
1 month	$1,636	7 months	$1,463	13 months	$ 665
2 months	1,628	8 months	1,330	14 months	532
3 months	1,620	9 months	1,197	15 months	399
4 months	1,612	10 months	1,064	16 months	266
5 months	1,604	11 months	931	17 months	133
6 months	1,596	12 months	798	18 months	- 0 -

In determining the number of months (a) fractional months shall be treated as whole months and (b) Equipment shall be repurchased on a "first-in, first-out" basis (i.e., the computation shall be made with respect to the oldest units of Equipment purchased by Dealer and not sold by Dealer, regardless of serial number). The computations shall be based upon the period commencing on the date the Equipment is received by Dealer and terminating on the date the Equipment is received by **ABC.** Units sold by Dealer shall be determined by serial number.

3.   (a)**ABC** 's obligations to repurchase Equipment shall apply only if ninety (90) days have elapsed from the last order for Equipment placed by Dealer with **ABC.**

(b) If Dealer delivers the Equipment to **ABC** during the ninety (90) day period described in paragraph 3(a), **ABC** shall not be required to make such payment until the expiration of sixty (60) days from the date of the last delivery of Equipment from **ABC** to Dealer. If Dealer orders Equipment during such sixty (60) day period, **ABC** shall, at its election, deliver to Dealer either the unit of Equipment returned by Dealer or new Equipment, at no additional charge to Dealer.

(c) If Dealer orders Equipment from **ABC** within thirty (30) days from the date of **ABC** 's payment to Dealer pursuant to paragraph 4(b), Dealer shall refund to **ABC** in full the amount paid by **ABC** hereunder, and **ABC** shall, at its election, deliver to Dealer either the unit of Equipment returned by Dealer or new Equipment, at no additional charge to Dealer.

(d) This Agreement shall not apply to any units of Equipment delivered to Dealer pursuant to Paragraphs 3(b) or 3(c), unless Dealer pays the full purchase price described in paragraph 1 with respect to such Equipment.

4.   (a) The provisions of this Agreement shall not apply unless Dealer has fully paid for each unit of Equipment which has been delivered by **ABC** to Dealer.

(b) If Dealer is in excess of 30 days past due in payment of other accounts to **ABC, ABC** may, at its election, apply the payments due to Dealer hereunder toward payment of such accounts, in which event Dealer shall pay the full purchase price with respect to units of Equipment ordered pursuant to paragraphs 3(b) and (c).

Exhibit 3-d (page 1)

(c) If **ABC** receives Equipment from Dealer during a period when paragraph 4(a) is applicable, the Equipment shall, for purposes of paragraph 2, be deemed to have been received on the day next following receipt by **ABC** of payment of the amount owed by Dealer with respect to all Equipment received by Dealer.

5.   **ABC** shall have no obligation to repurchase any Equipment which has been sold by Dealer. As used in this Agreement, a sale includes, but is not limited to, any sale on open account, conditional sale, installment sale, sale subject to a security agreement, or lease defined as a sale in accordance with Paragraph 4 of Opinion No. 27 of the Accounting Principles Board entitled "Accounting for Lease Transactions by Manufacturer or Dealer Lessors," a copy of which is attached hereto. Any questions concerning the applicability of these provisions should be directed to **ABC** Corporation - Main Street - NYC, NY. **Att,** Vice President/Controller.

6.   Dealer hereby grants **ABC** the right to audit Dealer's records as to serial numbers, names of customers, location of machines and related information during normal business hours on at least 24 hours written notice.

7.   **ABC** shall not be required to repurchase any Equipment which is not in the same condition in which it was delivered to Dealer, ordinary wear and tear excepted.

8.   This Agreement may be terminated or the terms and conditions hereof, including, but not limited to, repurchase prices and periods, may be cancelled, modified or amended by **ABC** at any time, on notice to Dealer; provided, however, that no such termination or modification shall affect Dealer's rights hereunder with respect to Equipment purchased by Dealer.

IN WITNESS WHEREOF, the parties hereto have duly executed this Agreement.

Albert Bakers   CORPORATION

Date:_____   By_____

Date:_____   By_____

(Z-2-56) 19-053-1M-1

Exhibit 3-d (page 2)

HOME OFFICE		
STANDARD OPERATING PROCEDURE		
Subject:	**Number** C-30	
APPLICATION OF CASH RECEIPTS	**Page** 1	**of** 3
	Effective Date 9/1/	
Supersedes Cor. No. 6 **Page C-30**	**Dated 1/3/**	**Related S.O.P./H.O.P**

PURPOSE OF PROCEDURE: To establish and maintain accurate internal control over cash receipts and deposits; to deposit cash on same day as receipt.

METHOD:

1. Mail Room—will open envelopes:

   a) Do not remove contents

   b) Hand carry to Accounting Department

2. Accounting Department—will:

   a) Tape net cash receipts and count checks

   b) Staple all papers accompanying checks to the checks and discard envelopes

   c) Pass checks and attachments to Accounts Receivable Department

3. Accounts Receivable Department—will:

   a) Savicopy checks

   b) Document accompanying information

   c) Sort Savicopies by district

4. Accounts Receivable Department—will:

   a) Endorse checks

   b) Prove out the numerical count in the endorsing meter, the number of Savicopies and the original count by the Accounting Department

   c) Not withhold any check from the daily deposit unless it is legally imperfect

   d) Hand carry checks to the Accounting Department for immediate deposit

5. Accounts Receivable Department—will utilize Savicopies of checks and customer remittance advices to:

   a) Apply cash to the Accounts Receivable turnaround forms

   b) Key off the trial balance

6. Accounts Receivable Clerks—will adhere to the following standard procedures:

Correction 27
Page 1 of 3

C-30

Exhibit 3-e (page 1)

HOME OFFICE		
STANDARD OPERATING PROCEDURE		
Subject:	**Number** C-30	
	Page of 2 3	
APPLICATION OF CASH RECEIPTS		
	Effective Date 9/1/	
Supersedes Cor. No. 6 Page C-30 Dated 1/3/	**Related S.O.P./H.O.P.**	

a) A remittance advice is to be made for every check, recording full details of the application, and a copy of this remittance advice given to the Data Processing Department when applying an "on-account" or "unapplied" remittance.

b) "Unapplied payments" are to be credited against the oldest open aging column on the trial balance:

1 — A form letter should be sent to customer advising him of application

2 - Do not reduce original accounts receivable card. Instead, use the same invoice number, but apply as a credit, and show both original invoice and on-account payment on trial balance.

3 - Show date paid, not original invoice date, on remittance advice.

d) System/360 transaction codes are to be used at all times.

e) All checks are to be qualified at once and any adjustments made immediately. Only where this is impossible will the check be placed in "suspense" account, each deposit therein to carry an individual account number.

f) The standard letter of "information and/or inquiry" is to be sent to the payor when there is any question as to correct application of the check.

g) The amount of the check (and any general ledger adjustment under $25) is to be entered in the space provided on the turnaround document.

h) Any journal entry of $25 or over must be approved by the Credit Department Manager and countersigned by the Assistant Controller and must be written up on a special journal entry form.

i) The net total of all checks is to be taped (by district) from Savicopies.

j) A net total of the credit to Accounts Receivable as reflected by turnaround forms is taped by district. The total net cash tape (i) must balance with the turnaround form credits to Accounts Receivable, less general ledger adjustments.

k) The final cumulative tape total of the net cash deposit (all districts) must reconcile with the original Accounting Department tape and with the Data Processing daily net cash run.

Correction 27
Page 2 of 3

C-30

Exhibit 3-e (page 2)

HOME OFFICE		
STANDARD OPERATING PROCEDURE		
Subject:		**Number** C-30
	APPLICATION OF CASH RECEIPTS	**Page** of 3 3
		Effective **Date** 9/1/
Supersedes Cor. No. 6 Page C-30	Dated 1/3/	**Related** **S.O.P./H.O.P.**

l) The miscellaneous general ledger adjustment total is reflected on the IBM run in the general ledger column of the Daily Cash Receipts Report (See i and j).

m) Turnaround Forms, together with the appropriate remittance advices, are transmitted to the Data Processing Department, upon completion of each individual day's application.

n) All *customer remittance advices* are filed daily with the check Savicopies. The Accounts Receivable Department *remittance advice books* are maintained by district in chronological sequence.

Correction 17
Page 3 of 3
Date Prepared: 9/28/

C-30

Exhibit 3-e (page 3)

DATE OF RUN 10/01/   A / R   A G E D   T R I A L   B A L A N C E   R E P O R T   SUMMARY PAGE

BILLING THRU 08/31/
PAYMENT THRU 08/31/

	CURRENT	1 TO 30	31 TO 60	61 TO 90	91 OVER	T O T A L
REGULAR RETAIL	2723894.66 **	1267720.32 **	612947.91 **	283918.42 **	1016518.82 **	5905000.13 **
REGULAR DEALER	1061960.00 **	1098907.08 **	346667.05 **	222320.34 **	872215.47 **	3602069.94 **
DOUBTFUL RETAIL	34825.02 **	26927.87 **	15948.82 **	10732.23 **	695770.80 **	784204.74 **
DOUBTFUL DEALER	2125.59 **	429.20CR **	571.85 **	13848.91 **	148767.92 **	164885.07 **
REGULAR RETAIL	.00 **	.00 **	.00 **	.00 **	.00 **	.00 **
REGULAR DEALER	.00 **	.00 **	.00 **	.00 **	.00 **	.00 **
DOUBTFUL RETAIL	.00 **	.00 **	.00 **	.00 **	.00 **	.00 **
DOUBTFUL DEALER	.00 **	.00 **	.00 **	.00 **	.00 **	.00 **
TOTAL A / R	3822805.27 ***	2393126.07 ***	976135.63 ***	530819.90 ***	2733273.01 ***	10456159.88 ***

Exhibit 3-f

45-607 EYE-EASE
45-707 20/20 BUFF
Made – U S A

A CORP.
AGED TRIAL BALANCE SUMMARY.
($ 000's)

	Month	Current	%	1-30 days	%	31-60 days	%	61 days and over	%	Total	%
Retail	Jan 19	3013	40.4	2343	31.4	685	9.2	1425	19.0	7466	100.0
	Feb	2847	36.8	1922	24.9	1432	18.5	1535	19.8	7736	100.0
	Mar	2991	38.2	1668	21.4	1171	15.0	1982	25.4	7812	100.0
	Apr	3959	50.8	955	12.2	819	10.5	2068	26.5	7801	100.0
	May	3119	42.5	1672	22.8	460	6.2	2093	28.5	7344	100.0
	Jun	2459	33.7	1982	27.1	945	12.9	1926	26.3	7312	100.0
	Jul	3404	45.1	948	12.6	1210	16.1	1977	26.2	7539	100.0
	Aug	2444	34.6	2054	29.1	456	6.4	2117	29.9	7071	100.0
	Sep	2145	31.0	1664	24.0	1135	16.4	1983	28.6	6927	100.0
	Oct	2489	37.6	1241	18.7	818	12.4	2076	31.3	6624	100.0
	Nov	2089	33.1	1722	27.2	604	9.6	1905	30.1	6320	100.0
	Dec	1732	29.3	1471	24.8	923	15.6	1789	30.2	5915	100.0
Dealer & Foreign	Jan 19	1106	31.0	837	23.5	580	16.3	1041	29.2	3564	100.0
	Feb	1012	28.0	928	25.6	546	15.1	1132	31.3	3618	100.0
	Mar	1290	32.9	917	23.4	527	13.5	1182	30.2	3916	100.0
	Apr	971	26.0	1052	28.1	568	15.2	1148	30.7	3739	100.0
	May	1661	38.2	941	21.6	689	15.9	1059	24.3	4350	100.0
	Jun	1076	23.4	1602	34.8	694	15.1	1233	26.7	4605	100.0
	Jul	1251	25.6	939	19.2	1271	26.0	1427	29.2	4888	100.0
	Aug	1263	24.5	1067	20.7	1015	19.7	1807	35.1	5152	100.0
	Sep	1271	26.6	1140	23.9	756	15.9	1603	33.6	4770	100.0
	Oct	1802	34.5	1205	23.0	850	16.3	1369	26.2	5226	100.0
	Nov	1584	28.8	1536	28.0	908	16.5	1469	26.7	5497	100.0
	Dec	1467	24.8	1604	27.2	1129	19.1	1705	28.9	5905	100.0
Total	Jan 19	4119	37.3	3180	28.8	1265	11.5	2466	22.4	11030	100.0
	Feb	3859	34.0	2850	25.1	1978	17.4	2667	23.5	11354	100.0
	Mar	4281	36.5	2585	22.0	1698	14.5	3164	27.0	11728	100.0
	Apr	4930	42.7	2007	17.4	1387	12.0	3216	27.9	11540	100.0

Exhibit 3-g

Sales To Cash Analysis
(In thousand of dollars)

HBJ 1/2/
Revised 11/18/

19__	Sales $M	Cash $M	3 Month Composite Sales $M	Cash (60 day lag) $M	Difference $M (4-5)	Cumulative Cash under (over) Sales ÷3
Mar	3500					÷3
Apr	4100					
May	2886	3715	10486	10525	(39)	(13)
Jun	2771	3342	9757	10609	(852)	(297)
July	3581	3468	9238	10646	(1408)	(766)
Aug	3727	3799	10079	10917	(838)	(1045)
Sept	3165	2379	10473	10545	(72)	(1069)
Oct	3827	3739	10719	10442	277	(977)
Nov	3911	3427	10903	11199	(296)	(1076)
Dec	4590	3276	12328	11425	903	(775)
Jan 19__	4037	4496	12538	11901	637	(563)
Feb	3770	3653	12397	11785	612	(359)
Mar	4440	3752	12247	12649	(402)	(493)
Apr	4290	4380	12500	12437	63	(472)
May	4390	4517	13120	11872	1248	(56)
June	3920	3540	12600	11209	1391	408
July	3937	3815	12247	11986	261	495
Aug	3626	3854	11483	12422	(939)	182
Sept	3130	4317	10693	12725	(2032)	(495)
Oct	4798	4251	11554	12093	(539)	(675)
Nov	3821	4157	11749			
Dec		3685				

Exhibit 3-h

Percentage of 61 plus days old to total A/R

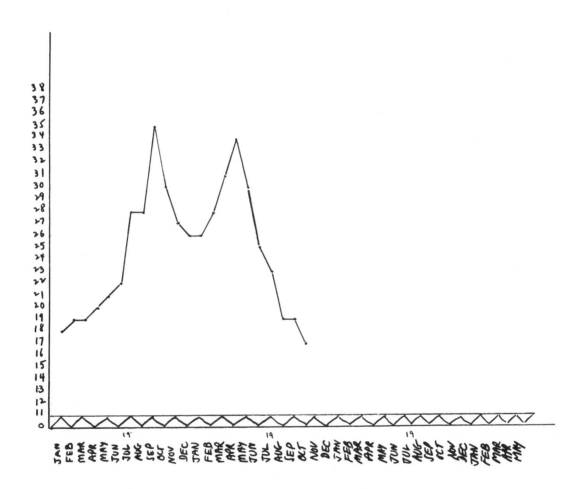

Exhibit 3-i

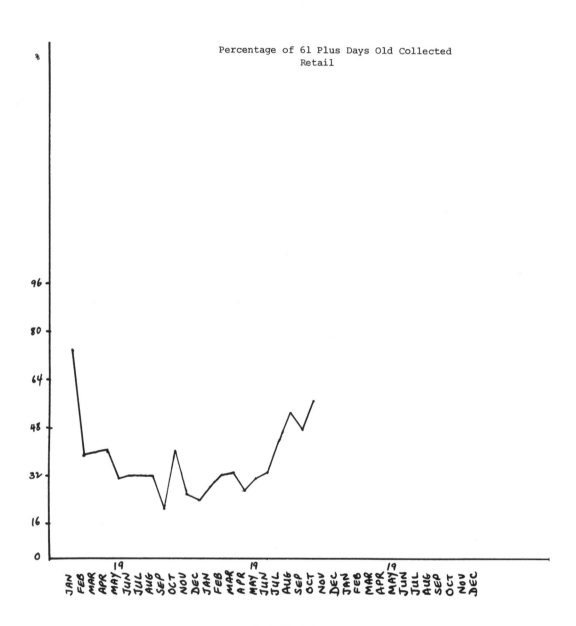

Percentage of 61 Plus Days Old Collected
Retail

Exhibit 3-j

MONTHLY ANALYSIS DOUBTFULS RETAIL (columns 1-6)
(3÷2)

DEALER

	MONTH ENDING	TOTAL DOUBTFUL	TOTAL $ COLLECTED	% OF TOTAL $ COLLECTED TOTAL DBTFL	ADDED TO DOUBTFULS	TOTAL DBTFL BAD DEBT WRITE-OFF	TOTAL DBTFL BAD DEBT WRITE-OFF	
1	197_							1
2	JAN.	605326	14859	2	55229	58427		2
3	FEB.	623669	16949	3	44846	10362		3
4	MARCH	799186	21048	2	73296	39783		4
5	APRIL	928328	40122	4	41165	60020		5
6	MAY	870186	38520	4	52211	28005	-0-	6
7	JUNE	760559	84803	11	39223	22376	124377	7
8	JULY	787889	26574	3	86424	24251	-0-	8
9	AUG.	784205	32303	4	164027	24070	-0-	9
10	SEPT.	772707	34481	4	92977	45412	-0-	10
11	OCT.	891801	42415	5	72821	40542	-0-	11
12	NOV.	873395	35783	4	84222	18251	1791	12
13	DEC.	956864	32709	3	70294	36754	-0-	13
14	197_							14
15	JAN.	988299	41471	2	24930	23947	-0-	15
16	FEB.	1 208702	36755	3	87167	13676	2563	16
17	MARCH	1 233675	40010	3	99215	20750	-0-	17
18	APRIL	1 226240	51647	4	109696	32434	-0-	18
19	MAY	1 278912	42310	3	75083	39728	-0-	19
20	JUNE	1 256768	51682	4	112843	28400	-0-	20
21	JULY	1 335901	51158	4	109859	40046	-0-	21
22	AUG.	1 250818	46259	4	82149	55901	-0-	22
23	SEPT.	1 290570	37132	3	72322	24436	-0-	23
24	OCT.	1 363211	50850	4	157770	26728	-0-	24
25	NOV.	1 484200	34099	2	89571	34099	-0-	25
26	DEC.							26

Exhibit 3-k

	Initials	Date
Prepared By		
Approved By		

45-807 EYE-EASE
45-907 20/20 BUFF
NATIONAL Made in U.S.A.

DOUBTFUL VS. BAD DEBT RESERVE
MONTHLY ANALYSIS

Month END	DEALER Doubtful	Retail Doubtful	Total Doubtful		BAD DEBT RESERVE	
APRIL	446820	1005560	1452380		1753695	
MAY	454096	926234	1380830		1784086	
JUNE	433819	866776	1300595		1085093	
JULY	425775	845450	1271225		1795379	
AUGUST	421530	815730	1237260		1827417	
SEPT.	428486	734434	1162920		1814818	
OCTOBER	412900	700332	1113232		1821707	
NOVEMBER	404138	723307	1127445			
DECEMBER						

Exhibit 3-I

A. CORP.

Schedule of Bad Debts Reserve - Annual

			PROVISION	A/R WRITE-OFF	BALANCE	% Col.5 ÷ Col.7	TOTAL A/R TRADE
Balance	5-1-	00			23410	5.1	462000
FYE	4-30	01	11866	-	35276	4.9	720000
FYE	4-30	02	26500	8638	53138	3.8	1406000
FYE	4-30	03	127114	5252	175000	8.4	2074000
FYE	4-30	04	159837	149837	185000	6.8	2716000
FYE	4-30	05	128467	14793	298674	7.2	4124000
FYE	4-30	06	371843	120517	550000	8.6	6390000
FYE	4-30	07	261600	251600	560000	7.5	7437000
FYE	4-30	08	288307	213191	635116	8.0	7930000
FYE	4-30	09	1100580	660696	1075000	10.0	10696000
FYE	4-30	10	1082994	832614	1325380	10.0	13242000
4 mos ended	8-31-	11	297821	223554	1399647	9.1	15404000

Exhibit 3-m

RECEIVABLE ANALYSIS

Product Line A

MONTH ENDED	SALES $M	#DAYS SLS/REC	TOTAL REC'S	AGEING				COLLECTIONS			
				C-60		P/D 61 +		TOTAL C-60		P/D 61 +	
				AMT.	%	AMT.	%	AMT.	%	AMT.	%
197___											
JANUARY	519	1 5 5	3454	1 346	39	1 444	42	679	22.9	544	73
FEBRUARY	622	1 8 2	3815	1 711	45	1 990	31	443	22.8	309	21
MARCH	784	1 5 5	3027	1 896	63	1 130	37	638	26.7	443	37
APRIL	874	1 2 4	2997	2 044	68	954	32	696	22.9	341	30
MAY	522	1 2 3	3046	1 946	64	1 100	36	646	21.5	417	44
JUNE	703	1 2 6	2906	1 857	64	1 049	36	694	22.7	388	35
JULY	633	1 4 4	2890	1 707	59	1 183	41	623	21.4	420	40
AUGUST	461	1 9 1	2676	1 499	56	1 178	44	675	23.3	358	30
SEPTEMBER	504	1 4 5	2327	1 494	64	833	36	652	24.3	468	40
OCTOBER	779	1 0 1	2533	1 576	62	957	38	548	23.5	294	35
NOVEMBER	535	1 2 3	2410	1 527	63	883	37	659	26.0	313	33
DECEMBER	752	1 0 4	2517	1 578	63	941	37	645	26.7	258	29
197___											
JANUARY	742	1 1 0	2538	1 616	64	923	36	662	26.3	332	35
FEBRUARY	682	1 0 9	2630	1 826	69	804	31	538	21.1	293	32
MARCH	811	1 0 7	2793	1 890	68	903	32	645	24.5	335	42
APRIL	1 140	9 4	3418	2 400	70	1 018	30	358	13	394	44
MAY	314	2 8 8	2885	2 159	75	726	25	762	22.2	375	37
JUNE	366	2 0 6	2479	1 779	72	700	28	780	28.8	450	38
JULY	550	1 6 0	2874	1 896	66	978	34	787	24.7	560	80
AUGUST	941	1 0 1	3040	2 231	73	808	27	532	46	620	63
SEPTEMBER	844	1 2 0	3379	2 635	78	744	22	527	56	358	44
OCTOBER	1 083	9 3	3173	2 442	77	731	23	395	33	501	67
NOVEMBER	1 299	8 0	3470	2 668	77	802	23	220	24	554	75
DECEMBER	964	9 6	2979	2 115	71	864	29	353	49	411	51
197___											
JANUARY	990	1 0 7	3326	2 344	70	982	30	601	55	386	44
FEBRUARY	976	1 0 1	3445	2 377	69	1 068	31	476	53	465	47
MARCH	1 067	1 0 6	3604	2 484	69	1 120	31	398	70	316	30

Exhibit 3-n

HOP/SOP MEMO

TO BE FILED WITHIN CORRESPONDING PROCEDURE
_____

Memo To: Distribution   Subject: Credit Analysis (CRAN)

From: Eff. Date: 5/1/
_____

HOP [ ] No.: _____   Title: Order Processing

SOP [x] No.: _C-22_____

HOP [ ] Last Correction No.:_____   HOP [ ] New Correction No.: _____

SOP [ ] Last Correction No.:_____ SOP [x] New Correction No.: ___436_____

Paragraph # _Exhibit G_____   Page # __24__   Affected
_____

Use of the Credit Analysis Code is to be reinstated. The purpose of this code
is to identify and categorize all credits issued. This code is to appear in
the space just above the Credit Memo. No. as follows:

CODE   REASON FOR CREDIT

Ø   Defective Parts
1   Home Office Processing Error
2   Branch Processing Error
3   Valhalla Warehouse Error
4   Defective Paper
5   Machine Cancellation
6   Machine Replacement
7   Dealer Reimbursement-GSA
8   Dealer Reimbursement - Retail
9   Customer Error
A   Service Call Adjustment
B   Salesman Error
C   Tax, Freight or Insurance Claim
                  Adjustment Refund
D   Maintenance Agreement Cancellation

INQUIRIES: Manager, Order Billing

DISTRIBUTION: List 12.0 SOP Manual Holders
                     8.0 Branch Administrators

Exhibit 3-o

COMPANY	NO. OF POLICY	AMOUNT	TERM	EXPIRES MO.	EXPIRES DAY	EXPIRES YEAR	PREMIUM	COVERAGE
Federal	FMPO69000703	Various*	Cont.	Anniversary			$45,268.00	Commercial Property Policy *see separate summary of this policy. Annual premium adjustment.
Federal	FXL77742900	$ 10,000,000.—	1 Yr	5 7	1 15		$ 2,991.00	Umbrella Excess Liability Policy Retained Limit: $10,000.—
Federal	(74)11403043	various $100,000/300,000—bodily injury 50,000—property damage 5,000—medical payments uninsured motorists cov. $ 50 deductible Comprehensive Fire/Theft $100 deductible Collision Towing coverage $25	1 Yr	8	1		$ 2,572.00	Automobile Insurance Mercedes Benz Mercedes Benz Dodge Van Citroen Cadillac Note: Oldsmobile eliminated 10/31/
Federal	99990108	$ 2,450,000.—	1 Yr	5	9		$12,250.00	Contingent Business Interruption Fire, Ext. Cov., Vandalism, Earthquake Volcanic eruption. Loc: Atsugi City, Kanagawa Pref., Japan
Ins. Co. of North America	10HF2048	$ ' 2,450,000.—	3 Yrs	5	19		Annual $11,596.67	Contingent Business Interruption Fire, Ext. Cov., Vandalism, Earthquake. Loc: Atsugi City, Kanagawa Pref., Japan
Ins. Co. of North America	16142	$750,000.—under deck 50,000.—on deck 50,000.—aircraft	Continuous				as per repts	Marine Open Cargo Policy "all-risk" per policy terms/conditions Warehouse to warehouse coverage.

Exhibit 4-a (page 1)

INSURANCE RECORD AS OF November 30, 19____

INSURED _____

LOCATION _____

COMPANY	NO. OF POLICY	AMOUNT	TERM	EXPIRES MO.	DAY	YEAR	PREMIUM	COVERAGE
Federal	(74)76322616	statutory	1Yr	5	1		Deposit $49,080.00	Workmens Compensation All States except 'monopolistic' states Experience modification 1.21 (California 1.97) Audit 5/1 -5/1/ $46,237. addl prem. Total Earned Prem 5/1/ $70,573.00.
INA Life Ins Co of New York	NYD11948	statutory	Cont. Until Canc.				as per repts	New York State Disability
Lloyds London	to be assigned	various	1 Yr	10	15		to be determ. 'quoted prem' $15,731.75	Aircraft Insurance Hansa Jet 320HFB Industrial Aid Use.

Hull

$575,000.—Hull "all-risk" coverage; agreed amount basis.
1% hull deductible applies in Flight, Taxying, and ingestion.
$500 hull deductible applies on ground.

Liability

$ 10,000,000.—Combined single limit Bodily Injury & Property Damage, Passenger Liability.
5,000.—Medical Payment coverage any one person including crew.
100,000.—Admitted Liability coverage any one person including crew.
1,000,000.—Combined single limit Bodily Injury & Property Damage, Passenger Liability: NonOwned Aircraft Liability

Pilots

—Asst Pilot (Can act as Chief Pilot upon being type rated in aircraft)

Geographical Limits

Central America, South America, Carribbean, Bahamas, Bermuda, USA, Canada, Mexico.

Note: Pro-rata, earned premium to follow as respects Argonaut Insurance Co. policy #H-5-682, covering policy period 8/24/ to 10/15/. (annual premium $7,957.00.) Lloyds London policy replaced Argonaut policy effective 10/15/

Exhibit 4-a (page 2)

289

INSURANCE RECORD AS OF ___November 30, 19___

INSURED _____

LOCATION _____

COMPANY	NO. OF POLICY	AMOUNT	TERM	EXPIRES MO.	EXPIRES DAY	EXPIRES YEAR	PREMIUM	COVERAGE
Federal	80352291	various	Cont. Anniversary	9	14		Annual $ 6,050.00	Comprehensive Bond
		Limits $500,000.—Commercail Blanket Employee Dishonesty 250,000.—Depositor's Forgery 25,000.—Credit Card coverage						Deductibles $10,000.—Employee Dishonesty on Merchandise 2,500.—Employee Dishonesty excl. Merchandise 2,500.—Depositor's Forgery
Peerless	805-37493	$500,000.—	1Yr	9	23		$ 380.00	General Term Bond for Entry of Merchandise Various Ports of Entry.
Aetna Cas.	72SB6381	$ 1,000.—	1Yr	3	10		$ 10.00	Continuous Bid & Perf. Bond Obligee: County of Los Angeles, Cal.
Aetna Cas.	72SB6669	$ 500.—	1Yr	5	19		$ 10.00	Franchise Tax Bond Obligee: State of Texas
Aetna Cas.	72SB25823	$ 5,000.—	1Yr	7	16		$ 50.00	Annual Bid & Perf. Bond Obligee: State of Kansas
Aetna Cas.	72SB25834	$ 5% Bid	1Yr	8	10		$ 5.00	Bid Bond Service Undertaking Obligee: City of Kansas City, Mo.
USF & G	2001-71	$5,595.06	1Yr	8	24		$ 112.00	Appeal Bond Obligee: XYZ (Kansas City, Mo.)
USF & G	1417-71	$5,000.—	3Yrs	6	7		$ 187.00	Concessionaire Bond Obligee: University of Minnesota
USF & G	2704-70	$500.—	5 Yrs	8	18		$ 40.00	Concessionaire Bond Obligee: NY State Dept of Soc Svcs
USF & G	1063-71	$100.—	5Yrs	4	29		$ 60.00	Concessionaire Bond Obligee: NY State Dept of Soc Svcs

Exhibit 4-a (page 3)

290

INSURANCE RECORD AS OF November 30, 19____

INSURED _____

LOCATION _____

COMPANY	NO. OF POLICY	AMOUNT	TERM	EXPIRES			PREMIUM	COVERAGE
				MO.	DAY	YEAR		
Federal Ins Co	FMPO6900703	various	Cont. Anniversary	5	1		$45,268.00	COMMERCIAL PROPERTY POLICY
								"All-Risk" Coverage per policy terms/conditions.
		Named Locations						$22,091.00 = Pers. Property Deposit
								23,177.00 = All other premium portion
	Limits of Liability							$45,268.00
	$ 3,500,000.—Columbus Avenue,							Annual premium adjustment/repts of value.
	500,000.—Clairemont Avenue,							
	2,000,000.—1212 44th Ave.,							Policy Deductible:
	1,000,000.—43 Park Lane,							$1,000. deductible applies to all losses/damages.
	2,000,000.—13811 Artesia Blvd..							$10,000. deductible applies to all Transit Losses.
	1,500,000.—9710 W. Foster Ave.,							
	500,000.—19433 E. Walnut Dr.,							Comprehensive General Liability $250 deductible
	450,000.—1465 NW 21st Terr..							$1,000,000.—Personal Injury Liability
	750,000.—11742 W. 86th Terr.,							250,000.—Property Damage Liability
	300,000.—14650 Southlawn Lane,							1,000,000.—Aggregate Pers. Inj.—Products Liab.
	500,000.—131 Beverly St.,							250,000.—Aggregate Prop. Dam.—Products Liab.
	1,000,000.—136-140 Horton Ave..							500,000.—Bod. Inj.—Contractual Liab.
	250,000.—at any other location (un-named) within the territorial limits of policy.							250,000.—Prop. Dam.—Contractual Liab.
	60,000.—while in Transit.							500/1,000.—Bod. Inj. NonOwned Auto Liab.
								1,000,000.—Prop. Dam. NonOwned Auto Liab.
	Building Coverage							Products Liability includes Broad Form Vendors
	$ 1,380,000.—							
	115,000.—							Additional Expense Coverage
	100,000.—							$100,000.—limit @ NY Location
	32,500.—							25,000.—limit @ all other locations.
	75,000.—							
								Additional Insured's coverage
	Fire Damage Legal Liability Coverage							Per location schedule as required by lease agreen
	$50,000.—limit; Blanket-All locations							

Exhibit 4-a (page 4)

291

INSURANCE RECORD AS OF ____November 30, 19___

INSURED _____

LOCATION _____

Property Covered Under Policy:

1) Personal property of every kind and description (except as excluded) usual to the conduct of the assured's business, the property of the assured, or the property of others while in the actual or constructive custody of the assured and for which the assured is legally liable.

2) Improvements and Betterments to buildings occupied by, but not owned by the assured.

Property Not Covered on Policy

1) Animals, currency, money, notes, securities, stamps, deeds, letters of credit, tickets . . .

2) Furs, jewels, precious metals

3) Aircraft, watercraft, vehicles licensed or designed for highway use.

4) Property sold under conditional sale, trust agreement, installments or other deferred payment plan.

5) Import/Export shipments.

Advertisers Liability Coverage
$100,000.–limit

Valuable Papers and Records Coverage
$250,000.–limit, NY location only

Earthquake & Flood Coverage
$ 25,000.–limit Deductible $1,000.–
Earthquake—California locations only
Flood—All locations

Exhibit 4-a (page 5)

292

INSURANCE RECORD as of November 30, 19

Insured_____

Location_____

PREMIUM ANALYSIS: COMMERCIAL PROPERTY POLICY
                 Federal Insurance Company Policy #FMP06900703
                 Policy Period: May 1, 19 to May 1, 19

Personal Property - Deposit portion of Premium....................$ 22,091.00
                 Named Locations $16,813.
                 Unamed Locations   5,278.
                                  $22,091.

All Other Premium portion - not subject to adjustment.............$ 23,177.00
Buildings: Valhalla, NY............$ 1,617.
           Chicago, Ill............   521.
           Hartford, Conn.........   205.
           Indianapolis, Ind.......   117.
           City of Industry, Cal...   182.
                                   $ 2,642.

General Liability:
           Premises Liability......$ 3,553.
           Products Liability...... 8,457.
           Fire Legal Liability....   500.
           Auto NonOwnership Liab..   506.
                                   $ 13,016.

Additional Expense Coverage......$ 350.

Valuable Papers & Records........$ 669.

Earthquake & Flood...............$ 1,000.

Transit Coverage.................$ 5,500.

                          Total Annual Premium including
                          Deposit premium portion = $ 45,268.00

Nov. 30, 19

Exhibit 4-a (page 6)

INSURANCE RECORD AS of NOVEMBER 30, 19

Insured _____

Location _____

COMMERCIAL PROPERTY POLICY #FMPO 6900703   PREMIUM SUMMARY

	May 1, 19	May 1, 19	May 1, 19	May 1, 19	May 1, 19
POLICY PERIOD					
ACCOUNT RATE	.76	.65	.56	.336	.357
AVERAGE PERS. PROP. VALUES	$3,839,734.	$7,258,969.	$7,971,680.	$6,188,270.	5 mos. $7,705,177.
DEPOSIT PREMIUM	$ 15,307.	$ 24,958.	$ 40,650.	$ 26,792.	$ 22,091.
ALL OTHER PREMIUM	9,210.	18,071.	21,128.	20,300.	23,177.
ADJUSTMENT PREMIUM	13,875.	15,692.	3,991.	(6,000.)	to be det.
TOTAL	$ 38,392.	$ 58,721.	$ 65,769.	$ 41,092.	$ to be det.

Nov. 30, 19

Exhibit 4-a (page 7)

STANDARD OPERATING PROCEDURE	
Subject: FREIGHT CLAIMS	**Number** B-6a
	Page of 1 1
	Effective **Date 2/9/**
Supersedes S.O.P. No. Page Dated	**Related** **S.O.P.**

Purpose: To have branches initiate paper work for processing of freight claims through the home office.

Method: Freight claims for short deliveries, damaged merchandise, merchandise lost in transit or freight claims of any other nature are to be handled through the home office in the following manner:

Branch Office Secretary-

1. Obtain proof of shortage or damage in the form of bill of lading indicating the problem.

2. Write a covering letter to home office Purchasing Department requesting that claim be placed and enclosing proof in 1 above.

Home Office Purchasing Department-

1. Place claim

2. Advise branch office of disposition of damaged merchandise.

3. Will replace merchandise if lost in branch transfer.

For parcel post claims see procedure titled "Parcel Post Insurance" page B-21.

Inquiries: For inquiries contact the home office Purchasing Department.

DISTRIBUTION: Branch office secretaries/Home Office Purchasing Department

DLG:2/9/

Exhibit 4-b

CLAIMS' PROCEDURES

A. NON DELIVERY, SHORTAGE (CARRIER)

    1. Form letter to carrier requesting proof of delivery.

        a. Second request if no answer in fifteen days.

    2. Letter to consignee requesting copy of freight bill
       or affidavit.

    3. Claim filed after thirty days if no answer or notification
       of loss from carrier.

        a. Form letter to carrier of intention to file
           claim with:

            1. Certified Copy of Original Invoice
            2. Original Bill of Lading
            3. Original Freight Bill
            4. Consignee's Copy of Freight Bill
            5. Other Supporting Documentation

              Plus standard form attached!

        b. Form letter to Insurance Broker with attachment

           Copies of the above: a) 1, 2, 3, 4, 5 plus copy of
           letter to carrier.

B. DAMAGE (CARRIER)

    1. Form letter to carrier noting shipment was received damaged,
       of intention to file claim, and request for an inspection
       report (notify consignee, unless otherwise directed, to hold
       shipment pending inspection).

    2. Second request if no answer in fifteen days.

    3. Upon receipt of inspection report, or after thirty days,
       attach copy to form letter to our Insurance Broker with copies
       of all items listed under A3a above. (If inspection report is
       not returned, attach form letter noting unanswered second request.)

0-95

Exhibit 4-c (page 1)

C. <u>NON DELIVERY, SHORTAGE, DAMAGE (MAIL, PARCEL POST)</u>

   1. Proof of loss form, cover form letter to consignee.
      (Second request, two weeks.)

   2. Post Office Form No. 1510 to Post Office with form letter.
      (Second request, two weeks; third request, one month.)

   3. Upon receipt of above, attach with Certified Copy of Original
      Invoice to form letter to Insurance Broker. (If forms are not
      returned from Post Office, allow final two weeks and send form
      letter noting unanswered third request.) Form No. 1510
      applicable only on insured mail.

NOTES:

    <u>Emergency Tracing Procedure</u>:

    Phone Tracing Department, or Customer Service Department at
    terminal of pick-up carrier. Supply shipper's name and location,
    consignee's name and location, date of shipment, number of cartons,
    commodity, weight, and freight bill number.

    Certification to read:

    "I hereby certify that this is a true copy of the_____
    dated_____."

                              Signed_____
                                    Customer Service Manager

    Damage claims are to be reported within 72 hours. Loss and damage
    claims must be filed within nine months.

    Our Insurance Broker should pay all claims in from four to six
    weeks and advise consignee as to disposition of damaged merchandise.

Exhibit 4-c (page 2)

HOP/SOP MEMO

TO BE FILED WITHIN CORRESPONDING PROCEDURE

Memo To: List 8.0, Branch Administrators
From: Daniel L. Gotthilf, Controller

Subject: Insurance Claims—
          Liability on Property Damage
Eff. Date: March 2, 19___

HOP [ ] No.: _____

Title: INSURANCE CLAIMS – LIABILITY ON
                    PROPERTY DAMAGE

SOP [ ] No.: B-7a

HOP [ ] Last Correction No.: _____   HOP [ ] New Correction No.: _____

SOP [ ] Last Correction No.: _____   SOP [ ] New Correction No.: ____365_____

Paragraph #   Page #   Affected

Insurance claims from customers, or others, for damage to property or persons, are handled by the Controller's office. To substantiate a claim, we need:

1. A letter from customer, or other claimant, giving a complete explanation of how the accident occurred, and date, time, place, witnesses.

2. A memo from our salesman or serviceman who witnessed the accident, explaining how and why it occurred, also giving date, time and place.

3. If our salesman or serviceman was not present at time of accident, a serviceman must make a service call to verify the damage and the machine problem, if any, and should prepare the memo in 2, above.

4. A copy of the Service Call Report, if any, from 2 or 3, above.

Branch Administrator should:

a. Investigate salesman's or serviceman's claim;

b. Forward items 1, 2 or 3, and 4 to Controller's office;

c. Advise customer that claim takes about three weeks to process for payment (if under $100);

d. Advise customer we are not responsible for claims arising from their own error, carelessness, or negligence. In short, we are responsible only for damage caused by a defect in our machine (such as a leaky tank).

e. Send a cover memo with documents in b, recommending for or against payment of the claim, based on all the facts and an interrogation of salesman or serviceman, in a above.

INQUIRIES: Controller
DISTRIBUTION: List 12.0, SOP Manual Holders

Exhibit 4-d

Projected Statement of Changes in Financial Position
Fiscal Year 19   & 19
(000)

	6 Mos. Ended	
	4-30-	4-30-
Funds provided by:		
Income	$3,411	$2,792
Add (deduct) expenses and revenues not involving working capital:		
Depreciation and Amortization:		
Building and equipment	685	1,812
Other	24	48
Working capital provided from operations	4,120	4,652
Investment in	90	120
Sale of Common Stock	390	-
Other Net	500	-
	5,100	4,772
Funds Used for:		
Purchase of Property, Plant & Equipment, Net; Principally rental machines	1,467	3,852
Long Term Borrowing	60	120
	1,527	3,972
Net Increase (Decrease) in working capital	$3,573	$800
Changes in Elements of Working Capital increase (decrease):		
Cash	$2,568	$ -
Accounts and Notes Receivable	474	30
Inventories	(1,055)	(450)
Notes and Loans Payable	788	(641)
Accounts Payable and Accrued Expenses	11	109
Other, Net (Prepaid Exp.)	787	1,752
Net Increase (decrease) in working capital	$3,573	$ 800

Exhibit 5-a

Projected Cash Requirements Statement
Fiscal Year 19__
(000)

	May	June	July	August	Sept.
Sources of Funds:					
Receipts from Operations:					
Sales & Rentals - Retail & Dealer - *(1)	$4,347	$4,420	$4,420	$4,474	$4,528
Sales - Canada & Foreign - *(2)	382	382	382	382	382
Royalty Income - *(3)	235	279	348	265	365
Lease Financing Income - *(2)	5	5	5	5	5
Misc. Income - *(2)	5	5	5	5	5
TOTAL REVENUE RECEIPTS	$4,974	$5,091	$5,160	$5,131	$5,285
Cost of Sales	$2,670	$2,679	$2,689	$2,698	$2,707
Operating & Reclassed Expenses	2,154	2,169	2,184	2,199	2,214
Interest Expenses	224	224	224	224	224
R & D Expenses	33	33	33	33	33
	$5,081	$5,105	$5,130	$5,154	$5,178
Non-Cash Items					
Prepaid Comm. - Amort Effect	$ (146)	$ (146)	$ (146)	$ (146)	$ (146)
Depreciation (excepting rental mach.) and Amort.	28	28	28	28	28
Depreciation - Rent. Mach. A	26	26	27	27	27
Depreciation - Rent. Mach. B	35	39	43	47	51
Depreciation - Rent. Mach. C	40	40	41	41	41
Other Amortization - *(4)	58	58	58	58	58
TOTAL NON-CASH ITEMS	$ 41	$ 45	$ 51	$ 55	$ 59
Cash from Operations	$ (66)	$ 31	$ 81	$ 32	$ 166
Equity in Sub.	10	10	10	10	10
TOTAL SOURCES OF FUNDS	$ (56)	$ 41	$ 91	$ 42	$ 176
Uses of Funds					
Inventory	$ (100)	$ (100)	$ (100)	$ (100)	$ (50)
Fixed Assets - A	25	25	25	25	25
Fixed Assets - B	259	259	259	259	259
Fixed Assets - B(a)	7	7	7	7	7
Fixed Assets - C	24	24	24	24	24
Capital Expenditures	6	6	6	6	6
Other Notes Payable	10	10	10	10	10
Other Taxes Payable	10	10	10	10	10
TOTAL USES OF FUNDS	$ 241	$ 241	$ 241	$ 241	$ 291
Cash Required (Excess)	$ 297	$ 200	$ 150	$ 199	$ 115
Cum. Cash Required	$ 297	$ 497	$ 647	$ 846	$ 961
Cash Requirements fulfilled by:					
Increase in Bank Borrowing to 17MM and Cash on Hand at start	$5,318	$5,318	$5,318	$5,318	$5,318
Cash Towards Bank Balances	5,021	4,821	4,671	4,472	4,357
Cash Balances Required	$3,400	3,400	3,400	3,400	3,400
Dec. Bank Debt or Reduction in Balances	$1,621	$1,421	$1,271	$1,072	$ 957

Exhibit 5-b

Projected Ratios
Fiscal 19__ & 19__

Profitability	19__	19__
Sales Growth	.228	.081
Gross Profit Margin	.436	.466
Operat Exp/Sales	.449	.425
Pre-Tax Margin	.099	.059
Aft. Tax Margin	.397	.148
Return on Avg. Net Worth	.346	.194
Return on Total Assets	.105	.054
Earnings Before Interest & Taxes/Total Assets	.175	.122

Turnovers (To Sales)		
Receivables	2.964	3.378
Inventory	4.691	5.270
Accounts Payable	9.502	10.468
Working Capital	3.734	3.835
Fixed Asset	6.079	4.676
Net Worth	3.229	3.012

Liquidity		
Quick Ratio	1.018	.996
Current Ratio	1.686	1.706

Exhibit 5-c

PROJECTED COLLECTIONS OF ACCOUNTS RECEIVABLE

(000's Omitted)

	Sales	Allowance for Un-Collectible Accounts	Estimated Collectible Balance	January	February	March	1st Quarter	2nd Quarter	3rd Quarter	4th Quarter	Balance Dec. 31 of Next Year
ACCOUNTS RECEIVABLE AND ALLOWANCE FOR UN-COLLECTIBLE ACCOUNTS AT DECEMBER 31 OF THE CURRENT YEAR:											
Prior to 4th Quarter	$ 596	$ 62	$ 534	$ 125	$ 124	$ 165	$ 414	$ 40	$ 40	$ 40	
4th Quarter	3,259	15	3,244	1,996	998	250	3,244	-	-	-	
Total	$3,855	$ 77	$ 3,778	$ 2,121	$ 1,122	$ 415	$ 3,658	$ 40	$ 40	$ 40	
PROJECTED SALES:											
January	$1,155	$ 2	$ 1,153	$ 231	$ 461	$ 346	$ 1,038	$ 115	$ -	$ -	
February	1,330	3	1,327	-	265	531	796	531	-	-	
March	1,915	4	1,911	-	-	382	382	1,529	-	-	
1st quarter	$ 4,400	$ 9	$ 4,391	$ 231	$ 726	$1,259	$ 2,216	$2,175	$ -	$ -	
2nd quarter	6,555	13	6,542	-	-	-	-	3,707	2,835	-	
3rd quarter	7,460	15	7,445	-	-	-	-	-	4,219	3,226	
4th quarter	8,185	16	8,169	-	-	-	-	-	-	4,629	$ 3,540
Total	$26,600	$ 53	$26,547	$ 231	$ 726	$1,259	$ 2,216	$5,882	$7,054	$7,855	$ 3,540
GRAND TOTAL	$30,455	$ 130	$30,325	$ 2,352	$ 1,848	$1,674	$ 5,874	$5,922	$7,094	$7,895	$ 3,540

Exhibit 5-d

PROJECTED PAYMENTS FOR MATERIAL PURCHASES

(000's Omitted)

	Purchases	Discount on Purchases	Estimated Balance	Payments Jan.	Feb.	March	1st Quarter	2nd Quarter	3rd Quarter	4th Quarter	Balance Dec. 31 of Next Year
PAYABLES BALANCE JANUARY 1 OF NEXT YEAR	$ 320	$ 3	$ 317	$ 274	$ 43	$ -	$ 317	$ -	$ -	$ -	
ESTIMATED PURCHASES:											
January	$ 461	$ 5	$ 456	$ 218	$ 201	$ 37	$ 456	$ -	$ -	$ -	
February	544	6	538	-	257	237	495	44	-	-	
March	412	4	408	-	-	195	195	213	-	-	
1st quarter	$ 1,417	$ 15	$ 1,402	$ 218	$ 458	$ 469	$ 1,145	$ 257	$ -	$ -	
2nd quarter	1,469	15	1,454	-	-	-	-	1,162	292	-	
3rd quarter	1,927	20	1,907	-	-	-	-	-	1,524	383	
4th quarter	1,790	19	1,771	-	-	-	-	-	-	1,419	
Total	$ 6,603	$ 69	$ 6,534	$ 218	$ 458	$ 469	$ 1,145	$1,419	$ 1,816	$ 1,802	
GRAND TOTAL	$ 6,923	$ 72	$ 6,851	$ 492	$ 501	$ 469	$ 1,462	$1,419	$ 1,816	$ 1,802	$ 352

Unearned discount $ 2
$ 354

Exhibit 5-e

303

ESTIMATED PAYMENTS FOR OPERATING EXPENSES

(000's Omitted)

Department	Annual Budget	Jan.	Feb.	March	1st Quarter	2nd Quarter	3rd Quarter	4th Quarter
MOLDING								
Total expenses	$ 3,118	$ 216	$ 216	$ 262	$ 694	$ 606	$ 909	$ 909
Less-Non-cash charges								
Supplies	$ 719	$ 51	$ 51	$ 60	$ 162	$ 143	$ 207	$ 207
Depreciation	220	18	18	19	55	55	55	55
Insurance	60	4	4	5	13	11	18	18
Taxes	32	2	2	2	6	6	10	10
Vacation pay	57	4	4	4	12	11	17	17
Total	$ 1,088	$ 79	$ 79	$ 90	$ 248	$ 226	$ 307	$ 307
Cash outflow	$ 2,030	$ 137	$ 137	$ 172	$ 446	$ 380	$ 602	$ 602
FABRICATION								
Total expenses	$ 1,168	$ 89	$ 89	$ 104	$ 282	$ 244	$ 333	$ 309
Less-Non-cash charges								
Supplies	$ 136	$ 11	$ 11	$ 12	$ 34	$ 30	$ 37	$ 35
Depreciation	175	15	14	15	44	44	43	44
Insurance	6	1	-	-	1	2	2	1
Taxes	3	-	-	-	1	-	1	1
Vacation pay	38	3	3	3	9	7	11	11
Total	$ 358	$ 30	$ 29	$ 30	$ 89	$ 83	$ 94	$ 92
Cash outflow	$ 810	$ 59	$ 60	$ 74	$ 193	$ 161	$ 239	$ 217
ASSEMBLY								
Total expenses	$ 1,077	$ 74	$ 74	$ 92	$ 240	$ 204	$ 323	$ 310
Less-Non-cash charges								
Supplies	$ 44	$ 3	$ 3	$ 4	$ 10	$ 9	$ 13	$ 12
Depreciation	15	1	1	1	3	4	4	4
Insurance	12	1	1	1	3	2	4	3
Taxes	6	-	1	-	1	1	2	2
Vacation Pay	115	8	8	9	25	22	35	33
Total	$ 192	$ 13	$ 14	$ 15	$ 42	$ 38	$ 58	$ 54
Cash outflow	$ 885	$ 61	$ 60	$ 77	$ 198	$ 166	$ 265	$ 256
REPAIRS AND MAINTENANCE								
Total expenses	$ 600	$ 42	$ 42	$ 51	$ 135	$ 118	$ 175	$ 172
Less-Non-cash charges								
Supplies	$ 95	$ 6	$ 7	$ 8	$ 21	$ 18	$ 28	$ 28
Depreciation	12	1	1	1	3	3	3	3
Insurance	2	-	1	-	1	-	1	-
Taxes	2	-	-	-	-	1	-	1
Vacation pay	13	1	1	1	3	3	4	3
Total	$ 124	$ 8	$ 10	$ 10	$ 28	$ 25	$ 36	$ 35
Cash outflow	$ 476	$ 34	$ 32	$ 41	$ 107	$ 93	$ 139	$ 137

Exhibit 5-f (page 1)

ESTIMATED PAYMENTS FOR OPERATING EXPENSES

Department	Annual Budget	Jan.	Feb.	March	1st Quarter	2nd Quarter	3rd Quarter	4th Quarter
PURCHASING								
Total expenses	$ 91	$ 7	$ 7	$ 8	$ 22	$ 21	$ 24	$ 24
Less Non-cash charges-								
Supplies	$ 5	$ -	$ -	$ 1	$ 1	$ 1	$ 1	$ 2
Depreciation	2	-	-	-	-	1	-	1
Insurance	1	-	-	-	-	-	1	-
Vacation pay	2	-	-	-	-	1	-	1
Total	$ 10	$ -	$ -	$ 1	$ 1	$ 3	$ 2	$ 4
Cash outflow	$ 81	$ 7	$ 7	$ 7	$ 21	$ 18	$ 22	$ 20
GENERAL FACTORY								
Total expenses	$2,643	$ 201	$ 201	224	$ 626	$ 575	$ 729	$ 713
Less Non-cash charges-								
Supplies	$ 144	$ 10	$ 10	$ 12	$ 32	$ 27	$ 43	$ 42
Depreciation	248	21	20	21	62	62	62	62
Insurance	28	2	3	2	7	7	7	7
Taxes	55	5	4	5	14	14	14	13
Vacation pay	45	4	3	4	11	11	12	11
Total	$ 520	$ 42	$ 40	$ 44	$ 126	$ 121	$ 138	$ 135
Cash outflow	$2,123	$ 159	$ 161	$ 180	$ 500	$ 454	$ 591	$ 578
SELLING & SHIPPING								
Total expenses	$4,267	$ 444	$ 381	$ 368	$1,193	$ 868	$ 1,247	$ 959
Less Non-cash charges-								
Supplies	$ 2	$ -	$ -	$ -	$ -	$ -	$ 1	$ 1
Depreciation	9	1	-	1	2	2	3	2
Insurance	9	1	1	-	2	2	3	2
Taxes	30	2	2	3	7	8	7	8
Vacation pay	31	2	3	2	7	8	8	8
Professional fees	53	2	3	4	9	13	15	16
Bad debts	34	3	3	3	9	8	9	8
Total	$ 168	$ 11	$ 12	$ 13	$ 36	$ 41	$ 46	$ 45
Cash outflow	$4,099	$ 433	$ 369	$ 355	$1,157	$ 827	$ 1,201	$ 914
GENERAL AND ADMINISTRATIVE								
Total expenses	$1,392	$ 228	$ 108	$ 107	$ 443	$ 326	$ 312	$ 311
Less Non-cash charges-								
Depreciation	$ 25	$ 2	$ 3	$ 2	$ 7	$ 6	$ 6	$ 6
Insurance	25	2	2	2	6	6	7	6
Taxes	11	1	1	1	3	3	2	3
Vacation pay	26	2	2	2	6	7	7	6
Professional fees	123	10	10	10	30	31	31	31
Total	$ 210	$ 17	$ 18	$ 17	$ 52	$ 53	$ 53	$ 52
Cash outflow	$1,182	$ 211	$ 90	$ 90	$ 391	$ 273	$ 259	$ 259

Exhibit 5-f (page 2)

ESTIMATED PAYMENTS FOR OPERATING EXPENSES

Department	Annual Budget	January	February	March	1st Quarter	2nd Quarter	3rd Quarter	4th Quarter
OTHER EXPENSES								
Total expenses	$__107	$____9	$____9	$__9	$___27	$___27_	$___27	$___26
Less Non-cash charges-interest	$__107	$____9	$____9	$__9	$___27	$___27_	$___27	$___26
Cash outflow	$___-_	$___-_	$____-_	$__-_	$____-_	$____-_	$____-_	$____-_
SUMMARY -- ALL DEPARTMENTS:								
Total expenses	$14,463	$1,310	$__1,127	$1,225	$_3,662	$_2,989	$_4,079	$_3,733_
Less Non-cash charges-								
Supplies	$1,145	$ 81	$ 82	$ 97	$ 260	$ 228	$ 330	$ 327
Depreciation	706	59	57	60	176	177	176	177
Insurance	143	11	12	10	33	30	43	37
Taxes	139	10	11	11	32	33	36	38
Vacation pay	327	24	24	25	73	70	94	90
Professional fees	157	13	13	13	39	39	40	39
Bad debts	53	2	3	4	9	13	15	16
Interest expense	__107	_____9	_____9	____9	_____27	_____27	_____27	_____26
Total	$2,777	$__209	$____211	$__229	$____649	$____617	$____761	$____750
Cash outflow	$11,686	$1,101	$____916	$__996	$_3,013	$_2,372	$_3,318	$_2,983_
DIRECT LABOR -- All departments	$4,769	$__327	$____327	$__410	$_1,064	$___892	$_1,434	$_1,379_
TOTAL CASH OUTFLOW FOR OPERATING EXPENSES	$16,455	$1,428	$__1,243	$1,406	$_4,077	$_3,264	$_4,752	$_4,362_

Exhibit 5-f (page 3)

MISCELLANEOUS CASH REQUIREMENTS

(000's Omitted)

	Next Year's Payments (1)	Janaury	February	March	1st Quarter	2st Quarter	3rd Quarter	4th Quarter	Balance Debit (Credit) Dec. 31 of the Current Year	Total (1)+(2)	Next Year's Expirations and Accruals	Balance Dec. 31 of Next Year
Professional and other service fees payable	$ 200	$ 100	$ -	$ -	$ 100	$ 100	$ -	$ -	$ (200)	$ -	$ (157)	$ (157)
Notes Payable	500	500	-	-	500	-	-	-	(1,500)	(1,000)	-	(1,000)
Payroll Payable	300	300	-	-	300	-	-	-	(300)	-	-	-
Taxes — other than Federal income tax	141	-	-	-	-	-	-	141	(141)	-	(139)	(139)
Vacation pay reserve	300	-	-	-	-	300	-	-	(150)	150	(327)	(177)
Miscellaneous expenses accrued	250	250	-	-	250	-	-	-	(250)	-	-	-
Other assets:												
Prepaid interest	-	-	-	-	-	-	-	-	100	100	(50)	50
Prepaid insurance	146	146	-	-	146	-	-	-	47	193	(143)	50
Supplies inventory	1,245	311	-	-	311	311	311	312	100	1,345	(1,145)	200
Federal income tax	1,264	-	-	419	419	419	213	213	(838)	426	(951)	(525)
Loans—banks	350	-	-	-	-	-	-	350	(350)	-	-	-
ACCRUED interest payable	57	-	-	-	-	28	-	29	-	57	(57)	-
Total	$4,753	$1,607	$ -	$419	$2,026	$1,158	$524	$1,045	($3,482)	$1,271	($2,969)	($1,698)

Exhibit 5-g

307

AUTHORIZATION FOR CAPITAL EXPENDITURE
(SEE SOP A8)

AUTHORIZATION NO.	DATE	FIELD SALES OFF. OR DEPT.	FOR HOME OFFICE USE ONLY TOTAL BUDGET FIELD SALES OFFICE		
CAPITAL EXPENDITURE BUDGET DATA		FIXED ASSETS	LEASEHOLD IMPROVEMTS.	FIXED ASSETS	LEASEHOLD IMPROVEMTS.
1. Total amount approved in the capital program for calendar year.					
2. Total authorizations previously approved - year to date.					
3. Total amount requested in this authorization.					
4. Balance remaining in approved capital expenditure budget.					

5. Reason(s) for Request

( ) Replacement ( ) New or Changed Product ( ) Hazard Elimination

( ) Reduction in Cost ( ) Increased Facilities ( ) Other - Explain Below

6. Does this Authorization involve a budget deviation? ( ) Yes, ( ) No If deviation, show total amount of excess: $ Explain necessity for budget deviation:	7. Description of Item:
	Life in Years: Cash Inflows (if any) Yr. 1 $_____ 2 _____ 3 _____ 4 _____ 5 _____

8. Vendor's Quotation						H.O. INSTRUCTIONS
Item No.	$	Local Vendor	Item No.	$	H.O. Vendor	
						Requisition No. Purchase Order No.:

SIGNATURES	TITLE	DATE
ORIGINATOR		
RECOMMENDED	PURCHASING MANAGER	
RECOMMENDED	OTHER	
RECOMMENDED	PURCHASING MANAGER	
ENDORSED OR APPROVED	CONTROLLER	
ENDORSED OR APPROVED	OTHER	
ENDORSED OR APPROVED	OTHER	

Exhibit 5-h

CASH BUDGET

	January	February	March	1st Quarter	2nd Quarter	3rd Quarter	4th Quarter
CASH BALANCE -- Beginning	$1,664	$ 7	$ 59	$1,664	$ 97	$ 82	$ 158
RECEIPTS:							
Collections -- trade account	2,352	1,848	1,674	5,874	5,922	7,094	7,895
Other income	8	8	8	24	24	24	24
Redemption of treasury bills	-	-	750	750	100	150	-
Loans from officers and stockholders	60	-	-	60	-	-	-
Total cash available	$4,084	$ 1,863	$2,491	$8,372	$ 6,143	$ 7,350	$ 8,077
PAYMENTS:							
Material purchase	$ 492	$ 501	$ 469	$1,462	$ 1,419	$ 1,816	$ 1,802
Operating expense	1,428	1,243	$1,406	$4,077	$ 3,264	$ 4,752	$ 4,362
Property additions	550	-	-	550	120	-	500
Dividends	-	-	100	100	100	100	100
Loans from officers and stockholders	-	60	-	60	-	-	200
Miscellaneous cash requirements	1,607	-	419	2,026	1,158	524	1,045
Total cash payments	$4,077	$ 1,804	$2,394	$8,275	$ 6,061	$ 7,192	$ 8,009
CASH BALANCE -- Ending	$ 7	$ 59	$ 97	$ 97	$ 82	$ 158	$ 68

Exhibit 5-i

BUDGET CALENDAR

1. Budget forms issued to Field Offices and Home Office
    Depts. Goals are communicated.   6/30/

2. a) Branch budgets to District/Zone Offices for
        review and approval   7/21/
    b) Home Office budgets to superior for approval   7/21/

3. Zone Offices and Home Office Depts. send approved
    budgets to Accounting Dept.   7/28/

4. Accounting Dept. reviews and sends budgets to
    Data Processing for key punching   8/4/

Following dates are dependent on completion of step 4:

5. Data Processing completes key punching and sends
    print-out to Accounting Dept.   6 days

6. Budget Section edits print-out and returns to D/P
    for correction.   4 days

7. Data Processing corrects and prints out individual
    and consolidated budgets.   2 days

8. All budgets to Budget Committee for review, approval
    or adjustment.   5 days

9. Data Processing adjusts budgets, if necessary, and
    sends approved budgets (6 copies) to Accounting Dept.   2 days

10. Budget Section issues approved budgets.   1 day

Exhibit 6-a

ORGANIZATION AND OPERATIONS

Man depends on communication. His progress hinges on his ability to communicate with other men rapidly and conveniently. As technological progress makes the world smaller, man's need for information grows greater. Whether he desires to copy directly, or translate the language of computers and other electronic devices for other men, he has a vital need for devices that make images. This is our field . . . and our future.

To carry out the far-reaching objectives Savin has set for itself requires:

1. A well-staffed organization, capable of functioning smoothly as our markets and products continue to expand.

2. Products that meet current and anticipate new market demands. This section describes our organization, how we operate, our products and their uses.

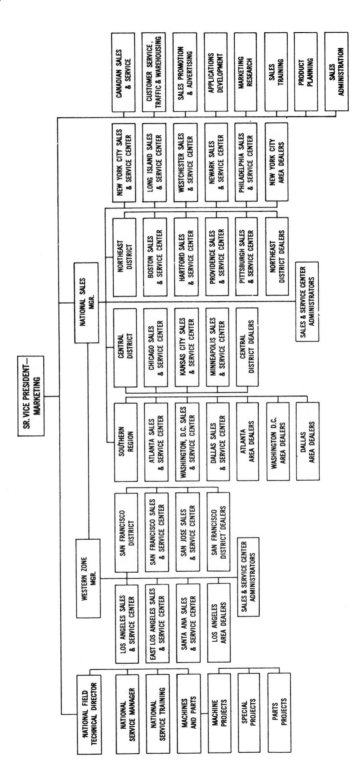

Exhibit 6-b

Chart of Accounts
FYE 4/30/

First Digit (High Order) – Position in Financial Statements

    1. Assets
    2. Liabilities
    3. Capital Stock and Surplus
    4. Sales and Operating Revenues
    5. Sales Returns and Allowances and Discounts
    6. Cost of Sales
    7. Operating Expenses
    8. Non-Operating and Royalty Income
    9. Non-Operating, Royalty, and R&D Expense

Second Digit – (Sub-Position in Financial Statements)

1	1. Current Assets
	2. Fixed Assets
	3. Deferred Assets
	4. Other Assets
2	1. Current Liabilities
	2. Long Term Liability
	3. Other Liabilities
3	1. Capital Stock Issued
	2. Capital Surplus
	3. Retained Earnings
4,5,6	1. Electrostatic
	2. Xerograpic Products
	3. C Paper
	4. Diffusion Products
	5. Other Operating Revenues or Expenses
	6. Discounts
7	1. Selling Expenses
	2. Service Expenses
	3. Traffic and Warehouse Expenses
	4. General and Administrative Expenses
8,9	1. Royalties
	2. Interest
	3. Research and Development
	4. Miscellaneous

Third and Fourth Digits – (Major Descriptions)
Fifth and Sixth D igits – (Minor Descriptions or Branches)
Seventh Digit (Low Order) – (Reserve for Future Use)

Exhibit 6-c

ACCOUNTS PAYABLE VOUCHER

TRANS A – B	VENDOR NAME	VENDOR NUMBER	A/P		– S –
			FREIGHT		– F –
			WEEKLY A/P		– W –
			(PLEASE CHECK ONLY ONE BOX)		

DUE DATE	CODING APPROVAL (If $500 & Code 3)	PURCHASE MONTH/YEAR	IBM Keypunch
			By Date

INVOICE DATE	LOC CODE	INVOICE NO.	QUAN.	PROD. CODE	INVOICE AMOUNT (BRACKETS=CREDIT AMT.)	CASH DISC.	GEN. LEDGER ACCT. NO.

TRANS CODES

A	B
1. Inventory Item	5. Vendor Invoice
2.	6. Vendor Credit Memo
3. Expense or Misc. Item	7. Charge Back to Vendor
4.	8. Credit Back to Vendor

GROSS INVOICE AMT.	
DISCOUNT AMT.	
NET AMT.	

Approved By

                        Accounting

Instruction: A1. Inventory Control initiates form, reocrds Vendor Name, our log no.
if applicable, inventory code, quantity, converted units.

Exhibit 6-d

Corporation

PPD BY _____

APPVD BY _____

Signature   Date

Card Code [Z] (3)

Profit & Loss Budget for Period Ended — Field Office

($000 Omitted — Hundreds in Decimals — Example 4.1 = $4,100)   (1-2)

Li. No. (4-5)	Description	M O N T H S (1) (6)	(2)	(3)	(4)	(5)	(6)	Total 6 Months Budget (7)	Estimate for Next 6 Mos. in Total (8)	Total 12 Months (9)
	Sales									
01	– Machines (Sch. I)									
02	– Paper (Sch. I)									
03	– Other (Sch. I)									
04	**Total Net Sales**									
05	**Less: Cost of Sales** (Sch. II)									
06	**Gross Profit on Sales**									
07	Add: Dealer Handling Charges									
08	Less: Parts & Machine Destruction									
09	**Total Operating Income**									
	Less Branch Budgeted Expenses:									
10	Cleaning & Maintenance									
11	Personnel Recruitment									
12	Postage									
13	Salaries									
14	Sundry									
15	Telephone & Telegraph									
16	Travel & Entertainment									
17	Training									
18	**Total Branch Budgeted Exp.** (Sch. III)									
	Allocated Budgeted Area Exp.:									
19	Administrative (Sch. III)									
20	Service (Sch. III)									
21	Warehouse (Sch. III)									
22	**Total Allocated Budgeted Area Expenses**									
23	**Total Budgeted Expenses**									
24	**Contribution to Non-Budgeted Expenses**									

Column reference numbers: (6) (10) (11) (15) (16) (20) (21) (25) (26) (30) (31) (35) (36) (41) (42) (47) (48) (53)

(0-8-101)

Exhibit 6-e (page 1)

Corporation

Sales Budget for Period Ended

($000 Omitted — Hundreds in Decimals — Example 4.1 = $4,100)

Field Office _____

Schedule I Page 1 of 2

☐ Retail   ☐ Dealer

Do Not Post Dealer Sales To Branch P&L.

PPD BY _____
APPVD BY _____
Signature   Date

Card Code ☐ (3)

L.I. No. (4-5)	Description	M (1) (6)	O (2) (11)	N (3) (16)	T (4) (21)	H (5) (26)	S (6) (31)	Total 6 Months Budget (7) (36)	Estimate for Next 6 Mos. in Total (8) (42)	Total 12 Months (9) (48)
	Machine Sales (Net of Returns & Allowances)									
01	203 Sales – Units									
02	203 Returns – Units									
03	Net 203 Sales – Units									
04	**203 – $ (Net of Allowances)**									
05	215 Sales – Units									
06	215 Returns – Units									
07	Net 215 Sales – Units									
08	**215 – $ (Net of Allowances)**									
09	220 Sales – Units									
10	220 Returns – Units									
11	Net 220 Sales – Unit									
12	**220 – $ (Net of Allowances)**									
13	230 Sales – Units									
14	230 Returns – Units									
15	Net 230 Sales – Units									
16	**230 – $ (Net of Allowances)**									
17	20-21 Sales – Units									
18	20-21 Returns – Units									
19	Net 20-21 Sales – Units									
20	**20-21 – $ (Net of Allowances)**									
21	Other Machine Sales (incl. 200) – Units									
22	Other Machine Returns – Units									
23	Net Other Machine Sales – Units									
24	**Other Mach. Sales – $ (Net of Allow)**									
25	**Total Net Sales – Units**									
26	**Total Machine Sales – $ (to Br. P&L line #1)**									
	MUP (Units Only)									
27	220 – Units Placed									
28	220 – Units Returns									
29	Net 220 – Units Placed									
30	230 Units – Placed									
31	230 – Units Returns									
32	Net 230 – Units Placed									
33	Other – Units Placed									
34	Other – Units Returns									
35	Net Other – Units Placed									
36	**Total Net MUP Units**							(53)		

(0-8-102)

Exhibit 6-e (page 2)

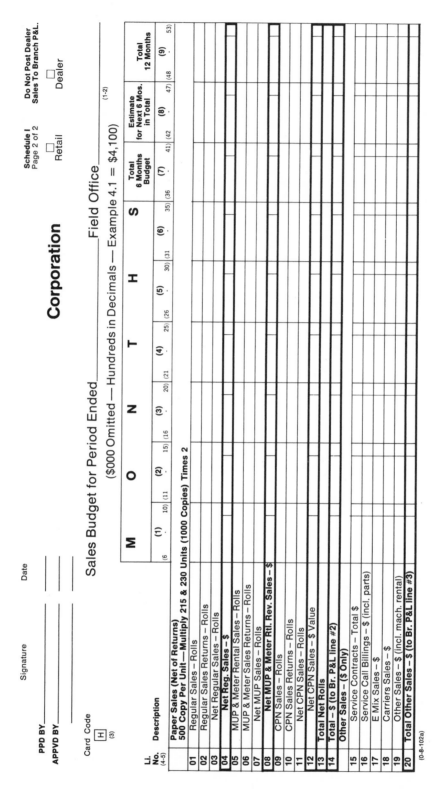

Exhibit 6-e (page 3)

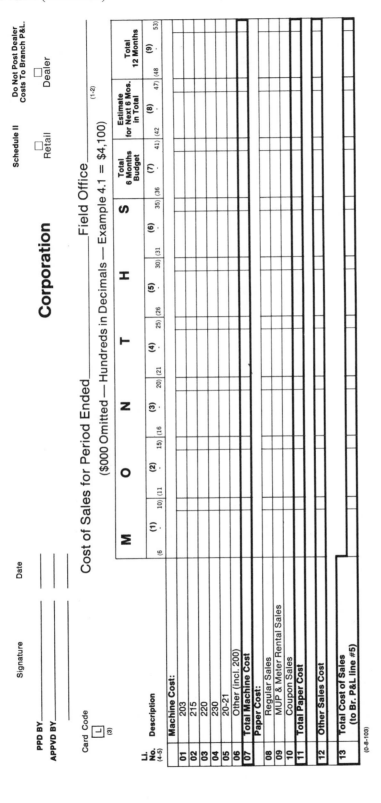

Exhibit 6-e (page 4)

Corporation

Schedule III

_____ Field Office

Expense Budget for Period Ended _____ (1-2)

($000 Omitted — Hundreds in Decimals — Example 4.1 = $4,100)

PPD BY _____   APPVD BY _____   Signature _____   Date _____

Card Code | P | (3)

Li. No. (4-5)	Description	M (1)	O (2)	N (3)	T (4)	H (5)	S (6)	Total 6 Months Budget (7)	Estimate for Next 6 Mos. in Total (8)	Total 12 Months (9)
		(6	(11	(16	(21	(26	(31	(36	(41	(47	(48	(53
01	Cleaning & Maintenance									
02	Personnel Recruitment									
03	Postage									
	Salaries:									
04	Managers									
05	Office Salaries									
06	Servicemen									
07	Warehouse									
08	Dealer Reps (Zone Only)									
09	Office Temps									
10	Total Salaries									
11	Sundry									
	Telephone & Telegraph:									
12	Telex & Cable									
13	Long Distance									
14	Base Charge									
15	Local Calls									
16	Other									
17	Total Tel. & Tel.									
	Travel & Entertainment:									
18	CR Reps									
19	Salesmen (incl. QMTM'S or MKTG. REPS) $100 Std. Trav. Allow									
20	Servicemen									
21	Managers									
22	Field Office – Administrative									
23	Dealer Reps (Zone Only)									
24	MTM's									
25	Other									
26	Total Travel & Entertainment									
27	Training									
28	Total Branch Budgeted Expenses (to Br. P&L line #18)									
	Allocated Budgeted Area Expenses:									
29	Administrative									
30	Service									
31	Warehouse									
32	Total Allocated Budgeted Area Expenses									
33	Total Budgeted Expenses									

(0-8-104)

Exhibit 6-e (page 5)

Schedule IV

PPD BY _____
APPVD BY _____
Signature _____ Date _____

Corporation

Employee Forecast (Head Count) for Period Ended _____ Field Office _____

Li. No.	Description	M (1)	O (2)	N (3)	T (4)	H (5)	S (6)
	Sales:						
01	Zone Manger						
02	Assistant Zone Manager						
03	Regional and District Manager						
04	Branch Manager						
05	Dealer Manager						
06	Salesmen (incl. sales reps & trainees)						
07	Marketing Reps						
08	Senior Marketing Reps						
09	QMTM's						
10	MTM's						
11	CR Reps						
12	Dealer Reps						
13	National Accounts Salesmen						
14	Telephone Solicitors						
15	Other (identify)						
16	**Total Sales Personnel**						
	Service:						
17	Zone Service Manager						
18	Dealer Service Manager						
19	Branch Service Manager						
20	Servicemen						
21	Other (identify)						
22	**Total Service Personnel**						
23	**Branch Warehousemen**						
	Administrative:						
24	Zone Administrator						
25	Branch/Area Administrator						
26	Office Employees						
27	Office Temps						
28	Other (identify)						
29	**Total Administrative Personnel**						
30	**Total Field Personnel**						

(0-8-105)

Exhibit 6-e (page 6)

Standard Branch Profit & Loss Statement
(Expenses are Expressed as a Percentage of Sales and Not as Dollar Amounts)

Sales			100.00%
Cost of Sales			45.00
Gross Profit			55.00
Expenses:			
Advertising		.02	
Amortization & Depreciation		1.45	
Business Taxes		*	
Car Rental Expense		1.44	
Coin-Op Commissions		*	
Cleaning Maintenance		.32	
Cost of Capital Invested – A/R		.55	
Credit & Collection		.63	
Dues & Subscriptions		*	
Equipment Rental		*	
Freight Out		1.10	
Payroll Taxes		1.83	
Personnel Rct Ads		.35	
Postage		.44	
Rent		1.30	
Salaries & Commissions:			
Branch Off. Sal.	4.12		
Salesmen	16.42		
Servicemen	5.74		
Branch Warehouse	.89		
Total Salaries & Commissions:		27.17	
Sales Incentives		.01	
Sundry		.57	
Supplies		.47	
Training		**	
Travel & Entertainment:			
Salesmen	2.00		
Servicemen	1.20		
Other	.04		
Total Travel & Entertainment		3.24	
Telephone & Telegraph		1.92	
Utilities		.19	
Total Expenses			43.00
Net Operating Profit Before Taxes			12.00
Less: Provision for Taxes			6.00
Net Operating Profit After Taxes			6.00%

 * The expense was either insignificant percentagewise, or nonexistent for the
   sample branches during the test period. However, these expenses will probably
   occur sometime during the year for some or all branches.

** Training expense is only incurred at the zone level.

Exhibit 6-e (page 7)

Standard Branch Profit & Loss Statement
(Expenses are Expressed as a Percentage of Sales and Not as Dollar Amounts)

Sales		100.00%
Cost of Sales		45.00
Gross Profit		55.00
Less Budgeted Expenses:		
Cleaning & Maintenance	.32	
Personnel Recruitment	.35	
Postage	.44	
Salaries	13.35	
Sundry	.57	
Telephone & Telegraph	1.92	
Travel & Entertainment	3.24	
Training	**	
Total Budgeted Expenses		20.19
Contribution to Non-Budgeted Expenses		34.81
Less Non-Budgeted Expenses:		
Advertising	.02	
Amortization & Depreciation	1.45	
Business Taxes	*	
Car Rental Expense	1.44	
Coin-Op Commissions	*	
Cost of Capital Invested - A/R	.55	
Credit & Collection	.63	
Dues & Subscriptions	*	
Equipment Rental	*	
Freight Out	1.10	
Payroll Taxes	1.83	
Rent	1.30	
Salaries & Commissions	13.82	
Sales Incentives	.01	
Supplies	.47	
Utilities	.19	
Total Non-Budgeted Expenses		22.81
Net Profit Before Taxes		12.00
Less: Provision for Taxes		6.00
Net Profit After Taxes		6.00%

* The expense was either insignificant percentagewise or nonexistent for the sample branches during the test period. However, these expenses will probably occur sometime during the year for some or all branches.

** Training expense is only incurred at the zone level.

Exhibit 6-e (page 8)

P & L Explanations

PURPOSE

This booklet has been compiled to provide a definition and interpretation of all items which comprise the Branch Profit and Loss Statements (P & L's) and includes the following subjects:

1. Sales
2. Cost of Sales
3. Adjustment to Gross Profit
4. Expense items
5. Allocation of expenses for Area Offices and some Warehouse
6. Standard Branch P & L's

1. SALES

Branch P & L's include all sales shown on the Invoice Register (branches) and Temporary PABST (zones) (PABST - Product Analysis by Sales Territories), as well as coin-op sales which are based on cash receipts deposited into corporate bank accounts.

Usual trade-up allowances which are included in the Invoice Register and Temporary PABST as deductions are added back to sales for Branch P & L purposes. Non-comp. trade-ups are shown as deductions in the Invoice Register, Temporary PABST and Branch P & L's. See Cost of Sales section for trade-up allowance adjustments.

2. COST OF SALES

Sales of all products are costed at lowest dealer price less 17% except as follows:

A. Miscellaneous parts are costed at 60% of selling price.
   Labor and Service Contracts are considered to have no cost.
B. Docustat sales (receipts) are costed at 9%.
C. Coupon sales, regardless of size, are costed on the basis of 8 1/2" paper using lowest dealer price less 17%.
D. Freight-Out (charged to the shipping branch) on shipments from one branch to another.

Adjustment for trade-up allowances on Savin Equipment:

For trade-up on allowances below the lowest dealer cost less 17%, the branch cost of sales (for the current sale on which the trade-in was taken) is reduced (profit is increased) by the difference between the allowance and the lowest dealer cost less 17%.

For trade-up allowances above the lowest dealer cost less 17%, the branch dost of sales (for the current sale on which the trade-in was taken) is increased (profit is reduced) by the difference between the allowance and lowest dealer cost less 17%.

Exhibit 6-e (page 9)

GENERAL BUDGET INSTRUCTIONS

What is Budgeting?

The budget is a profit plan for the Branch, District, Zone, Department or Division. Each of these is called a "Profit Center." The budgets for all profit centers are combined into the profit plan for the Corporation. Budgeting is the exercise involved in creating meaningful documents which will express the plans to achieve sales and the expenses associated with achieving those sales.

Your budget should be your best estimate of the sales which you can attain and of all expenses which you expect to incur to achieve those same sales. Your sales budget is not something which is unattainable; it is not a quota or a standard which you hope to reach. It is, instead, your most prudent estimate of those sales which you should attain, after giving consideration to all of the factors which might conceivably affect your achieving of these sales. Such factors are the general economy, salesmen's turnover, the quality of your product, competition in the area, your own managerial ability, and corporate support for your objectives. Under-budgeting sales does not mean that you have done a better job of selling. It generally means that you did not properly plan your activities.

Similarly, the budgeting of expense is based on good judgment and best estimates of the various factors which might influence such expenses. Under-budgeting expenses is just as inaccurate as over-budgeting expenses and could have a deleterious effect on sales. For example, if you under-budgeted postage expense by not doing direct mailing, you would show a favorable variance on your postage expense, but would probably show less sales than you should have for the period. The result would be less profit.

Budgets are required for a variety of purposes:

1. To estimate cash requirements to finance budgeted operations;
2. To enable sufficient inventories to be ordered to sustain the budgeted operations;
3. To permit Staff Departments to plan their service needs - for example, Data Processing, to order the proper equipment to handle increased volume of data;
4. To plan manning requirements;
5. To determine, in advance, that a profitable operation can be maintained.

Budgeting utilizes standard tools which help you to be a better "budgeteer." These are listed on the following pages.

Exhibit 6-e (page 10)

GENERAL BUDGET INSTRUCTIONS

The Tools of Budgeting

The Budget Calendar

The Budget Calendar presents a schedule of time in which forms and budgets should be prepared, approved and formalized. Since every Branch, District, Zone, Department, Staff Manager, and Officer supplies budgets, it is important that these flow through the organization on a rigid time schedule. This will permit the results to be consolidated and formalized to attain the five objectives set forth in What is Budgeting?

Statement of Operations

These are the "actual" results of operation which are used for two purposes:

1. As a guide to preparing budgets of future operations;
2. For purposes of comparing actual operations to budgeted operations and explaining variances.

Explanation of Variances

In accordance with the Budget Calendar, actual figures are sent to all concerned, requesting an explanation of variances on the 22nd working day of the following month. Answers pertaining to these variances should be returned to the Budget Department on the 27th working day of the following month. Variance explanations are required for the following reasons:

1. To fix responsibility for budget changes;
2. To serve as a guide for the preparation of future budgets.

Incurring of Expenses Not Budgeted

Variance explanations will reveal Expenses which have not been budgeted. If you have not budgeted an item, this does not mean that you cannot make the expenditure. The budget is merely a formal plan for anticipating and controlling profits, based on your forecast of what your expenditures will be. If you have not forecast an item correctly, you may still make the expenditure in accord with existing procedures. However, the Manager should plan carefully and economically. An operation which is not planned and does not conform to budget may disorganize the operation and probably result in an inefficient one. Moreover, under-budgeting is just as inefficient at over-budgeting. Plan carefully, make adjustments wherever necessary, and make each succeeding budget more accurate than the previous one.

Forms for Budgeting

1. Sales Budget - Form number (0-8-26) 1-08-9-321 - Used for computing sales volume on machines, paper, and other supplies.

2. Expense Budget - Form number_____ - Used to record estimated expenses to be incurred, from the alphabetical listing.

3. Capital Expenditures (Form number____) and Leasehold Improvements (Form number____) - Used to budget expenditures over $100 for fixed assets and improvements to the premises (see page 10 for a complete description of these items).

Exhibit 6-e (page 11)

<u>GENERAL BUDGET INSTRUCTIONS</u>

4. Forecast of Employees - Form number_____ - Used to list the number
    of persons to be employed in each division (head counts, not dollars).

5. Sales and Expenses Budget Summary - Used to summarize the totals
    from item 1 (Sales Budget) and item 2 (Expense Budget).

6. Expense Comparison - Form number_____ - Used by the Budget
    Department to compare your budget expenses with your actual
    expenses, and to show the variances. This also shows the results
    for last month. It is sent to you monthly with a request to explain
    major variances.

7. Operating Budget Comparison - Form number_____ - Used by the Budget
    Department to summarize the figures from your Sales and Expense Budget
    Summary (No.5, above). The Budget Department will also add cost of
    sales, will compute gross profit on sales and net operating income.
    Each month, your actual figures will be plotted against your budgeted
    figures and the over-all variances will be shown.

Exhibit 6-e (page 12)

GENERAL BUDGET INSTRUCTIONS

PREPARATION OF PROFIT & LOSS BUDGET

General Instructions

All dollar amounts are to be rounded to the nearest hundred dollars, with hundreds shown as decimals. Following are examples:

4.1 = $4,050 thru $4,149 - 4.2 = $4,150 thru $4,249

Each column on the form has been numbered from (1) thru (9). For each line enter the sum of columns (1) thru (6) in column (7). In column (8) enter your estimate (in total) for the next six months for each of the budgeted items. In column (9) enter the sum of columns (7) and (8).

Instructions by Line No.

1.	Enter amounts from line 26, schedule I, page 1.
2.	Enter amounts from line 14, schedule I, page 2.
3.	Enter amounts from line 20, schedule I, page 2.
4.	Enter the sum of lines 1, 2 and 3.
5.	Enter amounts from line 13, schedule II.
6.	Enter difference between lines 4 and 5.
7.	Enter 10% of dealer shipments made from the branch. The branch does not get credit on dealer shipments made from Valhalla.
8.	Non-warranty parts and machines destroyed must have a parts destruct request or machine disassembly request form completed as per SOP #B-16. These forms are costed at 20% of retail price and should be included in cost when forms are fully approved.
9.	Add line 7 to line 6 and deduct line 8. Enter difference on this line.
10. - 18.	Enter amounts from lines 1, 2, 3, 10, 11, 17, 27, 28, and 29, schedule III.
19. - 22.	Enter amounts from lines 29, 30, 31 and 32, schedule III.
23.	Enter the sum of lines 18 and 22.
24.	enter the difference between line 9 and line 23.

Note: Non-budgeted items will be shown in comparative reports which will be sent to you after the end of each month.

Exhibit 6-e (page 13)

ORGANIZATION MANUAL

SECTION	Table of Contents
Section	Title
01	Organization Charts
02	Titles and Names
03	Committee Profiles
	Awards
	Banking
	Executive
	Options
	Product Development

Issued Date	Effective Date	REPLACES		Correction Number	Page Number
		Old Page Number	Dated (Effective)		
2-1-	2-1-				

Exhibit 7-a (page 1)

ORGANIZATION MANUAL

SECTION	Organizational Charts

INTRODUCTION

The enclosed charts show organizational relationships and are in no way intended to reflect relative importance of positions.

The purpose of this section is to show the organizational structure of the Company. The charts included herein reflect the relationships of all management personnel and staffs. The manual will be revised from time to time as changes occur. Pertinent changes should be sent to the Administrative Planning Department.

Issued Date	Effective Date	REPLACES		Correction	Page No.
		Old Page No.	Dated (Effective)	No.	
2-1-	2-1-				01.01.01

Exhibit 7-a (page 2)

ORGANIZATION MANUAL

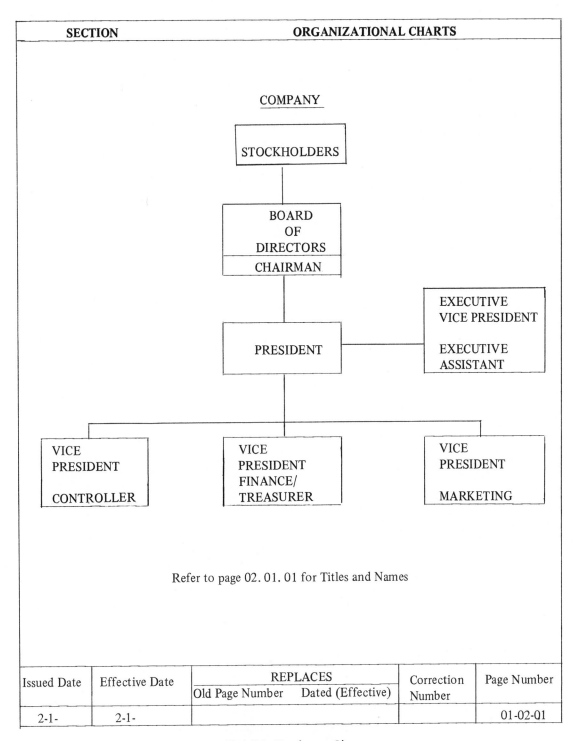

SECTION	ORGANIZATIONAL CHARTS

COMPANY

STOCKHOLDERS

BOARD
OF
DIRECTORS

CHAIRMAN

PRESIDENT

EXECUTIVE
VICE PRESIDENT

EXECUTIVE
ASSISTANT

VICE
PRESIDENT

CONTROLLER

VICE
PRESIDENT
FINANCE/
TREASURER

VICE
PRESIDENT

MARKETING

Refer to page 02. 01. 01 for Titles and Names

Issued Date	Effective Date	REPLACES		Correction Number	Page Number
		Old Page Number	Dated (Effective)		
2-1-	2-1-				01-02-01

Exhibit 7-a (page 3)

ORGANIZATION MANUAL

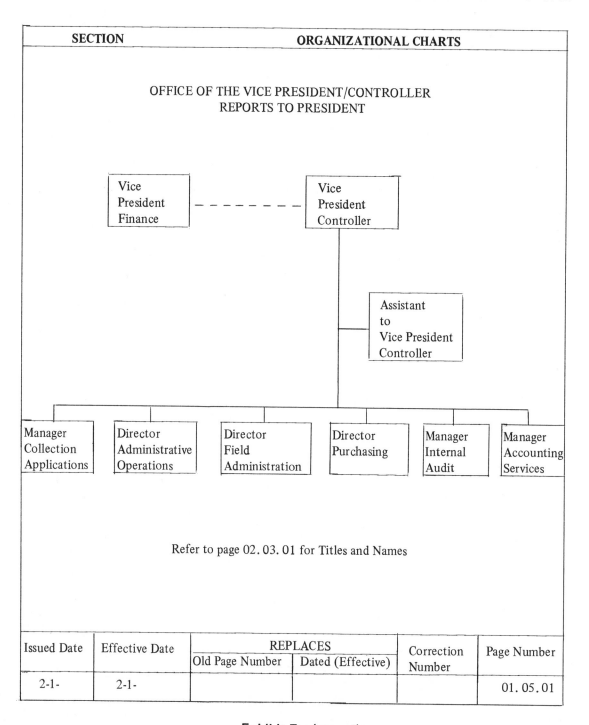

SECTION		ORGANIZATIONAL CHARTS			

OFFICE OF THE VICE PRESIDENT/CONTROLLER
REPORTS TO PRESIDENT

Vice President Finance – – – – – – – Vice President Controller

Assistant to Vice President Controller

Manager Collection Applications | Director Administrative Operations | Director Field Administration | Director Purchasing | Manager Internal Audit | Manager Accounting Services

Refer to page 02. 03. 01 for Titles and Names

Issued Date	Effective Date	REPLACES		Correction Number	Page Number
		Old Page Number	Dated (Effective)		
2-1-	2-1-				01. 05. 01

Exhibit 7-a (page 4)

ORGANIZATION MANUAL

SECTION	TITLES AND NAMES	
	CONTROLLER'S DIVISION	
	OFFICE OF VICE PRESIDENT/CONTROLLER . . . . NAME 1	
DEPARTMENT	TITLE	NAME
ASSISTANT TO VICE PRESIDENT		Name 2
MANAGER COLLECTION APPLICATIONS		Name 3
DIRECTOR ADMINISTRATIVE OPERATIONS		Name 4
DIRECTOR FIELD ADMINISTRATION		Name 5
DIRECTOR OF PURCHASING		Name 6
MANAGER/INTERNAL AUDIT		Name 7
MANAGER OF ACCOUNTING SERVICES		Name 8

Issued Date	Effective Date	REPLACES		Correction Number	Page Number
		Old Page Number	Dated (Effective)		
2-1-	2-1-				02. 03. 01

Exhibit 7-a (page 5)

(JOB DESCRIPTION FORMAT)

Effective Date:

TITLE: DIVISION:
                                                DEPARTMENT:
REPORTS TO: SECTION:
                                                UNIT:

SUMMARY OF FUNCTION:

MAJOR DUTIES AND RESPONSIBILITIES:

ORGANIZATIONAL RELATIONSHIPS:

EDUCATIONAL REQUIREMENTS:

EXPERIENCE REQUIREMENTS:

Exhibit 7-b

To: Distribution   Subject: Guidelines for Writing
                                              Job Descriptions
From: Office Services
                                          5/12/

Below you will find Guidelines for Writing Job Descriptions. Please follow this
procedure when writing job descriptions for those under your supervision.

Procedure

Drafts of job descriptions will be forwarded to the Personnel Department from
the supervising manager of that position.

The Personnel Department will edit and prepare final drafts of the job description
and submit it to the department head or executive for approval.

Job descriptions must receive final approval from the Personnel Department who
will then accept the responsibility for final typing, printing and distribution
to holders of a Job Description Manual and the person or persons filling that job.

All job descriptions will follow the same outline as indicated below (see example
attached):

TITLE: The title should be as simple and descriptive as possible; such as,
"Supervisor - Customer Service."

EFFECTIVE DATE: This is the date of completion of the latest revision of the
job description.

DIVISION: Indicate appropriate division; the major functional group headed
by a policy-making executive reporting directly to the President.

DEPARTMENT: Indicate the primary functional subdivision of a division
headed by an intermediate executive, usually but not necessarily supervising
other managers.

SECTION: Indicate secondary functional subdivision of a division; primary
functional subdivision of a department; a grouping of allied working units,
headed by an intermediate manager who may occasionally supervise another
manager.

UNIT: Indicate a group of closely related jobs within a section headed
by working supervisors.

Exhibit 7-c (page 1)

SUMMARY OF FUNCTIONS: This should be a one or two-sentence statement encompassing the basic function and objectives of this job, and should enable anyone reasonably familiar with the organization to understand the primary purpose of the position.

REPORTS TO: The title of the person to whom this job reports should be entered here. This assumes the hiring and firing responsibilities.

MAJOR DUTIES AND RESPONSIBILITIES: This section should describe as briefly as possible the specific, basic and major duties and/or responsibilities of the individual filling the job. Whenever possible the descriptive terms used should be related to the objectives of a particular function rather than to indicate merely what it is.

For example, the statement "supervises personnel processing customer orders for shipment and billing" would be better stated as follows, "supervises personnel in receiving phone and written communication from customers, and processes customer orders within 24 hours and insures customer satisfaction through prompt and courteous handling of customer complaints."

ORGANIZATIONAL RELATIONSHIPS: This section briefly outlines the contact, coordination and reporting relationships between the individual filling this position and other key positions. The statement should include the types and frequency of reports generated by this position and to whom the reports are made. It should also include the source and types of reports and other information which should be furnished to the person filling this position. This statement should also include the requirements for coordination with other persons involved with administration, controls or the decision making process related to this position.

EDUCATIONAL REQUIREMENTS: Indicate the minimum education requirements necessary to be able to fill the job (such as, number of years and/or completion of college, technical or trade schools, advanced degrees, seminars, etc.).

EXPERIENCE REQUIREMENTS: Indicate the minimum number of months or years of experience in specific job categories necessary to perform this job.

DISTRIBUTION: List 5.0 - General

Exhibit 7-c (page 2)

Branch Office Procedure

Title	
COMMISSION AND SALES VOLUME ADJUSTMENTS CHARGEBACKS, REINSTATEMENTS AND SPLITS	B.O.P Number: 4.02
	Page of 1 4
Vol. No. 4 Vol. Name: Financial Control	

PURPOSE:

To define the method and responsibilities for processing of adjustments, chargebacks, reinstatements and splits on Commissions and Sales Volume at the field level.

GENERAL NARRATIVE:

This procedure deals with the usage of the Commission Journal Entry to effectively process entries involving commissions and sales volume.

APPLICABILITY:

Commission Journal Entries are only to be used if the amount involved is $10.00 or more. Adjustments under $10.00 for one employee can be processed on a Commission Journal Entry provided that the aggregate total of the sums is $10.00 or more. Adjustments under $10.00 are covered on page 4 of this procedure.

PROCEDURE:

Branch Administration:

1) Completes a Commission Journal Entry Form (0-8-54) as follows: (Items are keyed to Exhibit "A".)

Item

A- Check applicable box-(if "split" box is checked, insert selling branch code and shipping branch code.

B- Print (or type) account name and address

C- Enter date journal entry is prepared

D- J.E. Number—Leave Blank

E- Branch Code: Insert two digit branch location code if split is involved enter selling branch code on first line and the shipping branch code on the second line.

F- Enter commission dollar amount to be charged or credited for first or only Salesman, Field Engineer or Customer Representative involved, carried to two (2) decimal places.

G- J.E. date-Enter date from item "C" above

H- Salesman number enter last two digits of employee (payroll) number for first or only Salesman, Field Engineer or Customer Representative involved.

Supersedes		Orig. Code	Release No.	Effective Date
B.O.P. No.(s). Page No.(s).		AP2	B.012	
				10/1/
Related Publications		Inquiries: Mgr. Administrative Control		

Exhibit 7-d (page 1)

COMMISSION JOURNAL ENTRY

☐ CHARGE BACK ☐ REINSTATEMENT ☐ ADJUSTMENT "A" ☐ SPLIT SELLING BR. _____

ACCOUNT NAME "B"
ADDRESS _____ SHIPPING BR. _____

DATE PREPARED "C"
J.E. NO. "D"
(H.O. USE ONLY)
27-32

(1) C C	(2-3) BRANCH CODE	(5-11) NX CREDIT (2 DECIMALS)	COMMISSION (5-11) X CHARGE (2 DECIMALS)	(12-16) J.E. DATE	(19-20) SALESMAN NO.	(21-26) INVOICE NO.	(33-40) ACCOUNT NO.
4 4	"E"	"F"	"F"	"G"	"H"	"I"	"J"

(41-44) PRODUCT CODE	QUOTA POINTS (45-48) X CHARGE (2 DECIMALS)	(45-48) NX CREDIT (2 DECIMALS)	SALES DOLLARS (49-56) X CHARGE (2 DECIMALS)	(49-56) NX CREDIT (2 DECIMALS)	(57-60) QUANTITY (2 DECIMALS)	(61) H.O. ONLY NON- PABST (N)	(80) TYPE
"K"	"L"	"L"	"M"	"M"	"N"	"O"	"P"

COMMENTS: "Q"

PREPARED BY "R"   TITLE "S"   APPROVED BY "T"   TITLE "U"

ORDER/BILLING DEPT.   DATE   KEYPUNCHED BY   DATE

ORDER/BILLING/DATA PROCESSING

Exhibit 7-d (page 2)

CORRECTION CHECKLIST

Upon receipt of a corrected page, circle or
cross out the appropriate number.

1	41	81
2	42	82
3	43	83
4	44	84
5	45	85
6	46	86
7	47	87
8	48	88
9	49	89
10	50	90
11	51	91
12	52	92
13	53	93
14	54	94
15	55	95
16	56	96
17	57	97
18	58	98
19	59	99
20	60	100
21	61	101
22	62	102
23	63	103
24	64	104
25	65	105
26	66	106
27	67	107
28	68	108
29	69	109
30	70	110
31	71	111
32	72	112
33	73	113
34	74	114
35	75	115
36	76	116
37	77	117
38	78	118
39	79	119
40	80	120

Exhibit 7-e

<u>POLICY MANUAL</u>

<u>INTRODUCTION</u>

The general purpose of the manual is to establish, clarify, and otherwise state for all corporate personnel those guidelines set forth as corporate policy.

If a conflict between SOP, HOP, Policy Manual, or other related releases exists, the Policy Manual will take precedence.

Issuance and distribution of all policy manuals and subsequent policy releases throughout the organizational structure will be under the direction of the appropriate corporate officers.

Deviations from published policies will result in disciplinary review by a corporate officer.

Exhibit 7-f (page 1)

<u>POLICY MANUAL</u>

<u>PURPOSE OF POLICY MANUAL</u>

<u>TABLE OF CONTENTS</u>

<u>SECTION</u>	<u>TITLE</u>
I	ADMINISTRATIVE
II	FINANCIAL
III	PERSONNEL A. ADVANCEMENT B. BENEFITS C. COMPENSATION
IV	SALES A. ADVERTISING B. DISTRIBUTION C. SERVICE D. NEW PRODUCTS E. PRICING AND ORDERS
V	INDEX

Exhibit 7-f (page 2)

POLICY MANUAL			
Subject: Alcoholism - Drugs			Number: I 3
			Page of 1 1
Effective Date: 4/1/__	Date Prepared: 4/15/__	Supersedes Cor. No.:	Inquiries: Director of Personnel
Related Publications:			Correction No: 5

It is considered that employees under the influence of alcohol or drugs are not performing their job in the best interests of the company and, in addition, may be endangering the health and welfare of fellow employees.

It is a company rule that an employee will be charged with misconduct if they are in the possession of, or are involved in the transportation or the use of alcoholic beverages or narcotics in any form (unless prescribed by a licensed physician) on the job. This also includes reporting to work when under the influence of narcotics or hallucinogenic drugs, such as, marajuana, LSD, etc., or alcohol, or in possession of the above items on company property. The parking lot and grounds are considered company property.

Employees involved in the use of any of the above will be subject to immediate discharge.

Employees involved in giving, trading or selling any of the above items will be reported to the appropriate authorities and subject to immediate discharge.

Exhibit 7-f (page 3)

ACCOUNTING MANUAL

Major Account Salaries and Wages	Minor Account Purchasing	Sub Account	Number 114

DEFINITION:

Those personnel engaged in producing goods and services used
in the manufacture incidental to the manufacture of development of the company's products.

INCLUDING:

Personnel administering the purchasing function, negotiating
with suppliers, determining economical purchase quantities
from the cost standpoint, placing orders with suppliers and
following up on shipment and defective goods received.

EXCLUDING:

Those personnel who are preparing purchase requisitions
for submission to purchasing will not be included in this
category unless they are directly responsible to the purchasing function such as may or may not be the case with
a material or inventory control section.

MAJOR EXPENSE CLASSIFICATION:

Purchasing salaries and wages will be included in Manufacturing expense.

Issued By The Vice President and Controller	Date Issued	Supersedes Issue Date	Page 1 of 1

Exhibit 7-g

EXERCISE OF AUTHORITY - FIELD SALES OFFICES
(BOP B-10)   Effective

ITEM (BOP & FOOTNOTES)	EVP & V.P. DLR. DIR. DIVISION	DIR. OF MKTG. DIR. F.O./ DLR. DIV.	AREA MGRS. & BR. GEN. MGRS. COMB. BRANCHES	BR. GEN. MGRS. W.M. ONLY BR.	OTHERS POSITION	LIMITS
Contributions: Misc. local contributions (C)	$ 25	$ 25	$ 25	$ 25		
Credit & Collection Fees & Serv.	2,500	1,000	500	500	Credit & Coll. Mgr.	Requirements
Credit memorandum approval & pymt. of accounts receivable balances related to adjustments for: a) Returned saleable merchandise & correction of invoicing errors A-3,A-30,C-3D-3	---To the extent of the original invoice or error being corrected---				Office-Cr. Mgr. or Supv.	100
b) Return & allowance for defective merchandise & the like A-3,A-30, C-3,D-3	5,000	2,000	500	500		
c) Refund or accounts receivable credit balances	---To the extent of the open balances ---				Credit & Collection Mgr. Approve:	
Credit Terms	---Per Published Corporate Procedures Only ---					
Delivery expense	1,000	750	500	500		
Employment agency fees	---To be paid by Employee through Payroll Deductions ---					
Entertainment (see Bus. Expense)						
Fees - Consulting	3,000	2,000	500	500	Division Officer	Requirement

Exhibit 7-h

Report #BVA230 Run Date 4/11

Branch # 40 Los Angeles

PROFIT & LOSS BUDGET
FOR PERIOD ENDING 04/30

------- M O N T H -------				Line		----- Y E A R T O D A T E -----			
Current Budget	Current Actual	Current Variance %	Last Year Actual	Number		Current Budget	Current Actual	Current Variance %	Last Year Actual
				01	Machines (Sched I)				
				02	Paper (Sched I)				
				03	Other (Sched I)				
				04	Total Net Sales				
				05	Less:Cost of Sale(Sched II)				
				06	Gross Profit on Sales				
				07	Add-Dealer Handling Charges				
				08	Less-Parts&Mach.Destruction				
				09	Total Operating Income				
					Less: Branch Budgeting Expense				
				10	Cleaning & Maintenance				
				11	Personnel Recruitment				
				12	Postage				
				13	Salaries				
				14	Sundry				
				15	Telephone & Telegraph				
				16	Travel & Entertainment				
				17	Training				
				18	Tot Br Budgtd Exp(Sched III)				
					Allocated Budgeted Area Expense				
				19	Administrative (Sched III)				
				20	Service (Sched III)				
				21	Warehouse (Sched III)				
				22	Tot Allocat Budgtd Area Exp				
				23	Total Budgeted Expenses				
				24	Contribution to Non-Budgtd Exp				
				25	Less: Non-Budgeted Expenses				
				26	Net oper'g Prof./Loss Bef. Tax				

Exhibit 8-a

PAGE __1__ OF __1__
DATE ___12/5/_____

BACK ORDER INFORMATION REPORT

INVENTORY CONTROL ONLY

DESCRIPTION	PART/ITEM NUMBER	QTY	NO. OF ORDERS	DATE OF OLDEST ORDER	COMMENTS	P/O DATE	ETA WHSE	EST QTY	COMMENTS
220 Console	4194 9597	56	26	11/19/___		11/19___	12/23	140	
Carry Case Console	4940	4	3	11/19/___		Will advise			
Offset E-Mix	7702	48	4	10/20/___		10/21	12/5	96	
Cpn bk pad	0-2-8	62	6	9/15/___		11/18	12/12	150 pads	
Bill Stuffers	z-2-580	4,000	6	9/9/___		Shipping	12/9		
750 Price List	0-2-154	1,000	2	11/10/___		11/10	12/5	5M	
750 Spec. Sheets	0-2-155	7,100	13	11/13/___		12/5	12/23	50M	
750 Mailer	0-2-160	43,000	13	11/21/___		Will advise			
750 Brochure	0-2-162	16,000	15	11/21/___		Will advise			
215 Ser. Man.	0-12-57	5	2	11/26/___		Will advise			
Label for Cass. Tape	0-13-29	1,200	2	11/14/___		Will advise			
Coupon bk. env.	0-14-46	1,500	2	10/15/___		Shipping	12/9		
App. for Emp.	0-16-6	50	1	11/18/___		12/3	12/30	2M	
Letterhds.		7,000	2	11/10/___		11/10	12/20	7M	

FROM PURCHASING: Branch Administrators   **RELEASE DATE FRIDAY**
                          Customer Service Manager
                          Vice President/Administration   Report reflects status
                          Controller   through Thursday P.M.
                          Inventory Control
                          Warehouse Manager
                          Director of Field Admin.
                          Dealer Managers list 7.0

                                          Inventory Control   Date

                                          Purchasing Dept.   Date

Exhibit 8-b

MEMO TO: Executive Vice President   SUBJECT: Shipping Survey

FROM: Customer Service Manager   DATE: March 26, 19__

A survey was conducted for the period February 17 through February 21
with the following results.

361 orders were processed as follows:

Shipped same day as received   28 - 8%
Shipped next day after received   127 - 35%
Shipped second day after received 160 - 44%
Shipped third day after received   46 - 13%

In addition to these orders, 33 others were processed outside of the
normal schedule as follows:

28 orders unable to ship as items were out of stock.
3 orders held for future delivery.
1 order was held awaiting export documents.
1 order in customer repair.

Note: Due to the Washington's Birthday holiday which fell on Friday
       this year, we lost one full day of shipping due to the fact
       that none of our order pickers worked nor did the vast majority
       of the common carriers.

We will continue to work towards maintaining this schedule and in
improving wherever we can.

JK/GS

sc: Warehouse Manager
     District Manager
     Controller
     Vice President/Marketing.

Exhibit 8-c

DATE OF RUN 9/05

CRAN
ANALYSIS OF SOURCE OF CREDITS
FOR THE MONTH ENDED   7/31

TAB BY BRANCH WITHIN ANALYSIS CODE

BR	CODE	SOURCE OF CREDIT	AMOUNT
10	C	CUSTOMER ERROR	3,848.01
10	D	MAINTENANCE OR SERVICE ADJUSTMENT	413.40
10	F	SALESMAN ERROR	280.90
10	G	TAX, FREIGHT OR INSUR. CLAIM ADJUSTMENT REFUND	272.96
10	H	UNSATISFACTORY OTHER THAN PAPER PARTS OR MACH.	206.70
10	1	ORDER DEPARTMENT PROCESSING ERROR	1,971.35
10	2	BRANCH PROCESSING ERROR	2,194.91
10	3	MAIN WAREHOUSE ERROR	764.00
10	6	MACHINE CANCELLATIONS	1,372.70
10	7	MACHINE REPLACEMENTS	1,619.50
		TOTAL	12,944.43*
12	A	DEALER REIMBURSEMENT-RETAIL	110.00
12	C	CUSTOMER ERROR	2,469.22
12	D	MAINTENENCE OR SERVICE ADJUSTMENT	1,550.88
12	E	RENTAL TERMINATION OR RENTAL ADJUSTMENT	65.71
12	G	TAX, FREIGHT OR INSUR. CLAIM ADJUSTMENT REFUND	10.10
12	H	UNSATISFACTORY OTHER THAN PAPER PARTS OR MACH.	5.75
12	2	BRANCH PROCESSING ERROR	3,809.99

Exhibit 8-d

CABARE - CALL BACK REPORT

CUSTOMER BY BRANCH WITHOUT PAPER PURCHASES OVER 60 DAYS

BRANCH CODE	BRANCH NAME	3 MOS.	4 MOS.	5 MOS.	6 MOS.	7 MOS.	8 MOS.	9 MOS.	10 MOS.	11 MOS.	12 MOS.
10	MIDTOWN/N.Y.	53	28	19	20	9	16	6	10	9	54
12	BOSTON	79	28	19	15	14	27	12	8	9	51
13	NEWARK	36	23	5	8	9	14	10	8	6	49
15	PHILADELPHIA	29	17	15	9	7	14	3	8	3	28
18	WASHINGTON	27	20	18	12	16	7	2	7	4	58
20	CHICAGO	14	11	5	6	8	8	4	3	3	18
22	KANSAS CITY	26	8	10	13	9	4	3	3	1	9
30	ATLANTA	14	23	15	10	9	7	1	1	3	17
40	LOS ANGELES	38	31	20	45	27	19	15	20	7	60
41	E. LOS ANGELES	2	19	3	0	0	2	0	0	0	0
42	SAN FRANCISCO	43	31	29	16	10	10	11	4	0	42
43	SANTA ANA	5	13	5	3	2	8	7	7	0	3
48	SANTA CLARA	11	4	4	4	4	4	3	0	0	12
62	HARTFORD	2	6	5	2	3	5	1	0	2	3
72	PROVIDENCE	7	3	4	1	4	3	2	1	1	10
82	LONG ISLAND	16	9	10	12	10	37	6	6	0	29
83	WESTCHESTER/N.Y.	7	5	6	5	5	14	5	4	1	21
	GRAND TOTALS	409 *	279 *	192 *	181 *	146 *	199 *	91 *	90 *	49 *	464 *
	DISTRIBUTION - D.L.G. G.S.C. R.K.L. A.M.										
	11/30		380	261	223	177	232	110	110	55	576
	10/31			339	273	198	257	124	108	57	597
	9/30				396	277	318	151	134	63	682
	8/31					398	423	208	175	92	792
	7/31						555	271	213	114	854

Exhibit 8-e

RUN DATE 08/24/XX

KEVOL
KEYVOLUME REPORT
3 MONTHS ENDING JUNE 19XX
CUSTOMERS OVER 1.00%

BRANCH #	ACCOUNT #	CUSTOMER NAME	3 MONTHS TOTAL UNITS	3 MONTHS TOTAL %	BRANCH UNITS
22	000517	HALMARK CARD CO	508	10.39	4,890
	000962	CHURCHILL TRUCK LINES INC	80	1.64	
	000996	MEDCO JEWELRY	60	1.23	
	001432	IDEAL TRUCK LINES INC	60	1.23	
	204002	COMMERCE TRUST CO	90	1.84	
	601009	MILWAUKEE KANSAS CITY	310	6.34	
	603054	MISSION PHOTO	88	1.80	
	699953	PROCTOR & GAMBLE	70	1.43	
	791131	SMITHVILLE COMMUNTY	60	1.23	
	901300	U S SAFETY SERVICE	146	2.99	
	941009	WHITAKER CABLE CORP	92	1.88	
22		* BRANCH TOTAL *	1,564	31.98	4,890

TYPE OF PAPER	U/M	# OF COPIES	KVOL U/M
200	1 ROLL	500	1 UNIT
215	1 BOX	1000	2 UNITS
220	1 ROLL	500	1 UNIT
230	1 ROLL	1000	2 UNITS

Exhibit 8-f

REPAP DATE OF RUN MAR. 25, 19XX

RETAIL 200 PAPER SHIPMENTS FOR THE PERIOD BEGINNING MAR. 1, 19XX to FEB. 29, 19XX
INCLUDES COUPON SHIPMENTS BUT NOT COUPON SALES

	19XX MAR.	19XX APR.	19XX MAY	19XX JUNE	19XX JULY	19XX AUG.	19XX SEP.	19XX OCT.	19XX NOV.	19XX DEC.	19XX JAN.	19XX FEB.	STD. 3 ROLLS PER MACH.	AVER. ROLLS FIRST QTR.	AVER. ROLLS 2ND QTR.	AVER. ROLLS THIRD QTR.	AVER. ROLLS 4TH QTR.
BRANCH																	
MACHINES IN THE FIELD																	
N.Y.C. PAPER SHIPPED																	
10 MACHINES IN THE FIELD																	
L.I. PAPER SHIPPED																	
82 MACHINES IN THE FIELD																	
WESTCH. PAPER SHIPPED																	
83 MACHINES IN THE FIELD																	
HOUSE PAPER SHIPPED																	
11 MACHINES IN THE FIELD																	
BOSTON PAPER SHIPPED																	

Exhibit 8-g (page 1)

349

DATE OF RUN MAR. 25, 19XX

RETAIL 200 PAPER SHIPMENTS FOR THE PERIOD BEGINNING MAR. 1, 19XX to FEB. 29, 19XX
INCLUDES COUPON SHIPMENTS BUT NOT COUPON SALES

BRANCH	MAR. 19XX	APR. 19XX	MAY 19XX	JUNE 19XX	JULY 19XX	AUG. 19XX	SEP. 19XX	OCT. 19XX	NOV. 19XX	DEC. 19XX	JAN. 19XX	FEB. 19XX	STD. 3 ROLLS PER MACH.	AVER. ROLLS FIRST QTR.	AVER. ROLLS 2ND QTR.	AVER. ROLLS THIRD QTR.	AVER. ROLLS 4th QTR.
12 MACHINES IN THE FIELD																	
HTFD. PAPER SHIPPED																	
62 MACHINES IN THE FIELD																	
PROV. PAPER SHIPPED																	
72 MACHINES IN THE FIELD																	
NEWARK PAPER SHIPPED																	
13 MACHINES IN THE FIELD																	
PHILA. PAPER SHIPPED																	
15 MACHINES IN THE FIELD																	
WASH. PAPER SHIPPED																	
18 MACHINES IN THE FIELD																	
CHICAGO PAPER SHIPPED																	

Exhibit 8-g (page 2)

Travel and Response Time

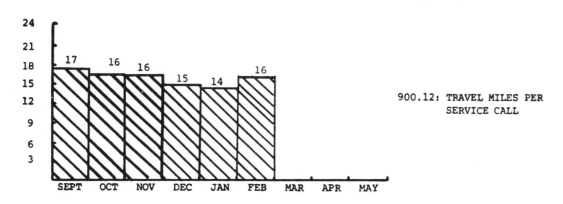

900.12: TRAVEL MILES PER
SERVICE CALL

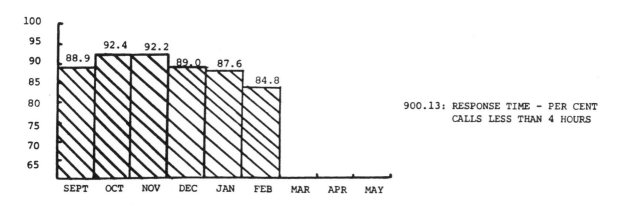

900.13: RESPONSE TIME - PER CENT
CALLS LESS THAN 4 HOURS

Exhibit 8-h

Service Analysis - Product A Data
February, 19

A. Product Performance Input:
   1. Average monthly volume per machine . . . . 10220 lines
   2. Lines between service calls . . . . 14600 lines
   3. Calls per machine per month 0.70
   4. Hours per machine per month 1.30
   5. Machine load per man 31

B. Labor Expense Recapitulation:
   1. Monthly labor cost* $1100.00
   2. Labor cost per machine 35.48
   3. Labor cost per line 0.003

C. Parts Expense Recapitulation:
   1. Parts expense per machine . . . .$ 9.20
   2. Parts expense per line 0.0009

D. Product Expense Summary:
   1. Total expense per machine . . . .$ 44.68
   2. Total expense per line 0.004

E. Contract Revenue:
   1. Maintenance contract @ $25.00 per copy. . . . .$ 25.00

F. Profit (Loss) Machine/Month:
   1. Profit (Loss) per machine per month . . . .$ (19.68)

      *Includes management and fringe.

                         Exhibit 8-i

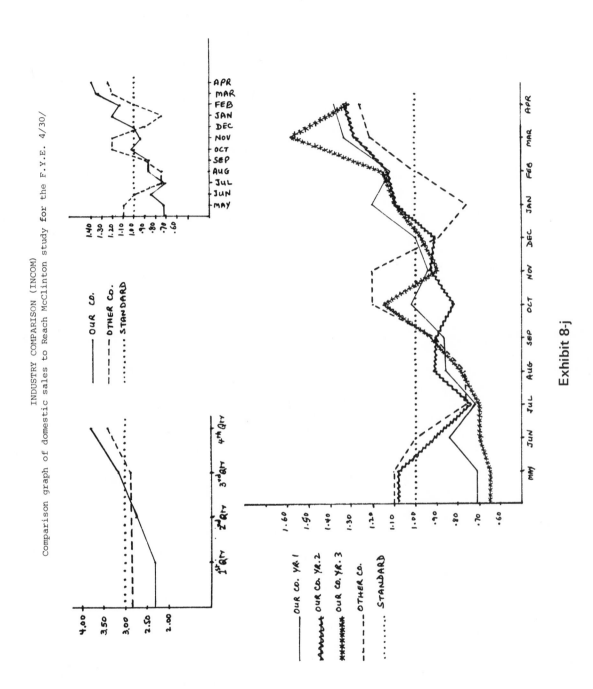

INDUSTRY COMPARISON (INCOM)

Comparison graph of domestic sales to Reach McClinton study for the F.Y.E. 4/30/

Exhibit 8-j

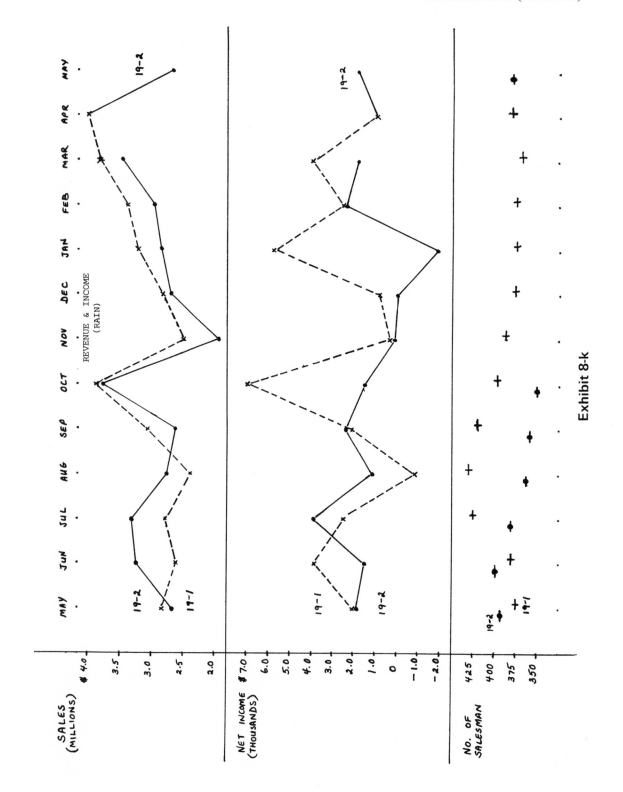

Exhibit 8-k

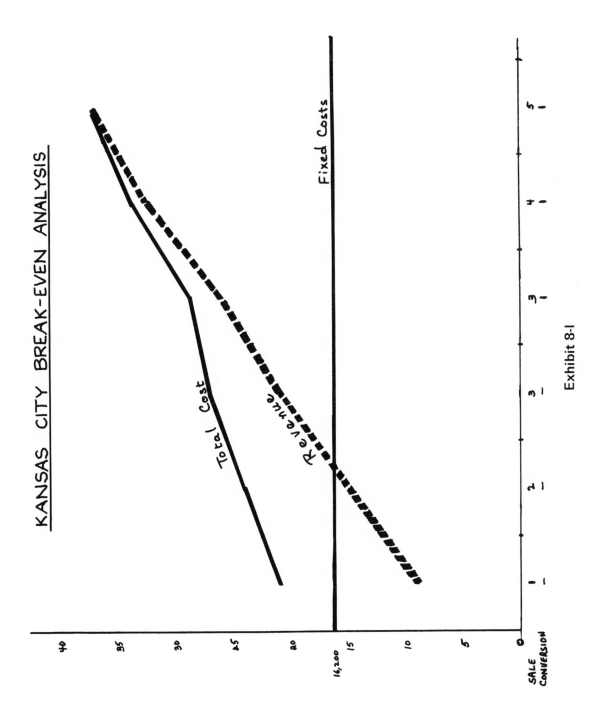

Exhibit 8-1

BOX SCORE
BRANCH 22   KANSAS CITY

	MAY 19—	JUN 19—	JUL 19—	AUG 19	SEP 19—	OCT 19—
Sales $ (000's)	40	48	36	48	48	39
Net Income after taxes, $(000's)	3	.4	—	4	2	(1)
Machines in field	847	853	858	867	873	886
Machines sold	7	6	5	8	6	13
# of Salesman	5	5	6	7	9	8
Machines sold per man	1.4	1.2	.8	1.1	.7	1.6
Gross Profit $ (000's)	24	29	23	26	26	23
%	59.6	58.8	61.6	55.5	54.2	59.9
Operating Exps $ (000's)	23	23	26	24	26	27
%	56.5	48.0	70.0	51.4	54.0	70.4
# of Rolls sold	1576	2200	1496	2342	2278	1698
Rolls sold per machine	1.9	2.6	1.7	2.7	2.6	1.9
# of Employees						
Salesmen	5	5	6	7	9	8
CR?	2	2	2	2	2	2
Servicemen	5	5	5	5	5	5
Adm.	3	3	3	3	3	3
W/House	1	—	1	1	1	1
Machines in field, per serviceman	169	171	172	173	175	177
# of Invoices	379	476	404	444	417	426
Invoices per Adm. personnel	126	159	135	148	139	142
Telephone soliciting Hrs	48	76	60	48	48	88
MUP – Machines:						
Cumulative	68	68	68	69	70	72
Current Month	—	—	—	1	1	2
MUP – Paper:						
Rolls sold last month	986	1018	503	970	931	764
" " per machine	14.5	15.0	7.4	14.1	13.3	10.6
Machines sold next month	6	5	9	6	13	17

Exhibit 8-m (page 1)

BOX SCORE LEGEND

1. <u>Sales</u>: Per Branch Profit and Loss Statement.

2. <u>Net Income after Taxes</u>: Per Branch Profit and Loss Statement.

3. <u>Machines in Field (Including MUP)</u>: Per Repam Retail Machine Report, adjusted to agree with periodic physical inventories.

4. <u>Machines Sold (Including MUP)</u>: Per Branch cost of sales by Product (COSBAB) MUP are per Repam Retail Machine Report.

5. <u>Number of Salesmen (Including MTM)</u>: Per actual Payroll records as at month end.

6. <u>Machines Sold Per/Man (Including MUP)</u>: A ratio computed by dividing the number of machines sold (including MUP) by the number of salesmen (including MTM).

7. <u>Gross Profit on Sales</u>: Per Branch Profit and Loss Statement and is reflected before dealer handling credit.

8. <u>Operating Expenses</u>: Per Branch Profit and Loss Statement.

9. <u>Rolls (in 500 sheets quantity) sold (Including MUP)</u>: Per Branch Cost of Sales by Product (COSBAB).

10. <u>Rolls (in 500 sheets quantity) sold Per Machine in Field</u>: is a ratio computed by dividing the number of rolls sold (including MUP) by the number of machines in field (including MUP).

11. <u>Number of Salesmen (Including MTM)</u>: Per actual Payroll Records as at month end.

12. <u>Number of CR's</u>: Per actual Payroll Records as at month end.

13. <u>Number of Servicemen Including Managers</u>: Per actual Payroll Records as at month end.

14. <u>Number of Administrative Personnel Including Branch Administrator</u>: Per actual Payroll Records as as month end.

15. <u>Warehousemen and Drivers</u>: Per actual Payroll Records as at month end.

16. <u>Machines in Field Per Servicemen</u>: is a ratio computed by dividing the number of machines in field (including MUP) by the number of servicemen.

17. <u>Number of Invoices</u>: Per Data Processing Work Counts Report.

Exhibit 8-m (page 2)

PAYROLL DISTRIBUTION
PAY PERIOD ENDING 12/31/

S U M M A R Y

T DISTRIBUTION CATEGORY	GROSS $	EMP. COUNT	\multicolumn{6}{c}{PRODUCT-LINE COUNT}					
			0	1	2	3	4	5
CORPORATE OFFICE	90,671.17	164	159	4			1	
OTHER OFFICE	39,341.16	128	126				2	
TOTAL OFFICE	130,012.33	292	285	4			3	
CORPORATE WAREHOUSE	2,761.54	5	9					
OTHER WAREHOUSE	6,489.00	20	20					
TOTAL WAREHOUSE	9,250.54	25	29					
CORPORATE SERVICE	9,513.82	20	14	2			3	1
OTHER SERVICE	111,862.74	285	15	136			73	65
TOTAL SERVICE	121,376.56	305	29	138			76	66
DEALERS	13,015.44	18	18					
BRANCH MANAGERS	38,821.70	41	18	8			15	
ZONE PRODUCT SALES MGRS	.00							
BRANCH SALES MANAGERS	.00							
QUOTA SALES MANAGERS	.00							
NATL ACCTS SALESMEN	1,246.16	2	1	1				
SALESMEN	67,614.93	194		94			100	
CUSTOMER REPRESENTATIVES	5,470.03	29		29				
S S R	13,222.40	39					39	
TELEPHONE SOLICITORS	705.50	4	4					
MISCELLANEOUS	2,833.45	8	8					
TOTAL PAYROLL	403,569.04	965	392	274			233	66

Exhibit 8-n

358

SUPPORT SYSTEM

SALESMAN SUPPORT REPORT
BY BRANCH
2 WEEKS ENDING 02/28/XX and Y.T.D.

	# OF SALESMAN	BI-WEEKLY					YEAR TO DATE		
		ACCOUNTS VISITED	AMT OF SUPPORT	BRANCH SUPPORT	DST/ZNE SUPPORT	NATIONAL SUPPORT	ACCOUNTS VISITED	TOTAL SUPPORT	BRANCH SUPPORT
Midtown	14	19	3	1	2	0	19	3	1
Elmsford	18	8	5	4	0	1	8	5	4
Wall Street	13	0	0	0	0	0	0	0	0
Lake Success	16	0	0	0	0	0	0	0	0
Cranford	8	19	4	3	1	0	19	4	3
Metro Region	69	46	12	8	3	1	46	12	8
Boston	9	46	15	5	10	0	46	15	5
Hartford	7	19	2	2	0	0	19	2	2
Providence	7	11	3	3	0	0	11	3	3
New England Region	23	76	20	10	10	0	76	20	10
Philadelphia	17	60	17	16	1	0	60	17	16
Wilmington	11	24	7	0	7	0	24	7	0
Baltimore	12	6	6	6	0	0	6	6	6
Mid-Atlantic District	40	90	30	22	8	0	90	30	22
Atlanta	8	0	0	0	0	0	0	0	0
Miami	0	0	0	0	0	0	0	0	0
Tampa	0	0	0	0	0	0	0	0	0
Jacksonville	0	0	0	0	0	0	0	0	0
Southeast District	0	0	0	0	0	0	0	0	0
Eastern Zone	140	212	62	40	21	1	212	62	40
Chicago O'Hare	8	6	3	0	3	0	6	3	0
Chicago Loop	10	0	0	0	0	0	0	0	0
Chicago District	18	6	3	0	3	0	6	3	0
Detroit	3	0	0	0	0	0	0	0	0
Ann Arbor	0	0	0	0	0	0	0	0	0
Detroit District	3	0	0	0	0	0	0	0	0
Pittsburgh	8	30	10	10	0	0	30	10	10
Minneapolia	9	5	5	1	4	0	5	5	1
Kansas City	7	14	8	2	6	0	14	8	2
Cincinnati	6	18	15	11	4	0	18	15	11
Central Zone	51	73	41	24	17	0	73	41	24
Los Angeles	18	47	16	16	0	0	47	16	16
East L.A.	6	33	17	17	0	0	33	17	17
Santa Ana	12	17	7	7	0	0	17	7	7
Long Beach	6	1	1	1	0	0	1	1	1
L.A. District	42	165	79	65	14	0	165	79	65
San Francisco	14	70	31	31	0	0	70	31	31
Oakland	6	22	9	9	0	0	22	9	9
San Jose	10	27	13	12	1	0	27	13	12
Denver	6	42	20	19	1	0	42	20	19
San Francisco Region	36	161	73	71	2	0	161	73	71
Dallas	14	0	0	0	0	0	0	0	0
Houston	6	4	1	0	0	0	4	1	0
Memphis	2	71	14	14	0	0	71	14	14
New Orleans	5	0	0	0	0	0	0	0	0

Exhibit 8-o (page 1)

```
COPIES:  President
         Executive Vice President
         Vice President/Marketing
         Director Field Operations
         Director Field Administration
         General Sales Manager


FROM:  Manager, Systems & Programming, Headquarters
TO:    DISTRIBUTION
DATE:  3/15/__

SUBJECT:  Field Support Reports:  How to Analyze
```

Page 1 - Salesman's Support Report

    Taking Midtown as the example:

1.   Number of active salesmen in branch: 14
2.   Number of accounts visited by salesmen and support personnel: 19
3.   Number of salesmen supported during the period: 3
4.   Of the 3 men supported, 1 was by branch personnel (either branch manager, branch service manager, or an M.T.M.)
5.   Of the 3 men supported, 2 were supported by zone or district management (zone manager, A.Z.S.O., district manager, or zone service manager)
6.   There was no national support for Midtown salesmen (V.P.'s, national managers or product managers)

Page 2 & 3 - Servicemen and CR Reps are Analyzed as per Page 1

Page 4 & 5 - Type of Call Report

Taking Midtown as the example:

1.   Of the 27 accounts visited (19 salesmen, 8 CR Reps, 0 servicemen),

3 were presentations	1 was goodwill
4 were demo's	2 were new accounts (CR)
1 was a sale	4 were active accounts (CR)
6 were cold calls	2 were inactive accounts (CR)
1 was a new Coupon Book Account	
3 were new Major Users	

Page 6 & 7 - Combined Support Report by Individual

    Using National Sales Manager as an example:

1.   Number of accounts visited with salesmen: 6
2.   Number of salesmen supported: 2
3.   No servicemen supported
4.   Number of accounts visited with CR Reps: 8
5.   Total of CR Reps supported: 1
6.   Total of accounts visited: 14
7.   Total men supported: 3

Exhibit 8-o (page 2)

DAILY   19
Date Prepared

CUMULATIVE RETAIL PAPER REPORT

BRANCH	Men	Mach In Field			2nd Prior Mo.			1st Prior Mo.			Current Month AT ___ AM/PM			BRANCH
		200	210	220	200	210	220	200	210	220	200	210	220	
ANA														ANA
ATL														ATL
BOST														BOST
CHI														CHI
DAL														DAL
HART														HART
K.C.														K.C.
L.A.														L.A.
L.I.														L.I.
NWK														NWK
NYC														NYC
PHIL														PHIL
PROV														PROV
S.F.														S.F.
SJO														SJO
WASH														WASH
WEST														WEST
TOTAL														

* Mach In Field is cumulative at start of current month.

INSTRUCTIONS:
   Figures shown are paper shipments - both regular and coupon:
     Shipping branches - From daily Telex or switchboard.
     Non-shipping branches - From order log before shipments.

DIST: EPC; RKL; GSC; DLG -   Mon., Wed., Fri.
         Zone Mgrs.   -   Friday PM (Their branches only)

Exhibit 8-p

COST/PRICING PRODUCT SHEET

PRODUCT_____

( ) NEW PRODUCT   ( ) CHANGE   DATE:___/___/___   BY:_____   PRODUCT CODE_____

UNIT OF MEASURE / UNIT OF MEASURE

	CONTROL PROD. NO:	ACCOUNTING	MARKETING	APPROVED PRICING	DIRECT COSTS - EXCLUDING COMMISSIONS TO SALESMEN			
					COST ELEMENT	RETAIL	DEALER	OTHER

RETAIL - SALES — UNIT OF MEASURE

RECOMMENDED PRICE (S) .	$.			
% GROSS PROFIT	. %			
% MARK-UP ON COST	. %			
% COMMISSION	. %			
$ COMMISSION	$.			

RAW COST (EFF DATE, VENDOR, FOB POINT, CURRENCY BASIS, UNIT)

RETAIL - RENTALS — UNIT OF MEASURE

RECOMMENDED PRICE (S) .	$.			
% GROSS PROFIT	. %			
% MARK-UP ON COST	. %			
% COMMISSION	. %			
$ COMMISSION	$.			

UNIT OF MEASURE

BROKERAGE

DUTY AT   %

INSURANCE & HANDLING TO MAIN WAREHOUSE

DEALER

RECOMMENDED PRICE (S) .	$.			
% GROSS PROFIT	. %			
% MARK-UP ON COST	. %			
% COMMISSION	. %			
$ COMMISSION	$.			

FREIGHT - IN TO MAIN WAREHOUSE

ROYALTY: %or$; BASE: ; NAME:

ROYALTY: %or$; BASE: ; NAME:

ROYALTY: %or$; BASE: ; NAME:

MAJOR ACCOUNT — UNIT OF MEASURE

RECOMMENDED PRICE (S) .	$.			
% GROSS PROFIT	. %			
% MARK-UP ON COST	. %			
% COMMISSION	. %			
$ COMMISSION	$.			

FREIGHT - OUT - MAIN WAREHOUSE TO BRANCH

FREIGHT - OUT - TO CUSTOMER

SPECIAL PACKING, HANDLING, OR RIGGING

SALES OR OTHER TAX IF UNBILLED TO CUST.

GSA - SALES — UNIT OF MEASURE

RECOMMENDED PRICE (S) .	$.			
% GROSS PROFIT	. %			
% MARK-UP ON COST	. %			
% COMMISSION	. %			
$ COMMISSION	$.			

GSA - RENTALS — UNIT OF MEASURE

RECOMMENDED PRICE (S) .	$.			
% GROSS PROFIT	. %			
% MARK-UP ON COST	. %			
% COMMISSION	. %			
$ COMMISSION	$.			

OTHER_____ — UNIT OF MEASURE

RECOMMENDED PRICE (S) .	$.			
% GROSS PROFIT	. %			
% MARK-UP ON COST	. %			
% COMMISSION	. %			
$ COMMISSION	$.			

TOTAL COST

GROSS PROFIT = PROFIT/PRICE

PRICE APPROVED

( )	( )	( )	( )	( )	( )	( )	( )
V. P. MKTG.	EXEC. V. P.	PROD. MGR.	V. P./CONTR.	PRES.	DLR. MGR.		

MARK-UP ON COST = PROFIT/COST

COST APPROVED

( )	( )	( )	( )
PURCH. MGR.	ACCTG. MGR.	V. P./CONTR.	

O-8-76

Exhibit 8-q

Purchasing Department   **1 /24/XX**   Dist:
                                                                     Date   Purch
                                                                                  Prod. Mgr.
FLASH COST CHANGE REPORT   SM
                                                                                  VP/Mkt.
VENDOR(S) _____ B. Corp. _____   DP Mgr.
                                                                                  Cont.
                                                                                  VP/Adm.
Effective Date of Change   2 / 1/XX   EVP

Annual Purchase Quantity   4000 _____   ea. _____   Annual Cost Increase
                               Quantity   Unit of Measure $109,760.00

Product	Present Cost	New Cost	$ Change	% Change
Roller A	103.28	130.72	27.44	26.57%

Product Code
439

Retail Profit Effect

Old Cost vs. New Cost

Present List Price	Mark-up Above Present Cost	Mark-up Above New Cost	Present Cost Markup Difference — New Cost Markup	
$180.00	$76.72 42.62%	$49.28 27.37%	$27.44 15.24%	X

				Annual Sales Qty Projected	Annual Profit Decrease
				2000	$54,880.00

Present Block Price	Mark-up Above Present Cost	Mark-up Above New Cost	Present Cost Mark-up Difference — New Cost Mark-up	
$____	$ %	$ %	$ %	X

Dealer Profit Effect

Old Cost vs. New Cost

Present Highest Dealer Price	Mark-up Above Present Cost	Mark-up Above New Cost	Present Cost Mark-up Difference — New Cost Mark-up	
$144.00	$40.72 28.28%	$13.28 9.22%	$27.44 19.06%	X

				Annual Sales Qty Projected	Annual Profit Decrease
				2000	$54,880.00

Present Lowest Dealer Price	Mark-up Above Present Cost	Mark-up Above New Cost	Present Cost Mark-up Difference — New Cost Mark-up	
$____	$ %	$ %	$ %	X

Exhibit 8-r

45-607 EYE-EASE
45-707 20/20 BUFF
NATIONAL Made in U.S.A.

DEPARTMENTAL REPORTS
Non-Accounting Generated

	Responsible Department	Working Day Due	ACTUAL DATE		
			January	February	March
Avg. No. Sales & MUP/ Salesman	O/B	13	13	14	13
Advertising Budget	Purch	14	14	13	14
Word Processor Budget	Purch	14	14	14	14
Dacom Monthly Report	Rapifax	15	15	14	15
Delco Collections Summary	Credit	15	15	15	15
Branch A/R Summary	Credit	15	16	15	16
Doubtfuls to Reserve	Credit	15	15	15	16
Recourse Lease	Credit	15	15	15	16
GSA Leases	O/B	15	15	15	16
Paper Sales to Murritt	CSD	19	18	18	20
Position for Paper & Chemicals	Purch	20	20	19	20

Exhibit 8-s

Year	STRAIGHT-LINE		DECLINING-BALANCE				SUM-OF-THE-YEARS-DIGITS	
	Annual Deduction	Cumulative Cost Recovered	Annual Deduction 150%	200%	Cumulative Cost Recovered 150%	200%	Annual Deduction	Cumulative Cost Recovered
1	$10	$10	$15	$20	$15	$20	$18	$18
2	10	20	13	16	28	36	16	34
3	10	30	11	13	39	49	15	49
4	10	40	9	10	48	59	13	62
5	10	50	8	8	56	67	11	73
6	10	60	6	7	62	74	9	82
7	10	70	6	5	68	79	7	89
8	10	80	5	4	73	83	5	94
9	10	90	4	3	77	86	4	98
10	10	100	3	3	80	89	2	100

As a general rule, *no matter what useful life is involved,* after half the useful life, you recovered only: $1/2$ the cost under the straight-line method; about $2/3$ under the double declining-balance method; and close to $3/4$ under the sum of the years-digits method.

≫TAX GUIDE→ Consider decelerated depreciation.—In your earlier low-income years you may wish to take less depreciation and save the lion's share for later higher bracket years.

How decelerated depreciation works.—Essentially it can be the sum of the years-digits method in reverse. For instance, if in the sum of the years-digits method equipment you just bought is going to last 5 years, you add up the digits for each year $1 + 2 + 3 + 4 + 5 = 15$. Then for the first year you deduct $5/15$ of your cost less salvage value; for the second you deduct $4/15$; for the third $3/15$ and so on. *Now to reverse the procedure:* If in the first year you deduct $1/15$ of your cost less salvage; in the second $2/15$; for the third $3/15$; for the fourth $4/15$ and for the fifth $5/15$, you come out with progressively higher deductions.

Will it work.—While the Code or Regulations don't specifically approve this method, there's nothing to prevent you from using it. And you should be able to justify use of the method, particularly where use of your equipment increases as time goes on.

Exhibit 9-a

DEPRECIATION METHODS

1. Straight-line
   a) Time related
   b) Output related
       i. Service hours
      ii. Units of production

2. Decreasing charge
   a) Arbitrary assignment (first 2/3 life = DD)
   b) Fixed percentage of declining balance
   c) Sum of the digits $\dfrac{(n \times (n+1))}{2}$
   d) Appraisal

3. Retirement and replacement

4. Interest
   a) Annuity
   b) Sinking fund

5. Appraisal (going-concern value)

Exhibit 9-b

FOREIGN SUBSIDIARY ALTERNATIVES

I. INFORMATION
   a) Tax treaty
      1. Avoids double tax
      2. Lower W/T on dividends

   b) Embassies and trade offices

   c) Accounting firms - here and abroad
      1. Communication
      2. Local taxes
      3. Non-tax considerations
      4. Forecast alternative income streams

II. FORM
   a) Branch - for early losses
      1. Avoids tax problems
      2. Avoids intercompany pricing problems
      3. Saves 1/2 the cost of starting-up

   b) WHTC
      1. Substantially all business in Western Hemisphere
      2. 95% gross income outside U.S.
      3. 90% gross income from "active" business
      4. 30% + tax saving
      5. Consolidated return & 100% dividends received credit
      6. Tax-free property transfers, including goodwill
      7. Sec. 367 gains need "clearance"
      8. Tax payable now and intercompany pricing problems
      9. Individual shareholder avoids double tax
      10. Capital gain on liquidation or sale of shares

   c) USPC
      1. 80% gross income in a possession
      2. 50% gross income from "active" business
      3. No tax until income is returned as dividends
      4. P/R tax benefits
      5. Individual shareholder avoids double tax
      6. Capital gain in liquidation or sale of shares

   d) CFC
      1. Over 50% stock control
      2. High tax rate obviates deferral as tax credit eliminates U.S. tax
      3. Manufacture abroad
         a) No tax
         b) Second tier or sub-subs
         c) "Minimum distribution" method of sub part-F relief (43% of income)
         d) 30% of gross income can be sub part-F type w/o being taxed as "deemed paid"
      4. Buy U.S. components and finish
         a) No U.S. tax until dividends paid
         b) Foreign tax credits available on gross-up basis
         c) Sec. 367 gains need "clearance"
         d) 30% of gross income can be sub part-F type w/o being taxed as "deemed paid"
      5. Buy U.S. and sell abroad
         a) Dividend is deemed paid
         b) No tax benefit

   e) DISC
      a) 95% gross receipts from exports
      b) 95% of assets must be qualified
      c) Liberal intercompany pricing rules
      d) DISC is exempt, but profits taxed to stockholders
      e) No WHTC reduction
      f) No consolidation
      g) Tax on 50% of profits is postponed 10 years

Exhibit 9-c

ADVANTAGES AND DISADVANTAGES OF

LIFO METHOD OF INVENTORY COSTING

Advantages of LIFO:

1. Improved cash flow from reduced taxes.

2. It serves to hedge a company's future earnings
    from future price declines.

Disadvantages of LIFO:

1. Impact on reported earnings and on a company's

    financial position.

2. Comparison of relative performance with other companies

    in the same industry that may not be on LIFO.

3. Possible adverse impact on the conventional application

    of a multiplier to earnings.

4. Modification or waiver of various restrictive covenants on loan

    indentures and other credit agreements restricting the amount of

    retained earnings available for cash dividends, reacquisition of

    stock and borrowing formulas.

5. Impact on existing bonus and profit sharing plans.

6. Inventories must be stated at cost, any market, obsolescence, or

    comparable reserves must be reinstated for federal income tax

    purposes, thereby generating income.

7. Some of the economic advantages of LIFO are lost in subsequent

    years if inventory quantities are reduced.

Exhibit 9-d

PRENTICE-HALL

Tax Calendar of Fixed Dates

JANUARY, 19

CALENDAR OF ANNUAL, SEMI-ANNUAL AND QUARTERLY DATES FOR ALL STATES FOR JANUARY, 19

For acts to be performed or payments to be made monthly, see pages 1401 et seq.

In the items below if neither foreign nor domestic corporations are specifically mentioned, both are included, but the mention of domestic corporations is equivalent to the exclusion of foreign corporations, and vice versa. Dates below indicate last day for action. In the entries below, no cognizance is taken of Saturdays, Sundays or holidays, it being usually true that a return or payment due on such dates can be made on the following business day.

ALA.—Property taxes—Levy on personalty for nonpayment [¶ 31,685] .**Jan. 1**
Sleeping car cos.—Annual license tax to Dept. Rev. [¶ 49,500] .....**Jan. 1**
Electric, hydroelectric utilities license tax—Report, pay ¼ to Dept. Rev. [¶ 49,484.10] ....**Jan. 14**
Street, interurban RRs, water, gas, pipeline, heating companies license tax—Report, pay ¼ to Dept. Rev. [¶ 49,482] ....**Jan. 14**
Income tax—Individual's declaration and/or installment to Dept. Rev. [¶ 11,535] ....**Jan. 15**
Express companies—Exclusive intrastate businesses pay flat fee [¶ 49,-498] ....**Jan. 15**
Property taxes—Return on assessor's demand between Jan. 1 and this date; fee 50¢, thereafter penalty (3rd Mon.) [¶ 31,555; 31,580] .....**Jan. 21**
Tax on shares, domestic corp.—Report to Dept. Rev. and duplicate to local assessor (3rd Mon.) [¶ 31,920; 31,923] ....**Jan. 21**
Use tax—Quarterly return, pay Dept. Rev. [¶ 21,379] ....**Jan. 20**
Forest products severance tax—manufacturers and exporters, report and pay Dept. Rev. [¶ 45,712; 45,717] ....**Jan. 30**
Lodgings tax—Report to Dept. Rev. [¶ 21,167] ....**Jan. 30**
Income tax—Employer's withholding statement to employee; report, pay, quarterly withholding tax to Dept. Rev. [¶ 11,555] ....**Jan. 31**
Motor carrier's fuel use tax—Quarterly report, pay Dept. Rev. [¶ 45,284] ....**Jan. 31**

ALASKA.—School tax—Due date [¶ 31,500] ....**Jan. 1**
Property tax—Assessment date [¶ 31,345] ....**Jan. 1**
Personal income tax—Pay 4th estimate installment to Comr. of Rev. [¶ 10,-317; 10,350] ....**Jan. 15**
Income tax—Report and pay to Comr. of Rev. tax withheld (plus school tax if any) during quarter ending Dec. 31 [¶ 10,360; 12,285.10; 31,500] **Jan. 31**
File annual withholding reconciliation [¶ 10,360; 10,634] ....**Jan. 31**
Business license tax—Renew license [¶ 21,227] ....**Jan. 31**
Income tax—Information return to Dept. Rev. by fish buyer and processor [¶ 10,335] ....**Jan. 31**
Property tax—Apply to Assr. for farm assessment [¶ 31,365] ....**Jan. 31**

ARIZ.—Property tax—Property assessed as of this date [¶ 31,540] ....**Jan. 1**
Telegraph, telephone companies—Personalty ownership inventory as of this date (report April 1) [¶ 49,422] ....**Jan. 1**
Property tax—Lien attaches (1st Mon.) [¶ 31,750] ....**Jan. 7**

Reprinted from Prentice-Hall State and
Local Taxes Service, All States Unit.

Exhibit 9-e

PRENTICE-HALL
Tax Calendar of Recurring Monthly Dates

All items in this calendar show acts to be performed or payments to be made at a definite date each month. For items that occur less frequently (annually, quarterly, etc.) than monthly, see pages preceding these.

In the items below if neither foreign nor domestic corporations are specifically mentioned, both are included, but the mention of domestic corporations is equivalent to the exclusion of foreign corporations, and vice-versa.

ALA.—Alcoholic beverage tax—Wholesalers and distributors report to Alcoholic Beverage Control Board [¶ 41,584] 10th

Tobacco use tax—Report, pay to Dept. Rev. [¶ 38,450] 10th

Gasoline and lubricating oil taxes—Carriers, warehouse and transfer companies report to Dept. Rev. [¶ 45,245; 45,250; 45,385; 45,390] 15th

Motor carriers tax—Report, pay to Dept. Rev. [¶ 49,264; 49,266] 15th

Oil and gas conservation and privilege taxes—Producers report pay Dept. Revenue [¶ 45,812; 45,817; 45,845; 45,850] 15th

Coal production tax—Report, pay Dept. Rev. [¶ 45,542] 20th

Gasoline inspection fee—Report, pay to Comr. of Agric. [¶ 45,450] 20th

Gasoline tax—Report, pay to Dept. Rev. [¶ 45,235; 45,260] 20th

Gasoline tax—Airport managers report to Dept. Rev. [¶ 45,235] 20th

Transient accommodations—Report, pay Dept. Rev. [¶ 21,167] 20th

Iron ore production tax—Report, pay Dept. Rev. [¶ 45,515; 45,525] 20th

Iron ore production tax—Transportation Co. report to Dept. Rev. [¶ 45,-515] 20th

Petroleum products inspection fee—Report and payment to Comr. Agric. [¶ 45,450] 20th

Lubricating oil tax—Report, pay to Dept. Rev. [¶ 45,380; 45,415] 20th

Motor fuel (non-gasoline)—Report, pay Dept. Rev. [¶ 45,320; 45,330] .20th

Sales tax—Report, pay to Dept. Rev. [¶ 21,379; 21,421] 20th

Leasing—Report, pay Dept. Rev. [¶ 21,221] 20th

Tobacco tax—Wholesalers, report-pay (also report purchases—applies to retailers) to Dept. Rev. [¶ 38,450] 20th

ALASKA—Alcoholic beverages-Report-pay [¶ 41,210; 41,215] ......Last day

Cigarette tax—Report, pay for previous month [¶ 38,300] ....Last day

Motor fuel tax—Report, pay Comr. Rev. [¶ 45,420; 45,425] ......Last day

Oil, gas production tax—Report, pay Comr. Rev. [¶ 45,507] ......Last day

Oil conservation tax—Report-pay Comr. Rev. [¶ 45,512] ....Last day

ARIZ.—Property tax (unsecured personalty)—Pay Co. Treas. [¶ 31,705] ....2nd Mon.

Alcoholic beverages wholesalers—Report, pay Dept. Rev. [¶ 38,518] ..10th

Use tax—Report, pay Dept. Rev. [¶ 21,379; 21,380] 15th

Sales tax—Report, pay Dept. Rev. [¶ 21,379; 21,380] 20th

Common, contract carrier—Report, pay MV Supt. [¶ 49,270] 25th

Private motor carriers—Report to MV Supt. [¶ 49,275] 25th

Gasoline—Distributors report, pay; carriers report to MV Supt. [¶ 45,-200] 25th

Motor fuel users—Report, pay MV Supt. [¶ 45,654; 45,655] 25th

Rental occupancy tax—Landlords report, pay Dept. Rev. (eff 12-31-74) [¶ 21,221] ....Last day

Reprinted from Prentice-Hall State and Local Taxes Service, All States Unit.

Exhibit 9-f

DATE DUE	TYPE OF FEDERAL TAX	TYPE OF DEPOSIT FORM	FINAL DATE FOR PAYMENT OF:	PORTION DUE	NOTES
Jan. 6, 1975	Payroll	501	Withheld Income & FICA Tax for December 23-31, 1974	All	(a)
Jan. 10	Payroll	501	Withheld Income & FICA Tax for January 1-7, 1975	All	(a)
Jan. 20	Payroll	501	Withheld Income & FICA Tax for January 8-15, 1975	All	(a)
Jan. 27	Payroll	501	Withheld Income & FICA Tax for January 16-22, 1975	All	(a)
Jan. 31	Payroll	501	All Undeposited 1974 Withheld Income & FICA Tax	All	(c)
Jan. 31	Excise	504	All Undeposited 1974 Excise Tax	All	(e)
Jan. 31	Unemployment	508	All Undeposited 1974 Unemployment Tax	All	(f)
Feb. 5	Payroll	501	Withheld Income & FICA Tax for January 23-31, 1975	All	(a)
Feb. 12	Payroll	501	Withheld Income & FICA Tax for February 1-7, 1975	All	(a)
Feb. 18	Payroll	501	Withheld Income & FICA Tax for January, 1975	All	(b)
Feb. 20	Payroll	501	Withheld Income & FICA Tax for February 8-15, 1975	All	(a)
Feb. 26	Payroll	501	Withheld Income & FICA Tax for February 16-22, 1975	All	(a)
Feb. 28	Excise	504	Excise Tax of January, 1975	All	(d)
Mar. 5	Payroll	501	Withheld Income & FICA Tax for February 23-28, 1975	All	(a)
Mar. 12	Payroll	501	Withheld Income & FICA Tax for March 1-7, 1975	All	(a)
Mar. 17	Payroll	501	Withheld Income & FICA Tax for February, 1975	All	(b)
Mar. 17	Corporate Income	503	1st Installment of 1974 Corporate Income Tax	50%	(g)
Mar. 19	Payroll	501	Withheld Income & FICA Tax for March 8-15, 1975	All	(a)
Mar. 26	Payroll	501	Withheld Income & FICA Tax for March 16-22, 1975	All	(a)
Mar. 31	Excise	504	Excise Tax of February, 1975	All	(d)
Apr. 3	Payroll	501	Withheld Income & FICA Tax for March 23-31, 1975	All	(a)
Apr. 10	Payroll	501	Withheld Income & FICA Tax for April 1-7, 1975	All	(a)
Apr. 15	Corporate Income	503	1st Installment of 1975 Estimated Corporate Income Tax	25%	(h)
Apr. 18	Payroll	501	Withheld Income & FICA Tax for April 8-15, 1975	All	(a)
Apr. 25	Payroll	501	Withheld Income & FICA Tax for April 16-22, 1975	All	(a)
Apr. 30	Payroll	501	All Undeposited 1st Quarter 1975 Withheld Income & FICA Tax	All	(c)
Apr. 30	Excise	504	All Undeposited 1st Quarter 1975 Excise Tax	All	(e)
Apr. 30	Unemployment	508	1st Quarter 1975 Unemployment Tax	All	(f)
May 5	Payroll	501	Withheld Income & FICA Tax for April 23-30, 1975	All	(a)
May 12	Payroll	501	Withheld Income & FICA Tax for May 1-7, 1975	All	(a)
May 15	Payroll	501	Withheld Income & FICA Tax for April, 1975	All	(b)
May 20	Payroll	501	Withheld Income & FICA Tax for May 8-15, 1975	All	(a)
May 28	Payroll	501	Withheld Income & FICA Tax for May 16-22, 1975	All	(a)
June 2	Excise	504	Excise Tax of April, 1975	All	(d)
June 4	Payroll	501	Withheld Income & FICA Tax for May 23-31, 1975	All	(a)
June 11	Payroll	501	Withheld Income & FICA Tax for June 1-7, 1975	All	(a)

NOTES AND REQUIREMENTS

(a) Assumes cumulative undeposited payroll tax liability reached $2,000 or more during the quarter-monthly period shown. See below: "REQUIREMENTS FOR DEPOSITING PAYROLL TAXES".

(b) Assumes monthly payroll tax liability was at least $200 but less than $2,000. See below: "REQUIREMENTS FOR DEPOSITING PAYROLL TAXES".

(c) Assumes undeposited quarterly payroll tax liability was under $2,000. See below: "REQUIREMENTS FOR DEPOSITING PAYROLL TAXES".

(d) Assumes excise tax liability exceeded $100 for the month shown. Deposits of $100 or less are permissible but not required. See below: "REQUIREMENTS FOR DEPOSITING EXCISE TAXES".

(e) Assumes undeposited excise tax liability for the calendar quarter exceeded $100 (applies to all excise taxes except air transportation and communication taxes). See below: "REQUIREMENTS FOR DEPOSITING EXCISE TAXES".

(f) Assumes cumulative undeposited unemployment tax liability exceeded $100 for the quarter or for a period of two or more quarters within the same calendar year. See below: "REQUIREMENTS FOR DEPOSITING UNEMPLOYMENT TAXES".

(g) Assumes the corporation is a calendar-year taxpayer. The portion due assumes corporation elected to pay its Corporate Income Tax (the amount still due after estimated tax deposits) in two equal installments. Fiscal-year taxpayers that elect to pay the tax in two equal installments must deposit the first installment on or before the 15th day of the third month following the close of the fiscal year. The second installment is due on or before three months after such date. Corporations can pay the entire amount due on the first due date.

(h) Assumes that the corporation is a calendar-year taxpayer and that the $40 minimum estimated tax requirement was met prior to the fourth month of the year. See below: "REQUIREMENTS FOR DEPOSITING ESTIMATED CORPORATE INCOME TAX".

REQUIREMENTS FOR DEPOSITING PAYROLL TAXES

These rules for depositing Withheld Income and FICA tax became effective February 1, 1971. Under these rules employers may be classified in one of three deposit categories depending on when the employer reaches certain accumulated tax liabilities during the calendar quarter.

CATEGORY I. Employers with a cumulative liability of $2,000 or more on the 7th, 15th, 22nd, or last day of the month must deposit the accumulated Withheld Income and FICA taxes within three banking days of these dates.

CATEGORY II. Employers with a monthly liability of at least $200 but less than $2,000 are required to make a deposit on or before the 15th day of the succeeding month in the case of the 1st or 2nd month of each quarter. The deposit for the last month of a quarter must be made on or before the last day of the month following the close of the quarter.

CATEGORY III. (a) Employers with cumulative quarterly liability under $200 may remit the total liability with the quarterly return which is due on or before the last day of the month following the close of the quarter.

Exhibit 9-g (Federal Tax Calendar, page 1)

371

(b) If the cumulative liability by the close of the second month of a quarter exceeds $200, but was less than $200 at the close of the first month, the employer must deposit the accumulated tax by the 15th day of the third month of the quarter. The liability for the third month may be remitted with the quarterly return.

(c) If the cumulative liability reaches $200 during the third month of the quarter, the total quarterly liability can be deposited, or paid with return, by the last day of the month following the close of the quarter.

REQUIREMENTS FOR DEPOSITING UNEMPLOYMENT TAXES

Under these rules employers may be classified in one of three deposit categories depending on when the employer reaches certain accumulated tax liabilities during the calendar year.

CATEGORY I. Employers with a total tax liability of more than $100 during a calendar quarter must make their deposit by the last day of the month following the close of the quarter.

CATEGORY II. Employers with quarterly tax liabilities of $100 or less must make deposits by the last day of the month following the calendar quarter in which the accumulated tax for any two or more quarters exceeds $100.

CATEGORY III. Employers with cumulative tax liabilities of $100 or less at the close of a calendar year may deposit the full amount or pay it with the annual return.

REQUIREMENTS FOR DEPOSITING ESTIMATED CORPORATE INCOME TAX

A corporation must deposit estimated tax during the current tax year if it can reasonably expect its estimated tax for the year will be $40 or more. Estimated tax is total expected tax liability less allowable tax credits and the statutory exemption. Corporations may be classified under one of four depositing categories depending upon when during its taxable year its estimated tax reached the $40 minimum.

CATEGORY I. Corporations that meet the minimum prior to the 4th month of the taxable year must deposit 25% of the estimated tax liability by the 15th day of the 4th, 6th, 9th and 12th month of the taxable year.

CATEGORY II. Corporations that meet the minimum prior to the 6th month of the taxable year (but after the 3rd month) must deposit 33⅓% of the estimated tax liability by the 15th day of the 6th, 9th and 12th month of the taxable year.

CATEGORY III. Corporations that meet the minimum prior to the 9th month of the taxable year (but after the 5th month) must deposit 50% of the estimated tax liability by the 15th day of the 9th and 12th month of the taxable year.

CATEGORY IV. Corporations that meet the minimum prior to the 12th month of the taxable year (but after the 8th month) must deposit 100% of the estimated tax liability by the 15th day of the 12th month of the taxable year.

REQUIREMENTS FOR DEPOSITING EXCISE TAXES

Under these rules, taxpayers with excise tax liabilities of $100 or more in any calendar quarter are required to make semimonthly, monthly or quarterly payments depending on their tax liabilities.

SEMIMONTHLY.—If excise taxes for any month of a calendar quarter exceeded $2,000, all excise taxes for the following quarter, regardless of amount, must be deposited semimonthly as follows: (semimonthly periods are the first through the fifteenth, and the sixteenth through the last day of a month).

June 16	Payroll	501	Withheld Income & FICA Tax for May, 1975	All	(b)
June 16	Corporate Income	503	2nd Installment of 1974 Corporate Income Tax	50%	(g)
June 16	Corporate Income	503	2nd Installment of 1975 Estimated Corporate Income Tax	25%	(h)
June 18	Payroll	501	Withheld Income & FICA Tax for June 8-15, 1975	All	(a)
June 25	Payroll	501	Withheld Income & FICA Tax for June 16-22, 1975	All	(a)
June 30	Excise	504	Excise Tax of May, 1975	All	(d)
July 2	Payroll	501	Withheld Income & FICA Tax for June 23-30, 1975	All	(a)
July 10	Payroll	501	Withheld Income & FICA Tax for July 1-7, 1975	All	(a)
July 18	Payroll	501	Withheld Income & FICA Tax for July 8-15, 1975	All	(a)
July 25	Payroll	501	Withheld Income & FICA Tax for July 16-22, 1975	All	(a)
July 31	Payroll	501	All Undeposited 2nd Quarter 1975 Withheld Income & FICA Tax	All	(c)
July 31	Excise	504	All Undeposited 2nd Quarter 1975 Excise Tax	All	(e)
July 31	Unemployment	508	2nd Quarter 1975 Unemployment Tax	All	(f)
Aug. 5	Payroll	501	Withheld Income & FICA Tax for July 23-31, 1975	All	(a)
Aug. 12	Payroll	501	Withheld Income & FICA Tax for August 1-7, 1975	All	(a)
Aug. 15	Payroll	501	Withheld Income & FICA Tax for July, 1975	All	(b)
Aug. 20	Payroll	501	Withheld Income & FICA Tax for August 8-15, 1975	All	(a)
Aug. 27	Payroll	501	Withheld Income & FICA Tax for August 16-22, 1975	All	(a)
Sep. 2	Excise	504	Excise Tax of July, 1975	All	(d)
Sep. 4	Payroll	501	Withheld Income & FICA Tax for August 23-31, 1975	All	(a)
Sep. 10	Payroll	501	Withheld Income & FICA Tax for September 1-7, 1975	All	(a)
Sep. 15	Payroll	501	Withheld Income & FICA Tax for August, 1975	All	(b)
Sep. 15	Corporate Income	503	3rd Installment of 1975 Estimated Corporate Income Tax	25%	(h)
Sep. 18	Payroll	501	Withheld Income & FICA Tax for September 8-15, 1975	All	(a)
Sep. 25	Payroll	501	Withheld Income & FICA Tax for September 16-22, 1975	All	(a)
Sep. 30	Excise	504	Excise Tax of August, 1975	All	(d)
Oct. 3	Payroll	501	Withheld Income & FICA Tax for September 23-30, 1975	All	(a)
Oct. 10	Payroll	501	Withheld Income & FICA Tax for October 1-7, 1975	All	(a)
Oct. 20	Payroll	501	Withheld Income & FICA Tax for October 8-15, 1975	All	(a)
Oct. 27	Payroll	501	Withheld Income & FICA Tax for October 16-22, 1975	All	(a)
Oct. 31	Payroll	501	All Undeposited 3rd Quarter 1975 Withheld Income & FICA Tax	All	(c)
Oct. 31	Excise	504	All Undeposited 3rd Quarter 1975 Excise Tax	All	(e)
Oct. 31	Unemployment	508	3rd Quarter 1975 Unemployment Tax	All	(f)
Nov. 5	Payroll	501	Withheld Income & FICA Tax for October 23-31, 1975	All	(a)
Nov. 12	Payroll	501	Withheld Income & FICA Tax for November 1-7, 1975	All	(a)
Nov. 17	Payroll	501	Withheld Income & FICA Tax for October, 1975	All	(b)
Nov. 19	Payroll	501	Withheld Income & FICA Tax for November 8-15, 1975	All	(a)
Nov. 26	Payroll	501	Withheld Income & FICA Tax for November 16-22, 1975	All	(a)

Exhibit 9-g (Federal Tax Calendar, page 2)

372

Dec. 1	Excise	504	Excise Tax of October, 1975	All	(d)
Dec. 3	Payroll	501	Withheld Income & FICA Tax for November 23-30, 1975	All	(a)
Dec. 10	Payroll	501	Withheld Income & FICA Tax for December 1-7, 1975	All	(a)
Dec. 15	Payroll	501	Withheld Income & FICA Tax for November, 1975	All	(b)
Dec. 15	Corporate Income	503	4th Installment of 1975 Estimated Corporate Income Tax	25%	(h)
Dec. 18	Payroll	501	Withheld Income & FICA Tax for December 8-15, 1975	All	(a)
Dec. 26	Payroll	501	Withheld Income & FICA Tax for December 16-22 1975	All	(a)
Dec. 31	Excise	504	Excise Tax of November, 1975	All	(d)
Jan. 6, 1976	Payroll	501	Withheld Income & FICA Tax for December 23-31, 1975	All	(a)
Feb. 2	Payroll	501	All Undeposited 1975 Withheld Income & FICA Tax	All	(c)
Feb. 2	Excise	504	All Undeposited 1975 Excise Tax	All	(e)
Feb. 2	Unemployment	508	All Undeposited 1975 Unemployment Tax	All	(f)

IMPORTANT: The above Timetable and Notes are for your information and are advisory only. We believe the information to be correct as of September, 1974 but cannot warrant accuracy since the United States Internal Revenue Service may alter its requirements without prior notice.

(a) Air transportation and communications tax must be deposited within three banking days after the end of the semimonthly period for which it was collected.

(b) Taxes on manufactured sugar or on policies issued by foreign insurers must be deposited on or before the first day of the following month for the first semi-monthly period of a month, and on or before the 15th day of the following month for the second semimonthly period.

(c) All other excise taxes not described above in (a) or (b) must be deposited by the 9th day of the following semimonthly period.

MONTHLY— If excise taxes for each of the first two months of a quarter exceed $100, they must be deposited by the last day of the following month. If the unde-posited excise taxes at the end of a quarter exceed $100, the entire amount must be deposited by the last day of the first month of the following quarter (last day of the second month for air transportation and communications taxes).

QUARTERLY— If cumulative undeposited excise tax liability for a calendar quarter is $100 or less, the entire amount may be deposited or paid with the return.

NOTE: Each date shown is the prescribed last day for filing the return or making the payment of tax indicated. However, if such date falls on a Saturday, Sunday or legal holiday, the due date is on the next succeeding day which is not a Satur-day, Sunday, or legal holiday (national or state-wide in the state where the return is to be filed).

Exhibit 9-g (Federal Tax Calendar, page 3)

Tax Calendar - April 19.
States   *Page 1 of 4*

					Date Due	Date Submitted	Date Mailed
1	WHTC Corp.						
2	Fed. W/H & FICA - 941				4/30	4/18	4/29
3	N.Y.S. Unemp. Ins. 1st Qtr.				4/30	4/18	4/29
4	Fed. W/H & FICA - April Deposit				4/30	4/18	4/29
5	DISC CORP.						
6	Fed. W/H & FICA - 941				4/30	4/29	4/29
7	N.Y.S. Unemp. Ins. 1st Qtr.				4/30	4/29	4/29
8	Fed. W/H & FICA - April Deposit				4/30	4/29	4/29
9	PARENT CORP.						
10	SALES TAX						
11	Alabama 1st Qtr.				4/20	4/14	4/17
12	Arizona				4/15-30	4/14	4/17
13	City - Tucson Rental ④ Retail	None None			4/15	4/14	4/14
14	Phoenix				4/15	4/14	4/14
15	Arkansas				4/15-30	4/12	4/12
16	California 1st Qtr. Recon.				4/30	4/29	4/29
17	Colorado						
18	City - Arvada				4/20	4/14	4/14
19	Aurora Boulder				4/20 4/20	4/17 4/17	4/17 4/17
20	Commerce				4/20	4/14	4/14
21	+ Co. Denver				4/15	4/14	4/14
22	Connecticut 1st Qtr.				4/30	4/21	5/1
23	District of Columbia				4/20	4/17	4/18
24	Florida				4/20	4/17	4/20
25	Georgia				4/20	4/14	4/14
26	Illinois				4/30	4/21	5/1
27	Indiana				4/30	4/21	4/29
28	Kansas				4/30	4/17	4/27
29	Kentucky				4/20	4/14	4/17
30	Louisiana				4/20	4/17	4/18
31	City - New Orleans				4/20	4/17	4/18
32	Co. - Jefferson Parish				4/20	4/14	4/14
33	Maryland - Baltimore				4/21	4/17	4/18
34	- Rockville				4/21	4/17	4/18
35	Massachusetts				4/20	4/20	4/24
36	Michigan Incl. W/H (SWT)				4/15	4/14	4/17
37	Minnesota				4/25	4/17	4/18
38	Missouri				4/15	4/15	4/15
39	Mississippi 1st Qtr.				4/20	4/17	4/17
40	New Jersey				4/20	4/17	4/18

Exhibit 9-h

AUTHORIZATION FOR PAYMENT

7/19/
(DATE)

Payee _Tax Collector — City of Hartford_

Amount _$597 46/xx_

Reason _1st Qtrly. Pymt. — Pers Prop. Tax - 19_

A/c Charged _74-05-62 0002_

Method of Repayment _____

Approved _pd_ _____

Date Payment Completed _Chemical Bk Ck.# 2246_

(Use this form for all advances to salesmen, loans to employees, exchanges, or payments without invoices.)

(0-8-56)

Exhibit 9-i

CONTROL SHEET

PERSONAL PROPERTY TAX PAID

V. E. 4/30/

PAGE 1 OF 4

	1	2	3	4	5	6	7
1	ARIZONA						
2	MARICOPA COUNTY		✓	553829		6/7/74	10338
3					553829		
4							
5	CALIFORNIA						
6	ALAMEDA COUNTY		✓	184346		7/30/74	5629
7	CITY OF ALAMEDA			216		4/23/75	2632
8	"			216		6/8/74	2175
9	HUMBOLDT COUNTY			5598		7/1/74	2278
10	KERN COUNTY			2099		11/4/74	2231
11	LOS ANGELES COUNTY			2657568		3/6/75	5675
12	" " "			159568		8/1/74	10870
13	" " "			1418177		5/21/74	1027
14	MARIN COUNTY			2200		8/1/74	3169
15	ORANGE COUNTY			60514		6/11/74	2279
16	" " "			228072		6/13/74	10378
17	COUNTY OF SANTA CLARA			355636		6/13/74	10400
18	COUNTY OF SAN MATEO			455941		8/1/74	1024
19	COUNTY OF SAN LUIS OBISPO			1186		8/1/74	2232
20	SHASTA COUNTY			2969		8/1/74	2223
21	SONOMA COUNTY			1486		5/30/74	1043
22	VENTURA COUNTY			5362		5/6/74	2133
23					5538647		
24							
25	COLORADO						
26	ALAMOSA COUNTY		✓	10003		2/12/75	2539
27	COLORADO SPRINGS			8575		1/1/75	2456
28	CITY & COUNTY OF DENVER			205743		1/21/75	1502
29					224321		
30							
31	CONNECTICUT						
32	SHELTON		✓	4557		7/19/74	2248
33	STAMFORD			72528		7/19/74	2242
34	STONINGTON			23180		3/14/75	2581
35	WETHERSFIELD			6160		7/19/74	2248
36	HARTFORD			59743		3/20/75	2586
37	"			119486		12/21/74	6134
38	"			59746		7/19/74	2246
39	DANBURY					7/19/74	2271
40	EAST HARTFORD					7/19/74	2245

Exhibit 9-j

ACCOUNTING AND AUDITING

Overseeing the Internal Audit Function
A Checklist for Executives and Directors

The internal audit function is assuming ever-increasing importance as corporations expand and their accounting systems become more complex. Pressures, moreover, continue to mount on executives and boards of directors, requiring them to maintain the utmost vigilance over all aspects of their companies' operations, including audit procedures. Equally important, a properly functioning internal audit system can help pinpoint areas of potential revenue improvement and cost reduction. As a basic guide, directors and executives may wish to use the following as a minimum checklist of internal audit procedures:

Organization

□ The board of director's audit committee should participate in approving the audit schedule, guiding the work of the internal audit staff in a broad sense, and overseeing the coordination of internal and external audit operations.

□ The manager in charge of the internal audit function should report to an upper echelon executive who can ensure that deficiencies are considered promptly and that corrective action is monitored.

□ The internal audit schedule should be established annually, in consultation with the company's external auditors.

Qualifications

□ Appointments to the internal audit staff should be on the basis of capacity to advance to higher positions.

□ Internal auditors, like their external counterparts, should engage in continuous training and self-improvement.

□ Internal auditors should be in a position to maintain independence in matters they review.

Performance Guides

□ Internal auditors should not be overly burdened with routine tasks.

□ Internal auditors should have full access to all areas of the company that their work requires.

□ The internal audit schedule should provide for coverage of all physical facilities within a reasonable time cycle.

□ Internal auditors should submit periodic reports, which permit management to evaluate progress in terms of the established schedule.

□ Internal auditors should observe generally accepted auditing standards as incorporated in the Statements on Auditing Procedure issued by the American Institute of CPAs.

□ The team's work should be guided by written programs.

Exhibit 10-a (page 1)

Performance Guides *(Continued)*

☐ Audit programs should be responsive to changing control conditions.

☐ The audit staff's workpapers should include comprehensive documentation of all tests, stating what was examined, procedure followed, and results.

☐ All audit programs should be signed off to indicate completion of steps.

☐ The results of each examination should be expressed in a written report oriented towards management and suitable for follow-up.

☐ The follow-up should include a mechanism to ensure that all control deficiencies signaled by the internal audit are corrected as soon as possible.

☐ The internal audit staff should review operational and administrative controls on a cyclical basis, with special attention to areas of potential revenue improvement and cost reduction.

Exhibit 10-a (page 2)

POSITION DESCRIPTION	
TITLE FIELD AUDITOR	DATE 7/24/
ORGANIZATIONAL UNIT Controller	JOB NUMBER

FUNCTION

Responsible to the Controller for auditing the accounting and administrative control functions at field, sales and service centers; for reporting the audit results in comparison with approved audit procedure; for providing recommendations for field procedural changes; for coordinating the initial interviewing and subsequent training of Branch Administrators.

RESPONSIBILITIES

1. *Interviewing*-Coordinate with the Training Manager (who interviews Branch Administrators for hire) in establishing definitive hiring criteria. Conduct preliminary interviews of Branch Administrators in the field, when requested by Training Manager, for new hires for replacement purposes. Recommend two to three interviewees to the Zone Manager for final interviewing and selection by the Zone Manager.

2. *Training*-Schedule training of new Branch Administrators for an initial 2-week period, at a smoothly-functioning Branch. Upon completion of field training, spend three days in SOP manual training with new Branch Administrators, discussing concepts involved.

3. *Auditing*-Schedule unannounced audits on field, sales and service centers at least once in every nine months. Conduct audits in accord with Internal Audit Questionnaire and Internal Audit Program. Complete Audit Report after each audit and supply the Summary Audit Appraisal each six months, to the Controller, covering all sales and service centers previously audited.

4. *Maintain Field Levels of Performance*-Retrain Branch Administrators wherever necessary. Fill in for Branch Administrators in emergency cases.

5. *Procedures*-Recommend updating and changes in procedures, based on field audit work. Write recommended new procedures where applicable.

Exhibit 10-b

MEMO TO: Distribution   SUBJECT: Field Audit Announcement

FROM: Controller   DATE: June 26, 19

Marketing Memo #148 dated June 12th, provided that Branch
Administrators would report directly to Branch Managers.

In accord with this change, the Controller's Division has
established a field auditing procedure as follows:

   1. Field Auditor's Position - This describes the
functions and responsibilities of the Field Auditor.

   2. Internal Audit Program - At Home Office - This
indicates the review work to be done by the Field Auditor,
prior to his field trip.

   3. Internal Audit Program - At Branch Office - This
indicates the work to be done by the auditor in the field
and is an extension of the work done in the Home Office,
No. 2, above.

   4. Internal Audit Questionnaire - These are questions
which will be asked by the Field Auditor, prior to his
beginning the audit, in No. 3, above.

   5. Audit Report:

            a) Detailed Report - Sent from Auditor, with
            copies to Controller, Branch Administrator,
            Zone Managers and Regional Managers.

            b) Summary Audit Report - A summary based on a)
            sent to Executive Vice President and Vice President
            for Marketing.

            c) Audit Appraisals - A summary each six months
            of all reports with A, B, C, or D ratings ad-
            dressed to Executive Vice President, with copies
            to Vice President for Marketing.

Field audits are unannounced approximately once every nine months,
to each Branch. Each audit will include all points noted on the
previous audit report.

Within 30 days of the audit, the report provided for in MM #148
should be submitted by the Branch Administrator to the Regional
Administrator, stating the corrective measures that have been taken
in response to the audit report.

Exhibit 10-c

INTERAL AUDIT PROGRAM FOR _____ CORPORATION

BRANCH _____ OFFICES

AUDIT PROCEDURES -- AT HOME OFFICE

BRANCH OFFICE # _____ LOCATION _____

MONTH AND YEAR _____

A. PETTY CASH

    1. Examine last two petty cash reconciliations.

        a. Approve arithmetic.

        b. Check petty cash fund balance to general ledger.

        c. Examine propriety of signatures on petty cash vouchers.

        d. Check names of all payees on Expense Report reimbursements to payroll records to verify employment as a serviceman. Verify mileage to leased car.

        e. Examine each petty cash voucher for propriety of expenditure.

    2. Review accounting distribution of expense items.

    3. List all items paid, over the two months which are not in compliance with petty cash procedure S.O.P. 24.

    4. Number of times petty cash was reimbursed in last two months.

Exhibit 10-d (page 1)

B. <u>SALES</u>

1. Review Invoice Register for the Branch for the last month and do the following:

   a. Determine that bill only numbers are being used in sequence. Check with invoice control section to make sure that missing numbers are accounted for and carried as outstanding.

   b. List twenty-five machine transactions (go to the second prior month if necessary) indicating date, invoice number, model number, and sales amount. Allow room on work sheet for customer name, serial number, machine order, confirmation call, and delivery receipt. List must include two trade-ins.

   c. Examine posting copies of invoices for these transactions and slot in customer name and serial number of machine. Mark "L" for leased sales.

   d. Trace names into customer alphabetical file, record by checkmark (✓) machine order, confirmation call and delivery receipt columns.

2. List last ten coupon transactions (go to previous month if necessary) indicating date, invoice number, type paper and unit price. Allow room on worksheet for customer name, coupon order form, terms of sale.

   a. Examine posting copies and list customer name, type paper and unit price.

   b. Trace these into customer's alphabetical file and record (checkmark) coupon order form and terms of sale *(terms not in accord with those on coupon order form).

3. Trace above ten coupon book numbers into Coupon Book Report and log. Verify sequential redemption of coupons. List below coupon book numbers and coupon numbers not redeemed in consecutive order. (Show name and original invoice number.)

4. Obtain numbering series of billings sent to branch.

5. Review terminology on 25 machine transactions (1.b., above) as to use of words "trade-in machine allowance," or "demo allowance," in accord with SOP C-35.

6. Compare Monthly New Order Report to DEPAM.

Exhibit 10-d (page 2)

C. INVENTORY

   1. Review Demo Materials Report from purchasing
       department. Note excessive use of paper and supplies
       per SOP C-6c. Review monthly purchase requisitions
       with the purchasing manager. Determine that
       merchandise is ordered for delivery in the following
       month, or three months hence, in accord with S.O.P.
       E-6. Test methods of calculating quantities requisitioned
       for conformity to the procedure. Verify receipt of
       BT's by all Branches.

D. FIXED ASSETS

   1. Review fixed assets schedule for branch and compare total
       per schedule to control accounts. Investigate difference.

   2. List five to ten items of major value from fixed assets
       schedule to physically verify presence and serial numbers
       at the branch office.

E. PAYROLL

   1. Obtain copies of weekly payroll time sheets for most
       recent period:

       a. Check to see if branch administrator has approved
           the record.

       b. Make copies and use at the branch offices as a
           verification of actual presence of employees.

   2. Review copies of last five Change of Status Notices
       sent in by Branch:

       a. Determine that all start-up papers are supplied in
           accord with SOP B-2.

       b. Are the Change of Status Notices sent in on a
           timely basis, after date of hire?

       c. Are "Additional Comments" completed with reasons
           for hire?

Exhibit 10-d (page 3)

F. COUPON LIABILITY

    1. Obtain tabulation of unredeemed coupons rep-
        resenting coupon liability for field veri-
        fication of detailed support.

    2. List coupon books issued last year with no redemptions.

    3. List twenty accounts for field verification-
        ten shipments; ten new orders.

ACCOUNT NUMBER	ACCOUNT NAME	CPN. SALE DATE	INV. NO.	ORIG CPNS	CPNS REDEEMED

BAL. OF CPNS.	ORIG. AMT.	AMT. REDEEMED	BALANCE OF AMT.

Exhibit 10-d (page 4)

G.   GENERAL LEDGER

   1. Review general ledger accounts at end of most current
       month. Investigator will obtain the following infor-
       mation:

       a. Analyze balances with account numbers which are
           not listed on the chart of accounts and determine
           the adjustment required.

       b. Analyze debit accounts with credit balance and
           vice-versa to determine reason for unusual balance.

       c. Analyze self balancing accounts to explain balances:
           i.e. exchanges, with copy, taxes payable.

       d. Analyze year to date balances that are contrary to
           what the account would normally contain. (Example:
           Credit balance in an asset account or debit balance
           on a liability account etc.) Determine the ad-
           justment required.

       e. Review expense and income accounts - note and in-
           vestigate unusual balances or abnormally high
           amounts.

H.   CREDITS

   1. List credit number, names, dates of last ten credits
       on a worksheet. Allow a column for date of return of
       merchandise.

I.   BILLING

   1. Examine IBM billing correction log for the last month and
       record:

       a. Details of all errors made at the Branch during the
           preceding month, for later discussion at the field
           office.

   2. Examine five current days of billing packages from the
       field office. Test for conformity to billing procedure,
       SOP C-22, as to preparation of tapes, attachment of tapes
       to billing packages, use of addressograph plates, trans-
       mittal slip, account numbers of N/A, telephone number
       on new accounts, "flags" for coupon books, special in-
       structions for commission adjustments when required,
       "flag" for leases.

J.   ACCOUNTS RECEIVABLE

   1. Examine aging of accounts receivable at Branch for past
       six months, to determine trend in successful collections.
       Record these and discuss at field office. A bad aging
       may indicate failure to confirm calls (SOP C-4d), or im-
       proper confirmation calls, or improper follow-up of Credit
       Department correspondence and memos.

Exhibit 10-d (page 5)

K. LIMITS OF AUTHORITY

List last 20 disbursements and test whether approvals were proper within limits of Authority, SOP B-10. If last 20 items listed do not include items over $500 and over $1,000, locate two items over $500 and two items over $1,000 for similar test.

Vendor	Amount	SOP B-10 Page	Item	Proper Approval Yes	No

L. LEASED VEHICLES

List all leased vehicles in sales, service, warehouse, or administration. Complete last two columns at Branch:

Car No. or Serial No.	Driver Assigned	Examine Natl. Serv. Dept's Inspection Report On Hand (Yes) (No)	Describe Condition of Vehicle (A),(B) (C)or(D)	If (C) or (D) Remarks

Exhibit 10-d (page 6)

INTERNAL AUDIT PROGRAM FOR _____ CORPORATION
                BRANCH OFFICES

            AUDIT PROCEDURES - AT BRANCH OFFICE

    BRANCH OFFICE #_____ LOCATION _____

            MONTH AND YEAR_____

A. CASH

    Count and list all cash on hand upon arrival:

    1. Petty Cash - Note any vouchers in excess or contrary to limits
        established in SOP. Compare total to General Ledger account
        balance.

        a. Receipts from Cash Sales - Note by date of supporting in-
            voices of Bill Onlys if remittances are being made daily
            to Home Office, if not determine reason.

        b. Review and run tape of current day's receipts to be deposited
            to Petty Cash. Obtain a copy of deposit receipt from bank.
            After Bill Only copies have been pulled from the file, trace
            deposit receipts to pull outs. Observe if Bill Only copy
            is noted with "Cash Sale".

    2. Review servicemen't Expense Reports paid through Petty Cash
        and verify the following:

        a. The reports are prepared complete with approval indicated.

        b. Rate of reimbursement agrees with current company plan and
            stated amounts.

        c. Test that deductions are made from Expense Reports for
            portal to portal mileage.

        d. Verify that Servicemen with company cars are traveling the
            minimum mileage stated by company policy as required for
            servicemen.

B. ACCOUNTS RECEIVABLE

    1. Examine current Aged Trial Balance. Determine that large amounts
        represent the detail in customer alphabetical file.

    2. Review file of cash sales and COD's. Note that they are being main-
        tained on a current basis. Determine adequacy of internal control.

    3. List and investigate current balances long outstanding and note volume
        and practices used to resolve them.

    4. Investigate unusual debits, credits and product codings.

    5. Review and list last 10 leased sales and determine:
        a. Credit information is properly compiled and required reference
            and bank forms are completed.

Exhibit 10-e (page 1)

b. Both the lease and machine order form is signed.

c. Lease form is properly completed as to taxes, trade-ins, allowances, monthly payments.

d. Proper down payment has been obtained and monthly payment is properly calculated.

6. Review applicable credit and collection practices with procedural compliance. Select 10 representative accounts receivable to analyze:

a. Determine whether a shipment was made while account was past due.

b. Note if accounts receivables with outstanding balances over $500 are receiving special handling.

c. Determine that Home Office Credit Department Correspondence is answered promptly.

d. Establish that a collection tickler file or daily calendar follow up file has been established for collection purposes.

7. Review last 10 shipments against coupon orders and determine:

a. That coupons are being received with order or picked up on delivery.

b. That first coupon shipments on new orders are properly noted on original for deletion from coupon book when issued by the Home Office.

8. Review last 10 coupon orders and determine:

a. That all coupons in each book are issued in the same amount or value.

b. That each coupon represents a minimum of 10% of the total quantity or value.

c. That instructions on the original order for the deletion of the first coupon, if shipment has been made, are properly documented.

d. That terms are in accordance with the printed order.

e. That confirmation has been made as evidenced by Savicopy of checklist attached to Savicopy of order.

f. That originals of orders and confirmation have been sent to the Home Office and copies maintained in branch.

C. SALES

1. On a test basis review internal control of shipping orders and invoices as follows:

a. Review a selected group of the shipping - numerical copies of invoices for missing numbers. List numbers missing. Trace and record status. Refer unlocated shipping invoice numbers to branch office personnel for further follow up.

Exhibit 10-e (page 2)

b. Compare sequence of numbers with documented record of numbers sent from Home Office.

c. Determine that Bill Onlys and/or invoices are secured and available only to authorized personnel.

2. On a test basis, review internal control of credit memorandums as follows:

a. Review a selected group and record all missing numbers and locate them.

b. See if reason for the credit is clearly stated.

c. Note that Branch Administrator approves BCA as indicated on the form.

d. List a selected number of credit memorandums, or Bill Onlys, for trade-in allowances and verify the receipt or disposition of the equipment involved. Review method of internal control for trade-in machines. Examine perpetual care for trade-in machines. Follow up subsequent sale of trade-in machines and compare sale price to allowance. Determine that maximum allowance is in accord with SOP.

3. List 10 customer invoice numbers and date of transaction for deliveries made only by branch office personnel. Include 5 machine invoices in the test. Trace the delivery receipts.

D. INVENTORY

1. Conduct a tour of the warehouse and note the following:

a. Restrictions as to entry of unauthorized employees.

b. General condition and storage methods used for the merchandise.

c. Review with warehouse supervisor or manager methods and records employed in the receiving and shipping of merchandise.

2. Review the following files representing equipment and supplies not on the premises and not billed:

a. Shipments of merchandise to outside warehouses.

b. Shipments returned to other branches or main warehouse on Branch Transfers - See if Branch Transfer file is maintained on a current basis and note unresolved transactions dating back for an unreasonable length of time.

c. Equipment signed for by salesmen. Note dates, and reason for being outstanding for more than 60 days. Obtain serial number list from each salesman and compare to salesman's demo sheets. Examine overall method of controlling shipment and return of salesman's demo machines. Verify to Mach. Activity List Cards.

d. Equipment out on demonstration with customers not billed - ascertain that this situation does not exist.

3. Take or observe and assist in the taking of major items of physical inventory, including all machines, 8½" paper 11" paper and 8½" x 11"

Exhibit 10-e (page 3)

and 8½" x 14" cut sheet paper and all supplies. Review support for all reconciling items pertaining to inventory. Reconcile all physical inventory to perpetual inventory cards. Trace last twenty entries on each inventory card to shipping copy of invoice from which posted. Test twenty other entries at random for each card. Verify "PIENT" stamp on each.

4. Reconcile physcial machine inventory to Mach. activity list. Physically locate all equipment in the warehouses or determine its whereabouts.

5. Review the following reports relating to machines:

    a. Rental Billing Control - Compare to Mach. Activity List Rental Cards.

    b. Obtain at Home Office and compare to local demo and rental list.

E.   FIXED ASSETS

1. Verify the existence of vehicles listed at the Home Office. Complete schedule.

F.   PAYROLL

1. If checks arrive at the branch office during the audit, distribute them to employees; if not, verify by observation each employee listed on the time sheet from Home Office.

2. Review employee time sheet for several pay periods and note the following:

    a. Agreement with stated company policy in regard to standard hours of work. See S.O.P. and Personnel Handbook.

    b. Completeness of date, recording of hours and approval indicated.

    c. Possible violations of state laws relating to overtime limitations pertaining to female help.

G.   ACCOUNTS PAYABLE

1. Examine all vendor invoices awaiting receiving reports, noting any amounts outstanding for any undue length of time.

2. Examine all receiving reports awaiting invoices, noting any amounts outstanding for any undue length of time.

H.   SERVICE DEPARTMENT

1. Review internal control for accounting of service call reports used as follows:

    a. Select a block of numbers and list all missing numbers.

    b. Investigate and attempt to locate missing numbers, review practices being followed to locate missing numbers.

    c. Security provisions for unused Service Call Report.

Exhibit 10-e (page 4)

2. **Examine Service Department Index Card Files** for seventy day follow-up and one year follow-up on service contracts. Verify conformity to established procedures.

3. **Trace twenty Service Call Reports** into numerical machine files and into monthly Service Call Report File.

4. **Test twenty Service Call Reports** for proper entries in the Rental, Service Contract or Warranty boxes.

5. **Test last ten billable Service Call Reports** to Bill Only File. Verify timeliness with which they were billed.

6. **Test time required to dispatch** twenty service calls at random. List all calls requiring more than six hours to complete.

7. **Review parts log**, as to entries; including receipt and disbursement of parts on service calls. Verify that there is a part received for every part distributed.

8. **Review Perpetual Inventory Cards** to determine that entries are made on receipt of parts branch transferred and on disbursement of parts on Bill Onlys and on Service Call Reports. Determine that "Car Stock" of servicemen's parts is recorded. Review card entries for internally used parts.

9. **Test "Car Stock"** of one serviceman to entries on Perpetual Inventory Record.

10. **List serial and model numbers** below of inoperable machines, length of time inoperable and reason.

Model Number	Serial Number	Date Inoperable	Reason

11. Review work sheets for internal work in numerical machine file.

I. **COUPON LIABILITY**

1. **Test last ten coupon deliveries** to determine that shipment is not made without receipt of coupon.

2. **List coupon books issued** prior to the current year under review which show no redemption activity during the current year. Review with branch manager.

J. **GENERAL**

1. **Examine Permanent and Working Files** to determine that they are neat, up-dated and current. (SOP A-45)

2. **Determine that R.M.F.'s and Receiving Reports** are made out currently on receipt of merchandise. Examine merchandise awaiting forms. Establish elapsed time from receipt to preparation of form.

Exhibit 10-e (page 5)

3. Examine R.M.F.'s awaiting issuance of B.C.A.'s. Is B.C.A. issued timely?
   Test last ten B.C.A.'s to date of receipt of merchandise.

4. Open Bill Only File - Examine pink copies awaiting receipt of I.B.M.
   invoices. Are follow-ups made every ten days? Are copies dated in
   upper-right hand corner indicating follow-up date?

5. Examine completed files to determine that completed Bill Onlys, Branch
   Transfers, Receiving Reports and Bills of Lading are filed numerically.

6. Is Call Back Report filed with comments as to results?

7. Test last ten shipments of machines to the Mach. Shipments Report.
   Ascertain that the report is prepared on a daily basis.

8. Examine End of Month Closing Reports in S.O.P. A-14 to determine that all
   closing is made in conformity with procedure on a timely basis.

9. Verify that daily billing, during audit periods, is sent to Home Office
   daily.

10. If audit covers a period over the fifteenth or last day of the month,
    ascertain that billing is sent to Home Office at the close of the day,
    by special delivery mail and air mail, if required.

11. Examine all vendors invoices ready for Headquarters payment. Trace them to
    petty cash to determine payment has not been made by branch. Examine
    statements and consignees memos to be sure that there are no approvals
    on them. Verify that they are sent to Home Office Daily.

K. ORDER PROCESSING

1. Examine ten new accounts and ten reorder accounts for the following:

    a. Telephone number on Bill Only on new accounts.

    b. Bill of lading attached to all accounts.

    c. Purchase order number must appear.

    d. Test old accounts to Aged Trial Balance to determine delinquency,
        and proper credit approval.

    e. D. & B. rating or bank and two credit references on new accounts.

    f. Is tax collected on new accounts or tax exemption certificate attached?

    g. If lease, is check made out to leasing company in proper amount?

    h. Are terms in accordance with company procedures?

    i. Examine branch administrator's approvals. Are these done daily
        rather than in groups?

    j. Is confirmation call report attached, if applicable?

    k. Is proper order form used; that is, machine order form, coupon
        order form or N.C.R. salesman's order form.

Exhibit 10-e (page 6)

  l. Is customer's signed order attached on new accounts?

  m. Is equipment lease form accompanied by signed order form?

  n. Is salesman's order neat and legible; is Bill Only neat and legible; is master item terminology used? Test name and address of all accounts to master account list for proper entry.

  o. Are all orders properly approved by branch administrator, initialed and dated?

  p. Is commission properly computed on all accounts?

  q. Is shipping date on Bill Only.

  r. If rental, does per diem rate appear?

  s. Is shipping date of Bill Only same as bill of lading date; trace Bill Onlys to transmittal sheets to determine that date of transmittal sheet is same as Bill Only.

  t. If Q.D.A., is copy of Q.D.A. attached? Check rate of annual usage to specs.

  u. If conversion from rental, is rental allowance properly computed?

2. Examine advice to Home Office on termination of salesman regarding list of rental accounts to be credited to new salesman.

3. If no rentals were included in test in 1 above, examine last three rental orders for per diem dates and copies of rental agreements attached.

4. If no conversion from rental to sale was included in 1 above, examine last three conversions for proper computation of rental allowance.

5. Examine two trade-ins of   equipment (one of which is a lease) for proper computation of trade-in allowance and commission compensation.

6. Examine one loan machine to a paper user for computation of commission adjustment.

7. Review date of receipt of last ten machine orders at Branch and check date of delivery. Record delay in delivery dates more than one day after receipt of orders.

  Invoice No.   Customer   Reason for Delay

Exhibit 10-e (page 7)

L. **BILLING**

1. Check open transmittal slips to determine that they are kept current and that billing is completed and mailed to Home Office, within 24 hours of shipment.

2. Review file of tapes to determine that they are held for the time period, as required by SOP C-22. Are tapes headed up properly?

3. Determine that billing is split and mailed on the same day as typed.

4. Is addressograph file properly updated?

5. Are master item list definitions used in typing line items?

6. Is telex from Home Office confirming price attached to the paperwork to cover all dealer shipments from the Branch?

7. Verify sequence of credit memos.

8. Verify sequence of invoices.

M. **LEASED VEHICLES**

Visually examine all vehicles listed on schedule prepared at Home Office. Rate cars A, B, C, or D, and if rated C or D, fill in reasons as to why. Note on schedule and investigate cars listed, not on hand, and vice versa.

Exhibit 10-e (page 8)

INTERNAL AUDIT QUESTIONNAIRE FOR _____ _____ _____ INCORPORATED

BRANCH OFFICES

(Audit Procedures --- At Branch Offices)

BRANCH OFFICE:

LOCATION:

DATE OF AUDIT:

DATE OF PREVIOUS AUDIT:

OFFICE HOURS:

AUDITOR:

Exhibit 10-f (page 1)

I. GENERAL

   A. EVALUATION OF INTERNAL CONTROL

	Yes	No	Comments
1. Is fireproof and locked storage provided for:			
a. Personnel Files			
b. Customer Alphabetical Files			
c. Perpetual Inventory Records			
d. Service Department Numerical Machine File			
e. Customer Wheeldex or Kardex			
f. Bill of Lading Duplicate Warehouse copies			
g. Mach. Activity List Cards			
h. Employee Time Sheets			
i. Working Folders for Branch Administrator and Secretary			
j. Service Follow-up File			
k. One Year Service Contract File			
l. Service Call Report Nightly File			
2. Does the inventory and other Fixed Assets, including leaseheld improvements in the branch sales office, exceed $50,000 per each location?			
3. If so, is the excess reported to the Controller for additional insurance coverage?			
4. Is the record retention plan in A-29 being maintained?			
5. Do the files appear to be in good order?			
6. Does the work appear to be on a current basis?			
7. Names of Employees who have keys to the office and/or warehouse (Indicate o, w, or b for both with the name): and title.			
List Names:			

Exhibit 10-f (page 2)

	Yes	No	Comments

7a. Are monthly staff meetings held with the branch administrator, the branch manager, service manager and warehouse manager?

7b. Does service manager inspect all leased cars, those of salesmen and servicemen, quarterly?

7c. Inspect two leased cars at random. Are they in a state of repair?

7d. Inspect sales offices. Are lead cards filed away?

7e. Inspect general offices. Are all papers and files removed from desks at night?

7f. Inspect warehouse. Is stock neat and orderly on pallets?

Are shelves neat and orderly?

Are shipping supplies neatly arranged?

Are returned cartons carefully secured?

7g. Inspect service area. Are tools secure?

Are unused machines crated or covered?

Are work benches neat?

Are premises clean and orderly?

8. Names of employees who have keys to locks on file cabinets:

9. Does the branch administrator periodically review the work of his subordinates?

10. Who performs janitorial services? If outside agency, are outside personnel monitored? Is liability insurance carried by agency?

11. Is the lease for the premises available for inspection at the branch?

12. Are orderly files of Marketing Memos and Sales Slants maintained?

13. Is the SOP manual kept current? Is the Correction Checklist current?

14. Is the price book kept current? Is the price book correction checklist current?

Exhibit 10-f (page 3)

	Yes	No	Comments

15. Are interim procedures (prior to formal SOP changes) noted in proper sections of the SOP manual?

16. Are lead cards filed neatly by salesmen?

17. Are numerical files maintained for Return Authorizations, Branch Transfers Out, Purchase Orders, Mach. Shipment Reports, Shipping Copy of Bill Only, Bills of Lading, machine folders in the Service Department, Returned Merchandise Forms?

18. Is Call Back Report file being maintained?

II. CASH

    A. EVALUATION OF INTERNAL CONTROL

       1. Is a petty cash checkbook used?

       2. Is actual cash on hand other than checks locked? Is the cash box secured? Names of persons having access to petty cash:

       3. Are check receipts accompanied by a transmittal slip sent to home office daily?

       4. Are remittance advices mailed to the home office - If not, how often is check receipt examined for application advice? If not, is it prepared at branch for transmittal to home office?

       5. Names of employees who:

          a. open the mail

          b. file Customer Copy of Invoice

          c. transact cash sales

          d. account for consecutive invoice numbers

          e. approve service billings

       6. Are any customer checks being withheld from remittance to the home office?

       7. Have separate boxes been provided for cash sales and petty cash storage?

       8. Is the practice of not making advances, loans, or I.O.U.'s, or cashing personal checks being followed?

Exhibit 10-f (page 4)

	Yes	No	Comments

III. ACCOUNTS RECEIVABLE

    A. Evaluation of Internal Control

        1. Are Aged Trial Balance held for at least three months?

        2. Is the A.T.B. examined before approving every order for credit?

        3. If not, how are customer orders approved for credit prior to processing?

        4. Are credit department memos answered promptly?

        5. Is the credit approval stamp being used for all orders where applicable? Are the bank and trade references checked on machine orders? Are credit department forms evidencing this attached to the order?

IV. INVOICES AND CREDITS

    A. EVALUATION OF INTERNAL CONTROL

        1. Do the customers sign purchase orders pertaining to sales of equipment?

        2. Is the Rental Billing Control Sheet used to insure follow-up on monthly rental billing?

        3. Is the seventy-day follow-up file and the one-year follow-up file for service contracts being used on a current and timely basis to insure billing service contracts?

        4. Are invoices checked for accuracy of prices and commission computations? How and by whom?

        5. Are all original documents attached to order normally sent to the home office with copies attached to the branch copy? Is master account list checked for proper name and address, account number and tax code?

        6. If not, what check is made? Is master item list used to type proper description of items?

        7. If not, what is used?

Exhibit 10-f (page 5)

	Yes	No	Comments

8. Are back orders held on unnumbered orders?

9. Are back orders cross-referenced on the preceding and following bill only?

10. Is the Machine Order Form and Coupon Order Form used where applicable?

11. Are confirmation calls made on all machine and coupon orders?

12. Are confirmation checklists completed for each call?

13. Are conditional orders held and not billed?

14. Are signed machine orders obtained even on leased sales?

15. Are rental accounts reviewed quarterly to test paper usage or possible additional shipment?

V. INVENTORY

   A. EVALUATION OF INTERNAL CONTROL

      1. Does a central shipping and receiving point exist for all incoming and outgoing merchandise?

      2. Is merchandise for resale stored behind partitions separating stock areas from passageways and all other parts of the building?

      3. Are the partitions from the floor to the ceiling?

      4. Is access limited to the branch manager, the branch administrator, and warehouse manager only?

      5. Have unauthorized personnel been observed in the stockroom area?

      6. Is the stockroom area kept locked and separate from the office at all times?

      7. Is the person responsible for the merchandise always in the area?

      8. Which of the following are responsible for the repair parts inventory?

Exhibit 10-f (page 6)

	Yes	No	Comments

a. Shipping supervisor
b. Warehouse manager
c. Appointed serviceman
d. None of the above
e. Who?

9. Are Receiving Reports, Return Merchandise Forms, or Branch Transfer Receipts prepared for incoming merchandise? Are copies filed in numerical order in the Warehouse or office for the following:

   a. Merchandise returned from customer for credit

   b. Trade-in equipment

   c. Customer equipment in for repairs

   d. Equipment returned from demonstration (unless salesman's demo machine)

   e. Inventory purchases

   f. Even exchanges

10. Are Return Authorizations completed to cover the return or pickup of merchandise as follows:

    a. Merchandise returned from customer for credit

    b. Trade-in equipment

    c. Customer equipment in for repairs

    d. Equipment returned from demonstration (unless salesman's demo machine)

    e. Inventory purchases

    f. Even exchanges

11. Are Return Merchandise Forms marked NCI (No Credit Issued) for even exchanges? And all retail parts Returns?

12. Are Bill Only's marked with an 00 code in the shipping location column of even exchange shipments?

13. Is movement of outgoing merchandise supported by standard pre-numbered Bill Only's?

14. Are materials and supplies removed for

Exhibit 10-f (page 7)

	Yes	No	Comments

internal use or salesmen's demonstration use supported by unnumbered orders
properly approve by branch administrator?

15. Are unnumbered orders in 14 above tallied
and posted off Perpetual Inventory Cards
monthly? Is Demo Materials Form competed
monthly?

16. Are signed bills of lading received to
cover the shipment of all machines from the
warehouse?

17. Are signed delivery receipts kept on demos
and turned in by the salesman when a demon-
strator is converted to a sale, and attached
to original order?

18. Is issuance of repair parts to servicemen
covered by postings off Perpetual Inventory
Cards? Are unnumbered orders used for this
purpose filed by date, monthly?

19. Are machine movements posted to Mach.
Shipments Report?

20. Are conversions from demo to sale posted
on Mach. Shipments Report?

21. Are all machine movements or conversions
posted to Mach. Activity List cards?

22. Is the monthly physical inventory of machines
checked to Mach. Activity List card count?

23. Is master Machine Inventory Control Card
checked to Physical Machine Inventory
Count, monthly?

24. Are signed salesman's demo sheets reconciled
to Mach. Activity List Card counts?

25. Is Rental Billing Control List reconciled
monthly to Mach. Activity List Rental Cards?

26. Is a monthly list of customer loan and demo
machines prepared for the branch manager and
reviewed by him?

27. How many loan machines have been out
more than 60 days? Reason:

28. Is any customer-owned merchandise on
premises clearly identified as customer-
owned?

29. Are trade-in machines inventory cards
kept current?

Exhibit 10-f (page 8)

	Yes	No	Comments

30. Is oldest merchandise used first to
    fill orders?

31. Are 100-ft. rolls, only, used for 8½" & 11"
    demonstration materials? If no, reason:

VI. FIXED ASSETS

A. EVALUATION OF INTERNAL CONTROL

1. Were any disposals made during the
   year? List:

2. What, if any, vehicles are Company-
   leased, or Company-owned?

Vehicle	Year and Model	Use	Driven By	His Position	Condition

VII. PAYROLL

A. EVALUATION OF INTERNAL CONTROL

1. Before distribution, does the branch
   administrator or branch manager review
   checks for reasonableness of pay and is
   he or she personally making distribution?

2. Determine hours of work limitation for
   female help, as covered by State Law.

3. Have all employees filled out
   insurance enrollment cards, W-4 forms,
   application, Wonderlic test, Blue Cross/
   Blue Shield cards? Compare W-4 signature.

4. Have all sales personnel read and signed
   Corporate Trust Policy and Restrictive
   Covenant? Is this counterinitialed by
   branch manager or branch administrator?

5. Do sales and telephone sales personnel
   sign the employment letter when hired?

VIII. ACCOUNTS PAYABLE

A. EVALUATION OF INTERNAL CONTROL

1. Are vendor invoices sent to Home Office
   promptly for payment?

Exhibit 10-f (page 9)

	Yes	No	Comments

2. Are purchase orders for under $50 placed at the Branch Office by using a special purchase order containing this limitation?

3. Are most items under $50 bought and paid for through petty cash?

4. Are all items under $10 bought and paid for through petty cash?

IX. PURCHASING

A. EVALUATION OF INTERNAL CONTROL

1. Test inventory levels of two major items (8½" and 11" paper) to required inventory level as per SOP E-6.

Exhibit 10-f (page 10)

ONE DAY FIELD AUDIT PROGRAM

HOME OFFICE

A. PETTY CASH (A-24, B-10)

    1. Trace fund balance to general ledger $ _____

    2. Review reasonableness of expenses and distribution there of.

    3. Review field engineer expenses, as follows:

        a. Reports complete with approval

        b. Rate of reimbursement agrees with current company plan, those with car insurance receiving 1¢/mile less.

        c. Test that deductions are made for portal to portal mileage.

        d. Verify employment   Schedule ____|____

    4. Reimbursement of fund limited to once a month?

    5. Query petty cash clerk for any immediate problems requiring follow up at branch. (Note below)

B. SALES/ACCOUNTS RECEIVABLE/CREDIT (C-22, C-25)

    1. Review invoice register for consecutive numeric sequence of invoices. Copy H/) accounting schedule of missing numbers for follow up at branch   Schedule ____|____

    2. Discuss any immediate problems with respective department heads...

        a. Retail sales with order/billing

        b. Dealer sales with dealer service

        c. Lease charge backs with credit's doubtful account collection desk

    3. Copy current D5 letters held by credit correspondent for follow up at branch. Indicate in margin of letter type of branch action being taken.

Exhibit 10-g (page 1)

C. INVENTORY

   1. Review demo usage report (purchasing department)
       if excessive copy for review at branch   Schedule _____|_____

   2. Copy branch inventory projections and requests.
       Valid at branch, follow up consistent shortages, etc.

D. PAYROLL

   1. Copy most recent time sheet and verify to payroll
       records   Schedule _____|_____

   2. If present at branch on payday, arrange that pay-
       checks be sent to auditor's attention. Have payees
       sign for checks. Retain and return for further re-
       view all undistributed checks   Schedule _____|_____

   3. Check out personnel ratios against "Box Score" held
       by budget manager

   4. Review sales personnel payroll records for proper
       employment letters

   5. Review past sales personnel termination payroll drop
       sheets for disposition of demo machines trace into
       inventory records at branch. Sight, if necessary. Schedule _____|_____

Exhibit 10-g (page 2)

ONE DAY FIELD AUDIT PROGRAM

_____ BRANCH OFFICE

A. PETTY CASH (A-24, B-10)

1. Perform a quick reconciliation, as follows:
    check book balance
    Add: Prior period reimbursement (if in transit)
         unreimbursed vouchers on hand
         cash on had (should be minimal)
         salesman advances (even if unauthorized)
    Total (should equal general ledger balance
    If difference between total (above) and general
    ledger balance is two (2)% of less, write off through
    countersigning a voucher with the branch administra-
    tor for difference. Mark voucher "cash short." If
    difference is greater, complete remaining audit and,
    if time permits, investigate.   Schedule ____|____

B. ACCOUNTS RECEIVABLE/CREDIT (C-25)

    1. Spot check ATB for long overdue balances. Note
        volume and explanations. Resolve.   ____|____

                                                                Y   N

    2. Credit department approval obtained when doubtful
        accounts are shipped?   [   ]   [   ]

    3. Home office credit correspondence answered prompt-
        ly with follow up of D5 letter?   [   ]   [   ]

    4. Is ATB checked before each order is shipped?   [   ]   [   ]

C. BILLING (C-18b)

    1. Major user log

        a. all pertinent information entered in log
            (name, address, customer #, machine #s, etc.)

        b. Trace machine # to SAL

        c. Is paper shipped automatically each month?
            Attach examples of non-compliance   Schedule ____|____

        d. If not, is it at customer request?

        e. at expiration of contract, is customer billed
            the difference in price per roll in event of
            purchase of less than contracted amount?
            Attach examples of non-compliance   Schedule ____|____

        f. Trace last five paper shipments to invoice,
            then to perpetual inventory records. Is post-
            ing copy marked "Pient"?   Schedule ____|____

Exhibit 10-h (page 1)

2. Coupon Books (CPN 5/18/72)

    a. All pertinent information entered in log? ☐ ☐

    b. All coupons issued in same amount for paper? ☐ ☐

    c. Each coupon represents a minimum of 10% of total quantity purchased? ☐ ☐

    d. Coupons redeemed sequentially? Attach example of non-compliance.

    e. Trace redumption of coupon to perpetual inventory records.

3. Billing/Order Processing (C-22, C-25)

    a. Are all orders billed and shipped within twenty-four hours? Verify

    b. Follow up missing invoice numbers called from invoice register in home office   Schedule ____|____

    c. Review daily invoicing (before bursting) for proper numeric sequence.   Schdule ____|____

    d. Review credits (A-3, A-5)

        1. Trace most recent IMF to actual returned merchandise

        2. Trace IMF to credit invoice and investigate any untimely delay

        3. If machine, trace to SAL and perpetual inventory

        4. Dealer returns should be supported by proper paper work (RA, IMF, etc.)

    e. B/Lading attached to invoice? ☐ ☐

    f. Bank and two credit references appended to new account? ☐ ☐

    g. Account number assigned? Trace to Rollex file.

    h. Confirmation call attached to machine and coupon book orders? ☐ ☐

D. INVENTORY (A-16, A-21, A-32)

1. Determine that all merchandise is accounted for:

    a. Branch transfers in transit?

    b. Outside warehouses

Exhibit 10-h (page 2)

        1. Review executive permission

        2. Sight warehouse receipt/billing

    c. Machines on loan (from SAL). Note length of time out.   Schedule _____|_____

    d. Machines on demo (C6c, C6d)

        1. Compare SAL and salesman demo sheets. Follow up discrepancies.   Schedule _____|_____

        2. Demo sheet signed by salesman and counter-signed? ☐ ☐

    e. Total machines in SAL should equal count plus all machines infield save sales and leases

2. Spot count 8½" 220 and 230 paper and reconcile with perpetual records

3. Compare rental billing control with SAL, all rentals billed beginning of each month? ☐ ☐

4. Trace recent inter branch and receiving IMF's to perpeutal inventory records.

5. Count and reconcile some high cost parts to perpetual inventory.

E. FIELD ENGINEERING (A-38, A-39, B-25c)

1. Select some service history cards at random

    a. Trace machine number to service numeric file and satisfy that card data agrees with latest call report

    b. Service contract expired? New one automatically billed?

    c. No contract, custom billed? Timely? Labor and parts billed at current retail price?

    d. Number of inoperative machines in service appear excessive? Explain

F. PAYROLL

1. Head count branch personnel against most recent time sheet.

2. If present on pay day, follow procedures in home office payroll program RE: Check off.

Exhibit 10-h (page 3)

ONE DAY FIELD AUDIT PROGRAM

EVALUATION OF INTERNAL CONTROL

A. FILES AND GENERAL REVIEW   YES   NO

   1. Fireproof and locked storage provision

      a. Personnel files

      b. Customer alpha files

      c. Perpetual inventory records

      d. Service numerical machine file

      e. Customer rolldex

      f. Warehouse duplicate b/ladings

      g. Savin activity list (SAL) cards

      h. Employee time sheet

      i. Service contract follow up file

      j. Service contract file

      k. Major user control log

      l. Coupon book control log

      m. Salemen's demo sheets

      n. Price books

   2. Files appear to be in good order?

   3. Paper work current?

   4. Orderly files of marketing memos, training memos, and new product fliers maintained?

   5. SOP manual and correction check list current?

   6. Price book and correction check list current?

   7. Are interim procedures (prior to formal SOP changes) noted in proper sections of SOP manual?

Exhibit 10-i (page 1)

8. Are numerical files maintained for:

    a. Return authorizations

    b. IMFS

    c. Purchase orders

    d. Shipping copy of invoice

    e. B/Lading

    f. Machine folders in service area

9. Inspect sales and general offices

    a. Sales lead card filed?

    b. All paper work and files cleared from desks
       at day's end?

B. WAREHOUSE

1. Inspect

    a. Stock neatly stacked and palletized?

    b. Shelves neat and orderly?

    c. Packing and shipping supplies neat?

    d. Are returns kept separate and secure before
       replacement into inventory?

    e. Repacking of returns done?

2. Is saleable merchandise partitioned off and separate
    from passageways and all other parts of building?

3. Are partitions floor to ceiling?

4. Is access to warehouse limited to branch manager, branch
    administrator and warehouse personnal? Observe.

5. Any unauthorized personnel observed in stockroom area?

6. Is stock room area kept locked and separate from sales
    and general offices at all times?

7. Is person responsible for merchandise and parts always
    in his respective area?

Exhibit 10-i (page 2)

C. SERVICE   YES   NO

    1. Inspect

        a. Are tools secure?

        b. Unused machines crated and/ or covered?

        c. Are work benches neat?

        d. Area swept clean? Orderly?

        e. Are parts locked away?

    2. Does service manager, alone, have access to parts
        inventory?

    3. Who, of the following, is responsible for repair
        parts inventory?

        a. Warehouseman

        b. Service manager

        c. Appointed service man

        d. Someone else? Who?

D. SECURITY

    1. Name and title of employees who have keys to office
        and warehouse.

    2. Name and title of employees who have keys to file cabinets.

    3. Conduct tour of branch, check all outside windows and doors
        for proper locks and easy access. Note any areas requiring
        additional security.

Exhibit 10-i (page 3)

WAREHOUSE SECURITY & PROCEDURES
Effective Thursday, 11/12/

A. New Hours

8 A.M. - 4:30 P.M. No night work or overtime.

B. Our Trucks

1. To be loaded in the morning at 8 A.M. and on the road by 8:30 A.M.
    They are to return by 4:45 P.M.

2. All undelivered products to be taken off the truck, checked in by the
    plant foreman, and rescheduled for the next day's load. After unloading,
    affix original bill of lading and order to the load. Order is to be re-
    initialed in lower right-hand corner with a ② to the right of the
    initials, indicating that it was reloaded and rechecked for a second time.

3. There is to be no product on a truck overnight (this includes outside
    trailers).

    a) If, in an emergency, the truck cannot be unloaded, then a seal,
        logged and identified, must be affixed by the foreman in the evening.
        The following morning the foreman must verify that the seal was not
        broken, must break seal and make an entry in the log. The log will
        show the truck number or description, seal number, date sealed,
        initials, date seal broken, initials.

4. Trucks are to be inspected weekly by warehouse foreman to check all
    locks.

C. Doors

1. All warehouse personnel are to use the regular employee entrance.
    The northeast door will be locked.

2. All bay doors are to be kept in a closed position unless a truck
    is in place, loading or unloading.

3. All emergency doors are to be kept closed.

4. When closing, in the evening, all doors are to be locked by the foreman;
    these include bay doors, exit doors, warehouse office door. The follow-
    ing personnel will have keys to the above doors:

        a) Warehouse manager
        b) Warehouse foreman
        c) Director of personnel

No other personnel will have keys, nor may they borrow keys, without
the express written approval of the Controller.

5. All files are to be locked within the office, with particular
    attention to 4-drawer files storing invoices, copies of bills
    of lading and orders.

Exhibit 10-j (page 1)

6. Special files containing inventory control data on supplies and machines are to be locked and these separate keys are to be controlled by the inventory control group only. One key is to be held by the Accounting Services Manager, the other by the Inventory Control Manager. No other personnel will have keys, nor may they borrow keys without the express written approval of the Controller.

7. Main warehouse doors into the office area are to be locked, by the guard, when the lights are turned out, no later than 6 P.M. Foreman assists guard when he leaves.

8. Keys and locks for doors are to be changed every six months.

D. Internal

1. All product is to be moved only with the proper paperwork attached as follows:

Outgoing merchandise - Orders, Branch Transfers, with Bills of Lading
Incoming merchandise - Receiving Reports, Branch Transfers, RMF's
Internal transfers - Locator tickets

2. Clipboards are to be used, along with order picking trucks or fork lifts.

3. Reserve product or machines are to be released by inventory desk assigning specific location to pull product from.

4. Packing slips in self-adhesive envelopes are to be plainly visible on all shipments.

5. No bills of lading and orders are to remain in the office, but must be kept with pending orders to be released to office after shipment by common carriers or our own truck.

E. Order Picking

1. To be done by persons designated by plant foreman.

2. All orders are to be initialed in the lower left-hand corner.

F. Order Packing or Checking

1. To be done by another and different person chosen by the foreman.

2. Checker's initials are to be put on the bottom, middle of the order, or Branch Transfer.

G. Shipping or Truck Loading

1. To be finally done by a third party chosen by the foreman (to include the manager, foreman, assistant manager, or office designee).

Exhibit 10-j (page 2)

2. His initials are to be put on the bottom right side.

Summary: All orders are to have three sets of initials before it can be considered valid (including UPS shipments).

3. Our truck manifest should be signed by driver for unit count verification. Manifest is to be filed in date order and kept for one year.

4. Foreman should personally check at least one different load daily and supervise all other loading.

5. No outside trailers are to be loaded unless a cab is available for immediate shipment that day.

H. Receiving

1. All trucks and product received (including returned merchandise) is to be listed on a dock receiving log showing date, vendor, carrier, pro number, package count, and receiving report number, or RMF or Branch Transfer number, which can be posted no later than 24 hours later.

2. The 4-part detailed Receiving Report, RMF, or Branch Transfer, is to be made out within 24 hours on all items received. There are three approved locations for creating Receiving Reports, RMF's, or Branch Transfers:

a) Warehouse
b) Parts Department
c) Mail Room

The 24-hour exception will apply to large parts shipments only. However, a blank Receiving Report or RMF must be made out showing the vendor or customer, marked "Subject to detailed count."

Note: The foreman or a responsible person must sign Receiving Report, Branch Transfer, or RMF, after completion.

I. Storage

We have a fluid reserve storage system.

1. Any product can be stored in any vacant bay.

2. Locator cards must be created, affixed and turned into inventory control showing item stored, count, location, date and initials of warehouseman who put away. Where machines are stored only one ticket for the bay is necessary, but all serial numbers must be shown.

3. Locator tickets are to be matched with Receiving Reports, Branch Transfers, or RMF's and turned in together.

4. See foreman for method of writing up serial numbers.

Exhibit 10-j (page 3)

J. Inventory Usage

1. Inventory control is the only group allowed to assign product
    to be moved from reserve areas.

2. We are to use oldest product first, regardless of where stored.

K. Forward Storage Areas

Each product other than machines has been assigned a forward permanent
location from which orders are to be picked; when the forward bay runs
low or out, another unit from reserve must be put in place and straps
as well as corrugated material are to be removed. (Reserve unit can
only be released through inventory control.)

L. Returned Goods

1. Returned goods, prior to creating RMF, are to be in a fixed location,
    clearly marked. After the RMF is created, move to a second location,
    pending a decision as to whether the merchandise should be repacked
    or stored.

2. Foreman is to review daily receipts to determine whether product is
    resalable and can be put into the forward location, or if item is
    to be repacked and sent to a repack station.

3. Repacking shall be kept current on a weekly basis.

M. Uniforms

All warehouse personnel, including drivers and helpers, will wear uniforms.

N. Short Record

Deliveries which are made to customers and which are short are to be recorded
in a log, with a page for each driver, showing date, customer, product,
quantity short, and driver's initials. Drivers will be required to initial
this log personally.

O. Loading or Unloading

The warehouse manager, warehouse foreman, assistant manager, or office
designee is to be assigned to each "open bay" to cover all incoming or
outgoing trucks. An open bay with a truck or trailer in place, incoming
or outgoing, is never to be left unsupervised by one of these four persons.

P. Pickups

There is to be an RA number to cover all pickups.

DISTRIBUTION: Warehouse Manager; Audit Manager; Systems Manager; Controller.

Exhibit 10-j (page 4)

(FORMAT OF ACTUAL REPORT)

SUMMARY AUDIT REPORT

April 22, 19___

To: Executive Vice President
     Vice President for Marketing

An internal audit was performed at   Corporation, Atlanta Branch, in May 19   with the following results:

1. The plan of the Warehouse does not permit restricted entry;
2. A shortage of one machine and 40 rolls of inventory was
   observed;
3. Petty cash loans are made to employees, contrary to procedure;
4. Machine Order Forms are not being used.

Rating - The Branch is rated (C)

John Smith, Audit Manager

sc: Controller

Exhibit 10-k

(FORMAT FOR AUDIT REPORT)

AUDIT REPORT

CORPORATION

_____ BRANCH

Date Submitted: April 22, 19_
Written by: Auditor or Supervisor
Submitted by: Auditor

Copies to: Controller
             Branch Administrator
             Branch Manager
             Zone Manager
             Regional Manager
             (Show names, not titles)

Exhibit 10-I (page 1)

(FORMAT OF ACTUAL REPORT)

AUDIT REPORT

_____ CORPORATION

_____ BRANCH

April 22, 19.__

To: Controller

An internal audit was performed at   Corporation,
Atlanta Branch, in May 19 , and, unless otherwise indicated, was concerned
with assets and liabilities recorded as of April 30, 19 .

A. Synopsis of Principle Items

     All items covered by the audit are not included in this report. The
     following points are considered to be of significant interest to the
     readers:

1. Petty cash was not in balance and personal loans are being made to
    employees (SOP 123).

2. Access to the warehouse area cannot be restricted (SOP 456).

3. 40% of machine orders tested were not written on Machine Order Form
    (SOP 789).

B. Inventory

1. Access to the warehouse, with the exception of repair parts, cannot
    be restricted, due to the present layout of the premises. This could
    contribute to an inventory loss (SOP 123).

2. 8½" paper was 40 rolls short from Perpetual Inventory.

3. Salesman's demo sheets not countersigned by Manager, Administrator, or
    Service Manager. One machine could not be accounted for (SOP 456)

C. Service Department

1. Service Reports are not filed on a timely basis in the numbered machine
    file (SOP 123).

D. Rating - Branch is rated (C).

We wish to express our appreciation for the courtesy and cooperation extended
to us during the course of the audit.

                                   _____
                                   John Smith, Branch Auditor

Exhibit 10-I (page 2)

To: Executive Vice President   Subject: Audit Appraisals -
                                                          Office and Accounting
                                                          Functions at Branch
                                                          Offices

This report covers the appraisals of Branch offices audited during the
first six months of 1967. The appraisals are classified as follows:

(A) Conditions were appraised as generally satisfactory

(B) Conditions were appraised as generally satisfactory, with
     some areas being considered as less than satisfactory

(C) Conditions were appraised as generally less than satisfactory,
     with some areas being considered as satisfactory

(D) Conditions were appraised as generally less than satisfactory

(A)	(B)	(C)	(D)
Name	Name	Name	Name

Indicate, in a footnote, any exceptions to the standard or the procedures
which were not included for any particular Branch.

Copies of the summary audit reports are attached, for your referral.

                                        _____
                                              Audit Manager

sc: Vice President for Marketing
     Controller

                         Exhibit 10-m

INDIVIDUAL SYSTEMS REPORT

FREIGHT PAYMENT PLAN
AUDIT REPORT

Period of audit: Sept., Oct. & Nov. 19__
By: ,Field Auditor
To: ,Controller
                   ,Accounting Services Mgr.
Date submitted: January 6, 19__

General

A test check examination of the freight payment plan was performed
on the periods indicated. In an effort to further insure accuracy,
a roll-forward method was utilized from August 19

This report consists of two parts, as follows:

        Part I - Itemized deficiencies
        Part II - Itemized corrective recommendations

Exhibit 10-n (page 1)

Freight Payment Plan   -2-   Jan. 8, 19__

Part I

DEFICIENCIES IN APPLICATION OF PLAN

1. Sight drafts are not being received from First National City Bank on a daily basis.

2. Imprest balance of $10,000 appears excessive, as illustrated by aggregate deposits vs. monthly ending book balance.

Sept.	19__	$2,680.37	$9,413.43
Oct.	19__	4,400.00	6,728.92
Nov.	19__	4,500.00	7,780.96

3. Freight bills are not audited as to rates.

4. Copies of drafts are not being presented to Data Processing for key punching disbursements journal.

5. Voucher proof program is used by Data Processing as disbursement journal.

6. Control log of issued drafts, are not kept on current basis.

7. Duplicate copies of invoices are paid on a direct basis to freight companies under plan.

8. More than one vendor number is being issued to some vendors without justification.

9. Inaccurate clerical recording of vendor invoice numbers.

10. Procedure does not define internal security requirements for unissued drafts.

Part II

RECOMMENDED CORRECTIVE ACTION

1. November 12, 19__ plan should be revised to agree with common business practices of monthly statement being accompanied by cancelled drafts.

Exhibit 10-n (page 2)

Freight Payment Plan   -3-   Jan. 8, 19___

2. Due to the limited period covered and additions being made
   under the plan, a conclusion cannot be rendered. However, it
   is suggested that a review be made in the future by accounting
   to ascertain the most economical imprest amount.

3. ICC rates and rate changes should be maintained on a current
   basis, by accounts payable.

4. A detailed listing of vendor invoice numbers are necessary
   for internal control. Therefore, continuation of the existing
   run is justified.

5. Report should be reheaded as freight disbursement journal.

6. Procedure should be strictly adhered to.

7. Direct payments should be eliminated to all freight companies
   under the plan. Where duplicate payments were made, immediate
   follow-up is in order for reimbursement.

8. Accounting should conduct a review and eliminate duplicate
   numbers for vendors and report findings to Data Processing.

9. Detailed listing of disbursements furnished by Data Processing
   should be checked to original documents.

10. Unissued drafts should be kept in locked cabinet, with number
    control by authorized accounting personnel.

Exhibit 10-n (page 3)

AUDIT PROGRAM

I. Accounts receivable
    A) Obtain detailed aged trial balance, by customer, as of _____.
        If already reconciled* to General Ledger, obtain a copy of the
        reconciliation and foot and agree all items to proper corresponding
        books and records. Report detail trial balance.

    1) Review reconciling items; obtain details and all supporting
        documents therefor. Verify the accuracy of each.

    2) Select 20% (stratified selection - large accounts only) of open
        Accounts Receivable for position confirmation as of _____.

    3) Set up control worksheet and numerical systems to control the A/R
        confirmations.

    4) Test check 10% of smaller accounts (not selected for confirmation)
        to local telephone directory for name and address.

    5) Circularize receivables selected in step (2). Summarize results
        and follow up and note all exceptions.

    6) Age (or obtain an ageing of) open receivables according to current
        (0 - 30 days), 30, 60, 90, and over 120 days.
        1) Confirm (positive) all accounts over 60 days over $_____.

    7) Obtain an analysis of the Provision for doubtful accounts.
        1) Detail method of providing the bad debt write-off.
        2) Test the provision for adequacy against the results of previous tests.
        3) Review credit correspondence for further status of possible
            uncollectibles.

    8) Test trace subsequent collections (receipts) subsequent to A/R cutoff
        date.

* If not reconciled, reconcile!

Exhibit 10-o (page 1)

II. FIXED ASSETS

  A) Obtain detail of Fixed Assets Inventory (listing). Obtain copy
      of invoice support for major items.

  B) Analyze the various Fixed Asset accounts for the current year and
      fully detail the method of capitalizing (standards, etc.).

  C) Analyze the various Depreciation provision accounts. Fully detail
      the method of providing the depreciation reserve.

  D) Vouch all additions and deletions from the all fixed asset accounts.

  E) Examine the respective fixed assets recorded in the Automobile &
      Furniture & Fixtures and any copy machines located in Home Office
      and included as a Fixed Asset.
      1) Reconcile this inventory in value to the account records.
          Note and follow up significant differences.
      2) Compare to detail records, and test trace to purchase documents
          (vouchers) selected large items. Test pricing - cost.
      3) Note condition, age and where possible estimate value (replacement).

  F) For Rental and Major User Machines - Obtain a complete listing as
      of _____ reflecting the following data:
      1) Customer Name
          Address
          Type of Machine (description)
          Length of time in service (app)
          Machine serial number
          Monthly billing amount of rental
          Paper price
          Copy of Contract (if any exists)
          Average paper usage last 3 months (Asterisk if less then contract
          specifies)
      2) Accumulated depreciation on the equipment reflected in F) 1)
          above. Also, an explanation of depreciation method (life, method,
          etc.)

  G) See sales for additional tests of Rental (billing)

III. INVENTORY

  A) Supplies
      1) If a detailed perpetual inventory record exists, obtain (or
          extract) a listing of all supplies on hand.
      2) If no perpetual exists, physically verify (by count) the supplies
          inventory. Obtain clerical help/supreme court.
      3) Note the costing procedure and price out the supplies inventory
          on detailed worksheets. Test costing to invoices.

Exhibit 10-o (page 2)

4) Check cutoff procedures by controlling receiving reports and
shipping papers. ("Close down" shipping area while the physical
inventory is in process*). Note all items in transit, follow
up and document validity of these. Obtain details of any
cosignment (or other inventory out on loan, demo, trial, etc.)
and verify these. Obtain appropriate supporting documentation.
Remove from inventory items picked/ordered prior to inventory
date. Segregate these physically and do not count. Count all
other items and list these showing product description, code,
number of pieces, etc.

5) Check condition of inventory items
(Items B to E apply to dealer aquisition only)

B) <u>RIP</u>

1) If a detailed perpetual inventory record exists, obtain
(or extract) list of all machine inventory on-hand
(by serial number).

2) Verify that all inventory exists by physical count/match
to perpetual inventory; or list each machine by TYPE, Serial
No. etc.

3) List RIP machines by location if off premises, and type of
placement, i.e., rental, demo, major user.

4) Verify that all machines "sold" have been replaced;note
exceptions.

5) If foreign machine is included, cost a zero value.

6) Reconcile prices out inventory to General Ledger.

C) For (A) & (B) above, review all transactions (interim) from last
statement date to physical inventory date (on a broad basis to control
activity) work back to reconcilable figures. Similarly, to last
RIP replacement date.

D) Verify that all inventory - foreign has been either paid for or
reflected as a liability.

E) Note: If foreign inventory is saleable or non-saleable.

IV. SALES/A.R./OTHER

1. Sales cutoff/MUP & Rentals - Obtain copies of all contracts
(MUP or Rental if available).

   A. Check billing on MUP and Rentals (verify to F.A. - list).

   B. Trace to A/R statement / Sales.

   C. Less Broadly.

   D. Note unusual billing procedure, amount, etc.

Exhibit 10-o (page 3)

       E. Select locations and confirm these (use discretion for selection; positive confirmation).

   2. SALES / OTHER

      A) Obtain a master listing of all customers (including name, address and also type of machine, serial number, sale price, and any other pertinent marketing information if possible.

      B) Examine billing on a test basis and trace to data provided in A), & B) above. Also trace to A/R list; and test A) above to that list.

V. CASH

1. Determine amount and location of all cash funds, bank accounts, and other negotiable assets.

2. Review and investigate internal control procedures. Evaluate such procedures by identification of selected transactions.

3. Count all cash on hand.

4. Check all bank reconciliations. If incomplete, these should be completed.

5. Confirm bank balances.

VI. TAXES

1. Review the net income per books with taxable income to be reported in the current year's tax returns.

2. Summarize beginning and end-of-the-year balances of estimated liabilities and provisions not deductible for tax purposes.

3. Review computation of federal income taxes.

4. Review state and local taxes. Compare with last period.

5. Review withholding procedures and test their functioning. Check accruals.

VII. CONTINGENT LIABILITIES

1. Establish the existence or absence of any contingent liabilities.

2. Determine the effect of any existing or contemplated litigations.

3. List long term liabilities for leases.

4. Any other.

VIII. ACCOUNTS PAYABLE

1. Check verification procedures and authorizations.

2. Test monthly statements from vendors.

Exhibit 10-o (page 4)

3. Review unrecorded purchases of goods and services.

IX. <u>EXPENSES</u>

1. Review and test Internal Accounting Control and Check.

2. Review, analyze and test operating accounts. Compare with last period and obtain satisfactory evidence to explain changes.

3. Review travel expenses by tracing test transactions.

4. Review commission payments.

XI. <u>GENERAL</u>

1. Note details on operation with regard to number of employees. If possible, detail salary, job responsibility, etc.

2. List all service contract by customer, effective date, expiration date, asterisk those over 1 year and those on foreign equipment, model no., price and note any special conditions in remarks column.

3. Obtain a copy of all insurance policies covering inventory, fixed assets, autos.

XII. <u>SPECIAL PROCEDURES FOR SUBSIDIARIES</u>

1. Check minutes of directors and stockholder's meetings.

2. Reconcile surplus accounts.

3. Review inter-company profit eliminations.

4. Review reconciliations of inter-company accounts.

Exhibit 10-o (page 5)

**Functions Most Frequently Reassigned
from Treasurer to Controller**

Financial Management
Maintenance of equity position and working capital
  ratio
Analysis and interpretation of economic conditions

Capital Expenditure
Analysis of need for appropriations
Control of payments

Budgets
Preparation of budgets
Administration of budget program

Inventories
Maintenance of inventory control records
Taking and costing inventories

Cash Management
Handling petty cash
Formulation of disbursement procedures for:

  Accounts payable
  Payrolls
  Pension plan payments
  Interest
Cash budgets

Taxes
Preparation and filing of tax returns
Appraisal of effect of taxes on company

Accounting
General and cost accounting
Plant and equipment accounting

Auditing
Internal auditing and checking
Arranging for outside credits

Financial Statements
Preparation, issuance and interpretation of financial
  statements
Preparation of SEC report (Form 10K)

Office Management and Methods

Government Orders and Regulations
Compliance with government orders and regulations

Statistics
Assembly, preparation and analysis of statistics

Payrolls
Preparation of wage, salary and confidential payrolls

Exhibit 11-a

ACCOUNTING CALENDAR

DAILY
Temp. PABST.
Cash Summary & Loan Schedule
Cost of Sales Control
Manual Checks
Taping-Depositing
Cash Receipts

WEEKLY
Wed.—Car Maintenance Checks
Thurs.—Travel Exp. Checks
Fri.—Freight Checks
Fri.—Union Payroll Checks

BI-WEEKLY
Reg. Payroll Checks
Private Payroll Checks
Blue Book—Payroll Summary

MONTHLY
Correction to COSAS
Status Report
Branch Petty Cash Reimbursements

1. Rent Checks Hand CD Summary	2. Payroll Summary	3. Depository Receipts	4. Blue Book (P/R sum.)	5. Cash Reg. for 10th	6. Over-rides A/R.J.E.
7. C/R Summary	8. Life & Health Ins. Union Welfare Union Dues	9. Closing of Freight Plan	10. A/P Checks Closing of Purchases	11.	12.
13. Bank Recs. G.S.A. report	14. Bank Recs. Special A/R Schedule	15. P/R Tax- State-City Summary-Reconciliation of Aged A/R.	16.	17. Flash P-L Report Gross Profit % Sch. Machine sold per salesman Final Pabst	18. Depository Receipts Sch. of MLP paper sales
19. Cash Req. for 25th. Auto Leasing Report Sales Tax Returns	20. Sales-Service Comm.	21. Docustat cust. comm.	22. Consolidated Financial Statements	23. Sch. of Expenses Financial Statements—Senox —SBMCL —Natl Photo	24. Financial Statements —EBM —Docustat —DE. Co
25. A/P Checks Sales Tax Returns Sch.—Loans to —Travel Advances —Deposits —Sales Sal. to Retail Sales	26. Cash Req. for 1st Missing Billing Control Sch. of Royalty Income Cafeteria P-L	27. EBM—Halifax P-L Sch.—Average price on coupon shipments	28. Update Stock Options F.A. Schedules Patent Sch. Deferred Prod. Dev. Sch.	29. Inventory Evaluation for Insurance Co. Def. Prof. Fees. Sch.	30. Sales Tax Ret. Overrides Notes Rec. Sch.

QUARTERLY
Mr. Smith Interest
1/1, 3/1, 6/1, 9/1
Apr, July, Oct, Jan
-P/R Tax Return
-Royalty Exp. checks
-Financial Release
- Fed & State Est. Taxes (see tax calendar)
-Stock Purchase Plan
-Wage Continuation Insurance
-Correction to CASA
-Rolls Shipped per Machine
-Reconciliation of Rolls

SEMIANNUAL
Physical Inventory
CoSAS/CASA Reconciled

ANNUALLY
W2's, 1099, 1096, 3692,
Fed'l Ins.
ABC Min. Royalty- Jan
Fed'l Tax Return
Certified Audit
Hertz-Mileage Credit

Exhibit 11-b

LOAN AGREEMENT LETTER

FROM: Treasurer
TO: Employee
DATE: 10/30/

SUBJECT: Loan - $2,100

Effective October 19, 19   , we are making a $2,100 loan to you.
This loan will be evidenced by a demand note, in the amount of
$2,100, plus 6% per annum interest.

We understand that this loan is for personal purposes and that you
herewith authorize payroll deductions, over a 2 1/2 year period
(65 bi-weekly payroll deductions, to include principal plus interest).

If, at any time during the tenure of this loan, you exercise any of
your ABC stock options, you agree that ABC will hold this stock as
collateral for repayment of the loan. During this period, if you
sell shares of stock which we are holding for collateral, the
proceeds will be used to repay the loan and any balance will be
returned to you.

It is clearly understood that the purpose of this loan is not to
purchase option shares of ABC stock.

You further understand that this is a demand note which is callable
at any time, at ABC's option. It is not our present intention to
demand payment of this note as evidenced by the 2 1/2 years of
payroll deductions which are being made above, but ABC retains the
right to discontinue these payroll deductions and to call for payment
of the remaining balance on the demand note, at any time, at its
option.

_____
Treasurer

                                    AGREED TO AND ACCEPTED

                                    _____

                                    Date:_____

Exhibit 11-c

STANDARD OPERATING PROCEDURE				
Subject:			Number	HOP M-550
	PRODUCT PRICING		Page of I 8	
			Effective Date 7/2/	
Supersedes Cor. No. 246	Page 1	Dated 3/10/	Related S.O.P./H.O.P.	

PURPOSE: To establish a responsibility for the coordination of all phases of the introduction of a new product, and to provide a means for the establishment and approval and distribution of prices, price changes on all products, and assignment of product codes.

EXHIBITS: 1. Notification of Vendor Pricing, Exhibit A
2. Cost/Pricing Product Sheet, Exhibit B
3. Price Book Cover Sheet, Exhibit C
4. Price Book Pricing Sheet, Exhibit D

SUMMARY: This procedure deals with the responsibility for the coordination of all phases of a new product, from the introduction, product codes assignment stages, to establishing new pricing and changes to existing item/product pricing, the preparation of the required forms and subsequent distribution of same, to expedite the items/products introduction and established items/products pricing.

METHOD:
A. ROUTING OF NEW VENDOR PRICES AND ASSIGNMENT OF PRODUCT CODES

PURCHASING DEPT.:   1. Prepares a five (5) part Notification of Vendor Pricing Form (attached as Exhibit A), one form for each item/Product involved, upon receipt of a Vendor invoice changing a price for an existing item/product, or when a new item/product is ordered.

NOTE: For each item/product, a separate Notification of Vendor Pricing Form is required. Multiple items/products *are not* to be transcribed to a single Notification of Vendor Pricing Form.

HOP Correction No: 253
Date Prepared: 6/19/

HOP M-550

Exhibit 11-d (page 1)

STANDARD OPERATING PROCEDURE		
Subject:	Number	HOP M-550
PRODUCT PRICING	Page of 2 8	
	Effective Date 7/2/	
Supersedes Cor. No. 246 Page 2 Dated 4/2/	Related S.O.P./H.O.P.	

2. If a new item/product is involved, pulls the Purchasing Follow-up File copy (last) of the Notification of Vendor Pricing Form and forwards the balance of the set to Order/Billing for assignment of the appropriate Product Code.

3. Files the Purchasing Follow-up File copy (last) of the Notification of Vendor Pricing Form, in the Follow-up File, *two (2) working days* from the date of issuance.

4. If a change in price, holds for step 9, below.

ORDER/BILLING DEPT.:

5. Assigns Product Code and updates the Master List.

6. Issues memo to List 5.0 (Execs., Staff, & Dept. Heads) announcing Product Code assignment.

ORDER/BILLING DEPT.:

7. Dates and initials Purchasing/Data Processing Department copy (original) of Notification of Vendor Pricing Form in the space provided, signifying the Product Code assignment and:

   a. Posts the newly assigned Product Code to Order/Billing Departments Product Master File.

   b. Forwards balance of Notification of Vendor Pricing Forms to the Purchasing Department.

PURCHASING DEPT.:

8. Removes the Purchasing Follow-up File copy (last) of the Notification of Vendor Pricing Form from Follow-up File, and posts the newly assigned Product Code to same, and refiles in the Follow-up File.

9. Affixes all applicable back-up Vendor documentation (if applicable) to verify and support changes in item/Product price(s), to the balance of the Notification of Vendor Pricing Forms and forwards complete package to the Accounting Department.

HOP Correction No: 253
Date Prepared: 6/19/

HOP M-550

Exhibit 11-d (page 2)

STANDARD OPERATING PROCEDURE		
Subject: PRODUCT PRICING	Number HOP M-550	
	Page of 3 8	
	Effective Date 7/2&	
Supersedes Cor. No. 246	Page 3 Dated 4/2/	Related S.O.P./H.O.P.

ACCOUNTING DEPT.:

10. Reviews Notification of Vendor Pricing Forms and verifies costs submitted from the Purchasing Department by examining all applicable back-up documentation.
11. Obtains savicopy of quotations.
12. Requests back-up support when memos are submitted concerning costs.
13. Prepares a new Cost/Pricing Product Sheet (attached as Exhibit B) for:
    a. New Items/Products
    b. Items/Products having a sufficient change in cost to affect profitability.
14. Calculates appropriate duty and freight.
15. Establishes retail, dealer, and Murritt prices using standard margins and markups.
16. Submits completed new Cost/Pricing Product Sheet to the appropriate Product Manager, for approval.
17. Retains balance of Notification of Vendor Pricing Forms and attached applicable back-up Vendor documentation.

B. ESTABLISHMENT OF NEW PRICES AND PRICE CHANGES

PRODUCT MANAGER:

18. Reviews submitted prices on Cost/Pricing Product Sheet and either approves or recommends changes to prices, indicating same on the Cost/Pricing Product Sheet.

PRODUCT MANAGER:
    Con't

19. Submits the Cost/Pricing Product Sheet to the Executive Vice President for approval.

EXECUTIVE VICE PRESIDENT:

20. Reviews existing prices, recommended changes thereto, and new prices on the basis of:

HOP Correction No: 253
Date Prepared: 6/19/

HOP M-550

Exhibit 11-d (page 3)

STANDARD OPERATING PROCEDURE		
Subject: PRODUCT PRICING	Number HOP M-550	
	Page of 4 8	
	Effective Date 7/2/	

Supersedes Cor. No.
            246
	Page
	         4
		Dated
		          4/2/
			Related
			S.O.P./H.O.P.

        a. Increase or decrease in costs.

        b. Increase or decrease in Sales volume.

        c. Unsolicited comments from Customers.

        d. Competitive Prices.

        e. Current economic conditions.

21. Confers with the Sales and Marketing Divisions to determine approval of recommended pricing.

22. Approves or changes submitted prices, indicating same on the Cost/Pricing Product Sheet.

23. Advises the President if recommended pricing is in accordance with established margins or higher than the established margins.

24. Confers with the Accounting and Marketing Divisions if price recommendations submitted by Accounting differ from Marketings.

25. Reviews recommended price changes for approval.

26. Submits recommended price changes with applicable backup papers to the President for approval.

PRESIDENT:

27. Reviews submitted price changes for approval.

28. Returns approved or changed prices with Cost/Pricing Product Sheet to the Executive Vice President.

EXECUTIVE VICE PRESIDENT:

29. Reviews approved or changed prices.

30. Returns approved or changed prices to the Accounting Department.

31. Notifies the Customer Service Department, applicable Product Managers, and Director of Advertising of new and/or changes to prices.

ACCOUNTING DEPT.:

32. Upon receipt of approved or recommended price changes to the Cost/Pricing Product Sheet from the Executive Vice President, retrieves balance of the Noti-

HOP Correction No: 253
Date Prepared: 6/19/

HOP M-550

Exhibit 11-d (page 4)

STANDARD OPERATING PROCEDURE		
Subject:	Number	
	HOP M–550	
PRODUCT PRICING	Page of	
	5 **8**	
	Effective Date 7/2/	
Supersedes Cor. No. 246	Page 5	Dated 4/2/	Related S.O.P./H.O.P.

fication of Vendor Pricing Forms, dates and initials Purchasing/Data Process-Department copy (original) of Notification of Vendor Pricing Form/package and affixes all backup Vendor Price/change documentation and Cost/Pricing Product Sheet to Notification of Vendor Pricing Forms.

ACCOUNTING DEPT.:
Con't.

33. Forwards the complete Notification of Vendor Pricing Forms package and attached backup documentation *(Cost/Pricing Product Sheet & Vendor Price/Change documentation)* to the Vice President/Controller for approval.

VICE PRESIDENT/ CONTROLLER:

34. Reviews Notification of Vendor Pricing package (Cost/ Pricing Product Sheet & Vendor Price/Change Pricing documentation) and either approves or disapproves, recommended pricing.

35. *If the Notification of Vendor Pricing package is disapproved:* confers with the Executive Vice President to resolve pricing.

36. *If the Notification of Vendor Pricing package is approved:* indicates same in the appropriate space provided, and forwards complete package to the Accounting Department.

ACCOUNTING DEPT.:

37. Enters the established (approved) *Retail and Lowest Dealer Prices* to the Purchasing/Data Processing Department copy (original) of the Notification of Vendor Pricing Form and dates and initials in the appropriate space provided.

38. Pulls and retains for Accounting files, the Accounting Department copy of the Notification of Vendor Pricing Form, and the Cost/Pricing Form, and forwards to the Order/Billing Department, for reference and file.

HOP Correction NO: 253
Date Prepared: 6/19/

HOP M-550

Exhibit 11-d (page 5)

STANDARD OPERATING PROCEDURE		
Subject:	Number	HOP M-550
PRODUCT PRICING	Page of	6 8
	Effective Date	7/2/
Supersedes Cor. No. 246	Page 6 Dated 4/2/	Related S.O.P./H.O.P.

39. Removes the Order/Billing Department copy of the Notification of Vendor Pricing Form, and forwards to the Order/Billing Department, for reference and. file.

C. DISTRIBUTION OF PRICE CHANGES

ACCOUNTING DEPT.:

40. Distributes specifications, costs, applicable Vendor/ Price change backup documentation, and prices to the Purchasing Department, for costs keeping and further/ future pricing.
41. Forwards the balance of the Notification of Vendor Pricing Forms to the Data Processing Department, for completion of master items list/cards containing costs and product codes from Order/Billing Department.

DATA PROCESSING DEPT.:

42. Keypunches applicable information *(Cost, Lowest Dealer Price, List Price, Product Code, and item/ product description)* from the Notification of Vendor Pricing Form, and updates Product Files.

DATA PROCESSING DEPT.: Con't.

43. Initials and dates Notification of Vendor Pricing Form, bursts from, and returns the Purchasing/Data Processing Department copy (original) to the Purchasing Department.
44. Retains the Data Processing Department copy (2nd) of the Notification of Vendor Pricing Form for Data Processing Files.

PURCHASING DEPT.:

45. Clears follow-up file, and files Purchasing/Data Processing Department copy (original) of J Notification of Vendor Pricing Form in permanent Files.

CUSTOMER SERVICE DEPT.: 46. Prepares a new pricebook release or a correction to the pricebook announcing the new prices.

HOP Correction No: 253
Date Prepared: 6/19/

HOP M-550

Exhibit 11-d (page 6)

STANDARD OPERATING PROCEDURE		
Subject:	Number	
	HOP M-550	
	Page of	
PRODUCT PRICING	7	8
	Effective	
	Date 7/2/	
Supersedes Cor. No. Page Dated	Related	
246 7 4/2/	S.O.P./H.O.P.	

47. Distributes new Price Book Pricing Sheet (Exhibit D) with Price Book Cover Sheet (attached as Exhibit C) to the Executive Vice President, Vice President/Marketing, Vice President/Controller, Accounting Services Manager, appropriate Product Manager, and President, for approval initials on the Price Sheet.

48. Distributes initialed pricebook additions as follows:
a. *Dealer Prices:*
List 5.0-Exec., Staff & Department Heads
List 7.1-Dealers
List 8.1-Br. Admins & Br. Managers
List 10.1-Overseas Affiliates
b. *Retail Prices:*
List 5.0-Exec., Staff & Department Heads
List 8.1-Br. Admins. & Br. Managers
List 9.1-Service Managers

PRODUCT MANAGER/ DIRECTOR OF ADVER-TISING

49. Coordinates with the Executive Vice President on preparing Marketing Memos, Production Specification Sheets and Advertising requirements.

50. Prepares Marketing Memos, Product Specification Sheets, and Advertising releases as required.

51. Distributes Marketing Memos and Product Specification Sheets as follows:
a. List 6.0-Field Sales Personnel
b. List 9.0-Field Service Personnel

CREDIT DEPT., CUSTOMER SERVICE DEPT. ORDER/ BILLING DEPT. PARTS DEPT. OF WAREHOUSE, AND BRANCHES:

52. Screens all orders held, such as Standing Orders, Quarterly Orders, Advance Orders, Credit Hold Orders, Back Orders, and adjust price as follows:

Exhibit 11-d (page 7)

STANDARD OPERATING PROCEDURE		
Subject:	Number	HOP M-550
	Page of	8 8
PRODUCT PRICING	Effective Date	7/2/
Supersedes Cor. No. 246	Page 8 Dated 4/2/	Related S.O.P./H.O.P.

CREDIT DEPT., CUSTOMER SERVICE DEPT. ORDER/ BILLING DEPT., PARTS DEPT. OF WAREHOUSE, AND BRANCHES:
    Con't.

52. a. *Price Increase*-No adjustment necessary if order date prior to effective date of the increase.
    b. *Prior Decrease*-Adjust prices in Customer's favor.

D. SPECIAL PRICES-RETAIL

BRANCH MANAGER:

53. May authorize deviations from published prices within the guidelines set by the applicable zone *General Manager,* or set forth in SOP.

E. SPECIAL PRICES-DEALER

DISTRICT MANAGER: (DEALER REPRESENTA-TIVE)

54. Prepares Dealer Change of Status Form requesting Special Prices.
55. Forwards Dealer Change of Status Form in accordance with SOP C-6e.

EXECUTIVE VICE PRESI-DENT: MANAGER, NATIONAL DEALER MAN-AGER:

56. Reviews Dealer Price Book every six (6) months and continues or discontinues *Special Pricing* in effect.

F. NATIONAL ACCOUNTS

BRANCH MANAGER:

57. Forwards request for National Account Pricing upon request of Customer or salesman to the National Accounts Manager.

NATIONAL ACCOUNTS MANAGER:

58. Approves National Account pricing and prepares a National Account Memo and distributes to List 5.0, 7.1, and 8.1.

INQUIRIES: Executive

Executive Vice President, Vice President/Controller, and Director of Purchasing, Manager-Accounting Services.

DISTRIBUTION:

List 11.0 HOP Manual Holders

Exhibit 11-d (page 8)

NOTIFICATION OF VENDOR PRICING

FROM: _____   DATE: __/__/____

☐ NEW ITEM   ☐ PRICE CHANGE

⑥   ___(a)___   ___(b)___   ___(c)___   ___(d)___
     PRODUCT TYPE   VENDOR NAME   INVOICE NUMBER   INVOICE DATE

ACCOUNTING DEPARTMENT
ONLY

NEW RETAIL   NEW (LOWEST) DEALER

☐☐☐☐☐☐ ___(f)___   ☐☐☐☐☐ ___(h)___
13   18 EXISTING RETAIL   19   24 OLD (LOWEST) DEALER
     (e)   (g)

       PRODUCT CODE   ITEM/PRODUCT DESCRIPTION
(i)   ☐☐☐☐   ☐☐☐☐☐☐☐☐☐☐☐☐☐☐   (j)
       9   12   31   45

       NEW COST
(k)   ☐☐☐☐☐☐   ___(l)___
       25   30   OLD COST

ON HAND INVENTORY LEVEL: _____

ORDER/BILLING DEPT.:   DATE PRODUCT CODE ASSIGNED: __/__/__ BY ____
ACCOUNTING DEPT.:   DATE PRICING APPROVED: __/__/__ BY ____
VICE PRESIDENT/CONTROLLER: DATE APPROVED: __/__/__ BY ____
DATA PROCESSING DEPT.:   DATE KEYPUNCHED: __/__/__ BY ____

INSTRUCTIONS

NEW ITEMS:

Purchasing Dept. prepares one form for each item involved and completes items a thru d, and j and k, above.

Order/Billing Dept. completes item i, above.

Accounting Dept. completes items e and g, above.

Data Processing Dept. kypunches items e, g, and i thru k, above.

PRICE CHANGES:

Purchasing Dept. prepares one form for each item involved and completes items a thru d, and i thru l, above.

Accounting Dept. completes items e thru h, above.

Data Processing Dept. keypunches items e, g, and i thru k, above.

DISTRIBUTION: 1) Purchasing/Data Processing Dept. 2) Data Processing Dept. 3) Account Dept.
                 4) Order/Billing Dept. 5) Purchasing Follow-Up File

(0-5-3)
                                                                   HOP M-550

Exhibit 11-d (page 9)

COST/PRICING PRODUCT SHEET

Product _____

( ) New Product　( ) Change　Date: __/__/__　By: _____　Product Code _____

Unit of Measure _____

	Unit of Measure	Control Prod. No:	Accounting	Marketing	Approved Pricing	Direct Costs Excluding Commissions to Salesmen			
Retail Sales						Cost Element	Retail	Dealer	Other
Recommended Price (S)	_____	$.				Raw Cost (Eff Date, Vendor, FOB Point, Currency Basis, Unit)			
% Gross Profit		. %							
% Mark-Up on Cost . .		. %							
% Commission		. %							
$ Commission		$.							
Retail - Rentals	Unit of Measure								
Recommended Price (S)	_____	$.							
% Gross Profit		. %							
% Mark-Up on Cost . .		. %							
%Commission		. %							
$ Commission	Unit of Measure	$.				Brokerage			
Dealer						Duty at ___ %			
						Insurance & Handling to Main Warehouse			
Recommended Price (S)	_____	$.				Freight - in to Main Warehouse			
% Gross Profit		. %				Royalty: % or $; Base: ; Name:			
% Mark-Up on Cost . .		. %				Royalty: % or $; Base: ; Name:			
% Commission		. %				Royalty: % or $; Base: ; Name:			
$ Commission		$.							
Major Account	Unit of Measure								
Recommended Price (S)	_____	$.							
% Gross Profit		. %							
% Mark-Up on Cost . .		. %							
% Commission		. %							
$ Commission		$.							
SA - Sales	Unit of Measure					Freight - out - Main Warehouse to Branch			
						Freight - out - to Customer			
						Special Packing, Handling, or Rigging			
Recommended Price (S)	_____	$.				Sales or Other Tax if Unbilled to Cust.			
% Gross Profit		. %							
% Mark-Up on Cost . .		. %							
% Commission		. %							
$ Commission		$.							
SA - Sales	Unit of Measure								
Recommended Price (S)	_____	$.							
% Gross Profit		. %							
% Mark-Up on Cost . .		. %							
% Commission		. %							
$ Commission		$.							
Her _____	Unit of Measure								
Recommended Price (S)	_____	$.							
% Gross Profit		. %							
% Mark-Up on Cost . .		. %							
% Commission		. %							
$ Commission		$.				Total Cost			

Gross Profit - Profit/Price　　　　　　　　Mark-Up Cost - Profit/Cost

Price Approved　　　　　　　　　　　　　Cost Approved

( )	( )	( )	( )	( )	( )	( )	( )		( )	( )	( )	( )
V.P. Mktg.	Exec. V.P.	Prod. Mgr.	V.P./Contr.	Pres.	Dlr. Mgr.				Purch. Mgr.	Acctg. Mgr	V.P./Contr	

Exhibit 11-d (page 10)

PRICE BOOK COVER SHEET
FOR
PRODUCT PRICING PROCEDURE
HOP M–550

PRODUCT NO. _____
DATE __/__/__

_____   ( ) NEW PRODUCT   ( ) CHANGE

_____   __/__/__
EXECUTIVE VICE PRESIDENT   DATE   ( ) APPROVED   ( ) CHANGED
COMMENTS:_____
_____
_____

_____   __/__/__
VICE PRESIDENT MARKETING   DATE   ( ) APPROVED   ( ) CHANGED
COMMENTS:_____
_____
_____

_____   __/__/__
VICE PRESIDENT/CONTROLLER   DATE   ( ) APPROVED   ( ) CHANGED
COMMENTS:_____
_____
_____

_____   __/__/__
ACCOUNTING SERVICES MGR.   DATE   ( ) APPROVED   ( ) CHANGED
COMMENTS:_____
_____
_____

( ) W.P.   ( ) FAX   ( ) COPIERS

_____   __/__/__
PRODUCT MANAGER   DATE   ( ) APPROVED   ( ) CHANGED
COMMENTS:_____
_____
_____

_____   __/__/__
PRESIDENT   DATE   ( ) APPROVED   ( ) CHANGED
COMMENTS:_____
_____
_____

FORWARD TO
( ) CUSTOMER SERVICE MANAGER

Exhibit 11-d (page 11)

PRICE BOOK

Subject:						Page	of
						Effective Date	
Supersedes Cor. No.		Page		Dated		Date Prepared	
Approved By:	Pres.	Exec. V.P. V.P./Mktg.	V.P./Contr.	Acctg./Svc.	Prod. Mg.	Correction Number	

Appropriate Product Manager's initials signifying approval of Product Pricing release.

Exhibit 11-d (page 12)

AUTHORIZATION FOR REPAYMENT OF EMPLOYEE LOANS

I herewith acknowledge that I am accepting my position
with   Corporation ("   ") on
a "No Fee Paid By Company" basis, and that the payment
of my employment agency fee is my sole responsibility.

I have requested, and herewith acknowledge receipt of,
a loan of $_____to pay this fee. I authorize
the employment agency listed below, and to record said
amount as a loan made to me.

I further authorize   to deduct twelve (12) equal
payments of $_____each from my bi-weekly pay for
repayment of the above loan. Deductions shall commence
starting with my first full pay period.

Should my employment with   terminate for any
reason, prior to repayment in full of the above loan,
I agree to authorize deductions of any balance from my
accrued vacation or severence pay, if any. If, after
these deductions, there is any remaining balance, I
agree to pay it forthwith.

NAME OF AGENCY: _____

ADDRESS: _____

                    By:_____
                        (Employee's Signature)

                    Date:_____

                        _____
                        (Location/Department)

Exhibit 11-e

TRAVEL AUTHORIZATION AND TRAVEL ADVANCE REQUEST

EMPLOYEE NAME_____POSITION_____LOCATION_____

PRODUCT LINE_____

DIVISION _____DEALER SALES _____RETAIL SALES _____SERVICE

_____ADMIN.   _____WHSE.   _____OTHER
                                                          (Specify)

PURPOSE OF TRAVEL_____

_____

DEPARTURE DATE:_____TRAVELLING TO:_____

IS AIR TRAVEL INVOLVED?   _____

    YES _____   _____

    NO_____   _____

                                              _____

NUMBER OF NIGHTS EXPECTED TO BE AWAY FROM HOME_____

TRANSPORTATION $_____

HOTEL, MEALS, ETC. $_____   PER AUTHORIZED EXPENSE LIST
                                             BOP 4.06.
OTHER (Explain) $_____

TOTAL ESTIMATED EXPENSES $_____

   TRAVEL ADVACE REQUESTED?

      NO
                                             ADVANCE MAY NOT EXCEED TOTAL
      YES   AMOUNT REQUESTED $_____   ESTIMATED EXPENSES BY MORE THAN 10%

IF YES, IS AMOUNT TO BE ADVANCED BY HOME OFFICE_____PETTY CASH_____

TRAVEL AUTHORIZED BY_____TITLE_____

AIR TRAVEL AUTHORIZED BY_____TITLE_____

ATTACH COPY OF APPROVAL TELEX IF APPLICABLE.

Exhibit 11-f

STATEMENT OF REIMBURSABLE EXPENSES

NOTE: Print or type.
See reverse side for instructions.

STAPLE RECEIPTS
BEHIND HERE

NAME | DIVISION | DEPARTMENT | LOCATION / FLOOR | BUDGET NUMBER | PERIOD ENDED

DATE		HOTEL ROOM *	BREAKFAST	LUNCH	DINNER	TAXIS	TELEPHONE AND TELEGRAPH	OTHER (Itemize)		TOTAL
MO	DAY							DESCRIPTION	AMOUNT	

TOTAL DAILY EXPENSES

TRANSPORTATION EXPENSES*

DATES		CARRIER	FROM	TO	PERSONAL AUTO		PURCHASED BY (✓)		CREDIT CARD	CHECK (✓) IF UNUSED (RETURN TO CO.)	AMOUNT USED
DEPART	RETURN				MILEAGE	RATE	EMPLOYEE	COMPANY			

ADD: TOTAL TRANSPORTATION USED

ADD: TOTAL BUSINESS MEETING EXPENSE (Carry over from reverse side)

TOTAL EMPLOYEE EXPENSES FOR PERIOD

DEDUCT: TOTAL ADVANCES AND AMOUNTS PAID BY COMPANY (Carry over from reverse side)

BALANCE DUE   ☐ COMPANY   OR   ☐ EMPLOYEE

Purpose of Business Travel

SIGNATURE | DATE | AUTHORIZED APPROVALS | AUDITED BY

*Attach receipts or bills.

(O-8-1)

Exhibit 11-g (page 1)

DETAIL OF BUSINESS MEETINGS EXPENSE

These expenses are to be shown in total in the space provided on the front side of this form. Each payment must be listed separately. All gratuities for porter, etc. are to be summarized on a daily basis. Tips in connection with an underlying expense, such as meals and taxis, are to be included with that expense. In order to comply with tax laws, the occupation of each person and the business purpose of the business discussion are to be described in sufficient detail so as to clearly establish the business relationship between the Company and the persons present at the business meeting. If related meetings take place with reference to a particular expenditure, state on succeeding lines the date, hours and place of the related meetings.

DATE	MEETING PLACE AND CITY	NAME, FIRM AND OCCUPATION OF PERSONS PRESENT	BUSINESS PURPOSE	DESCRIPTION OF EXPENSE	AMOUNT

TOTAL (Carry forward to front side of this Form.)

ADVANCES AND AMOUNTS PAID BY COMPANY (Include Transportation)

DATE	DESCRIPTION	AMOUNT
PREVIOUS BALANCE DUE COMPANY		

TOTAL (Carry forward to front side of this form.)

INSTRUCTIONS FOR THE USE OF THIS FORM

1. USE OF THIS FORM - This form is to be used to account for all authorized business expense reimbursements, including the use of credit cards, cash advances, and any direct payments which are to be made by the Company in behalf of the employee. If an independent contractor accounts to the Company for such expenses, this form must be used.

2. RECEIPTS - A receipt for each item of hotel expense, transportation expense, and each other expense item is to be attached to this report. Each payment is ordinarily considered to be a separate item. Tips should be included with the underlying expense. Cancelled checks, check stubs, and non-itemized credit card billings are not deemed to constitute receipts for this purpose.

Exhibit 11-g (page 2)

SECURITIES ANALYST REPORT

DATE_____   PERSONAL INTERVIEW_____

                                     TELEPHONE INTERVIEW_____

NAME_____COMPANY_____

ADDRESS_____

CITY_____STATE_____ZIP_____

TELEPHONE_____
          Area Code   Ext.

PARTICIPANTS IN INTERVIEW:_____

                          _____

                          _____

                          _____

                          _____

GENERAL NATURE OF INTERVIEW:_____

_____

_____

_____

_____

_____

_____

_____

_____

_____

_____

_____

_____

Exhibit 11-h

"Bardahl" Formula Defense

(accumulated earnings)

1. Yearly revenues	$3,937,894
2. Average accounts receivable	$354,767
3. Turnover rate of average accounts receivable (line 1 ÷ line 2)	11.10
4. Days in accounts receivable cycle (365 ÷ line 3)	33
5. Accounts receivable cycle as a percent of year (line 4 ÷ 365)	9.04%
6. Yearly expenses	$3,572,050
7. Expenses for one accounts receivable cycle (line 6 x line 5)	$322,913
8. Average accounts payable	$175,807
9. Turnover rate of average accounts payable (line 6 ÷ line 8)	20.32%
10. Days in accounts payable cycle (365 ÷ line 9)	18
11. Difference in accounts receivable cycle and accounts payable cycle (line 4 - line 10)	15
12. Non-deferred expenses for one accounts receivable cycle as a percent (line 11 - line 4)	45.45%
13. Operating capital needed for one business cycle (line 7 x line 12)	$146,764

Exhibit 11-i

Provisions of the Tax Law

Section 46   Amount of Investment Tax Credit
Section 47   Recapture of Investment Tax Credit
Section 172   Net Operating Loss Deduction
Section 269   Acquisitions Made to Evade or Avoid Income Tax
Section 302   Effect on Recipients of Distributions in Redemption of Stock
Section 306   Effect on Recipients of Dispositions of Certain Stock
Section 317   Definitions
Section 331   Gain or Loss to Shareholders in Corporate Liquidations
Section 332   Effect on Shareholders in a Complete Liquidation of a Subsidiary
Section 333   Effect on Shareholders in a One-Month Liquidation
Section 334   Basis to Shareholders of Property Received in Liquidations
Section 336   General Rule for Recognition of Gain or Loss to a Corporation in Liquidation
Section 337   Effect on a Corporation of Sales or Exchanges in Connection with a
                   Twelve-Month Liquidation
Section 341   Collapsible Corporations
Section 354   Recognition of Gain or Loss to Shareholders in a Reorganization
Section 356   Receipt of Additional Consideration by Shareholders in a Reorganization
Section 358   Basis to Shareholders in a Reorganization or Tax-Free Incorporation
Section 361   Nonrecognition of Gain or Loss to a Corporation in a Reorganization
Section 362   Basis of Property to Corporations
Section 368   Definitions Relating to Corporate Reorganizations
Section 381   Carryovers in Certain Corporate Acquisitions
Section 382   Special Limitations on Net Operating Loss Carryovers
Section 453   Installment Method
Section 483   Interest on Certain Deferred Payments
Section 1245   Gain from Dispositions of Certain Depreciable Property
Section 1250   Gain from Dispositions of Certain Depreciable Realty
Sections 1371-1378   The Electing Small Business Corporation (Subchapter S)

Exhibit 12-a

Utilization of Tax Loss Carryforwards by Acquirers

1) WE ACQUIRE

   a. Use "A" or "C" reorg.
   b. Reduce loss by 5% for each 1% that stock given is
      less than 20% of our stock (Sec. 382b)
   c. Sec. 269 applies

2) OUR SUB ACQUIRES:

   a. Use "A" or "C" reorg.
   b. No reduction in loss if value of our stock given is at least
      20% of the value of sub's stock. If not, Sec. 382b applies.
   c. Sec. 269 - Principal purpose cannot be to secure benefit of the loss.

3) CONTINUE OLD BUSINESS:

   I. a) We acquire them in "B" reorg, in a non-taxable purchase
       b) They continue to operate as a subsidiary
       c) Sec. 269 applies - Principal Purpose
       d) Lisbon shops applies - their losses cannot offset our profits

   II. a) We acquire in "A" or "C" reorg.
       b)
       c) Sec. 382b applies (reduction of losses if they give up
          more than 20%)
       d) Sec. 269, Principal Purpose applies, if we get more than
          50% control
       e) Lisbon applies - their losses cannot offset our profits

Exhibit 12-b

MEMO TO: Executive Vice President   SUBJECT: Acquisition Goals
           Treasurer
           Controller   DATE: November 5, 19__

FROM: President

1.   Produce increased earnings per share during the year of
     the acquisition.

2.   Improve the market diversification of net income.

3.   Develop and maintain a working environment which would
     enable us to attract and retain high-talent employees
     at all levels.

4.   Seek profitable markets where new technologies are needed.

5.   Our technological and/or marketing resources must make a
     significant contribution to the other company, and it to us.

6.   Good, skilled, experienced, loyal management that will
     remain with the Company.

7.   An industry which will be in the ascendency during the
     last third of the 20th century.

8.   A company that has grown faster than GNP for past three
     years.

9.   Growth rate must be equal to industry ratio.

10. For other than our own distributors, minimum sales will be
     $3 million and minimum earnings after taxes will be $150,000.

11. Minimum of 50% gross profit and 5% net after taxes. Minimum
     return on investment will be 15-20%. Minimum of three
     consecutive years of earnings.

12. Our net worth and working capital shall not be adversely
     affected and acquisition must have a favorable effect on
     the Company's cash flow.

Exhibit 12-c

SCHEDULE OF MERGER ANALYSES

	000 omitted	
	Qty	%

Per cent of dominance

Seller received_____our shares for_____of its shares
Our shares to be held by seller after merger

	Qty	%
Our shares held by us before merger	1,240	
Total our shares after merger		

Distribution of our shares to seller

	Qty	%
To principal stockholders		
To all other directors and management		
To minority group		
To minority group		
Total		100

Book Value (Equity)

	$ Amt.	Per Common Share
Seller's before merger		
Ours before merger	6,197	5
Merged company's		

Earnings (after tax)

	$ Amt.	Per Common Share
Seller's before merger		
Ours before merger	2,034	1.64
Merged company's		

Price

	X book value	X Earnings	Per Common Share
Seller's			
Ours	12	37	60

Book value traded

	$ Amt.	Per Common Share
Seller's book value received in merger		
Our book value traded away		

Earnings (after tax) traded

	$ Amt.	Per Common Share
Seller's earnings received in merger		
Our earnings traded away		

Interest compared to dividends

	$ Amt.	Per Unit
Seller's annual dividend before merger		
Seller to receive interest from bonds to be issued in merger		

Increase in market value to seller

	$ Amt.	Per Common Share
Market value of seller before merger		
Market value of us before merger	74,400	60
Combined market value before merger		
Per cent of shares to be held by seller (item 2) _____%		
Market value of seller after merger		
Market value of seller's option stock before merger		
Market value of seller's option stock after merger		

Working capital

		Ratio
Seller's before merger		
Ours before merger	6,509	4.9 to 1
Merged company's		

Return on investment

		%
Seller's before merger		
Ours before merger		33

Exhibit 12-d

ACQUISITION EVALUATION CHECKLIST

A. Vital Statistics

    1.   Company_____Phone_____

    2.   Address_____Zip Code_____

    3.   Type of Business_____

    4.   Annual Sales $_____Net Income$_____

    5.   Number of Employees_____Number of Plants_____

    6.   Location of Plants_____

         _____

    7.   Backlog$_____Inventory_____

    8.   State of Incorporation_____

    9.   Reason for Sale_____

    10. Terms_____

    11. Finder_____Phone_____

    12. Terms_____

B. Key Management Executives

    1.   Name_____8. Appraisal of current effectiveness

    2.   Age_____   _____

    3.   Title_____9. Growth Potential

    4.   Time with company_____ _____

    5.   Contract_____yes_____no   10. Approves of merger_____yes_____no

    6.   Terms_____   11. Willing to continue with new company

    7.   Shares beneficially owned_____   _____yes_____no_____

    12. Percentage total stock outstanding owed by officers, key

         executives_____%

C. Capitalization

                                          Par   Shares   Shares
    1. Shareholder's Equity   Value   Authorized Outstanding Equity

        Preferred   _____   _____   _____   _____

        Common   _____   _____   _____   _____

Exhibit 12-e (page 1)

2. Long-term Debt   <u>Amount</u> <u>Due Date</u>   <u>Terms</u>

    Issue   _____ _____   _____

    Issue   _____ _____   _____

3. Potential Dilution (number of shares)

    Convertibles _____   Options _____   Warrants _____

4. Securities Traded   New York Stock Exchange _____ American Stock Exchange ____

    Over the Counter   _____ Regional Exchanges   ____

D. <u>Financial Data</u>

1. Balance Sheet   Net Worth $_____   Current Ratio _____

    Fixed Assets $_____   Depreciation $ _____

2. Profit and Loss   Sales (current) $_____   Sales (last year) $_____

    Earnings (current) $____   Earnings (last year) $_____

    Per Share (current) $_____   Per Share (last year) $_____

E. <u>Plant & Equipment</u>

1. Facilities   Average Age _____years Obsolescense _____years

2. Annual investment in new plant and equipment per employee $_____

3. Annual investment in new plant and equipment per $ sales $_____

F. <u>Marketing</u>

1. <u>Principal Products</u>	<u>Markets</u>	% of <u>Market</u>	<u>Name of Competitors</u>	
_____	_____	_____	_____	
_____	_____	_____	_____	
_____	_____	_____	_____	
_____	_____	_____		

2. <u>Growth Potential</u>	<u>Market</u>	<u>Current</u>	Next 12 Months	Next 5 Years
_____	_____	_____	_____	_____
_____	_____	_____	_____	_____
_____	_____	_____	_____	_____
_____	_____	_____		

G. <u>Sales</u>

1. Number of sales personnel _____   Method of Compensation _____

2. Principal customers _____

3. Pricing Method _____   Industry Pricing Method _____

Exhibit 12-e (page 2)

4. Percent of selling price for: direct labor _____ % raw materials _____ %

                                       overhead _____ % selling expenses ___ %

                                       profit _____ %

5. Product Mix   Number of items _____ % Catalog _____   %Other _____

6. Sales support services: Advertising _____   Promotion _____

                                Brochures _____   Other _____

H. **Industrial Relations**

1. Compensation Review: 6 months _____ One Year _____ Other _____

2. Wage and Salary Structure: Above Industry _____ Below industry _____

                                           Average _____

3. Motivation Techniques   Yes   No

        Incentive and/or bonus   ___   ___
        Profit sharing   ___   ___
        Stock Purchase   ___   ___
        Stock Options   ___   ___
        Hospitalization benefits ___   ___
        Other   ___   ___

4. Management Development Program   Yes _____ No _____

5. Labor Conditions in Industry   Superior _____ Average _____ Poor _____

6. Relationship with union   Superior _____ Average _____ Poor _____

I. **Business and Legal Aspects**

1. Accounting

    Name of Auditor _____ Phone _____

    Address _____ Zip Code _____

    Contact _____

2. Legal

    Name of Counsel _____ Phone _____

    Address _____ Zip Code _____

    Contact _____

Exhibit 12-e (page 3)

J. Miscellaneous   (Checklist of available printed materials)

       Annual Report   _____   Proxy Statement   _____
       Prospectus   _____   Interim Financial Reports   _____
       Organization Chart   _____   Company Brochures   _____
       List of Customers   _____   List of Distributors   _____
       Licensing Agreements _____   Union Agreements   _____
       Leases   _____   Insurance Policies   _____
       Salary & Wage   _____   Benefit Plans   _____
         Structure
       Sales Catalogs   _____   Data Sheets   _____
       Internal Communication Media (house organ, etc.) _____

K. Acquisition Assessment

   1. Evauation of Business   Yes   No

          Technical Superiority   ____   ____
          Patent Protection   ____   ____
          Market Strength   ____   ____
          Industry Vitality   ____   ____

   2. Reason for Acquisition   _____

       _____

   3. Major Competitors   Company   Share of Market

                                _____   _____
                                _____   _____
                                _____   _____
                                _____   _____

   4. Alternate Acquisitions   Company   Share of Market

                                _____   _____
                                _____   _____
                                _____   _____
                                _____   _____

   5. Evaluation of Management   Yes   No

          Management Ability   ____   ____
          Leadership   ____   ____
          Creativity   ____   ____
          Stability   ____   ____
          Integrity   ____   ____
          Growth Potential   ____   ____

   6. Management Motivation and Goals

          Cash   ____   Income   _____   Financing _____
          Captial Gains _____   Retirement _____   Succession _____

Exhibit 12-e (page 4)

GUIDELINES FOR PREPARING FINANCIAL FORECASTS

MAS Forecasting
Guidelines
Issued

The AICPA's management advisory services executive committee has issued the third in its series of guidelines. Guidelines for Systems for the Preparation of Financial Forecasts provides direction to developers of forecasting systems and to preparers of financial forecasts so that due care is exercised in their preparation. The following summarizes the ten guidelines:

.. A financial forecasting system should provide a means for management to determine what it considers to be the single most probable forecasted result.

.. The system should provide management with the means to prepare financial forecasts using the accounting principles that are expected to be used when the events and transactions envisioned in the forecast occur.

.. Forecasts should be prepared with appropriate care by qualified personnel.

.. A financial forecasting system whould provide for seeking out the best information, from whatever source, reasonably available at the time.

.. The information used in preparing a financial forecast should reflect the plans of the enterprise.

.. The assumptions utilized in preparing a financial forecast should be reasonable and appropriate and should be suitably supported.

.. The financial forecasting system should provide the means to determine the relative effect of variations in the major underlying assumptions.

.. A financial forecasting system should provide adequate documentation of both the forecast and the forecasting process.

.. A financial forecasting system should include the regular comparison of the forecast with attained results.

.. The preparation of a financial forecast should include adequate review and approval by management at the appropriate levels.

Copies are available from the AICPA order department at $2.50, with usual member discounts.

The previous booklets in the series dealt with administration of an MAS practice and of MAS engagements.

Exhibit 12-f

SIX METHODS OF DETERMINING THE PURCHASE PRICE

Data: Net Assets $100,000
       Profits of last 5 years: $19,000, $19,500, $19,000, $21,500, $21,000
       Total $100,000
       Average $20,000

---

(1) "Years' purchase of past annual profits."
     Profits of second preceding year ....$ 21,500
     Profits of first preceding year 21,000
     Total, and price to be paid for goodwill ....$ 42,500

(2) "Years' purchase of average past profits."
     Average profits of last 5 years (as stated above) .... $ 20,000
     Multiply by number of years of purchase   2
                                          Goodwill .... $ 40,000

(3) "Years' purchase of excess profits."

		12 1/2% of	
Year Preceding Sale	Profits	Net Assets	Excess
Third	$19,000	$12,500	$ 6,500
Second	21,500	12,500	9,000
First	21,000	12,500	8,500
	Total payment for goodwill		$24,000

(4) "Years' purchase of average excess profits."
     Average profits of past 5 years ....$ 20,000
     Deduct 12 1/2% of $100,000 12,500
                                       Excess ....$ 7,500
     Multiply by number of years of purchase   3
                                       Goodwill ....$ 22,500

(5) "Capitalized profits, minus net assets."
     Capitalized value of average net profits, or total
       value of business $20,000 ÷ 12 1/2% $160,000
     Deduct agreed value of net assets other than goodwill ... 100,000
                                       Goodwill .... $ 60,000

(6) "Excess profits capitalized."
     Average profits of past 5 years .... $ 20,000
     Deduct profits regarded as applicable to net assets
       acquired - 12 1/2% of $100,000   12,500
     Remaining profits, regarded as indicative of goodwill .. $ 7,500

     Goodwill - $7,500 ÷ 25% (or 4 years) .... $ 30,000

Exhibit 12-g

STOCK ALLOTMENT TO THE ACQUISITION PRICE

Assumptions

1. Assume the preferred stock to be issued at 6%.
2. Assume the capitalization of goodwill to be on the basis of 20%.

Determination of Net Assets - Preferred Stock

	A	B	C	Total
Assets as valued	$100,000	$60,000	$150,000	$310,000
Liabilities	30,000	20,000	50,000	100,000
Net assets for which preferred stock should be issued	$ 70,000	$40,000	$100,000	$210,000

Capitalization of Excess Profits - Common Stock

	A	B	C	Total
Average annual net profits	$ 10,000	$15,000	$ 8,000	$ 33,000
Preferred dividends - 6%	4,200	2,400	6,000	12,600
Excess remainder	$ 5,800	$12,600	$ 2,000	$ 20,400
Capitalization of remainder at 20%..	$ 29,000	$63,000	$ 10,000	$102,000

Summary of Stock Allotment

	A	B	C	Total
Preferred stock	$ 70,000	$40,000	$100,000	$210,000
Common stock	29,000	63,000	10,000	102,000
Total	$ 99,000	$103,000	$110,000	$312,000

Exhibit 12-h

Memorandum of Agreement (Acquisitions)

OUR CORPORATION
ADDRESS

May 31, 19___

Mr. Jack Smith
ABC Company
Address

Dear Jack:

Confirming our discussion of May 8th, we are interested in purchasing your business on the following basis:

1. Purchase Price - The initial purchase price will be five times pretax earnings, for the last one-year calendar period ended December 31, 1976. These pretax earnings will be adjusted upward for profit sharing, cash bonus and profit sharing retirement expenses (approximately $13,000), and for personal expenses which need not be a charge against the new business operation (approximately $5,000 to $10,000). For example, if pretax earnings for the year ended December 31, 1976 were $27,000, add to this profit sharing bonuses and expenses of $13,000 and non-recurring personal expenses of $10,000, to arrive at adjusted pretax earnings of $50,000. Five times this equals $250,000, which would be the initial payment.

We would then offer a two-year earn-out period, with a required maintenance of earnings in the third year. We would pay seven times pretax earnings in excess of base year earnings for each of the two years. In the above example, the $50,000 of base year earnings would be adjusted to our accounting basis. These adjustments would include the deferral of service contract income and amortization over a 12-month period (you state that this will have very little effect, as you sold the same number of service contracts last year, as this year); coupon books - you are taking all these into income when sold. We would adjust these to reflect income when shipped or paid. Presumably, there should be very little effect if the amount of coupon books which you have sold this year is approximately the same as last year; depreciation - would be changed to our basis instead of your own 3-year basis, which would result in an increase in earnings.

Having arrived at adjusted pretax earnings, the base for first-year earnout would be these pretax profits which are recast on to our accounting basis, for the year ended December 31, 1976. The earn-out will be seven times the excess over that base for the year ending December 31, 1977, with a 40% escrow holdback. The base will then be increased for the second year earn-out and you will be paid seven times the excess pretax earnings over the second year base, again using our accounting basis. There will again be a 40% escrow holdback, but there will be adjustments if your earnings drop below the earn-out base and you must maintain earnings in the third year. Attached is a schedule of examples indicating how the earn-out will work.

For example, if your adjusted base for earn-out in the first year remains at $50,000 and if you were to increase earnings by $20,000 in each of the next two years, you would receive seven times $20,000 for each of these years, or $140,000 for each of the two years, a total earn-out of $280,000. Adding this to the

Exhibit 12-i (page 1)

Mr. Jack Smith
May 31, 1977
Page Two

initial payment of $250,000 would result in a total payment of $530,000 for the purchase. If your earnings only exceeded the $50,000 base by $10,000 each year; that is, $60,000 in the first year of the earn-out and $70,000 in the second year of earn-out, you would then earn $70,000 for each of the two years, a total of $140,000 which, added to the initial payment of $250,000, would result in a total purchase price of $390,000..

A final example, if you exceeded your base by $30,000 each year and showed earnings of $80,000 in the first year and $110,000 in the second year, your total earn-out for the two-year period would become $420,000 which, added to the $250,000 initial payment, would make a total purchase price of $670,000.

Prices for our merchandise which will be charged to you during the period of earn-out will be lowest dealer published prices.

ABC will operate as a subsidiary of our Corporation. As soon as practicable, our Corporation would be prominently displayed on all signs, letterheads, etc., and the ABC identification will be displayed in successively lesser prominence.

You would operate basically along the principles of our Corporation's branch offices throughout the United States. If our Corporation assumes responsibility for accounting functions which ABC is now doing, we will charge you at the cost to our Corporation, but no higher than ABC is now paying.

Legal and accounting expenses of the sale are the responsibility of the selling stockholders and will not be considered as expenses to be charged against ABC.

During the earn-out period, if you earn 20% below the earn-out base in any one year, our Corporation, at its option, may take direct control of operating its subsidiary.

You will be responsible for marketing our Corporation's products in your present territory.

Your board of directors will be asked to resign in favor of our Corporation's nominees. You will, of course, continue to be represented on the board, during the earn-out period.

2. <u>Piggyback Rights</u> - Our Corporation will give you one piggyback right for registration of your shares.

3. <u>Accounting</u> - You agree to utilize the services of accountants of our Corporation's choice, after the purchase, which we have indicated at this time to be Coopers & Lybrand. Such accounting charges during the earn-out period will be charged against ABC's operations, but will not exceed accounting charges incurred by ABC prior to acquisition.

4. <u>Operations</u> - You agree not to pay any sums to your employees except regular

Exhibit 12-i (page 2)

Mr. Jack Smith
May 31, 1977
Page Three

salaries, commissions, bonuses and reimbursement for reasonable expenses. You
will keep present insurance in effect and will not diminish it. You will use
your best efforts to preserve your business intact and to keep your employees
and to preserve your relationships to suppliers, customers and employees. You
will not make any charitable contributions. You will not mortgage, lien, or
encumber any of your assets, or sell, assign or transfer your assets, except
inventory in the normal course of business. You will not become liable for
legal accounting or other fees, except as approved by our Corporation. You
will establish banking relations as you deem desirable provided that, except
for payroll checks and checks payable to our Corporation, no check in excess
of $3,000 shall be drawn by ABC unless countersigned by our President or Vice
President/Controller. Salaries will continue to be drawn, as at present.

You will continue to devote your full time, skill and attention exclusively
to your work at ABC, during normal business yours. All developments, inventions,
trade secrets, improvements, discoveries, by ABC, or you, will belong to our
Corporation. You will not enter into any commitment of capital expenditures in
excess of $3,000 without prior permission from our Corporation, except purchases
from our Corporation and inventory items.

You agree to maintain secrecy concerning our Corporation's affairs and have
all the other obligations of an executive employee - to devote full time and
efforts to the business. For a period of five years after termination of employment, for any reason, you agree not to enter into competition with us, nor engage
in, as principal, agent, employer, stockholder, officer, or otherwise, any such
business.

This agreement is binding upon you and your successors and assigns.

Your employment may be terminated for a period of three consecutive months,
or five months, even though not consecutive, if you become mentally or physically
unfit, or otherwise unable to perform your duties.

Our Corporation may, at its election, take out and maintain life insurance
on you, as we deem necessary, and our Corporation shall be named the beneficiary,
and you agree to cooperate in the procurement of application for such life
insurance.

5. Stock Price - The price of the stock will be the average of the closing price
of our Corporation as traded on the New York Stock Exchange for the 30 days prior
to signing the contracts. The stock price for earn-out purposes, each year, will
be the average of the closing prices for the month of December of each year,
respectively, 1977 and 1978. There will be no upper or lower limit upon the
calculation of the price of the stock.

6. New Products - ABC will be granted distribution rights on all of our Corporation's new products, to the extent that these products are distributed through
dealers in the normal course of our Corporation's business.

Exhibit 12-i (page 3)

Mr. Jack Smith
May 31, 1977
Page Four

I trust this summarizes the discussions which we have had and our understanding. This is not an offer, but is subject to approval by the President and our Board of Directors, but I believe that it is a viable arrangement which they will, in my opinion, approve. If you have any questions concerning any portion of this, please feel free to call me.

Kindest personal regards.

Very truly yours,

_____

Vice President/Treasurer

copies: President
         Executive Vice President

Exhibit 12-i (page 4)

45-608 EYE-EASE
45-708 20/20 BUFF
NATIONAL

Earn – out Examples

	Pre-Tax Earnings	Initial Payment of "our corp" stock	Value of Stock Earned	Stock issued	Stock in or (out) of Escrow	
I Base Period Earnings	50000	250000				
Year 1 Earnings	70000		100000	60000	40000	
Year 2 Earnings	90000		100000	60000	40000	Base is 70M
Year 3 Earnings	90000		—	80000 ←⟨80000⟩		
or						
Year 3 Earnings	80000 *		—	20000 ←⟨80000⟩		60M To our Corp.
or						
Year 3 Earnings	74000 *		—	—	⟨80000⟩	80M To our corp.

*5 Times Amount below 90,000 base is returned to our Corporation, but not more than is in escrow.

II Base Period Earnings	50000	250000				
Year 1 Earnings	40000		—		Average for first 2 yrs is equal to or under base – Earn out Ends	
Year 2 Earnings	60000					

III Base Period Earnings	50000	250000				
Year 1 Earnings	60000		50000	30000	20000 →To our Corp.	
Year 2 Earnings	56000		—		⟨20000⟩ Earn out Ends	

IV Base Period Earnings	50000	250000				
Year 1 Earnings	70000		100000	60000	40000	
Year 2 Earnings	65000				⟨25000⟩ →To our Corp.	
Year 3 Earnings	65000 *			15000 ←⟨15000⟩		

* Third Yr. Base is 65,000 for full earn-out

V Base Period Earnings	50000	250000				
Year 1 Earnings	40000 *		—	—		
Year 2 Earnings	70000 **		50000	30000	20000	Base is 60M
Year 3 Earnings	55000			20000 ←⟨20000⟩		

* Must earn over 60,000 in 2nd year for any chance of additional Stock.
** Third year minimum is 55,000 (Average of years 1 and 2)
    or

Year 3 Earnings	52000			50000 ←⟨20000⟩→		15M To our corp.

Exhibit 12-i (page 5)

RECORD RETENTION PERIODS

Employees' applications (after
    termination)
Employees' tax withholding statements
Express receipts
Freight bills
Freight claims (after expiration)
Freight drafts
Labor contracts (after expiration)
Manifests
Remittance statements
Receiving reports
Sales slips
Salesmen's expense accounts
Service reports
Shipping tickets

5 to 6 years

Correspondence, license
Correspondence, purchase
Correspondence, traffic
Complaint reports
Credit memos
Employees' daily time reports
Equipment inventory records
Insurance, fire inspection reports
Internal audit reports
Monthly trial balances
Payroll, overtime
Photographs of installations, etc.
Price exceptions and adjustments
Safety reports
War contracts and all papers
    pertaining thereto

6 to 7 years

Bond registers
Bonds, cancelled
Claims, closed, against company
Contracts and agreements (expired)
Correspondence, war bonds
Credit files
Employee record (terminated)
Expense reports
Federal income tax returns
Insurance, group disability
Inventory, recaps

6 to 7 years

Invoices, copy of order
Invoices, paid

Patent assignments
Payroll, bonus
Payroll, general
Payroll, part time
Payroll, temporary
Price and policy bulletins (superseded)
Real estate records (after disposal of
    land and buildings)
Stock dividends checks, cancelled
Stockholder lists

7 to 8 years

Checks, payroll
Commission statements
Correspondence, production
Cost statements
Employees' earning record
Employees' salary & wage rate change
Insurance, pensions (after expiration)
Purchase orders for capital expenditure
Sales sheets
Specification sheets

8 to 9 years

Accident reports (after settlement)
Agreements, leases (after expiration)
Checks, dividend
Checks, general
Checks, petty cash
Compensation cases (after closing)
Engineering problems (killed)
Vouchers, cash
Vouchers, numeric copy

9 to 10 years

Vouchers, A-Z copy
Voucher register

10 years

Insurance claims after settlement
Payroll, Series E Bonds (life of bond)
Vouchers, capital expenditure

17 years

Agreements, licenses

Permanent

Agreements, deeds
Applications filed with regulatory
    agencies
Engineering and research project records
Ledgers and journals, cash
Ledgers and journals, customer

Exhibit 13-a

STANDARD OPERATING PROCEDURE		
Subject:	Number	
		HOP M-550
FILE RETRIEVAL	Page of	
	1	2
	Effective Date	4/1/__
Supersedes Cor. No. Page Dated	Related S.O.P./H.O.P.	

PURPOSE: To insure appropriate controls for the transmittal, storage, and retrieval of all filed documents, present and historical.

METHOD:

DEPARTMENT HEAD:

1. Completes Requisition for filed documents as follows:
   a. Checks block-"Other" and indicates "File"
   b. Date-current date
   c. Attention-To file clerk
   d. Date needed
   e. Requested by-Department name
   f. Approved by-Department Head's signature
   g. Description of document-title, date
   h. Special instructions
2. Forwards requisition to file clerk.

FILE CLERK:

3. Enters document in "File Retrieval Log" (see Exhibit A).
4. Pulls requested document from files.
5. Files requisition in place of original document to serve as "out card."
6. Prepares a Letter of Transmittal (see Exhibit B), attaches document(s), and forwards to Department Head.

DEPARTMENT HEAD:

7. Returns "File Retrieval Log" upon return of the document.
9. Pulls requisition from file, and refiles original document.
10. Destroys requisition.
11. Reviews "File Retrieval Log" daily for documents not returned within the 48-hour period, and prepares a "Document Return Request" (See Exhibit C).
12. Adjusts "File Retrieval Log" to reflect 24-hour extension date in "Date to be Returned" column.

Date Prepared: 6/13/__
Correction No. 88

Exhibit 13-b (page 1)

STANDARD OPERATING PROCEDURE		
Subject:	Number	
		HOP G-220
	Page of	
FILE RETRIEVAL	2 2	
	Effective	
	Date 4/1/	
Supersedes Cor. No. Page Dated	Related	
	S.O.P./H.O.P.	

DEPARTMENT HEAD: 13. Returns document to file clerk upon receipt of "Document Return Request."

FILE CLERK: 14. Processes per steps 8-10 above.

INQUIRIES: Office Manager
DISTRIBUTION: List 11.0-HOP Manual Holders

Date Prepared: 6/13/__
Correction No. 88

Exhibit 13-b (page 2)

FILE RETRIEVAL LOG

Date Out	Date to be Returned	Return Date	Document Title and Number	Document Date	Department For

0-6-8-) 1-069-2m-1

EXHIBIT A

Exhibit 13-b (page 3)

LETTER OF TRANSMITTAL

This is the document you requested. Please return to file department within 48 hours.

Document Date	Document Title	Document #

(0-6-9) 1-069-2m-1

EXHIBIT B

Exhibit 13-b (page 4)

DOCUMENT RETURN REQUEST

DATE: _____

DEPARTMENT: _____

SIGNED OUT DATE: _____

DATE TO BE RETURNED _____

DOCUMENT TITLE _____

DOCUMENT NO. _____

DOCUMENT DATE _____

ADDITIONAL COMMENTS _____

_____

_____

_____

(0-6-10) 1-069-2m-1

EXHIBIT C

Exhibit 13-b (page 5)

ORGANIZATION MANUAL

SECTION	ORGANIZATIONAL CHARTS

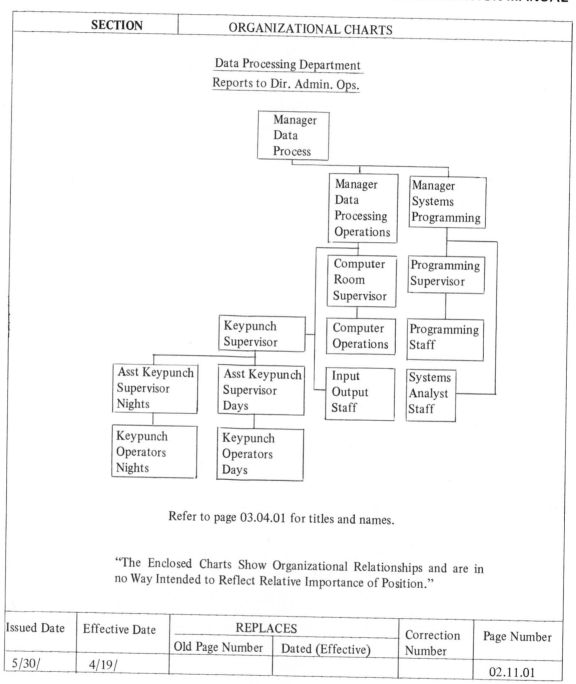

Data Processing Department
Reports to Dir. Admin. Ops.

Refer to page 03.04.01 for titles and names.

"The Enclosed Charts Show Organizational Relationships and are in no Way Intended to Reflect Relative Importance of Position."

Issued Date	Effective Date	REPLACES		Correction Number	Page Number
		Old Page Number	Dated (Effective)		
5/30/	4/19/				02.11.01

Exhibit 14-a

Performance Planning and Evaluation
for
Management by Objectives

CONFIDENTIAL

Employee Name (Last, First and Initial)		Serial Number	Date Employed
Position Title	Position Code—4 digit (Optional)		Date Assigned Present Position
Date Assigned to This Appraiser	Date of Performance Plan		Date of Performance Evaluation
Location	Office or Dept. Number		Division

Exhibit 14-b (page 1)

PERFORMANCE PLANNING

PERFORMANCE EVALUATION

RESPONSIBILITIES (Key words to describe the major elements of this employee's job.)	PERFORMANCE FACTORS AND/OR RESULTS TO BE ACHIEVED (A more specific statement of the employee's key responsibilities and/or goals he can reasonably be expected to achieve in the coming period.)	RELATIVE IMPORTANCE	ACTUAL ACHIEVEMENTS	LEVEL OF ACHIEVEMENT				
				FAR EXCEEDED	CONSISTENTLY EXCEEDED	EXCEEDED AT TIMES	MET	UNSATISFACTORY

CONTINUING RESPONSIBILITIES (Responsibilites, not covered at left, to be considered only when they have had a significant positive or negative effect on the overall performance.)

RELATIONSHIPS WITH OTHERS (JOB RELATED) (Significant positive or negative influence this employee has had on the performance of other employees.)

CHANGES IN PERFORMANCE PLAN (May be recorded anytime during the appraisal period.)

OVERALL RATING (Considering all factors, check the definition which best describes this employee's overall performance during the past period.)

Satisfactory
☐ Results achieved **far exceeded** the requirements of the job in **all key areas.**
☐ Results achieved **consistently exceeded** the requirements of the job.
☐ Results achieved **exceeded** the requirements of the job **at times.**
☐ Results achieved **met** the requirements of the job.

Unsatisfactory
☐ **Marginal** performance. Must improve to satisfactory.
☐ **Inadequate** performance. On Notice.

OPTIONAL ADDITIONAL PLANS (Where considered appropriate by manager and employee.)

ADDITIONAL SIGNIFICANT ACCOMPLISHMENTS

Exhibit 14-b (page 2)

474

COUNSELING SUMMARY

Employee Strengths   **Suggested Improvements**

1. _____   1. _____
2. _____   2. _____
3. _____   3. _____

SIGNIFICANT INTERVIEW COMMENTS

(Record here only those additional significant items brought up during rhe discussion by either you or the employee which are not recorded elsewhere in this document.)

_____

_____

_____

_____

_____

_____

_____

_____

_____ _____ _____
Manager's Signature   Print Name   Date of Interview

EMPLOYEE REVIEW

Optional Comments: If the employee wishes to do so, any comments concerning the performance plan or evaluation (for example, agreement or disagreement) may be indicated in the space provided below.

_____

_____

_____

I have reviewed this document and discussed the contents with my manager. My signature means that I have been advised of my performance status and does not necessarily imply that I agree with this evaluation.

_____ _____
Employee's Signature   Date

MANAGEMENT REVIEW

Optional Comments _____

_____

_____

_____

_____ _____ _____
Reviewer's Signature   Print Name   Date

Exhibit 14-b (page 3)

PROGRAMMING STANDARDS

PURPOSE: This standard specifies the procedures and techniques to
be used by SAVIN programmers. The use of these standards will optimize programs efficiency and improve communication in the Data Processing
group. Program maintenance is greatly simplified if programs are
adequately annotated and uniform techniques are used.

RESPONSIBILITY: It will be the responsibility of the Programming
Manager and the Documentation Administrator to enforce these standards.

STANDARDS:

1. No program assignment or program change is to be accepted without
    Standard Program Specifications acceptable to the Programming
    Manager.

2. These standards will be adhered to in all programs, unless specific
    authorization has been given by the Programming Manager.

3. All programs will be written in A.N.S. COBOL, unless otherwise
    specified by the Programming Manager.

4. Where a Source Statement book is available for a file, record
    or processing description, it must be used. Further, the programmer
    should use the actual book data-names and not an independent data
    description.

5. The program name assigned by the (Analyst) must be used for the
    PROGRAM-ID and for the source statement library entry. Program
    segments will use the program name, followed by a two-digit segment
    number (01 through 99). Each program change will be assigned a
    version number. The PROGRAM-ID must be held in a six-character
    data item immediately following the WORKING-STORAGE SECTION entry.

    e.g. WORKING-STORAGE SECTION.
          77   W-PROGRAM-ID   PIC X(6) VALUE 'APS101'

EACH TIME A NEW PROGRAM VERSION IS COMMENCED, THIS DATA ITEM
MUST BE CHANGED, AS WELL AS THE PROGRAM-ID. A REMARKS LINE SHOULD
BE ADDED TO DESCRIBE EACH CHANGE.

Exhibit 14-c (page 1)

PROGRAMMING STANDARDS
(As applied to Trainees)

1) Keep your Project Leader informed daily as to the status of all incomplete programs assigned to you.

2) Ask your Project Leader for help in setting up job(s) for testing. (Do not submit any program for testing without notification.)

3) After two hours of trying to debug a program, make certain that you get help. (Do not use 'TRACE' or 'EXHIBIT' statements unless asked to do so.)

4) Make ALL corrections to your source deck before resubmitting for another compilation/test; then resubmit as soon as possible.

5) Code all corrections to your program(s) if more than 10 lines.

6) Always inform your Project Leader of any problems encountered in obtaining compiliations, tests, etc.

7) When coding, use the general programming standards as set up by the department head.

8) Unless otherwise authorized, a flowchart must be drawn and the logic accepted by the Programming Manager before coding commences.

Exhibit 14-c (page 2)

A/R Cash Good Thru: 10/16
Billing Updated Thru: 10/15

Data Processing Report Schedule
For Month of ___ October ___

Control Code	Report Name	Input Due Date	Input Rec'd	Proof Due Date	Proof Rec'd	Report Due	Run Date	Rerun #1	Rerun #2	Date Mailed	Date Rec'd	Distribution	Comments
SAR85	A/R Dunning Letters					10/16	10-11			10-15			
SAR21	A/R Cash Update F.O.M.					10/16	10-12			10-14			
SAR31	A/R Reg. Cash Only E.O.M.					10/16	10-14			10-14			
SCA15	A/R Mthly Cash Receipts					10/16	10-15			10-15			
SCA20	A/R Mthly Cash by G/L					10/16	10-15			10-15			
SCA25	J/E by G/L					10/16	10-15			10-15			
SCA40	J/E Single Entry					10/16	10-15			10-15			
SCA50	A/R Mthly Cash Aging					10/16	10-15			10-15			
PRO200	P/R Master Updates 9/18 Union	10/15	10-15	10/16	10-16	10/16	10-15			10-16			
PRO300	P/R Adjustments 9/18 Union	10/15	10-15	10/16	10-16	10/16	10-15			10-16			
PRO600	P/R Checks 9/18 Union			10/16	10-16	10/16	10-16			10-16			
PRO700	P/R Register 9/18 Union					10/16	10-16			10-16			
GLS042	Freight Purchases by Dis. Code												
GLS042	Purchases by Dis. Code												
DBS810	Invoice Reg						10-16			10-17			
AP1096	A/P Bank Rec Proof						10-16			10-17			
	Master Billing Register					10/17							
	Master Billing Invoices					10/17							
COMO30	Commission J/E Proof					10/17	10-17			10-17			
AP0004	A/P Vendor Master Updates 9/28	10/16	10-16			10/17	10-17			10-17			
AP0019	A/P Details-Proof 9/28	10/16	10-16			10/17	10-17			10-17			
AP0023	A/P Cash Req. 9/28					10/18							
AP0022	A/P Checks 9/18					10/18							
AP015B	A/P Check Register 9/18					10/18							
COMO70	Commission Master Update					10/18							
	Br. Billing Close												

Exhibit 14-d

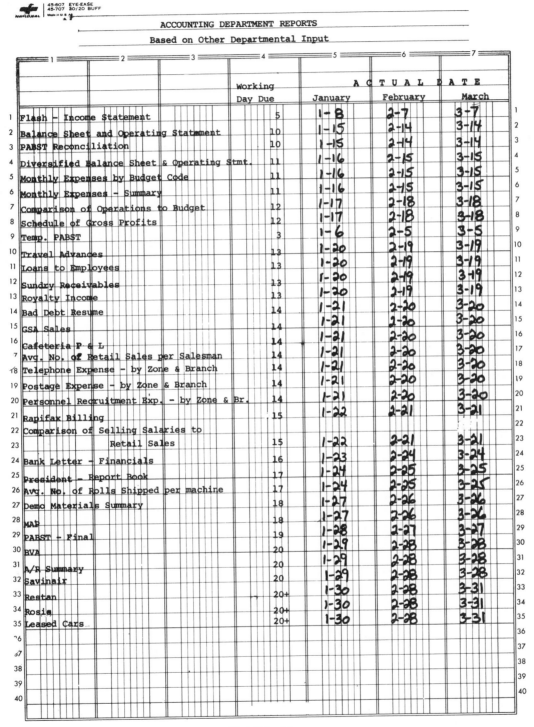

ACCOUNTING DEPARTMENT REPORTS

Based on Other Departmental Input

	Working Day Due	January	February	March
1 Flash – Income Statement	5	1-8	2-7	3-7
2 Balance Sheet and Operating Statement	10	1-15	2-14	3-14
3 PABST Reconciliation	10	1-15	2-14	3-14
4 Diversified Balance Sheet & Operating Stmt.	11	1-16	2-15	3-15
5 Monthly Expenses by Budget Code	11	1-16	2-15	3-15
6 Monthly Expenses – Summary	11	1-16	2-15	3-15
7 Comparison of Operations to Budget	12	1-17	2-18	3-18
8 Schedule of Gross Profits	12	1-17	2-18	3-18
9 Temp. PABST	3	1-6	2-5	3-5
10 Travel Advances	13	1-20	2-19	3-19
11 Loans to Employees	13	1-20	2-19	3-19
12 Sundry Receivables	13	1-20	2-19	3-19
13 Royalty Income	13	1-20	2-19	3-19
14 Bad Debt Resume	14	1-21	2-20	3-20
15 GSA Sales	14	1-21	2-20	3-20
16 Cafeteria P & L	14	1-21	2-20	3-20
17 Avg. No. of Retail Sales per Salesman	14	1-21	2-20	3-20
18 Telephone Expense – by Zone & Branch	14	1-21	2-20	3-20
19 Postage Expense – by Zone & Branch	14	1-21	2-20	3-20
20 Personnel Recruitment Exp. – by Zone & Br.	14	1-21	2-20	3-20
21 Rapifax Billing	15	1-22	2-21	3-21
22 Comparison of Selling Salaries to				
23 Retail Sales	15	1-22	2-21	3-21
24 Bank Letter – Financials	16	1-23	2-24	3-24
25 President – Report Book	17	1-24	2-25	3-25
26 Avg. No. of Rolls Shipped per machine	17	1-24	2-25	3-25
27 Demo Materials Summary	18	1-27	2-26	3-26
28 MAP	18	1-27	2-26	3-26
29 PABST – Final	19	1-28	2-27	3-27
30 BVA	20	1-29	2-28	3-28
31 A/R Summary	20	1-29	2-28	3-28
32 Savinair	20	1-29	2-28	3-28
33 Restan	20+	1-30	2-28	3-31
34 Rosin	20+	1-30	2-28	3-31
35 Leased Cars	20+	1-30	2-28	3-31

Exhibit 14-e

SYSTEMS AND PROGRAMMING
DEPARTMENT STATUS

As of Date 9/6/

Proj. Leader: BAM

STAFF STATUS

	Systems				Programming			
	Budgeted	Actual	Open	On Termination	Budgeted	Actual	Open	On Termination
	6	6			12	10		

PROJECT STATUS

Project Name	Scheduled Dates		Current Dates		Current Weeks Manpower Allocation				Total Mandays					Comments
	Start	Completion	Actual Start	Current Completion	Systems		Programming		Budgeted	Expended	% Complete To Date	Est. Act Final Total		
					People	Man Days	People	Man Days						
PR2070-P/R Master Update PGM.	8/16	9/6	8/19	9/6			1	1	14	7	100	—		Program is now Undergoing Extensive System Testing In 'Operations'
PR1200-State 941 Forms	8/19	9/13	8/19	9/20			1	0	15	5	70	15		
PR1300-Print Federal 941 Forms	8/19	9/13	8/19	9/20			1	0	15	3	30	15		
SAR110-A/R File Reload (New SAR91)	8/14	9/13	8/30	9/13			1	2	10	3	25	10		
Branch Number Processing Changes	8/20	9/20	8/20	9/20			2	5	20					
Docustat Program Maintenance	9/4	9/13	9/4	9/13			1	3	8	3	40	8		

Exhibit 14-f

480

NEW PROJECT REQUEST　　　　　　　　　　DATA PROCESSING
　　　　　　　　　　　　　　　　　　　　SYSTEMS & PROGRAMMING

REQUESTOR'S NAME	REQUESTING DEPT.	DEPT. MANAGER'S SIGNATURE

DATE REQUESTED	PRIORITY	TARGET DATE
/ /		/ /

GENERAL DESCRIPTION OF REQUEST

Attach sheet if space is insufficient

PROBLEMS OR DEFICIENCIES TO BE OVERCOME BY PROJECT

Attach sheet if space is insufficient

FOR SYSTEMS DEPARTMENT USE

PROJECT ASSIGNED TO	DATE ASSIGNED	ESTIMATE
		MANHOURS	COST
	/ /		

SUMMARY OF FINDINGS - PROJECT RECOMMENDATIONS

Attach sheet if space is insufficient

Exhibit 14-g

PROGRAM CHANGE REQUEST

REQUEST DATE
/ /

REQUESTOR'S NAME	DEPT HEAD'S SIGNATURE	REQUESTING DEPT

PROGRAM NO.	PROGRAM NAME

DESCRIPTION OF CHANGE

REASON FOR CHANGE

DATE REQUIRED
/ /

DOES THIS CHANGE AFFECT ANY OTHER DEPT?   yes no   ○ ○
IF YES, HAVE THEY BEEN INFORMED?   ○ ○

DATE RECEIVED	DATE ASSIGNED	ASSIGNED TO	ESTIMATE MANHRS COST
/ /	/ /		

DATE COMPLETED	PRODUCTION DATE		ACTUAL MANHRS COST
/ /	/ /		

COMMENTS, IF ANY

Exhibit 14-h

PROJECT STATUS NOTICE FORM

Systems & Programs

TO   :   PSN no. _____

SUBJECT: _____   ISSUED BY: _____

                                                                      DATE: _____

```
BASED ON MEMORANDUM
   FROM      DATED
```

ACTIVITY	DATE	REMARKS
1. Scheduled start		
2. Original estimated completion		
3. Revised estimated completion		
4. Completed as of		

Reason for revision (if applicable):

Remarks:

If you have any questions, please contact our Systems & Programs Dept. and refer to JOB NUMBER _____ and PSN no. shown above.

SYS R 00-034 : 04- 2C

Exhibit 14-i

**DATA PROCESSING
SYSTEMS & PROGRAMMING**

IMPLEMENTATION SCHEDULE			
FUNCTIONS	ASSIGNED TO	DATE PREPARTED / /	
		SECTION	PRIORITY

Exhibit 14-j

PROGRAM ASSIGNMENT FORM

NEW

CHANGE

ONE-TIME

SYSTEM IDENTIFICATION:	DATE PREPARED / /
PROGRAM IDENTIFICATION:	PROGRAM NUMBER:
REQUESTED BY:	DATE REQUESTED / /
SYSTEMS ANALYST:	PROGRAMMER ASSIGNED:
DATE ASSIGNED / /	DATE REQUIRED: / / ESTIMATED MANDAYS:

COMPLETION DATES

PROGRAM ANALYSIS:	FLOWCHART:	CODING:
KEYPUNCH:	COMPILED:	FIRST TEST:
TESTING COMPLETED:	PROGRAM ACCEPTED:	

INPUT: OUTPUT:

PROGRAM SPECIFICATIONS:

Exhibit 14-k

TROUBLE SCAN REQUEST

OPERATIONS REPRESENTED BY_____

REQUESTED (DATE)_____

```
EFFORTS BY OPERATION




```

TROUBLE DOCUMENTED WITH   ○ tape dump
                                   ○ disk file dump
                                   ○ run listings
                                   ○ spo messages
                                   ○ authorization forms

                                   ○ others _____

```
TROUBLE DESCRIPTION




```

```
SYSTEMS & PROGRAMMING FINDINGS and COMMENTS




```

SYS 00-036 5-72 1C

Exhibit 14-I

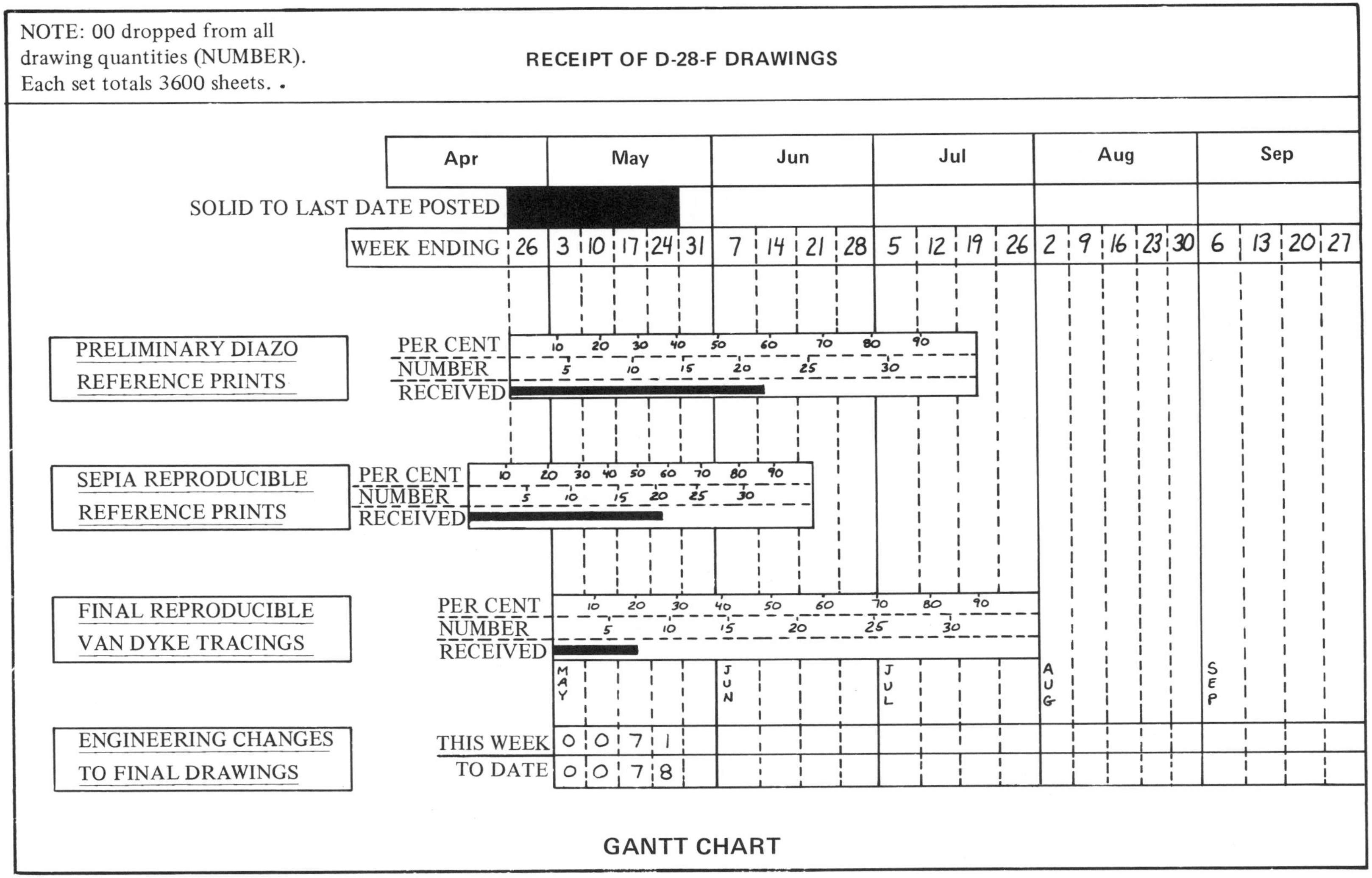
NOTE: 00 dropped from all drawing quantities (NUMBER). Each set totals 3600 sheets.
RECEIPT OF D-28-F DRAWINGS
Apr
May
Jun
Jul
Aug
Sep
SOLID TO LAST DATE POSTED
WEEK ENDING
26 3 10 17 24 31 7 14 21 28 5 12 19 26 2 9 16 23 30 6 13 20 27
PRELIMINARY DIAZO REFERENCE PRINTS
SEPIA REPRODUCIBLE REFERENCE PRINTS
FINAL REPRODUCIBLE VAN DYKE TRACINGS
ENGINEERING CHANGES TO FINAL DRAWINGS
PER CENT
NUMBER
RECEIVED
THIS WEEK
TO DATE
MAY
JUN
JUL
AUG
SEP
GANTT CHART

Exhibit 14-m

SYSTEMS AND PROGRAMMING   ○ New
DOCUMENTATION CHECK LIST   ○ Revised

JOB NO. _____   SYS. & PROG. CLEARING _____
DATE _____   OPERATIONS CLEARING _____

	S & P	OPER'S
○ ASSIGNMENT FORM		✕
○ SYSTEM FLOW		✕
RECORD LAYOUT ○ CARD		✕
○ TAPE		✕
○ DISK		✕
○ PRINTER LAYOUTS		✕
○ CARRIAGE TAPE (PRINTER)	✕	
○ COBOL LISTING WITH XREF.		✕
○ TEST RESULTS (CHECKED BY PROJECT LEADER)		✕
○ PROGRAM NARRATIVE		✕
○ KEYPUNCH INSTRUCTIONS	✕	
○ INPUT-OUTPUT CONTROL		✕
○ EXECUTE SETS	✕	
○ CATALOGED EXHIBITS		✕
○ SOURCE DECK		✕
○ RUN BOOK INSTRUCTIONS	✕	
○ OTHERS (TABLES, ETC.)		

Exhibit 14-n

SYSTEM/PROGRAMMING STANDARDS

OPERATIONS RUN BOOK

PURPOSE: This is an outline of the information which will be required
for the Operations Run Book before a system is accepted for production.
This is a preliminary draft and a more comprehensive description will
be provided later.

GENERAL OUTLINE:

Each data processing system will be maintained in a separate Run Book.
The Run Book will be divided into sections, with a separate section
for each subsystem or jobstream (Daily Processing, etc.).

Each section will contain the following:

(a)   Jobstream Flowchart.
(b)   File Retention Schedule.
(c)   Listing of any pertinent system codes.
(d)   File Backup Procedures for every file.
(e)   Run Instructions for each program.
(f)   Program Restart Procedures.
(g)   Report Distribution (not in Run Book).
(h)   System "Failure" Instructions.
(i)   File and Record Description including location of key data (physi-
      cal, not data).
(j)   Run Controls (balancing procedures, error action).

Each book will contain a Table of Contents.

PROGRAM RUN INSTRUCTIONS:

The run instructions for each program will include the following:

(a)   Run Sheet. This will contain an Input/Output diagram showing
      all files used and the physical devices assigned. If forms are
      printed, the form number and the corresponding carriage control
      tape must be identified. Indicates whether a control or date
      card is used. A brief (1 or 2 sentence) description of the pro-
      gram function is required. Note any special conditions (copy
      of first page of program narrative).

(b)   Control or Date card keypunch instructions.

(c)   List of all console error messages. Must indicate the reason
      for the message and the action to be taken (e.g., cancel). On
      the new systems these are not permitted (other than "JOB TERMINATED
      ABNORMALLY").

(d)   Sample printer output with alignment instructions.

The Run Book must contain an 80-80 listing of the jobstream JCL cards for
each job. Indicate where data cards are placed in the JCL. Sort control
cards must be listed with the JCL.

Exhibit 14-o

Form 3921
(Rev. Sept. 1971)
Department of the Treasury
Internal Revenue Service

Exercise of a Qualified or Restricted Stock Option
(U.S. information return under section 6039(a)(1) of the Internal Revenue Code)

For calendar year
19_ _ _ _

Copy A
For Internal
Revenue Service

1. Corporation Transferring Stock

a. Name and address (including ZIP code)

2. Name of corporation whose stock is transferred
(If different from corporation transferring stock)

b. Employer identification number ▶

3. Person to Whom Stock is Transferred

a. Name and address (including ZIP code)

b. Identifying number ▶

4. Date option granted

5. Date of transfer

6. Option price

7. Fair market value of stock at time option exercised

8. Place an "X" in the appropriate box to indicate whether the option exercised is:

a. A qualified stock option under section 422(b) . . . . ☐

b. A restricted stock option under section 424(b) . . . . ☐

9. No. of shares transferred ▶

Exhibit 15-a

19___ STOCK OPTION PLAN
of
SAVIN BUSINESS MACHINES CORPORATION

1. *Purpose of the Plan.* The purpose of this Plan (the "Plan") is to promote the interests of Savin Business Machines Corporation (the "Company") and its shareholders by permitting the Company to grant options to purchase shares of its Common Stock, $.10 par value ("Common Stock"), to key employees, including officers and directors who are also employees, of the Company and its subsidiaries, in order to attract and retain the services of such key employees and to provide additional incentive to such key employees by offering them a greater stake in the Company's success through increased stock ownership. Options which may be granted under the Plan include, but are not limited to, qualified stock options which meet the requirements of Section 422 of the Internal Revenue Code of 1954, as amended (the "Code").

2. *Stock Subject to the Plan.* Options may be granted under the Plan to purchase in the aggregate not more than 70,000 shares, subject to adjustment as hereinafter provided, of Common Stock, which shares may, in the discretion of the Board of Directors, consist either in whole or in part of authorized but unissued shares of Common Stock or shares of Common Stock held in the treasury of the Company. Subject to the foregoing limitation upon the number of shares which may be issued upon exercise of options, shares covered by the unexercised portion of any option may be subject to another option under the Plan and options may be granted which are exercisable on an alternative or mutually exclusive basis. Any shares subject to options which for any reason expire or are terminated unexercised as to such shares, shall again become available for options under the Plan.

3. *Administration of the Plan.* The Plan shall be administered by either the Board of Directors or a Stock Option Committee (the "Committee") consisting of three members of the Board of Directors. None of the members of the Committee shall be eligible to participate in the Plan. The Committee shall be appointed by, and shall serve at the pleasure of, the Board of Directors. A majority of the members shall constitute a quorum, and the acts of a majority of the members present at any meeting at which a quorum is present, and any acts approved in writing by a majority of the members without a meeting, shall be the acts of the Committee.

Subject to the express provisions of the Plan, the Board of Directors, or, if acting, the Committee shall have the authority, in its discretion, to determine the individuals to whom, and the time or times at which, options shall be granted; whether a grantee shall be granted a qualified stock option, a non-qualified stock option, or both; the number of shares to be subject to each option, which may be either a fixed number or a number expressed in terms of, and to be determined by, a formula under which the grant consists of the difference between a specified number of shares and all or a part of the number of shares issued upon past or future exercises of another option granted to the same individual; the option price per share; the period of each option; and the other terms and provisions of each option. Options need not be identical. The Board of Directors or the Committee may also interpret the Plan; prescribe, amend and rescind rules and regulations relating to the Plan; and make all other determinations necessary or advisable for the administration of the Plan. The determinations of the Board of Directors or the Committee, as the case may be, on the matters referred to in this paragraph shall be conclusive.

4. *Eligibility.* The Board of Directors or the Committee, as the case may be, may, consistent with the purposes of the Plan, grant options from time to time, within ten (10) years from the date of adoption of the Plan by the Board of Directors of the Company, to key employees, including officers and directors who are employees, of the Company or of any of its present or future subsidiary corporations (as defined

Exhibit 15-b (page 1)

in Section 425(f) of the Code, and, at times, called the "Subsidiaries"), and covering such number of shares of Common Stock as it may determine. No qualified or nonqualified stock option may be granted to an individual if he would own, immediately after the grant of said option, shares of stock possessing more than 5% of the total combined voting power or value of all classes of stock of the Company or any of the Subsidiaries. For the purposes of this paragraph, an employee shall be deemed to own shares of stock which he may purchase under outstanding options and shares of stock attributed to him under Section 425(d) of the Code or any comparable provision thereafter enacted. Employees, including those who have been granted options under stock option plans heretofore or hereafter adopted by the Company may receive more than one option under the Plan, subject to the above limitations.

5. *Option Price.* The purchase price of the Common Stock under each option shall be determined by the Board of Directors or the Committee, as the case may be, but shall not be less than the fair market value of the stock at the time of granting of the option. Such fair market value shall be taken by the Board of Directors or the Committee, as the case may be, as the average between the high and the low sale price, regular way, on the principal securities exchange on which the Common Stock is traded, on the date the option is granted, or, if there is no such sale on that date, then on the last previous day on which such a sale was reported; provided, however, that if such method is inconsistent with any regulations applicable to "qualified stock options" adopted by the Commissioner of Internal Revenue, then the fair market value shall be determined by the Board of Directors or the Committee consistently with such regulations.

6. *Term of Option.* The term of each qualified stock option granted pursuant to the Plan shall be for a period not exceeding five (5) years from the date of granting thereof and the term of each non-qualified stock option granted pursuant to the Plan shall be for a period not exceeding ten (10) years from the date of granting thereof. Options shall be subject to earlier termination as hereinafter provided.

7. *Exercise of Option.* The Board of Directors or the Committee shall have authority in its discretion to prescribe in any option agreement that the option will be exercisable in full or at any time or from time to time during the term of the option, or to provide for the exercise thereof in such installments at such times during said term as the Board of Directors or the Committee may determine. An option may be exercised at any time or from time to time during the term of the option as to any or all full shares which have become purchasable under the provisions of the option. The Board of Directors or the Committee may, in its discretion, accelerate the time or time at which an option may become exercisable.

Options granted hereunder shall be exercised by giving written notice to the Company at its principal office, presently Valhalla, New York 10595, specifying the number of shares purchased and accompanied by payment in full in cash of the aggregate purchase price therefor. Certificates representing the shares of stock purchased shall be issued as promptly as practicable thereafter. The holder of an option shall not have any rights of a shareholder with respect to the shares covered by his option until the date of issuance of a stock certificate to him for such shares. In no case may a fraction of a share be purchased or issued under the Plan.

8. *Prior Outstanding Options.* No qualified stock option granted hereunder may be exercised while there is outstanding (within the meaning of Section 422(c)(2) of the Code) any qualified stock option (or restricted stock option) to purchase shares of stock of the Company or any of the Subsidiaries which was granted to such option holder prior to the granting of such qualified stock option hereunder. For the purpose of the preceding sentence, and as provided at Section 422(c)(b) of the Code, a qualified or restricted stock option granted to such option holder prior to the granting of such qualified stock option shall not be deemed to be outstanding if such prior option is an option to purchase stock of the same class in the same corporation at a price (determined as of the date of grant of the qualified stock option being granted) not higher than the option price of the option being granted. This section shall not apply to the granting of nonqualified stock options under the Plan.

Exhibit 15-b (page 2)

9. *Termination of Employment.* Any option holder whose employment has terminated for any reason other than death may exercise his option, to the extent exercisable upon the effective date of such termination, at any time within three months after the date of termination, but in no event after the expiration of the term of the option, provided, however, that if his employment shall be terminated either (i) for cause or (ii) without the consent of the Company, said option shall (to the extent not previously exercised) terminate immediately. Options granted under the Plan shall not be affected by any change of employment so long as the holder continues to be an employee of the Company, of any of the Subsidiaries or of a corporation or its parent or subsidiary issuing or assuming a stock option in a transaction to which Section 425(a) of the Code applies.

10. *Death of Employee.* If an option holder dies while he is employed by the Company or any of the Subsidiaries or within three months after termination of his employment (unless such termination was either (i) for cause or (ii) without the consent of the Company) the option may be exercised, to the extent exercisable on the date of his death, by his executor, administrator or other person at the time entitled by law to his rights under the option, at any time within six (6) months after death, but in no event after the expiration of the term of the option.

11. *Stock Option Contract.* Each option shall be evidenced by an appropriate Stock Option Contract which shall provide, among other things, (a) that the employee agrees that he will, at the election of the Company, remain in the employ of the Company or any of the Subsidiaries for a period of at least one year from the later of (i) the date the option is granted to him and (ii) the date to which he is then otherwise obligated to remain in the employ of the Company or such Subsidiary, and (b) that in the event of exercise of such option, the shares subject to option will be acquired for investment and not with a view to distribution thereof. Anything herein contained to the contrary notwithstanding, the restrictions on resale or other distribution of the shares will be deemed removed and inoperative upon the registration under the Securities Act of 1933, as amended, of the shares of Common Stock in the Plan by the Company. Nothing in the Plan or in any option contract entered into pursuant hereto shall confer upon any employee any right to continue in the employ of the Company or the Subsidiaries, or interfere in any way with the right of the Company or the Subsidiaries to terminate his employment at any time without liability to the Company or the Subsidiaries.

12. *Listing and Registration of Shares.* Each option shall be subject to the requirement that if, at any time the Board of Directors or the Committee determines, in their discretion, that the listing, registration, or qualification of the shares subject to options granted hereunder upon any securities exchange or under any state or federal law, or the consent or approval of any governmental regulatory body, is necessary or desirable as a condition of, or in connection with, the issue or purchase of shares hereunder, the option may not be exercised in whole or in part unless such listing, registration, qualification, consent or approval shall have been effected or obtained and the same shall have been free of any conditions not acceptable to the Board of Directors or the Committee.

13. *Financial Assistance to Optionees.* The Board of Directors or the Committee may cause the Company or the Subsidiaries to give or arrange for financial assistance (including without limitation direct loans, with or without interest, secured or unsecured, or guarantees of third party loans) to an optionee for the purpose of providing funds for the purchase of stock pursuant to the exercise of an option granted under the Plan, when in the judgment of the Board of Directors or the Committee such assistance may reasonably be expected to be in the best interests of the Company, and provided that such assistance as may be granted shall be consistent with the Certificate of Incorporation and By-Laws of the Company and applicable laws, and will permit the stock to be fully paid and non-assessable when issued.

14. *Adjustments Upon Changes in Common Stock.* Notwithstanding any other provision of the Plan, in the event of any change in the outstanding Common Stock by reason of a stock dividend, share distribution, recapitalization, merger, consolidation, spin-off, split-up, combination or exchange

Exhibit 15-b (page 3)

of shares, or the like, the aggregate number and kind of shares available under the Plan and the number and kind of shares subject to each outstanding option and the option prices shall be appropriately adjusted by the Board of Directors, whose determination shall be conclusive.

15. *Amendments and Termination of the Plan.* The Board of Directors, without further approval of the shareholders, may, at any time, suspend or terminate the Plan or amend it from time to time in such respects as it may deem advisable in order that options intended to be qualified stock options granted hereunder qualify as "qualified stock options" under the Code or any comparable provisions thereafter enacted and conform to any change in applicable law or to regulations or rulings of administrative agencies, or may so amend it in any other respect not involving a substantial departure from the principles herein set forth; provided, however, that no amendment shall be effective without prior approval of a majority of the holders of the issued and outstanding shares of stock of the Company, which would: (a) except as specified in Paragraph 14, increase the maximum number of shares for which options may be granted under the Plan; or (b) change the eligibility requirements for individuals entitled to receive options hereunder. No termination, suspension or amendment of the Plan shall, without the consent of the holder of an existing option, adversely affect his rights under such option.

16. *Non-Transferability of Option.* No option granted under the Plan shall be transferable otherwise than by will or the laws of descent and distribution; and options may be exercised, during the lifetime of the holder thereof, only by him.

17. *Shareholders' Approval.* The Plan shall be subject to approval by the affirmative vote of the holders of a majority of the outstanding shares of stock of the Company at the next annual meeting of its shareholders and any options granted hereunder prior to such approval shall be conditioned thereon.

Exhibit 15-b (page 4)

QUALIFIED STOCK OPTION CONTRACT

        THIS QUALIFIED STOCK OPTION CONTRACT made as of the day of
19 , between Savin Business Machines Corporation, a New York corporation
(herein referred to as "Company") and

(herein referred to as "Optionee").

WITNESSETH

        1. The Company, in accordance with the allotment made by the Stock
Option Committee or the Board of Directors, and subject to the terms and
conditions of the Company's stock option plans, grants as of the date hereof,
to the Optionee an option to purchase an aggregate of   shares of the
Common Stock $.10 par value, of the Company at $ per share, being
100% of the fair market value of such stock on the date hereof.

        2. The option may be exercised prior to   19 , upon written
notice of exercise to the Company at its principal office, presently at
Valhalla, New York, 10595, specifying the number of shares purchased and
accompanied by payment in full of the aggregate purchase price for such
shares; provided, however, such option shall become exercisable up to 25%
of the aggregate number of shares originally subject thereto, commencing
one (1) year after the date of granting of the option; and as to an additional 25% after each succeeding anniversary of the date on which the
option first becomes exercisable, provided, further, that the right to
purchase shall be cumulative so that if the full number of shares purchasable in a period shall not be purchased, the balance may be purchased
at any time or from time to time thereafter but prior to the termination
of such option. The Board of Directors or the Committee may, in its
discretion, accelerate the time or times at which an option may become
exercisable.

        3. The Optionee agrees to make his services available to the Company
and its subsidiaries for a period of one year from the date hereof, provided,
however, that nothing in the Plan or herein shall confer upon the Optionee
any right to continue in the employ of the Company or its subsidiaries or
interfere in any way with the right of the Company or its subsidiaries to
terminate such employment at any time without liability to the Company or
its subsidiaries.

        4. An option may not be exercised by the Optionee while there is out-
standing (within the meaning of 422(c) (2) of the Internal Revenue Code of
1954, as amended) any qualified stock option (or restricted stock option)
to purchase shares of stock of the Company which was granted to the Optionee
prior to the granting of the within option.

        5. The Optionee represents and agrees that in the event of any exercise
of the option, the shares of Common Stock subject to option, will be acquired
for investment and not with a view to distribution thereof.

Exhibit 15-c (page 1)

6. In the event the Optionee ceases to be in the employ of the Company or its subsidiaries for any reason other than death, the option herein granted may be exercised, to the extent, if any, the Optionee was entitled to do so on the effective date of such termination, by the Optionee, within three (3) months after the effective date of such termination, provided, however, that if such employment shall be terminated either (i) for cause or (ii) without the consent of the Company, the option shall (to the extent not previously exercised) terminate immediately. In no event may an option be exercised after the date set forth in paragraph 2 hereof.

7. In the event the Optionee dies while in the employ of the Company or its subsidiaries, or within three (3) months after the termination of such employment (unless such termination was either (i) for cause or (ii) without the consent of the Company), the option may be exercised, to the extent exercisable on the date of his death, by his executor, administrator or other person at the time entitled by law to the Optionee's rights under the option, within six (6) months after the death of the Optionee, but in no event after the date set forth in paragraph 2 hereof.

8. The Company and the Optionee further agree that they will both be subject to and bound by the terms and conditions of the Qualified Stock Option Plan of Savin Business Machines Corporation, a copy of which is attached hereto and made a part hereof.

9. This contract shall be binding upon and enure to the benefit of any successor or assignee of the Company.

IN WITNESS WHEREOF, we have hereunto set our hands in duplicate at Valhalla, New York, as of the day and year first above written.

SAVIN BUSINESS MACHINES CORPORATION

By_____
　　　ROBERT K. LOW, President

_____
　　　(Optionee)

Exhibit 15-c (page 2)

Notes to Financial Statements

Stock option activity for the year ended April 30, 19__	NUMBER OF SHARES	OPTION PRICES
Outstanding at April 30, 19__	190,971	$11.88 to $63.38
Changes during the year:		
Granted	142,575	3.75 to 10.00
Exercised	—0—	— —
Terminated	85,322	7.75 to 55.00
Outstanding at April 30, 19__ (exercisable, 55,452 shares)	248,224	3.75 to 63.38

At April 30, 19__, Savin had received notices of election to convert options for 25,100 shares to nonqualified stock options and options for 7,000 shares were eligible for conversion to non-qualified stock options.

There were 19,482 shares reserved for future grants. On July 9, 19__, the Board of Directors authorized, subject to approval of the stockholders, the granting of options for an additional 50,000 shares.

Under Savin's amended Employee's Stock Purchase Plan eligible employees may purchase up to 75,000 shares of Savin's stock at the lesser of 85 percent of the market value on the offering date or at the end of the subscription period. At April 30, 19__, 267 employees of Savin had subscribed to purchase 21,448 shares under the plan and 5,529 shares had been purchased.

During fiscal 19__, Savin: a) entered into an agreement with Ricoh Company, Ltd. to 1) sell 20,000 shares of common stock at $4.875; 2) sell an additional 80,000 shares of common stock at $4.875 prior to December 17, 19__; and 3) issue warrants for the purchase of 150,000 shares of common stock at $7.70 per share expiring at the rate of 37,500 quarterly, commencing March 15, 19__; b) issued 5,529 shares of common stock purchased under the Employee's Stock Purchase Plan.

Exhibit 15-d

STOCK OPTION LEDGER
J. SMITH

GRANT CODE C

OPTION PRICE	DATE OF GRANT	NUMBER OF SHARES	# SHARES EXERCISED	# SHARES TERMINATED	DATE	BALANCE EXERCISABLE FUTURE	NOW
$ 17 00	6-23-03	1000			6-23-03	1000	
					6-23-04	750	250
	SPLIT	500			9-11-04		
$ 11 33		1500			9-11-04	1125	375
	SPLIT	1500			1-31-05		
567		3000			1-31-05	2250	750
					5-1-05	2250	750
					6-23-05	1500	1500
			1500		11-17-05	1500	—
					5-1-06	1500	—
					6-23-06	750	750
			750		4-02-07	750	—
					6-23-07	—	750
			750		8-02-07	—	—

Exhibit 15-e

EMPLOYEE STOCK OPTION SUMMARY
QUALIFIED STOCK OPTION PLAN

NAME: _J. Smith_   DEPARTMENT: _V.P._   LOCATION: _01_

REPORTS TO: _H. Jones_

GRANTS

Grant Code	# of Shares This Grant	Cumul.	Option Price This Grant	Date Granted
A	6,000	6,000	$ 2.92	7-21-01
B	6,000	12,000	8.50	6-23-02
C	3,000	15,000	5.67	6-23-03
D	1,000	16,000	39.1875	3-22-06
E	* 2,000	18,000	27.6875	8-02-07
F	2,000	20,000	11.875	3-20-09
G	* <2,000>	18,000	—	10-10-09
H	10,000	28,000	6.75	10-10-09
I	3,000	31,000	3.00	6-11-10
J				
K				
L				
M				
N				
O				
P				

*Transferred to Non-qualified

EXERCISES

Grant Code	# of Shares This Time	Cumul.	$ Amount This Time	Date Exercised $	Cumul. Amounts	Cumul. Shares Unexercised
A	3,000	3,000	8,760	PRIOR 4/30/04	8,760	12,000
A	1,500	4,500	4,380	7-21-04	13,140	10,500
Ⓐ	1,500	6,000	4,380	11-17-05	17,520	9,000
B	4,500	10,500	38,250	11-17-05	55,500	4,500
C	1,500	12,000	4,380	11-17-05	59,880	3,000
Ⓑ	1,500	13,500	12,750	4-02-07	72,630	2,500
C	750	14,250	2,190	4-02-07	74,820	1,750
E						3,750
Ⓒ	750	15,000	4,252	8-02-07	79,077	3,000
Ⓔ	2,000	TRANSFERRED TO	NON-QUALIFIED			1,000
						3,000
						13,000
						16,000

1. Insert grant code for option exercised.
2. Circle grant code when option is completely exercised.

(0-1-10)

Exhibit 15-f

Description of Financing under the "Special" Qualified Stock Options
----

"Special" Qualified Stock Options or Non-Qualified Stock Options arising from the rescinding of the former (as described in Paragraph 2 of the Explanation of 19 "Special: Qualified Stock Option Plan) will be available for "special" financing by the Company, on request. This financing will have the following features:

1. Senox Limited, our wholly owned subsidiary, <u>will lend you 30% of the market value</u> of the stock on the day you exercise your option. An example of the loan and the funds which you, yourself, would have to provide is set forth below:

1)	Date of grant	August 2, 19
2)	Option price at date of grant	$25 per share
3)	No. of shares granted	500 shares
4)	Percent eligible for exercise after each year	25%
5)	Value of grant (500 sh. x $25)	$12,500
6)	Amount eligible for exercise after each year ($12,500 sh. x 25%)	$ 3,125
7)	Assumed market value on August 2, 19	$ 30 per share
8)	Total market value on August 2, 19 of exercisable shares (125 sh. at $30)	$ 3,750
9)	Maximum Senox Loan ($3,750 x 30%)	$.1,125
10)	Funds you must supply (line 6 minus 9)	$ 2,000

2. In accord with regulations of the Federal Reserve Board, your total loan from the Company <u>may not exceed 35% of the market value</u> at any time. Note that in the example above we have made a loan of 30% of the market value. This would permit the price to drop as much as 15% before the Company must require that you place additional collateral with us, in the form of more stock or additional cash in sufficient amounts to keep your loan below the legally permitted 35% of market value. An example of a call for additional collateral is set forth below:

11)	Assumed market value 6 months after exercise on February 2, 19	$ 24 per share
12)	Total market value of shares previously exercised (125 sh. x $24)	$ 3,000
13)	Maximum legal loan ($3,00 x 35%)	$ 1,050
14)	Additional collateral required (line 9 minus 13)	$ 75*

   * This may be supplied to Senox in cash or stock. If in stock, it must have a market value of $75, for example 3.1 shares of Savin at $24 = $75.

3. On the other hand, if the market value of the stock rises by the time you exercised additional shares, Senox would lend you 30% of the value of all of the shares you would hold after your additional exercise. An example of this is given below. Note in this example that Senox would lend you $1,875 (line 20) as compared to the loan on the first exercise of $1,125 (line 9). This is the result of the increase in the market value of the shares to $40, in the example:

Exhibit 15-g (page 1)

Description of Financing.....(cont'd)
Page -2-

15)	Market value of date of 2nd exercise (8/2/)	$40
16)	Shares to be exercised on August 2, 19	125 shares
17)	Total shares to be owned after August 2, 19	250 shares
18)	Market value of shares to be owned (250 x $40)	$10,000
19)	Maximum Senox loan ($10,000 x 30%)	$ 3,000
20)	Additional Senox loan to be made August 2, 19 (line 19 minus 9)	$ 1,875
21)	Funds you must supply (line 6 minus 20)	$ 1,250

4. Security will be required for each loan made by Senox Limited in the form of a non-recourse note which you will be required to sign in favor of Senox. In addition, Senox will hold your stock as security for payment of the note. In short, this means that if you do not repay your loan to Senox, Senox may look only to the stock it holds for payment on the loan and will have no other recourse to you nor any of your assets.

5. Your holding period for capital gains begins on the date you exercise your stock options, despite the fact that Senox is holding these securities for repayment of your loans. You may sell stock at any time, concurrently with the payment of the loan to Senox, and you will receive any excess proceeds from Senox.

6. Additional financing assistance may not be supplied by Savin nor Senox in exercising these options. However, Savin will recommend to major banking facilities that additional loans be made available to you to assist you in financing 70% of the option price which is your obligation. However, you will be unable to place this stock as security with the banks and the purpose of these bank loans cannot be attributed specifically to acquiring the stock, but rather, must be attributed to your overall financial needs. There is no assurance that our banks will make these loans available to you. These loans will be contingent on the bank's usual credit review--including your own personal credit situation, your existing loans, the individual bank's lending requirements and the general money and economic situation.

7. Your request for financial assistance in the exercise of your options should be made to the treasurer's office, setting forth the date of the original grant, the number of shares originally granted, the price of the grant, the amount of shares you desire to exercise, and the date on which you desire to exercise your shares.

Exhibit 15-g (page 2)

SUBJECT INDEX